The Ris

MANCHESTER
UNIVERSITY PRESS

STUDIES IN EARLY MODERN
EUROPEAN HISTORY

This exciting series aims to publish
challenging and innovative research in all
areas of early modern continental history.
The editors are committed to
encouraging work that engages with
current historiographical debates, adopts
an interdisciplinary approach, or makes
an original contribution to our
understanding of the period.

SERIES EDITORS:
William G. Naphy and Penny Roberts

EDITORIAL ADVISORY BOARD:
Professor N. Z. Davis,
Professor Brian Pullan, Professor Joe Bergin
and Professor Robert Scribner

Already published in the series:

*A city in conflict: Troyes during the French wars
of religion*
Penny Roberts

Fear in early modern society
eds. William Naphy and Penny Roberts

Forthcoming

*Narratives of witchcraft in early modern
Germany: fabrication, feud and fantasy*
Alison Rowlands

The Duke of Lerma: a political life
Patrick Williams

The Rise of
RICHELIEU

Joseph Bergin

Manchester University Press

Manchester and New York

distributed exclusively in the USA by St. Martin's Press

First published 1991 by Yale University Press

This edition published 1997 by
Manchester University Press
Oxford Road, Manchester M13 9NR, UK
and Room 400, 175 Fifth Avenue, New York, NY 10010, USA

Distributed exclusively in the USA by
St. Martin's Press, Inc., 175 Fifth Avenue, New York,
NY 10010, USA

Distributed exclusively in Canada by
UBC Press, University of British Columbia, 6344 Memorial Road,
Vancouver, BC, Canada V6T 1Z2

British Library Cataloguing-in-Publication Data
A catalogue record for this book is available from the British Library

Library of Congress Cataloging-in-Publication Data applied for

ISBN 0 7190 5238 6 *paperback*

First published 1997

01 00 99 98 97   10 9 8 7 6 5 4 3 2 1

Printed in Great Britain
by Redwood Books, Trowbridge

Contents

For
Sylvia, Edward and Olivia

Preface

THE pages that follow were originally inspired, albeit in a somewhat ambiguous way, by the experience of reading, and in some cases re-reading, a number of biographies of Richelieu. The result of this activity was a rising sense that much of what they had to say about him had an air of unreality to it. The more I read the more I became intrigued by the relatively unproblematic portrayal of his eventful career and achievements, and even more so of the environment in which he lived. In particular, his route to ministerial office seemed inadequately charted, let alone accounted for. Although there was an abundance of factual detail, some of it highly embroidered, it rarely seemed to get the interpretation that it cried out for; in general, answers seemed in far greater supply than questions in these accounts. I supposed that if better questions could be asked, somehow better answers, too, could be found. This reaction proved both too simplistic and too optimistic, and writing this book has turned out to be infinitely more demanding than I ever imagined. Of course, the initial optimism was crucial to embarking on and, especially, finishing the enterprise. By the time I had completed it, the blithe confidence of the beginning had given way to a considerable sense of trepidation.

Any book dealing with the rise of a major historical figure must face the difficulty of how to stand back from the known outcome of events, and to ask questions which restore a sense of historical contingency to its subject matter. In the case of Richelieu, generations of writers have combined to produce a portrait of him which it is extremely hard to look at from a new perspective. Admittedly, there is nothing particularly novel about breaking off the analysis in 1624, when he assumed ministerial office for the second time. But doing so does enable one to reduce the measure of hindsight involved in tracing his career, and to become more conscious of a whole range of factors which either helped or impeded his progress. The following pages are therefore intended as an essay in reassessment, one which is based on a combination of old, relatively familiar, as well as some new sources. Above all, it tries to give due weight to a range of factors which had not, I felt, figured sufficiently in the standard accounts of his early career. Indeed, the more our perspectives on Richelieu are widened to include family traditions, the church, social relations and so on, the more he will appear as a real political figure operating within a time-bound framework rather than as the 'Man of State' of legend.

The reassessment which is offered here is one which has at times required the presentation of a good deal of factual, narrative material, which will not be readily familiar, even to those who know this period of French history reasonably well. I am conscious that this may create difficulties for some readers, making certain developments hard to follow, but I have tried to offset that by providing them with a chronology of events and genealogical tables.

As on previous occasions, I am keenly aware of how much I owe to friends, colleagues and institutions who make academic scholarship both possible and worthwhile. Their support and assistance persuades me that something like a community of scholars still exists despite growing pressures and incomprehension, which are not always confined to the wider world outside of academe. I shall not try to thank here all those whose help, especially in locating, deciphering and understanding documents, was of such value to me: I have endeavoured to thank them at the appropriate places in the notes to the text. Others followed the book's progress and in some cases asked me questions which, perhaps unknown to them, made me rethink my assumptions. But I would particularly like to express my continuing gratitude to Nigel Griffin who read the entire manuscript without complaint, and contributed enormously to improving both its style, such as it is, and especially its clarity. Mark Greengrass did likewise, and directed me towards problems and sources which I would never have discovered for myself. I also wish to thank Orest Ranum for a generous critical reading of the text at a late stage of its history, and for his many perceptive reflections on it. I should probably have had to write another book were I to give the observations of these reader–critics the attention they merit. None of them, I need hardly add, should be regarded as responsible for what has finally seen the light of day. Without Jeremy Lawrance's help, I would not have known how to prepare a manuscript capable of being typeset directly from two small disks. No less crucial to the outcome was the contribution of the University of Manchester, and specially its Grants Assessment Committee, which provided much-needed funds for the research which this project entailed.

Finally, my own family has proved extraordinarily tolerant of my increasing absorption with the past. Though the neglect which they suffered as a consequence cannot be repaired with a stroke of the pen, I happily dedicate this book to them.

Chronology

1585

9 Sept.   Birth of Richelieu in Paris

1586

5 May   Richelieu baptized at St Eustache church, Paris

1588

13 May   Day of Barricades, Henri III expelled from Paris
24 Dec.   Murder of Guises and arrest of Leaguer deputies at
               Estates General at Blois by François de Richelieu

1590

May–Sept.   First royalist siege of Paris
10 June   Death of François de Richelieu at Gonesse

1594

Feb.   Henri IV crowned at Chartres, enters Paris in March
Oct?   Richelieu enters College of Navarre

1600

Sept.   Royal decree reforming University of Paris
17 Dec.   Marriage of Henri IV and Marie de' Medici

1601

27 Sept.   Birth of Louis XIII

1602

?   Alphonse de Richelieu joins Carthusian order
Oct (?)   Richelieu nominated bishop of Luçon by Henri IV

1603

Oct?   Richelieu begins philosophy studies in Paris

1605

June?   Richelieu takes M.A. degree

1606

18 Dec.   Richelieu, in Rome, receives bulls for Luçon

1607

17 April   Richelieu consecrated bishop in Rome
2 June   Richelieu takes oath of fidelity to king at
               Fontainebleau
29 Oct.   Richelieu takes bachelor of theology examinations

31 Oct.	Richelieu fellow of the Sorbonne

1609

April	Spanish-Dutch Twelve Years' Truce
15 Dec.	Richelieu arrives in diocese of Luçon

1610

14 May	Assassination of Henri IV
15 May	Marie de' Medici regent for Louis XIII
22 May	Edict of Nantes confirmed
17 Oct.	Louis XIII crowned at Reims

1611

26 Jan.	Dismissal of Sully as finance minister
May–Sept.	Huguenot political assembly at Saumur
Nov.	Bérulle founds Oratory

1612

March	Henri Chasteignier de la Rocheposay bishop of Poitiers
25 Aug.	Franco-Spanish marriage treaty
1 Sept.	Provincial council of Sens condemns Edmond Richer's *De ecclesiastica et politica potestate libellus*
18 Oct.	Louis XIII engaged to infanta Ana

1613

19 Nov.	Concino Concini becomes maréchal d'Ancre

1614

10 Feb.	Princes begin withdrawing from court
15 May	Treaty of Ste Ménéhould with princes (approved on 25 May)
7 June	Convocation of Estates General
23 June	Bishop of Poitiers defies Condé
2 Oct.	Majority of Louis XIII
27 Oct.	Opening of Estates General
12 Nov.	Treaty of Xanten settling Cleves-Jülich dispute

1615

9 Jan.	Marriage of Henri de Richelieu to Marguerite Guiot
23 Feb.	Formal closure of Estates General. Richelieu addresses regent on behalf of clergy
23 March	Deputies to Estates ordered home by crown
June	Second revolt of princes
15 June	Treaty of Asti settling Mantua-Montferrat dispute
25 Nov.	Marriage of Louis XIII and Anne of Austria in Bordeaux
Nov.	Richelieu grand aumonier to new queen
Nov.–Dec.	Condé-Huguenot alliance

1616

21 Feb.	Crown opens negotiations with Condé and princes
3 May	Treaty of Loudun
Late May	Condé returns to Paris
May–Aug.	Ministerial reshuffle
1 Sept.	Arrest and imprisonment of Condé. New revolt of princes
14 Nov.	Death of Suzanne de La Porte, Richelieu's mother
26/30 Nov.	Richelieu secretary of state

1617

Jan.–April	Revolt of the princes
24 April	Assassination of Concini, dismissal of Richelieu and other ministers
3 May	Richelieu accompanies Marie de' Medici to exile at Blois
15 June	Richelieu exiled to Coussay
25 June	Decree restoring Catholicism in Béarn
25 June	Bertrand d'Eschaux archbishop of Tours
26 Oct.	Richelieu exiled to Luçon
12 Dec.	Death of Villeroy
Dec.–Jan.	Assembly of Notables at Rouen
Nov.	Publication of Richelieu's *Principaux points de la foy*

1618

March	Henri de Gondi first cardinal de Retz
7 April	Richelieu exiled to Avignon
23 May	Defenestration of Prague
Sept.	Cardinal de Retz president of council
9 Dec.	Guichard Déageant loses ministerial rank

1619

Jan.–April	Huguenot assembly at La Rochelle
27 Jan.	Épernon secretly leaves Metz for Angoulême
22 Feb.	Marie de' Medici escapes from Blois to Angoulême
7 March	Richelieu recalled from Avignon
20 March	Death of Emperor Mathias
27 March	Richelieu at Angoulême
April	Publication of Richelieu's *Instruction du Chrétien*
30 April/ 12 May	Treaty of Angoulême
8 July	Henri de Richelieu killed in duel
28 Aug.	Ferdinand II elected emperor
3 Sept.	Schomberg *surintendant des finances*
5 Sept.	Louis XIII and Marie de' Medici meet at Couzières
Sept.–April	Huguenot assembly at Loudun

20 Oct.	Liberation of Condé
9 Nov.	Declaration of Condé's innocence

1620

April–June	Negotiations between court and Marie de' Medici, defection of leading nobles towards queen mother
3 July	French-sponsored Treaty of Ulm
7 July	Louis XIII's military offensive against Marie de' Medici begins
July	Habsburg occupation of Valtelline
7 Aug.	Battle of Ponts-de-Cé near Angers
10 Aug.	Treaty of Angers. Richelieu and La Valette candidates for red hat
Oct.	Reunion of Béarn and France
26 Nov.	Marriage of Richelieu's niece to Antoine de Combalet
25 Dec.	Huguenot assembly at La Rochelle

1621

11 Jan.	La Valette cardinal
28 Jan.	Death of Pope Paul V
9 Feb.	Election of Gregory XV
31 March	Death of Philip III of Spain
3 April	Luynes constable of France
15 April	Franco-Spanish treaty of Madrid over Valtelline dispute
18 April	Louis XIII resumes anti-Huguenot campaign
17 May– 23 June	Siege of St Jean d'Angély
3 Aug.	Death of Guillaume du Vair, keeper of seals
18 Aug.	Siege of Montauban
22 Sept.	Death of duc de Mayenne
24 Oct.	Death of Archbishop du Perron of Sens
18 Nov.	Siege of Montauban lifted
8 Dec.	Battle of White Mountain, suppression of Bohemian revolt
14 Dec.	Death of Luynes
21 Dec.	Méric de Vic keeper of the seals; Schomberg de facto principal minister

1622

28 Jan.	Louis XIII back in Paris
31 Jan.	Queen mother in council
Late Jan.	Huguenot revolt led by Soubise
21 March	King resumes anti-Huguenot offensive
16 April	Victory over Soubise at Rié
April–Sept.	Richelieu and Marie de' Medici at Nantes

2 Aug.	Death of Retz
9 Aug.	Richelieu elected provisor of Sorbonne
1 Sept.	Siege of Montpellier
2 Sept.	Death of Méric de Vic keeper of the seals, succeeded by Lefebvre de Caumartin
5 Sept.	Richelieu made cardinal
6 Sept.	Cardinal de La Rochefoucauld in council
Late Sept.	Richelieu and queen mother at Lyon
Sept.	Habsburgs extend control of Valtelline and Grisons
9 Oct.	Condé leaves for Italy
19 Oct.	Peace of Montpellier with Huguenots
22 Dec.	Cardinal's barrette presented to Richelieu by Louis XIII

1623

21 Jan.	Death of Caumartin keeper of seals
23 Jan.	Schomberg dismissed as *surintendant*, replaced by La Vieuville
7 Feb.	Treaty of Paris: French alliance with Savoy and Venice
8 July	Death of Gregory XV
6 Aug.	Election of Urban VIII
Oct.	Olivares becomes principal Spanish minister

1624

1 Jan.	Sillery deprived of seals
6 Jan.	Étienne Aligre appointed keeper of seals
5/6 Feb.	La Vieuville ousts Brûlarts
29 April	Richelieu member of king's council
10 June	Treaty of Compiègne
13 Aug.	Arrest of La Vieuville, Richelieu principal minister
5 Sept.	Renewal of Treaty of Paris of Feb. 1623
Nov.	Coeuvres's expedition to Valtelline

Abbreviations

A.A.E.	Archives des Affaires Étrangères
A.A.W.	Archives of the Archdiocese of Wesminster
A.N.	Archives Nationales
A.S.V.	Archivio Segreto Vaticano
B.L.	British Library
B.N.	Bibliothèque Nationale
B.V.C.	Sorbonne, Bibliothèque Victor Cousin
M.C.	Minutier central des notaires parisiens
MS. Fr.	Manuscrit français
MS. Ital.	Manuscrit italien
MS. Lat.	Manuscrit latin
Nunz. Fr.	Nunziatura di Francia
P.R.O., SP	Public Record Office, State Papers series

All French currency values have been expressed in *livres tournois*, even though the official money of account between 1576 and 1603 was the *écu*, valued at 3 *livres*.

All dates from contemporary English sources have been given in 'new' style, i.e. ten days ahead of the dates used in the English calendar.

Introduction

'La gloire des grands hommes se doit toujours mesurer aux moyens dont ils se sont servis pour l'acquérir.'[1]

FEW would doubt that Richelieu deserves to belong in the Pantheon of great figures in French history. Whether alone or in association with Mazarin, Colbert and Louis XIV, his name has become a kind of shorthand for a crucial stage in the country's cultural as well as political development, which makes him one of the relatively few figures to be readily familiar to generations of people both inside and outside France. The general image of him is the more widely shared because it combines the visual and the historical: the first evokes the splendid portraits of him in his red, cardinal robes painted by that great master of spiritual and psychological insight, Philippe de Champaigne; the second, the figure of a clever, authoritarian, and rather Machiavellian statesman who managed to create something like a modern state out of a rather fractious, strife-prone kingdom. This broad general appeal complements rather than contradicts the particular attraction that Richelieu has always had for French élites, especially the political and bureaucratic ones. In their eyes, he has always clearly passed the acid-test which separates the select few from the many who engage in political activity: in the well-turned language of French politics, he was blessed with that rare but indispensable – and untranslatable – quality of possessing 'un grand sens de l'État'. Successive generations of those looking for historical models have had little difficulty, despite occasional reservations about some of his methods, in accepting him as one of the greatest of statesmen.

It is a truism to say that in history, as in life, winners tend to take all, and to impose a vision of their own achievements which posterity all too often limits itself to refining and endorsing. One of the most recent biographies of Richelieu begins with a startling claim – 'à chaque décennie son Richelieu!' – and ends with the assertion that the Cardinal was the 'most perfect specimen of the average French-

1 La Rochefoucauld, *Maximes*, ed. Jacques Truchet (Paris 1967), p. 41.

man with his vices and his virtues pushed to extremes'.[2] There has certainly been no scarcity of biographies over the centuries, easily enough to meet the requirement of at least one for each decade; but while it is also true that each generation rewrites history from its own particular vantage point, few have suggested it should be done quite so self-consciously as this. No doubt unintentionally, the claim cited above raises a series of difficult questions, but without offering much assistance as to how they should be answered, or how the contradictory demands of transient intellectual fashions and of historiographical priorities could be satisfactorily harmonized. Moreover, it is likely that one decade's 'Richelieu' does not necessarily differ very much from that of preceding ones, especially if he is to be regarded as an exemplar of the 'average Frenchman'. Although historical writing cannot altogether escape contemporary preoccupations, what has been called 'the search for a usable past' tends to generate more enthusiasm than enlightenment, and to confuse the historical record. It is hardly necessary to remark how prevalent such a search has been in countless studies of Richelieu; the classic example, one that can perhaps stand for many others of lesser value as historical documents, is Gabriel Hanotaux's six-volume *magnum opus*, in which an influential Third Republic historian-cum-politician vicariously pursued his personal quest for the kind of statesman-figure which he felt that his own generation so badly needed.[3] In the following generation, the more widely available work of Carl Burckhardt conveyed, albeit without adding much to our knowledge of Richelieu, a powerful sense of destiny in its portrayal of the Cardinal's career, and nowhere more so than in its interpretation of the 'Rise of Richelieu'.[4] Nearer to our own time, Elizabeth Wirth Marvick has brought a Freudian perspective to bear on Richelieu's development in her attempt to uncover the factors which, in effect, 'programmed' Richelieu for a leadership role in French politics; here, too, the sense of individual destiny is inescapable.[5]

The approach adopted in the present book had as its point of departure a response, perhaps an over-reaction, not merely to such expectations, but more generally to the assumptions and tone of many of the standard accounts of Richelieu's career. Perhaps for that reason, it is easier to say what it is *not* than what it is, and one of the

---

2 Michel Carmona, *Richelieu: le pouvoir et l'ambition* (Paris 1983), pp. 5, 719.
3 *Histoire du cardinal de Richelieu* (Paris 1893–1947), hereafter Hanotaux, *Richelieu*. Hanotaux did not live to finish this work, which was brought to completion by the duc de La Force. Hanotaux served as minister for foreign affairs between 1894 and 1898, was a member of the Académie Francaise, and a regular editorialist in the press.
4 Carl J. Burckhardt, *Richelieu and his Age*, 3 vols. English translation (London 1967–70).
5 Elizabeth Wirth Marvick, *The Young Richelieu. A Psychoanalytical Study in Leadership* (Chicago 1983).

things it is not intended to be is a biography in the usual sense of the term. As a genre, historical biography is beset by many pitfalls, most notably the kind of tunnel vision which results from focusing sharply on an individual while leaving context, background and other connected aspects relatively underdeveloped. The most common result tends to be a circularity in both narrative and interpretation; all too often, explanation tends to be extracted from the subject that actually requires it. In the case of Richelieu this is compounded by powerful and long-standing teleological reflexes, which tend to inflate even insignificant or uncertain aspects of his career. We may quote one example of this tendency, taken from an otherwise careful and sober study of French politics between 1614 and 1616. Examining the sudden arrest of the prince of Condé in September 1616, Berthold Zeller wrote:

> The name of Richelieu is nowhere to be found among those responsible for [the arrest]. But who can doubt that [he] . . . advised that it should be done? Who would hesitate to attribute to him the strong and effective measures which, in both civil and military affairs, guaranteed in such a firm and novel way, the new order of things? His recompense was, of course, commensurate to the services he rendered.[6]

Such an approach is all the more remarkable in that Zeller was writing of a period in which Richelieu was a minor political figure. Not surprisingly, it is his ministerial career which attracts privileged attention. By contrast, his pre-ministerial career seems to require much less analysis in its own right. Such an imbalance has frequently been reinforced by a tendency, especially among French writers, to depict Richelieu as a man of destiny, whose superior intellect and ability were the real and ultimate explanation of why he came to occupy such high office. Again, in such a perspective there seemed little of genuine importance to be learned from scrutinizing his preministerial years, except perhaps an appreciation of how badly governed France was before his ministry, or how far his progress had been thwarted by a political class desperate to keep him away from power. In such a perspective, serious understanding of him and his record begins rather than ends when he returned to ministerial office in 1624. This book ends in 1624.

The more one studies Richelieu and his time, the more the sheer weight of the historiographical tradition embodied in the many studies of him becomes apparent, and it would be foolish to pretend

6 Berthold Zeller, *Louis XIII, Marie de Medicis chef du conseil 1614–1616* (Paris 1898), pp. 321–2.

that the problems they raise are easily surmounted. Any attempt to confront them must begin with a discussion of the documentary foundations of that tradition. These fall into a number of categories. The first includes the early lives of the Cardinal – especially by de Pure, Aubery, Leclerc, and which to some degree drew on family lore or oral traditions generally; the second includes the earliest publications of documents, whether they be collections like Aubery's *Mémoires pour l'histoire du cardinal-duc de Richelieu*, or more celebrated texts like the *Testament Politique* or the so-called *Mémoires*.[7] The third, and by far the most voluminous category, consists of modern attempts to produce comprehensive editions of Richelieu's papers, as well as of familiar texts like the *Testament Politique* and the *Mémoires*.

It is important to realize from the outset that the corpus of essential material for the study of Richelieu's early career has remained relatively unchanged since 1853, when Avenel published the first of his great folio volumes of *Lettres, instructions diplomatiques et papiers d'état*, supplemented almost twenty years later by additional material gleaned partly from institutions such as the archives of the Quai d'Orsay.[8] The first document he printed dated from around 1609, just as Richelieu was about to take up residence in his diocese of Luçon. A substantial section of the first volume consisted of papers relating to Richelieu's brief career as secretary of state in late 1616 and early 1617; both before and after those dates, items of political interest were scattered, sometimes thinly, among a variety of private, ecclesiastical and business papers. But there was much more to Avenel's admirable contribution than the patient assembling of a notoriously difficult and dispersed corpus of sources. It is crucial for an understanding of the historiography of Richelieu to remember that Avenel's labours were infused with a thoroughly nineteenth-century belief in the primacy of high politics, particularly of foreign and military affairs, and, consequently, in the value of getting as close as possible to the thinking and intentions of great political figures as they grappled with the problems of their time. This meant, in the first instance, publishing the 'active' correspondence and papers of such men, while relegating their incoming, 'passive' correspondence to minor roles such as elucidating obscurities, establishing correct dates and so on, in the active correspondence. To have treated both kinds of material in the same manner would, no doubt,

---

7 These and other works are listed in the bibliography.
8 Denis-Louis-Martial Avenel, ed., *Lettres, instructions diplomatiques et papiers d'état du cardinal de Richelieu* [*Collection de documents inédits sur l'histoire de France*], 8 vols. (Paris 1853–76), referred to hereafter as Avenel, *Lettres*. Some of these institutions had been closed to him at the outset.

have been to cloud the role and action of someone in Richelieu's position. In addition, Avenel was one of the first to articulate the view that this objective could best be achieved by adopting the minutes of Richelieu's letters and papers as the basis of scholarly editing and publication: they had the singular advantage of showing precisely where Richelieu intervened, *la plume à la main*, to alter an idea or an expression, thus bringing the historian as near as was humanly possible to the making of policy and to the mental processes of a major political figure.[9] Though there was much less documentation relating to great affairs of state in the years before 1624, the effect of such a principle was the same – to detach the individual from his context, and to concentrate attention on his attitudes and behaviour to the virtual exclusion of other factors.

It need hardly be said that this philosophy, although expressed in the apparent obscurity of a scholarly edition, had a profound influence on biographers and historians of the Cardinal; the manner in which the sources were laid out before them made it all the easier to believe that the 'right' approach to Richelieu's career was, in the broadest sense of the term, the biographical one. Avenel's work had other, less noticeable drawbacks. His reliance on minutes rather than on originals, which was unavoidable in many instances, meant that quite a few of the documents he attributed to Richelieu turned out not to be by him at all, or were lacking in dates and the names of addressees; this has created many difficulties for historians which only a systematic new edition could clear up. But the pre-1624 years have been excluded from the modern edition of the Cardinal's political papers now in progress, though a comparison of the two approaches to the problem of editing them shows clearly how sharply perspectives have altered over the years. By publishing 'passive' and 'active' correspondence, as well as other papers relevant to particular political issues, the new edition conveys an invaluable sense of the political milieu in which Richelieu moved, and the extent to which he relied on his personal and political entourage to generate ideas and suggestions for debate and consideration; it thus enables the historian to exchange the sense of looking over Richelieu's shoulder as he first drafted, and then revised, his ideas, for that of eavesdropping on the wider political 'conversations' of his ministry.[10] By that yardstick, anyone studying the Cardinal's progress before 1624 must regard Avenel's work as no more than a part, though admittedly an essential one, of a larger but difficult documentary mosaic. The attempt

---

9 *Ibid.*, vol. I., for Avenel's preface.
10 *Les Papiers de Richelieu. Section politique intérieure: correspondance et papiers d'état*, ed. Pierre Grillon (6 vols. to date, Paris 1975–), vol. I., editor's introduction.

made in this book to see the mosaic as a whole inevitably leads to
certain changes of perspective on Richelieu's emergence as a leading
political figure by the 1620s.

A still more formidable problem is posed for this same period
of the Cardinal's career by the literary monument known as his
Mémoires. Their influence on historians of early seventeenth-century
France, and not merely of Richelieu, has been more direct and far-
reaching than that of his original papers; many accounts have followed, with relatively little modification, the narrative and interpre-
tive framework they established. There is no need to review here
the vexed question of the precise extent of Richelieu's own contribution to them, or of their authenticity as a statement of his personal
views.[11] They are neither the autobiographical recollections that we
expect memoirs to be, nor the loosely linked collections of state
papers and correspondence of which there were other examples in
the sixteenth and seventeenth centuries. It is worth noting that the
members of his entourage engaged in writing them always referred
to them simply as 'the History'. What the *Mémoires* obviously do
express is Richelieu's belief in the need for a quasi-official history of
France in the age of Louis XIII, one which would purvey a clearly-
defined vision – his own – of the events and great issues of his lifetime. If only for that reason, the *Mémoires* were clearly superior and
more persuasive than either the more conventional journals or the
often gossipy recollections produced by several contemporaries, and
it is not surprising that historians should have found them so attractive. Moreover, by incorporating, either verbatim or in paraphrase,
numerous letters or important memoranda, they also had the allure
of objectivity.

Of course, that 'objectivity' was constantly qualified by a highly
retrospective view of events and individuals, who were judged time
and again, and for the most part found seriously wanting. Of none is
this more true than of Richelieu's own predecessors in high office,
from Concini in 1616–17 to La Vieuville in 1624. Time and again,
however, many of the judgements thus expressed turn out, when
checked against sources which are not the product of hindsight, to
be seriously at variance with the attitudes and behaviour of Richelieu
himself at the times in question; and some of these sources, as we
shall see, emanate from Richelieu's own pen. For all their obvious
shortcomings, memoirs where no such ambition to write definitive
history was present can provide historians with material that is often
more revealing because less apologetic.

11 The results of the most intensive research on this subject were published in the *Rapports et
   notices sur l'édition des Mémoires du cardinal de Richelieu*, 3 vols. (Paris 1907–14).

Discrepancies of this kind obviously raise questions about the value of the *Mémoires* for the decade before 1624, as well as about the reliability of the historical accounts that follow them closely. What we know about the composition of the *Mémoires* makes it clear that their intrinsic value for these years is much less than for the years of Richelieu's ministry. Whole sections were put together from the semi-official *Mercure françois* and a variety of other occasional publications, as well as from the memoirs of certain other contemporaries, copies of which Richelieu had obtained from their authors. In some cases, he actually commissioned *relations* from individuals involved in events that were of particular interest to him personally – for example, Guichard Déageant on the fall of Concini and its aftermath, Cardinal La Valette on Marie de Medici's escape from Blois, and Louis de Marillac on the revolt of the summer of 1620. But however authoritative and first-hand they may be, these accounts were all written much later at the request of a powerful Cardinal-Minister whom the authors were clearly not anxious to offend. Having been a minister only briefly in 1616–17, Richelieu simply did not dispose of the kind of material for the years before 1624 that he would accumulate after that date. This is also the reason for another striking feature of the *Mémoires*: the great *avis au roi* and similar papers which have been the staple diet of generations of historians of Richelieu's ministry, are entirely absent before 1624. When allusions occur in the *Mémoires* to particular interventions by him or by Marie de' Medici in political debates, doubts about such contributions persist in the absence of any corroborative evidence.

Moreover, as we shall see in some detail, the facts of Richelieu's political career between 1617 and 1624 did not quite fit the image of himself that he wished to see transmitted to posterity. If the *Mémoires* become vague, allusive or virtually silent on many questions of primary interest to the historian of those years, it is generally because Richelieu's circumstances and actions frequently differed from the myth under construction. His subsequent efforts to secure possession of the papers of those who had served, or been associated with, him before 1624 point to a similar conclusion. The clearest single instance of this concern is represented by a letter to him from Pierre de Bérulle, only weeks after his appointment to the council in 1624:

I heard this morning of the sudden death of Monsieur Barbin, and the news led me to believe that I should write to you immediately and let you know that it might not be pointless to have his papers impounded, prudently and quickly, as they doubtless contain several things concerning the affairs of the queen mother – and indeed your own. I am certain that he was recently informed of

several things concerning you which you ought to be aware of,
and which would be better kept secret.[12]

That members of Richelieu's entourage like Bérulle should express
such solicitude for his reputation is no accident, and their behaviour
shows how far he had made his views known to them. Most of
the 'tours de souplesse' with which former associates would repro-
ach him in later years were drawn from this period of his career,
when he was entangled in factional opposition to Louis XIII and his
ministers.[13]

II

Exercises in *Quellenkritik* can all too easily become destructive, but
the intention behind the preceding pages has not been to depict
Richelieu as perpetrating a grand fraud on generations of trusting
devotees and misguided historians. There is no doubt that in their
conception, documents like the *Mémoires* and the *Testament Politique*
stemmed from a superior understanding, not merely of political
realities, but also of the value of forcing the hand of history itself
through such documents. But William Church's concluding remarks
about the Cardinal's *Mémoires* in his study of Richelieu's political
thought should serve as a necessary reminder of the Cardinal's
intentions: 'the inspiration . . . lay in his desire to leave behind him
a lengthy, comprehensive history of his ministry as part of his pro-
gram of self-justification'.[14] Any attempt to look afresh at the Cardinal's career must start from a realization of both the nature and the
limitations of even the most highly-prized sources.

If the effect of this is to relativize the sources for the study of
Richelieu, that in turn makes it possible to envisage a different
approach to his career. A critical analysis of the kind that will be
attempted in this book should begin by discarding the Olympian
view which sees his life as entirely of a piece, in which his success
in securing high ministerial office becomes the organizing principle
of everything that preceded that success. That approach owed much

12   *Correspondance de Pierre de Bérulle*, ed. Jean Dagens, 3 vols. (Louvain 1937–9), II.
     pp. 461–2, Bérulle to Richelieu, 18 May 1624. Claude Barbin was instrumental in gaining
     ministerial office for Richelieu in November 1616, and knew a great deal about one of
     the most obscure periods of his career. Barbin later became bitter at what he saw was
     Richelieu's failure to help him obtain his rehabilitation from disgrace, banishment, and
     imprisonment.
13   The phrase was used by Mathieu de Morgues, one of his earliest supporters who turned
     against him after the Day of the Dupes. See Maximin Deloche, *La Maison du Cardinal de
     Richelieu* (Paris 1912), ch. 3. See also Deloche, *Autour de la plume de Richelieu* (Paris 1920).
14   William F. Church, *Richelieu and Reason of State* (Princeton 1972), p. 473.

of its tenacity to the unstated assumption that from the very beginning of his career he had possessed political skills of an exceptional
kind, which he was ready to deploy to the full whenever suitable
opportunities arose. Richelieu's political skills, it will be argued
here, were not uniquely innate or God-given, but were gradually
developed through experience, which included making mistakes,
and, more crucially still, learning from those mistakes. The Richelieu who took office in 1624 was an infinitely more mature and
formidable figure than the Richelieu of, say, 1616 or 1620. This
point of view, it might be thought, should lead logically to close,
detailed attention to Richelieu's psychology and personal development. But the present study eschews any explicit attempt to develop
such a focus. There have been innumerable such studies over the
generations; more recently attempts have been made to subject the
young Richelieu – up to 1614 and beyond – to psychohistorical
treatment.[15] But it does not seem that the kind of documentation
which has survived offers much prospect of success to its practitioners. If the present work offers insights into Richelieu's personality, they do not derive from the application of psychological or
psychoanalytical theories, but from observing his behaviour not in
isolation, but in successive contexts, choices, and activities.

The focus of the chapters to follow is thus contextual and historical rather than simply biographical. They are based on the view that
the rise of Richelieu cannot be simply equated with his biography,
any more than, say, the Reformation can be equated with that of
Luther. Richelieu is emphatically not viewed as a *deus ex machina*, a
man of destiny sent to save France from the factious and the mediocre, but as a churchman who began his career without much money
or influence, and who gradually took advantage of the openings
which presented themselves over the years. Although the *terminus ad
quem* of the book is 1624, it will be suggested that Richelieu's later
ministerial record was strongly marked by the fact that he was a
priest and a bishop, by the manner in which he obtained office, and
by the political alignments without which he would not have played
any part at all in French political life.

Because both social and political historians have repeatedly shown
that French society contained few openings for the self-made or the
outsider, a proper understanding of a career like Richelieu's should
begin with an assessment of his family background, and its record of
action and service during the generations before him. Early modern
families like the Richelieus were repositories of traditions, especially
where the choice of a profession was concerned, traditions which

---

15 The most notable recent exercise in this genre is Marvick, *The Young Richelieu*.

constituted a kind of 'moral capital' in their eyes. This should not be taken to imply crude determinism or fatalistic acceptance of the past on their part, as is quite evident from their ability to seize new opportunities and add them to their stock of existing ones, but rather to indicate the extent to which generations thought and acted within patterns which they at once accepted and tried to fashion to their own advantage. Anyone attempting to uncover the previous history of the Richelieu family and the early years of its most famous scion must make do with sources that are highly fragmentary and scattered. Anecdotes abound, which is hardly surprising, and some of them may well have been borrowed from other contemporary families, since variations on them have been found elsewhere in the sixteenth century. What is noteworthy, however, is how disproportionately important a part they have played in explaining key events in the family's history. Genuine contemporary evidence, where available, leads to somewhat different interpretations, which perhaps rob traditional accounts of their familiar, dramatic character, but which open up perspectives which other scholars may be able to develop in due course. The career of Richelieu's own father is particularly rich in such mythical episodes; but, as will be seen, even his financial activities, which led to a well-known bankruptcy by the time of his death, contain unexpected surprises and remain highly difficult to explain satisfactorily.

Richelieu's early years, education and choice of an ecclesiastical career witness a repeat of this combination of oft-repeated anecdotes and independent sources which are relatively few and recalcitrant; the difficulties besetting a satisfactory historical reconstruction remain considerable. If the course of his career needs to be studied in the light of family history and the changing political context of his own time, equally the successive stages of that career need to be given due consideration. Thus Richelieu's activities as a bishop merit examination for their own intrinsic interest, rather than being viewed as a convenient ladder with which he managed to scale the political heights. Indeed, a central thesis of this book is that without this ecclesiastical dimension, his political career cannot really be understood at all. The experience he acquired, the problems he confronted, and the circles in which he moved identified him with the increasingly powerful reformist groups in the French church and in politics; between them they laid the foundations for his advancement, and although ultimately they were no guarantee of success, it is no accident that Richelieu consistently sought to reap as many political benefits as possible from his ecclesiastical status. This is often seen merely in terms of securing the cardinal's hat, but that, too, telescopes a wider variety of activities into one. Richelieu, it should be remembered, neither inaugurated nor terminated the age of the cardinal-ministers.

Finally, the broad political context of Richelieu's rise to power is equally indispensable. No doubt, it is naive to imagine that there has ever been an age of perfect political stability and continuity in government, but early seventeenth-century France has never enjoyed such a reputation. The political disturbances of the regency of Marie de Medici; the ministerial upheavals of the late 1610s and early 1620s; the uncertain hand of a well-meaning monarch endowed perhaps with more ability than has normally been assumed by historians, but whose judgement of men still seems to have been deficient; the real weaknesses of a government faced with difficult problems both at home and abroad – all of these generated political uncertainty and an unusually rapid turnover in ministerial ranks. By the same token, they created openings for those with the ambition, the backing, and the ability to take advantage of them. It remains to be seen why a younger son and an ecclesiastic should have been among the most successful in seizing the opportunities so offered.

Chapter 1
FAMILY TRADITIONS

'Songez, vous qui estes nez gentils-hommes, que Dieu vous a faicts naistre pour porter les armes, pour servir vostre prince, et non pas pour courre le lièvre ou faire l'amour. Quand la paix viendra, vous aurez vostre part du plaisir. Toutes choses ont leur temps et leur saison.'[1]

IN 1631, André Duchesne published a substantial folio volume entitled *Histoire de la maison royale de Dreux et de quelques autres familles*. He was an industrious genealogist and a eulogist of the French monarchy, one of those royal historiographers who have recently been described as 'artisans of glory'.[2] More at home perhaps in genealogy than in history, he made a living from placing his pen and learning at the service of the great – as witness the long list of works of both history and genealogy he produced before and after 1631. No doubt, demand for his talents increased as new men found their way into the upper ranks of French political and social life, bringing with them a consuming ambition to establish for themselves and their lineage a historical pedigree which would serve to explain and vindicate their sometimes rather too rapid elevation to eminence. By 1631, one such man – not exactly a favourite, even though many attributed to him the excessive powers of a typical favourite – felt a compulsive need to embellish his record and that of his family, especially as he had only that year been elevated to the ranks of the peerage. Thus it was that Duchesne included among the 'other families' alluded to in the title of his newest work an extensive genealogy of the Richelieu family. Because of Richelieu's known sensitivity on questions of pedigree, family and 'reputation', Duchesne's work was subjected to close supervision, but in return he was allowed to print carefully selected documents and information from the Cardinal's own archives. As befitted a politician who had recently established himself as undisputed chief minister, the burden of Duchesne's work was a twofold one: to highlight the long

---

1 Blaise de Monluc, *Commentaires 1521–1576*, ed. Paul Courteault (Paris 1964), p. 249.
2 See Orest Ranum, *Artisans of Glory. Writers and Historical Thought in Seventeenth-Century France* (Chapel Hill, N.C., 1980). Duchesne, though holding the title of historiographer royal, does not figure prominently in this study of seventeenth-century historians, but the list of his publications leaves no doubt as to his record.

record of unswerving service to the crown that had characterized the Richelieu family over many generations, and to insist upon their excellent noble pedigree, even to the extent of connecting them to the royal house of Dreux and ultimately tracing their ancestry all the way back to Charlemagne. Though such vainglorious excess drew barbed responses from some quarters, not all of which could be published, there could be no doubting the record's true purpose – to justify on the grounds of distinguished lineage and service the Cardinal's title to his political position.[3]

The seventeenth century's obsession with lineage and genealogy has been the nightmare of many a historian, laying false trails for the unwary and spawning half-truths of every kind. If most of the difficulties besetting critical history and genealogy seem to have sprung from the ambitions of new, usually office-holding, families to appropriate some older noble family tree, or graft themselves on to it – and were none too scrupulous as to the methods they employed – many older noble families themselves were by no means immune to the growing temptation to embellish family history. Social and political success proved a powerful incentive to rewrite family history in a way that would legitimate that success.

Where the diligence of historians has since managed to set the record straight, our understanding of the social and political history of the age has been considerably enhanced; in some instances, familiar commonplaces have been damaged beyond recognition.[4] The Richelieu family is only one of many French noble families to lack a wholly dependable critical history, based upon a sound genealogy established from authentic sources.[5] It is this continuing absence of such a history which has allowed both eulogists and detractors a free rein. It is not the purpose of the present study to make good this particular shortcoming, though it is one which should be borne in mind at the outset of any attempt to locate Richelieu's early career in the context which he himself chose, through André Duchesne, to emphasise in 1631.

Ideally, the historian should imitate the genealogist, and not limit his vision of the Richelieu family to a handful of perhaps arbitrarily-

---

3 B.N. Cabinet d'Hozier 271, dossier 7332, manuscript genealogy allegedly written in the mid-seventeenth century by Jean du Bouchet. See the discussion of this document in Marvick, *The Young Richelieu*, pp. 32–3 and p. 224, n. 10. Another unpublished genealogy, allegedly containing André Duchesne's real – and unflattering – views on Richelieu's origins, is in B.N. MS. Fr. 31808, pp. 1–12.

4 A fine recent example is Jean-Louis Bourgeon, *Les Colbert avant Colbert. Destin d'une famille marchande* (Paris 1973). More recently, Daniel Dessert has shown how the Fouquet family hijacked the pedigree of a homonymous family: *Fouquet* (Paris 1987), ch. 1.

5 Among the first and best modern studies is Aimé Martineau, *Le Cardinal de Richelieu*, vol. 1 (only vol. published) (Poitiers 1866).

chosen 'significant' members – say, the Cardinal himself, his father
or mother: a sixteenth-century family's 'capital' of tradition, attitudes and service would have been built on broader foundations
than that. But it is fortunate that anyone who is concerned with
the Cardinal's rise to power does not need to negotiate their way
upstream to the original sources of his family, and can legitimately
choose which individuals and features of its history deserve particular attention.

At the outset, it is fair to say that there is little in the history of the
Richelieus before the early decades of the sixteenth century to distinguish them from the mass of the French *gentilhommerie*, whose
noblesse might be undisputed, but who were not especially distinguished. Moreover, if we bear in mind that the French nobility was
not a historical constant composed of the same enduring families, it
will come as no surprise to learn that the Cardinal's ancestors did not
begin to acquire a clear family profile until the mid- to late-fifteenth
century. Before that, they and related families seem to have moved
around Poitou before finally settling in the neighbourhood of Chinon
and Loudun, where they intermarried with local families of similar
wealth and status.[6] In so doing, they inherited or exchanged both
lands and titles and, as they established themselves, became a typical
and integral part of a seigneurial society bound by ties of marriage,
service, and political interest. The lands and properties of the Richelieus reflected this history of mobility, marriage, exchange and
inheritance, and were a characteristically heterogeneous and geo-
graphically dispersed collection of the kind familiar to any reader of
the text of an act of *aveu et dénombrement*. Indeed, it was as a consequence of the marriage of Geoffroy du Plessis to a daughter of the
Clérambault family that the *seigneuries* of Richelieu and Beçay came
into du Plessis hands in 1488. The fact that from that point onwards
they adopted the title of *seigneurs* of Richelieu should suffice to
indicate the modesty of their rank and fortune prior to that juncture.
In one specific sense, they would remain relatively modest until as
late as 1631, when Richelieu was transformed at one stroke from a
mere *seigneurie* into a peerage; until that date their occasional use of
titles such as baron or marquis were either usurpations or harmless
fantasy, devoid of all legal foundation.[7] It may seem strange that the

---

6 For examples of this pattern from other parts of France, see James B. Wood, *The Nobility
   of the élection of Bayeux* (Princeton, N.J., 1980); E. Perroy, 'Social Mobility among the
   French *Noblesse* during the Later Middle Ages', *Past and Present* 21 (1962), pp. 25–38.
7 Neither Richelieu's father nor his elder brother ever called themselves anything other
   than *seigneur* of Richelieu. The Cardinal's own title of marquis du Chillou was an
   invention. See Joseph Bergin, *Richelieu: Power and the Pursuit of Wealth* (New Haven and
   London, 1985), p. 123.

marriage in 1506 of François III du Plessis, the Cardinal's great-grandfather, to Anne Le Roy, the daughter of a vice-admiral of France, brought no sudden elevation of the family, although she did add the *seigneurie* of Le Chillou to the family's collection of lands. It would appear that insofar as they extended their lands and wealth, it was at least as much the result of dowries or legacies from allied families as of their own services or ability.

But there is, of course, an equally obvious reason for this state of affairs, namely that the genealogy of the Richelieu family's services to the crown was for a long time limited and unremarkable. Their roots were overwhelmingly provincial, and an occasional marriage, like that with the daughter of Vice-Admiral Le Roy or, in the next generation, to a Rochechouart, did not suddenly transform their rank and interests; at most, what it did was to provide a window onto the wider world, especially of noble clientèles, and through them to establish an appropriate toe-hold at court. From the 1460s onwards, a number of Richelieus served in domestic posts in a variety of royal households, when royal residence in the towns and chateaux of the Loire valley made such office particularly accessible. But the most decisive fact is that for several generations, the family served the powerful house of Montpensier, whose seat at Champigny-sur-Veude was within a few miles of the Richelieu lands; prolonged service to this house enabled the Richelieus to fulfil their local ambitions and also to find a place within the clientèle of a family with national interests. The details of this relationship still remain obscure, but it was clearly already operative by the generation of the Cardinal's grandfather, Louis du Plessis. Thus, if the family gradually rose above the anonymous ranks of the mere gentlemen of their province, it was through a patiently-pursued combination of marriage alliances and traditional service to families like the Montpensier.

There is one notable feature of the Richelieu family's history which merits attention here, because it may partly explain the difficulties which prevented the family from taking full advantage of the opportunities available to it – that is its failure to develop into a well-knit clan. This failure, which was not uncommon among the French nobility, was essentially the result of its inability to spawn several collateral branches over a number of generations, the enduring fragility of the main line and, over three generations, the premature deaths of successive heads of the family. Louis I, the Cardinal's grandfather, was himself one of ten or eleven children and the eldest of five sons, yet he was the only son to produce children by the marriage he contracted with Françoise de Rochechouart in 1542. He died only nine years later, leaving three sons and two daughters. But, in turn, only one of these sons, Richelieu's father, married and had both sons and daughters, and although he was forty-two when he died, his death also came, as we shall see, at the worst possible time for his family. But there was worse to come, for the main line disappeared altogether with the Cardinal's eldest brother, Henri, who married late, left no children and died early from wounds received in a duel, in July 1619. We know how keenly Richelieu felt this void around him, and how dissatisfied he was with the mediocrity of some of the relatives he had to work with. One consequence of this was to make him more reliant than he might otherwise have been on individuals from his mother's family and its network of relations and clients, as well as on fellow ecclesiastics. But that void was itself not wholly new, and had almost certainly hampered the family's aggrandisement in earlier generations. A consequence of a different kind is that it inevitably focuses the history of the Cardinal's family background on the career and experiences of his father – and to a lesser extent, of his great-uncles. Although the Cardinal scarcely knew his father, both he and the rest of his generation were marked by his eventful career. So many incidents and features of that career have always been controversial that it demands close scrutiny; the portrait of the soldier, courtier, and financier presented here diverges considerably from the traditional accounts, not least from the one that his own descendants endorsed.

II

François IV du Plessis, one of five children and the second son of Louis de Richelieu, was born in 1548. His mother, Françoise de Rochechouart, was, despite her illustrious name, a *vieille fille* and, though resident at court throughout most of her life, apparently not regarded as a particularly good match: at the time of the marriage Louis de Richelieu was a lieutenant in her father's regiment, which may explain the union. Unfortunately, we do not know what effect his death, only three years after François's birth, had on the family's fortunes, but responsibility for his children was jointly assumed by their mother and their uncle, Jacques du Plessis, then abbot of La Chapelle-aux-Planches. One tradition, which seems plausible and in keeping with earlier family practice, has it that François and his elder brother, called Louis like their father, were sent as pages to the court of Catherine de' Medici and Charles IX; another holds that François himself was initially destined for a career in the church.[8] Whatever the truth of these claims, François first emerges from obscurity in circumstances which were, by all accounts, particularly dramatic, if

8   Marvick, *Young Richelieu*, p. 35, believes in the ecclesiastical option.

still not fully understood. The incident itself was too widely-known for the Cardinal's first biographer, Aubery, to ignore, but his treatment of it was oblique and apologetic: 'autre temps, autres moeurs'.

François's elder brother, Louis had succeeded to the family's land and titles, and had followed his father in the service of the Montpensiers when, probably in 1565, he was ambushed and killed by one of his neighbours with whom he had recently quarrelled, the *seigneur* of Brichetières.[9] The usual version of these events is that François, the second son, was summoned home from court by his proud and domineering mother to take his place as head of the family and to avenge his slain brother. If it is true that he was being groomed for an ecclesiastical career, this change of plan would provide a neat counterpoint to that of his most famous son, who was pushed *into* an ecclesiastical career for the good of the family and the protection of its interests. At any rate, François soon managed to avenge his brother in a calculated and clinical manner, cold-bloodedly killing his adversary in an ambush, after which, it is said, he had to leave his manor and the locality in order to escape the attentions of royal justice as it attempted to catch up with him. But to this day it is not clear whether a full trial for murder was ever conducted, and if so by whom. Some legal action against him was probably initiated, but we can discount many of the wilder embellishments of this chapter of the family's history. There is certainly no basis for the legend that, in order to escape from the law, François had to endure a long exile of nearly eight years during which he travelled to England, Germany and finally Poland, where it was his good fortune to meet the future Henri III of France, elected king of Poland in 1573, an encounter which would lay the foundations of his later career.[10] Instead of such a providential scenario, it seems altogether more likely that François, if he was indeed in serious trouble over his act of revenge, sought the king's pardon and obtained royal letters of remission to that effect, such a prosaic outcome being perfectly normal among nobles and others in his predicament.[11] It would have been relatively easy as Charles IX and his court, during their two-year progress through France between 1564 and 1566, actually stayed, in September 1565, at Champigny and Oiron, both within a stone's throw of Richelieu.[12]

9 Hanotaux, *Richelieu*, I, p. 33.

10 *Ibid.*, I, pp. 34–5; Maximin Deloche, *Les Richelieu. Le Père du Cardinal* (Paris 1923), pp. 4–6.

11 See Natalie Zemon Davis, *Fiction in the Archives* (Oxford 1988), a study based largely upon the contents of letters of remission. Robert Muchembled, *L'Invention de l'homme moderne* (Paris 1988), ch. 1, shows that rulers were sympathetic to appeals from individuals in a similar predicament to Richelieu.

12 Jean Boutier, Alain Dewerpe, Daniel Nordman, *Un Tour de France royal. Le voyage de Charles IX (1564–1566)* (Paris 1984), p. 141.

This outcome is the only one that is compatible with the one indisputable fact we know from these years. In August 1566, the marriage contract between François, 'gentilhomme ordinaire de la chambre du roy', and Suzanne de La Porte was signed before a Parisian notary, Claude Boreau. Not only is it hard to imagine that a fugitive from the law and his family could have openly negotiated a marriage in Paris at this point, but it is even less likely that his future father-in-law, François de La Porte, then at the height of his reputation as a lawyer in the *parlement* of Paris and enjoying the favour of Charles IX, would have pledged his only daughter to a criminal still under either suspicion or actual sentence. François was then eighteen years old, his intended spouse fifteen, and it seems that it was by the agreement of their parents that the marriage itself did not take place until 1569.[13] Thus, rather than wandering around foreign countries to avoid judicial reprisals, François probably spent most of his time during these years on his family lands; it is also likely that he saw military service with the regiment of Montpensier's son, the prince of Dombes, in which he had succeeded his elder brother as an ensign (*guidon*), and in which his disreputable uncle, Antoine, held the higher rank of lieutenant and, later, captain.

'A singular feature of the history of the lords of Richelieu is that they have always been fortunate in their choice of wives, having chosen all of them from noble and illustrious houses.'[14] This was André Duchesne's verdict on the early history of the family up to Louis de Richelieu's marriage to Françoise de Rochechouart; indeed, it was these noble wives, and not the direct Richelieu line, which enabled him to embellish the family's genealogy so effectively. However, Duchesne was prudent enough to abstain from commenting in the same vein on her daughter-in-law, Suzanne de La Porte. But from such a perspective, and given contemporary views on the subject, François de Richelieu's marriage to the daughter of a mere barrister, however well-known, was an undoubted *mésalliance*; the fact that it happened at all demonstrates that blue blood on its own was far from commanding unquestioning respect in a century which saw the traditional social hierarchy having to make room for many new names. The Richelieu family sought in the La Porte match just what other contemporary noble families did – money, service, and useful connections in the world of law. Given her pedigree, we can well believe the tradition that the Cardinal's grandmother, Françoise de Rochechouart, disapproved of the match, but families that were prepared to ignore, for whatever reasons, the stigma associated with

13   Deloche, *Le Père*, appendix 1.
14   *Histoire généalogique*, p. 45.

such marriages stood a better chance of thriving socially and econ-
omically than those that held to their principles and avoided them
altogether.[15] For her part, Suzanne de La Porte had previously been
sought at least once as a bride, and her family origins had even been
investigated by her prospective in-laws, but it is impossible to say
whether the decision not to go through with the marriage was based
on social considerations.[16]

Suzanne de La Porte not only brought to the marriage a dowry of
10,000 *livres*, but also several seigneurial lands to the north of Paris
which, as her mother's sole heir, she had already acquired. It is not
clear to what extent the Cardinal's father was able to put this wind-
fall to immediate positive use: there is no sign that it served to buy
office or land, as was commonly the case. The most likely reason is
that the Richelieu family debts were already proving difficult to
manage, and the marriage contract itself hinted at a possible need to
'alienate' some of Suzanne's property in order to pay them. That is
what duly happened, especially in 1571 and 1572, when François de
Richelieu explicitly justified several alienations of her assets by the
need to meet claims to unpaid dowries or jointures for members of
his own family going back as far as his great-grandmother! Then, in
September 1572, he formally acknowledged that the dower lands
had been sold and, in order to meet his contractual obligations to his
wife, he made over to her an inter vivos gift of a half-share in his
own *seigneurie* of Le Chillou – the estate from which their most
famous son would briefly take his fictitious title of marquis.[17] Also
in September 1572, François made his only known will, although
we can do no more than speculate on what induced him to do so just
then. But as no children had yet been born, he bequeathed all that
which he could to his wife, whom he also made his sole executrix.[18]

15 See Daniel Hickey, *The Coming of French Absolutism* (Toronto 1986), pp. 154ff, esp.
p. 158 for this argument at a provincial level, and the effects on the nobility of the
Dauphiné of a refusal of intermarriage.
16 Archives of the Order of Malta, vol. 3180, *preuves de noblesse* for entry to the Order by
Amador de La Porte, 17 Jan. 1584, testimony of Simon Bernard, who conducted the
investigation. The prospective husband was a certain sieur de Champmarin. I would like
to thank Dr David Allen for locating this important document for me in the Malta
archives.
17 M.C., VIII, 102, 11 Sept. 1572. Le Chillou was valued at 11,4000 *livres*, exactly the same
as the *propres* belonging to Suzanne of which Richelieu had just disposed. Deloche, *Le
Père*, p. 127, was puzzled by the lack of any later reference to these lands. Richelieu had
already undertaken, in accordance with the law and the undertakings given in his
marriage contract, to secure the *remploi* of his wife's personal property, which he had
quickly sold, as charges on his estates of Le Chillou and La Vervolière, provided that the
seigneurie of Richelieu itself remain unmortgaged for the eldest son of their marriage:
M.C., VIII, 98, 12 April 1571.
18 M.C., VIII, 102, 11 Sept. 1572. The testament is a short document of only two pages,
free of the grandiose formulae characteristic of wills at the time.

This is not the full record of the advantages that accrued to François de Richelieu from his marriage. It is usually claimed that La Porte demonstrated his goodwill and support by making further financial gifts to the young couple after their marriage, but these may well have been payments in respect of Suzanne de La Porte's not inconsiderable rights in the estates of her mother and grandparents. It is also widely held that he was the architect of his son-in-law's rise to favour and court office, and in particular that it was he who supplied the funds which enabled Richelieu to purchase the post of *grand prévôt* in 1578. Unfortunately, most of this is entirely without foundation, especially in relation to the office of *grand prévôt*. François de Richelieu's career, as we shall presently see, followed an altogether more conventional and prosaic route. Surprisingly little is known for certain about La Porte's career, who is usually viewed as an influential lawyer enjoying the personal favour of Charles IX. Yet quite how he rose from obscure origins to such eminence has never been explained, but the evidence suggests that it owed much to the Guises, who normally figure as bogeymen in Richelieu family history. Years after his death, it was claimed that La Porte had been 'chef du conseil de la royne d'Escosse et de Messieurs de Lorraine'.[19] There is independent evidence that in the mid-1560s, he was an 'ordinary' member of the Paris council of Mary Stuart, then dowager queen of France, but it is less clear when, or indeed if, he subsequently became president of that body.[20] There is no comparable evidence to show that he played in similar role in the affairs of the Guise family, but there must be a strong presumption that he did so: he certainly could not have served Mary Stuart in the way he did without active Guise patronage, as the cardinal of Lorraine held overall responsibility for her affairs.[21]

The advantages that La Porte drew from such exalted connections are far more difficult to discern. But rather than speculate on them, and on how far François de Richelieu might have been known to the Guises from an early age, we should note the simple but crucial fact that La Porte died in April 1572, less than three years after his daughter's marriage, and long before he could work the wonders for her and her husband so often attributed to him.[22] If his death de-

---

19 Archives of Order of Malta, vol. 3180, testimony of Philippe de Bras, 17 Jan. 1584.

20 A. Teulet, ed., *Relations politiques de la France et de l'Espagne avec l'Ecosse au xviᵉ siècle*, 5 vols. (Paris 1862), ii, pp. 268–81, at p. 271. His annual salary of 10 *livres* was far lower than that of other council members, suggesting that, in 1566 at least, his role was a relatively modest one.

21 See Mark Greengrass, 'Mary, Dowager Queen of France', *Innes Review* 38 (1987), pp. 171–94, for a well-documented study of Mary's complex interests in France after 1560.

22 M.C., VIII, 102, 24 April 1572. This document refers to La Porte's *inventaire après décès* begun on 10 April 1572, probably within a few days of his death. This document, which

prived the couple of a protector and mentor, in the short term it provided Richelieu with additional funds. Even though La Porte's estate had to be split between the children of his two marriages – a complex business which gave rise to much hard bargaining – François managed to secure for his wife the equivalent of around 15,000 *livres*.[23] Most of this, too, was quickly converted into cash and used to pay creditors, though he did spend 3,000 *livres* on a piece of land near his native estate.[24] Inherited debt, possibly on a quite substantial scale in relation to their resources at the time, was thus familiar to the Richelieu family long before the Cardinal's father could make his own singular contribution to the record.

Despite François de La Porte's early death, the benefits of the marriage to Richelieu were not simply material or financial. An advantageous marriage was one that procured social and professional relations that could be turned to account in a whole range of ways. La Porte was largely a self-made man, and therefore may not have had the opportunity to forge extensive family alliances among the Parisian élite. But both of his marriages were to be sources of significant support and influence in the history of the Richelieu family. His first wife was Claude Bochart, only daughter of Antoine Bochart and Françoise Gayant. Claude, like her own daughter, Suzanne, was an only child, but the Bochart family had developed a network of branches, and were already prominent among the Parisian office-holding class, enjoying greater status than La Porte, a mere barrister; they would rise still further and continue to distinguish themselves in both the church and the service of the crown during and indeed beyond the Cardinal's lifetime. Thus, his cousin, Jean Bochart de Champigny, was one of the two-man commission that administered the royal finances at the outset of Richelieu's ministry, between 1624 and 1626, while the Capuchin, Père Honoré de Champigny (Charles Bochart in civilian life), was an outstanding religious figure in early seventeenth-century Paris. La Porte's second wife, Madeleine Charles, was the daughter of Nicolas Charles, *seigneur* du Plessis-Piquet, a Poitevin family like La Porte's own; but equally significant was the fact that her mother was also a Bochart, thus making her and her step-daughter, Suzanne, cousins. These ties of blood between Madeleine, her children, and the Richelieu family proved to be of considerable value during the lifetime of the Cardinal's father. Madeleine Charles outlived her husband by many years, and there is

might have shed much valuable light on La Porte's career and his dealings with the Richelieu family, has not survived.

23 M.C., VIII, 102, 24 April 1572 (3 acts), 15 Sept 1572; M.C., LXXVIII, 90, 10 Feb. 1573, for some of the relevant acts relating to La Porte's estate.

24 M.C., VIII, 103, 15 March 1574, purchase of fief and *métairie* of Bournay, near Faye-la-Vineuse.

abundant evidence that she and François de Richelieu were on good terms, if we can judge by the extent to which she stood surety for him when he needed to borrow money or assumed some of his financial obligations.[25] Richelieu and his wife may even have lived in the same house as her for the first decade of their marriage, before acquiring a Parisian residence of their own, the hôtel de Losse, in 1579.[26] Moreover, as is well known, it was *her* children – the La Porte de La Meilleraye as they became known – who were to play important roles in the later history of the Richelieu family.

III

If a 'good' marriage, financial and otherwise, was essential for an ambitious young nobleman, it could not of itself map out a future career. That would have to emerge primarily out of a family's own capital of relations and traditions. It was one thing for the Cardinal to emphasize over half a century later his family's unbroken service of the crown, quite another to determine and hold to any such clear commitment during the 1560s and 1570s, when faction as much as religion plunged France into turmoil. The loyalties of the Richelieu family at this time are not easy to grasp, but they were almost certainly determined by their principal patrons, the Montpensiers. As a member of the king's council, and governor of Anjou, Touraine and Maine, Louis de Bourbon, duc de Montpensier, was a powerful political and military figure in western France right up to his death in 1582. He also emerged early during the wars of religion as leader of the Catholic Bourbons, and a scourge of the Huguenots. There were obvious advantages to being numbered among the retainers of such a powerful man, but for all the closeness of the connection with Montpensier, there is no direct evidence to show how far the Richelieu family adopted, or at least made public, the same fierce devotion to the Catholic cause, as distinct from serving and supporting the duke's ambitions.

What is clear is that it was above all the military developments of the 1560s and 1570s which gave the Richelieus a greater profile than they had previously enjoyed; it was primarily through continuing the family's military traditions, and not through fortunate accidents or reliance on his in-laws, that François de Richelieu rose to prominence. His ancestors had not achieved especial distinction during the

25 Abundant evidence of this support can be found in M.C., XC, vols. 140–6. The last known instance of it dates from 1586: M.C., XC, 146, 29 Sept.
26 M.C., LXXVIII, 118, 8 March 1578.

early Italian wars, but François's two uncles, François and Antoine, had sought fame and fortune beyond the Alps. In 1549, both were described as 'courounel des gens de pied françois au Piémont sous la charge du sieur de Bonivet', but it was apparently François, nicknamed Pilon, who distinguished himself most during the campaigns of the 1550s.[27] In recognition of his talents, he was given the command of one of the regiments of the reorganized and considerably reduced royal infantry in 1561. Had his career not been cut short by his death at the siege of Le Havre in 1563, he would probably have become the dominant figure, in political as well as military terms, in the Richelieu family.[28] After his death, it was his brother Antoine – nicknamed the Monk, as he had briefly been in a monastery in his early years – who was undoubtedly the best-known and certainly the most colourful figure among the Richelieu family. But his character and behaviour made him quite incapable of guiding the family's fortunes outside of the military sphere. Unmarried to the end, he began his career as an ensign in the regiment of the prince of Dombes, Montpensier's eldest son, rising to become successively lieutenant and captain. For many years, he appears to have been Montpensier's right-hand military man, and saw constant military action during the early wars of religion.[29] It was under the duke's aegis that he became governor of Tours in the early 1560s, and both were implicated in a massacre of Huguenots there in 1562 which was later publicly denounced by Coligny.[30] Antoine had an unsavoury reputation for cruelty and dissolute morals, and his death in a brawl outside a Parisian brothel in January 1576, was recorded for posterity by the diarist, Pierre de l'Estoile.[31] His nephew, who duly succeeded him as lieutenant of the regiment, had served his military apprenticeship under him, and although he would never flinch from his unpleasant duties as *grand prévôt* after 1578, he did not acquire the same reputation as Antoine.

There is every reason to suppose, therefore, that during the late 1560s and early 1570s, when not resident on his lands or in Paris, François de Richelieu was serving with his uncle in the Montpensier

27 M.C. XIX, 173, 14 Feb. 1549, *quittance* for loan. Admiral Bonnivet was one of the principal French commanders in northern Italy under Henri II. For 'captain' Richelieu's role in Italy, see Monluc, *Commentaires*, pp. 205, 237, 240–2. He is mistakenly called Louis in the notes to this edition.

28 A. de Brantôme, *Discours sur les colonels de l'infanterie de France*, ed. Etienne Vacheret (Paris/Montreal, 1973), p. 85.

29 *Archives Historiques du Poitou*, 12 (1882), p. 247, Henri duc d'Anjou to Comte du Lude, 21 May 1569.

30 *Histoire ecclésiastique des églises réformées*, ed. G. Baum and E. Cunitz, 3 vols. (Paris 1883), I, pp. 340–1; II, pp. 680–2, 693–4.

31 Pierre de L'Estoile, *Journal pour le règne de Henri III 1574–1589*, ed. L.-R. Lefèvre (Paris 1943), p. 105.

regiment. Given the prominent part played by the duke in the military campaigns of the third and fourth civil war, much of which took place in Poitou, it is quite likely that François participated in the successive battles and sieges undertaken under the overall leadership of the duc d'Anjou, the future Henri III. Unfortunately, stories about personal exploits at, for example, the battle of Moncontour, or at the sieges of St Jean-d'Angély or Fontenay-le-Comte, remain wholly unsubstantiated, and may well have been invented later to flatter the Cardinal.[32]

In view of the favour Richelieu later enjoyed under Henri III, it is tempting to assume some personal connection dating from the 1568–70 campaigns, but here, too, it has to be said that there is not a scrap of positive evidence. It is impossible to accept another long-standing tradition that derives from the Cardinal's first biographer, Antoine Aubery, and which is often thought of as the key to his subsequent career – that François's future 'fortune' was made when he won Anjou's favour on accompanying him to Poland after his election as king in May 1573. Aubery claimed that he was a member of the advance party which reached Poland ahead of the king, and that he played an important part in securing Henri III's escape and return to France.[33] In fact, the new king's party did not leave French soil until December 1573, and there is no mention of François in any of the extensive records relating to the king's household or the activities of the French party in Poland.[34] What *is* documented, however, is that he was present in Paris throughout the early months of 1574, attending to his personal affairs; and with the ailing Charles IX finally dying in May 1574, it is hard to see how or when Richelieu might have made even a brief trip to Poland.[35]

Once again, some less dramatic account, and one assuming a gradual advancement, seems more appropriate if we are to explain the favour Richelieu won with Henri III. First of all, it should be noted that during the three years it took Henri III, following his return to France, to reward him with the office of *grand prévôt*, there are no signs of rapid or unusual royal attention that could be construed as an obvious and routine result of the Polish interlude or

32 Pierre Champion, *Jeunesse de Henri III*, 2 vols. (Paris 1941–2), I, p. 213, for references to operations in region of Mirebeau, Ile-Bouchard, Faye-la-Vineuse, all within a stone's throw of Richelieu; Montpensier commanded a section of the army at Moncontour, *ibid.*, pp. 215–18.

33 See Deloche, *Le Père*, pp. 14–15, for references to the Polish connection, which he accepted as probable.

34 See Pierre Champion, *Henri III roi de Pologne*, 2 vols. (Paris 1943–51), a detailed account based on extensive sources. The name of Richelieu does not figure in the household list: I, pp. 303–22.

35 M.C., VIII, 103, acts dated 2 Jan., 15 and 19 March 1574.

some earlier connection. While one should be wary of taking at face value the formulaic expressions encountered in letters issued by the royal chancery, it may well be that Henri III was simply stating the plain facts, which he had no need to exaggerate, when, in his letters appointing François a *conseiller privé* in May 1578, he referred to 'the praiseworthy ('recommendables') services he has rendered our predecessors and ourselves in the late wars', and that the absence of any reference to Poland is no oversight. Moreover, the king then went on to mention, though without itemizing them, 'several other major and important duties related to the good of our service'.[36] These services, it seems clear, date especially from the crowded years 1576 and 1577, which saw a resumption of the wars, two unsuccessful edicts of pacification, serious trouble with the leading princes and nobles of the realm, and a meeting of the Estates General. Henri III found himself in a weak position, both politically and militarily, having to conduct negotiations with leaders of the Huguenots and the aristocratic Malcontents; as virtually all of them were absent from court, emissaries moved ceaselessly around France. The king and the court spent much of their time in Anjou and Poitou, one of the principal theatres of both warfare and politics in these years. It was probably his standing as an energetic and trusted Montpensier man – he succeeded his uncle, Antoine, as regimental captain in January 1576 and assumed a more prominent role – and as a *gentilhomme ordinaire de la chambre du roy*, that gradually brought Richelieu into closer touch with Henri III. Little by little, it seems, his usefulness and his abilities became apparent. Thus, in June 1576, he was one of the royal commissioners who invested the king's younger brother with the duchy of Anjou, an instance of his own provincial origins proving beneficial;[37] either he or his uncle had been involved in the preceding negotiations with the new duke.[38] By October 1577, as two rare surviving letters from his pen show, he was reporting directly to the king and to Villeroy, the secretary of state, on a mission to treat with political and military figures such as the prince of Condé for the implementation of the peace of Bergerac, and the pacification of Poitou and Aunis following the fall of the town of Brouage that August.[39] For several months thereafter, he continued

36 A.N., V⁵ 1225, fo. 246v, 11 May 1578.
37 Mack P. Holt, *The Duke of Anjou and the Wars of Religion* (Cambridge 1986), p. 70.
38 *Lettres de Catherine de Médicis*, ed. H. de La Ferrière and G. Baguenault de la Puchesse, 10 vols. (Paris 1880–1905). v, p. 179, letter to Brûlart, 16 Dec. 1575. Catherine expresses her satisfaction with the 'sieur de Richelieu' – Antoine or François? – just returned from talks with her son.
39 Deloche, *Le Père*, pp. 23–4, letter to king, 12 Oct. 1577; *ibid.*, p. 25, to Villeroy, same date. See Condé's letter of 4 Jan 1578 to Henri III about Richelieu's mission, in *Lettres de Catherine de Médicis*, VI, p. 94, note 1.

to shuttle between Paris, the itinerant court, and the western provinces in the service of the king. It was this kind of activity which
enabled him to display those qualities and characteristics that eventually decided Henri III, a shrewd judge of men, to offer him a post
which would attach him more firmly to his person and his service.

The general political context of these years is especially pertinent
to the king's decision to promote Richelieu. Shortly after his acces-
sion in 1574, Henri III found himself confronted with a whole series
of problems – the disaffection and ambitions of his brother, Alençon;
the failure to achieve a workable religious peace with the Huguenots;
the threat represented by leading nobles such as Damville who were
prepared to make common cause with the Huguenots, as well as by
the first Catholic League; and, above all, the influence of great aristocratic families (above all the Guises), from whose clutches he was
desperate to free himself. Much of his reign would be taken up with
the pursuit of this last goal, and with the search for loyal, trustworthy servants from among the ranks of the middling nobility who
were not compromised by the politics of the great aristocracy.
François de Richelieu was among the earliest to benefit from this
political conjuncture. In early 1578, Henri III persuaded the baron de
Sénecey to part with his office of *prévôt de l'hôtel du roi*, probably as
part of an effort to reduce the influence of the duc de Guise, his
patron.[40] On 28 February 1578, the king appointed François not only
to Sénecey's office, but also to that of *grand prévôt de France*, a post
which had been suppressed or, it would seem, vacant for more years
than anyone could remember.[41] There are signs that Sénecey himself
was reluctant to go, since the *grand conseil* refused to register Richelieu's appointment for several months, on the grounds that it ante-
dated Sénecey's formal act of resignation, and it took the king's
personal intervention in April 1578 to overcome these objections.[42]
The following month, Richelieu was one of those nominated, in one
of the king's reform ordinances, a *conseiller d'état* entitled to attend
council when the duties of his office rendered it appropriate.[43] This
nomination also entitled him to attend deliberations of the *grand
conseil* and the *parlement* of Paris. Around the same time, he became a
chevalier of a royal order of chivalry, doubtless that of St Michel,
though not, it should be noted, of that of the Holy Ghost, founded

40 Jacqueline Boucher, *La Cour de Henri III* (Rennes 1986), p. 59.
41 A.N. V⁵ 1225, fos. 244v-6r, 28 Feb. 1578. The letters patent refer to two previous
    holders of this office, but are extremely vague about the relevant edicts or ordinances
    governing its prerogatives and exercise.
42 *Ibid.*, fo. 246r-v, 20 April, *lettres de jussion*.
43 B.N. MS. Fr. 18,155, fo. 3v, 'des personnes desquelles les rois ont composé leurs
    conseils'.

later that year.[44] Richelieu would have to wait another seven years for that particular honour, a reminder that he had not yet established himself sufficiently to the be admitted to the deliberately limited new élite of chivalry.[45] No trace has come to light of any financial transactions concerning the office of *grand prévôt*, but it is not inconceivable that Henri III himself compensated Sénecey, as he is known to have done in other instances of a similar kind, for the loss of office sustained at the king's own insistence.[46]

In purely institutional terms, Richelieu's office was overshadowed by that of the duc de Guise as *grand maître de France*, a post which made Guise titular head of the king's own household. In previous decades, a succession of ordinances governing the life of the court and the royal household officers had been published, but these had not always been implemented. Contemporary commentators differed widely in their views on the French court, with some claiming it was orderly and magnificent, others that it was unregulated and undignified. The less than satisfactory state of the court probably had much to do with the confusion of roles and authority resulting from conflicting legislation, as well as from a tradition of relatively unrestricted access to the king himself. In the opening years of his reign, Henri III had fended off a determined bid by the duc de Guise to strengthen his grip on the household but, not wishing to antagonize Guise unnecessarily, he agreed, among other things, that the *grand prévôt* and his officials should obey the *grand maître*, albeit 'en ce seulement qui sera necessaire de faire pour la police de la maison de Sa Majesté, comme aussi feront pour le regard de la police'.[47] Henri III's later ordinances and actions, especially his efforts to reform both the court and his personal household, made it clear that he was determined to retain his own freedom of action. Given Guise's political record, and the broader political antagonism between the two men, this conflict was not limited to purely household matters and, during the following years, Henri managed to transfer some important court offices to non-Guise courtiers.[48]

The consequences of all this were, needless to say, of the first importance for the career of Richelieu who, had Guise had his way, might have found himself a mere cypher. In the event, it is not clear how far Guise, who spent much time away from the court after

44 A.N. V⁵ 1225, fo. 246v, 11 May, for first known mention of this title.
45 The first appointments to the new order were made in Dec. 1578: *Lettres de Henri III*, ed. Michel François, 4 vols. to date (Paris 1959–84), IV, nos. 3196 *seq*.
46 Boucher, *Cour de Henri III*, p. 60.
47 Pierre de Miraumont, *Le Prévost de l'hostel et grand prévost de France avec les édits, arrests, réglements et ordonnances concernans son iurisdiction* (Paris 1615), pp. 56–65.
48 Boucher, *Cour de Henri III*, pp. 59–60

1578, ever attempted to subordinate Richelieu to him. His only documented attempt to do so dates from mid-1588, after Richelieu had been in office ten years, but it had little to do with his earlier drive to impose his control over the royal household.[49] Evidence from the intervening years suggests that clear battle-lines, factional or ideological, were an occasional rather than permanent feature of political life at Henri III's court; we should be wary of accepting at face value later attempts – often based on a rewriting of recent history after the wars of religion – to classify contemporaries as either 'servants' or 'enemies' of the king.[50] One example of this may suffice here. On two occasions, in late 1583 and early 1584, the English ambassador became extremely worried by Richelieu's maritime activities: on the first occasion he described Richelieu as being 'bukell and thonge with the Duke of Guise' and, on the second, as being 'affected to the house of Guise'.[51] The ambassador's perceptions may not be entirely reliable – Richelieu's 'affection' for Guise may have been temporary and tactical – but it is beyond dispute that, both then and later, Richelieu worked in close co-operation with the duc d'Elbeuf, another member of the Guise clan.

The office of grand prévôt made its holder not only a kind of chief constable of the court, wherever it might be, but also conferred jurisdiction over civil and criminal cases relating to the court and its members. Seeing that the king's peace was kept by all those who lived and worked there was his primary responsibility. Because we cannot be sure how far royal ordinances are a satisfactory guide to actual practice, we can turn to the passages on the office of grand prévôt contained in a detailed account of the French court written in late 1584 by an English visitor, Richard Cooke. He devoted considerable space to it under the heading 'the order of the kinges court when it removeth or is in prograce', but it is clear that Richelieu's functions were not confined to periods of peregrination. Nor is the order of Cooke's remarks itself without interest:

> For the better orderinge of the trayne the kinges of Fraunce have thought good to create a certayne officer to be acknowledged cheife and superintendant over all his house. To this officer is geven power and authoritie to take cognizance of all causes and to

49 Deloche, Le Père, pp. 256–7, letter of 16 Sept. 1588.
50 For a specific instance of this, see Élie Barnavi and Robert Descimon, La Sainte ligue, le juge et la potence. L'Assassinat du président Brisson (Paris 1985), ch. 9.
51 The two letters are printed in full in William Murdin, ed. A Collection of State Papers relating to Affairs in the Reign of Queen Elizabeth from the year 1571 to 1596 (London, 1759), pp. 380–3, Stafford to Secretary of State Walsingham, 20 Dec. 1583; ibid., pp. 389–91, same to same, 18 Jan. 1584. The first is calendared in the C(alendar) of S(tate) P(apers) Foreign, (hereafter C.S.P. Foreign) XVIII, pp. 264–5.

doe justice for all sortes of crimes committed within the verge as well within the Court as without . . . He hath charge to keepe in goode order all the kinge's trayne of princes and others followinge the Court, and to compel everie one to kepe good rule and to paye justlie and trulye theire hostes for everie thinge they take. Allsoe he hath charge over the daughters of joy, that is to saie over all theire light weomen called theire fillez de joy who doe ordynarili followe the Court.

Cooke then goes on to describe in more detail the *grand prévôt*'s role in fixing prices and controlling markets in places where the court was resident, and he notes that the *grand prévôt* was expected to report to the king once a week on all matters appropriate to his charge.[52]

Even such a brief resumé conveys something of the range of the *grand prévôt*'s activities, and makes it clear that the office was no sinecure designed for popularity-seekers. The *grand prévôt* was actively involved in supervising and policing those spheres where the court and its members encountered the outside world, and it is not hard to imagine the difficulties he might have encountered in obliging great nobles and their households to pay for lodgings and other services wherever the court might happen to be at any moment. Complaints against the court and its inhabitants by townspeople were commonplace, and ensured that even those aspects of the *grand prévôt*'s job which did not involve criminal matters could be unpleasant and provoke friction. In addition, the court did not have its own *intendance*, and was therefore dependent on a peculiar category of entrepreneurs, 'les marchands à la suite de la cour', who were obliged by their status to follow it wherever it went to ensure regular supplies of food and other goods. Controlling them and fixing price-lists for the goods they supplied also fell within the province of the *grand prévôt*. And, as Cooke also notes at considerable length, he was also entitled to fix prices within the towns or areas where the court happened to be, to supervise their markets, and to prevent sales of food outside the market-place. In Paris, for example, it was he, in consultation with the officials of the Châtelet, who fixed the prices of foodstuffs sold in the city markets.[53] There was, then, no shortage of work for Richelieu and his staff of ninety-nine deputies, officials and archers recorded for the year 1585.

---

52 David Potter and P.R. Roberts, 'An Englishman's view of the court of Henri III, 1584–1585: Richard Cooke's "Description of the Court of France"', *French History*, 2 (1988), pp. 343–4. The editors' introduction to this document usefully summarizes our knowledge about Henri III's court and his efforts to reform it.

53 *Ibid.*, p. 344.

But it was the policing powers and the concomitant civil and criminal jurisdiction which were central to the *grand prévôt*'s office. Inevitably, Richelieu was unhappy about certain features of life at court, and he made suggestions for improvements to the Assembly of Notables held at Saint Germain in 1583, thereby seconding Henri III's own efforts to the same end.[54] Not only were those subject to his jurisdiction not enamoured of it, but rival courts like the *grand conseil* also tried to circumscribe his powers. In civil cases subject to him, appellate jurisdiction belonged to the *grand conseil*, but in criminal cases, no such jurisdiction existed and he was the sole judge of last resort.

Insofar as Henri III was breaking new ground by promoting Richelieu, he did so primarily by reviving the office of *grand prévôt de France* and coupling it with that of *prévôt de l'hôtel*. The functions of this office were all the vaguer as it had long been vacant, and the *prévôté*'s first historian confessed he could not find sources to define its attributions satisfactorily.[55] It was perhaps this very uncertainty which gave the king maximum flexibility: he employed his *grand prévôt* on numerous commissions and *chevauchées* throughout the kingdom, and while Richelieu was subject in theory to the authority of the marshals of France, whenever it was a question of arresting and bringing suspects to trial, the sweeping powers he enjoyed were such that existing courts were unlikely to welcome his intervention.[56] Missions carried out in his capacity as *grand prévôt* probably explain Richelieu's numerous recorded voyages to different provinces during the 1580s; it was he, for example, who was sent to Normandy in 1579 to put down a military rising there by the comte de la Roche-guyon.[57] When arrests had to be made, courtiers placed under surveillance, important prisoners to be escorted, criminals to be tried and executed, or other unpleasant tasks performed, the *grand prévôt* was usually called upon.[58] Although they may well have been on the

---

54   *Ibid.*, p. 320. These touched on questions of hygiene and the order of the court. An earlier petition to the king, dating from 1580, is to be found in Deloche, *Le Père*, pp. 151–8.
55   Miraumont, *Le Prévost de l'hostel*, pp. 147–8. The author was himself a former *lieutenant* in the *prévôté*, and thus well placed to know his subject.
56   *Ibid.*, pp. 144–5.
57   These missions can be tabulated from the receipts for the costs of travel to be found in B.N., Pièces originales, vol. 2302, dossier 52,053, Richelieu family. These were used extensively by Deloche in his *Le Père de Richelieu*, *passim*. Deloche (pp. 144–5) also refers to the 1579 expedition to Normandy.
58   Miraumont, *Le Prévost de l'hostel*, esp. pp. 22f, 172ff, 287–9, provides numerous original documents which illustrate the range of tasks he performed. Several traces of these activities can also be found in *C.S.P. Foreign*, XIV, p. 337, Cobham to secretaries of state, 12 July 1580; *ibid.*, XVI, p. 393, 27 Oct. 1582; *ibid.*, p. 432, Cobham to Walsingham, 14 Nov. 1582.

wane by the time Richelieu became *grand prévôt*, the court itself was a centre of some unseemly conflicts, murders and assassinations as the likes of Alençon, Marguerite de Valois and others took the lead in exacting revenge on those who had offended them.[59] In an age which experienced more than its share of cruelty and gruesome deeds, his was not an occupation for the squeamish, as can be seen from even a few examples. In March 1586, he publicly displayed the heads of certain military freebooters caught operating without commission but claiming to 'belong' to Montpensier *fils*, and whom he had promptly executed.[60] If he balked at participating in the murder of the Guise brothers at Blois in December 1588, he was on hand to arrest the leading Leaguers present at the Estates General there, an action singled out for denunciation by the leaders of the Parisian League.[61] Less than a year later, it was he who tried for murder the dead body of Henri III's assassin, Jacques Clément.[62] All contemporary accounts agree that François de Richelieu performed his duties conscientiously and with a vigour and grim determination that won him the sobriquet 'Tristan l'Hermite', and his reputation was sufficiently well-known for the pamphleteers of the League to single him out for criticism and pillory.[63] Having left Paris during the uprising of May 1588 with Henri III, whom he accompanied from place to place during the following year, he had no hesitation in rallying to Henri IV in August 1589 after Henri III's murder. With the 'court' now effectively reduced to the condition of a military camp, Richelieu's normal functions as *grand prévôt* were largely overtaken by those as a military captain, and his expenses and activities, which included numerous secret missions on the king's orders, increased sharply.[64] He fought energetically at Navarre's side during the campaigns and sieges of 1589 and 1590.[65] It is hardly surprising that Henri, whose brushes with assassins were numerous, should have picked a man of his resolution and firmness for the post of first

59 Boucher, *La Cour de Henri III*, pp. 48–9.
60 René de Lucinge, *Lettres sur la cour d'Henri III en 1586*, ed. A. Dufour (Geneva 1966), p. 118.
61 *Registre des délibérations du bureau de l'hôtel de ville de Paris*, ed. F. Bonnardot *et al.*, vol. IX (Paris 1902), pp. 232, 239–41, 243, letters of 8, 11 and 12 Jan 1589.
62 Miraumont, *Le Prévost de l'hostel*, pp. 22–3.
63 Deloche, *Le Père*, pp. 266ff.
64 B.N., P.O. 2302, dossier Richelieu, no. 22, 1 July 1588, Richelieu's receipt of 1,500 *livres* for his *estat extraordinaire* as *grand prévôt* for the month from 15 June to 14 July 1588. See Hélène Michaud, 'L'Ordonnancement des dépenses et le budget de la monarchie 1587–1589', *Annuaire-Bulletin de la Société de l'Histoire de France* (1970–1), p. 140, who records payments for no fewer than thirteen secret payments between Sept. 1588 and July 1589.
65 *Lists and Analysis of State Papers*, vol. I (Aug. 1589–June 1590), ed. R.B. Wernham (London 1964), p. 265, for a near-miss from a bullet at siege of Falaise, Dec. 1589.

captain of his guards. But his tenure was very brief indeed: his first 'quarter' of service began on 1 June 1590, but he died on 10 July 1590 at Gonesse, north of Paris, during the king's abortive first siege of the city.[66]

IV

Although the functions of the *grand prévôt* made the office more 'domestic' (as the Cardinal would have disdainfully said) than political, its greatest advantage was that it placed the incumbent in a position of close proximity to the monarch; by comparison with that, the formal duties of an office counted for little. Moreover, as Henri III was determined to reform his court, and to introduce a measure of order and distance there in order to protect the king's person and privacy, such proximity was even more valuable than it had been in the past. By the same token, the king was fortunate to have near him as his *grand prévôt* a man as tough and as loyal as François de Richelieu. There were limits, of course, and Richelieu did not enjoy anything like the unrestricted freedom of access allowed to successive favourites like Villequier, Joyeuse or Épernon. Equally, he never came remotely as close as his most famous son to taking a seat in the king's inner council and becoming a major voice in the shaping of royal policy. As *grand prévôt* and courtier, he figured prominently in the front rank of the second division. It is difficult, for example, to imagine how far a man like Richelieu, whose cultural and intellectual accomplishments were strictly limited, could have shared Henri's well-known passion for ideas and the arts.

François de Richelieu's promotion to *grand prévôt* inevitably curtailed his purely military or quasi-diplomatic activities, but it enabled him to develop others that are no less central to an understanding of his career in the service of the king. Henceforth, his presence would be required at court, which was increasingly resident in Paris during the 1580s, and the duties of his office ensured that he would be gradually absorbed by the concerns of the court. This is emphatically not to suggest that he turned into an effete dandy of the kind popularly supposed to have flourished under Henri III; both his reputation and his duties make it difficult to think of him as one of the king's *mignons*. But it is not always sufficiently emphasized that the court was much more than a mere social stage, even under Henri III, and that it was above all the hub of government, with all the

---

66 *Ibid.*, p. 288, Lyly to Stafford, 31 May 1590, for his appointment. Captains of the guard, like so many officials in royal service, served in turns on a 'quarterly' basis.

political and financial ramifications that this implies. A welcome consequence for us of Richelieu's more sedentary, if not exactly tranquil, existence is that more traces survive of his activities and pre-occupations during the 1580s. Some of the best evidence for these activities and connections at court is provided by the records of his financial affairs. These are far from complete, if only because of the confused state in which his finances were left at his death, and what we have is not always easy to interpret. But they add a great deal to what has previously been said and, without a consideration of them, the subsequent history of the house of Richelieu can hardly be understood.[67]

In the early years which followed his marriage, Richelieu was, as we have seen, primarily concerned to clear inherited and, in some cases, long-standing family debts. He seems to have been relatively successful in this, as no subsequent claims of this kind, apart from those of his mother for her jointure, have come to light. It is impossible to say how much this policy of setting his own house in order reduced his available capital; his reserves were probably limited, and there is no trace of unusual financial operations throughout most of the 1570s. His ambitions were, it appears, only finally released by his appointment as *grand prévôt*, which in turn greatly widened his scope to fulfil them. Something of this is suggested by his first major operation after becoming *grand prévôt*: the purchase, in July 1579, of the hôtel de Losse, situated in the rue du Bullouer, near the Louvre, which was to be the family's normal place of residence until the Day of the Barricades, in May 1588. Valued at 9,500 *livres*, it could not rival the splendid residences of the great nobles and financiers, but neither was it inexpensive, and it does seem to have been a wholly appropriate town residence for a nobleman-courtier of the second rank with formal duties and a numerous staff under his orders.[68] Over the years, the household would grow in size, the birth of the first of his children roughly coinciding with the purchase.

The surviving records of the 1580s lead to an unmistakable conclusion: François de Richelieu became an active member of a category of courtier which historians of seventeenth-century France would describe as an *affairiste*, or more charitably perhaps as a gentleman-financier. The former term refers to those who, in contemporary language, were 'intéressés dans les affaires du roi' – who were, in other words, investing or speculating in the royal finances. In this respect at least, the *grand prévôt* was making, rather than

---

67 For convenience, all monetary values will be given in *livres tournois*, although the legal tender between 1576 and 1602 was the *écu*, valued at 3 *livres*.

68 Deloche, *Le Père*, appendix 2, for text of sale contract, 21 July 1579.

following, family tradition; there is no sign than his uncles or other members of the family took a close interest in the royal finances.

The beginnings of Richelieu's financial 'career' are hard to pin-point, given his long absences from Paris during the mid- and late 1570s; the exceptions are his numerous, though in themselves perfectly ordinary, efforts to raise cash through private annuities (*rentes constituées*). But, by the early 1580s, there can be no doubt that he was increasingly associating with court nobles and financiers of the first rank. The financial drain on royal resources represented by the civil wars, as well as by Henri III's sometimes lavish attempts to purchase loyalty or reward service with cash, enlarged the customary scope for private enterprise, as well as the king's own dependence on it. New methods of raising money were required, and the ensuing 'affaires extraordinaires' played an important part in fuelling the bitter criticism of Henri III's régime.[69] They also provided a wide circle of courtiers like the *grand prévôt* with opportunities to speculate, to facilitate access to royal ministers, to act as brokers, and to secure shares in the ensuing financial operations. Such activities did not respect conventional 'party' or factional lines; they brought together in the pursuit of a wide range of material rewards men of otherwise differing backgrounds and commitments, and the most lucrative of them were a source of strong rivalries at Henri III's court.[70] Equally, it should be noted that it was strongly incumbent on members of a court often suffering from serious liquidity problems to use their own credit to assist the king. It is not always easy to draw a line between duty and speculation in this sphere, and it is clear that in the last years of Henri III's reign, Richelieu was one of those *fidèles* who was ready to lend money to a hard-up monarch.[71] Needless to say, the records of many of these financial operations are often either incomplete or deliberately opaque. For example, it is almost certainly the case that Richelieu occasionally merely 'lent his name' to transactions involving other principals; yet even where this was so, it reveals a role he could have played, and others, of course, did the same for him. What does not seem to be in doubt is that he was engaged in financial operations on an increasing, sustained, and quite massive scale.

The sheer variety of Richelieu's financial interests is no less striking, and it is better, rather than listing them indiscriminately, to group them together under a number of headings, beginning with

69 See Richard Bonney, *The King's Debts. Finance and Politics in France 1589–1661* (Oxford 1981), pp. 25–9.
70 See Boucher, *La Cour de Henri III*, pp. 83ff.
71 See Michaud, 'L'Ordonnancement des dépenses et le budget de la monarchie 1587–1589', pp. 119, 130.

the least complicated. The extent to which he was officially entitled to make money out of the prerogatives of his office was probably limited enough, yet his authority over the merchant-purveyors of the court was a legitimate source of profit; in 1587 we find him permitting many of them to resign their positions to persons of their choice (the privilege of *survivance*), and charging them fees varying between 120 and 300 *livres* for doing so. Unofficially, his office enabled him to do much more than that, and merchants anxious to become purveyors probably had to offer him some inducement if they were to succeed in their ambition. Moreover, if Richard Cooke was correct in reporting the *grand prévôt* as controlling the court's 'light weomen', it would be absurdly prudish to assume that that responsibility did not have its own financial rewards – though it should surprise no one that no actual record of profits has come to light! In addition, petitioners of various kinds had recourse to him, either directly or indirectly, as witness the case of a suitor who, even after the court had fled from Paris in 1588, offered to pay Richelieu 6,000 *livres* for his intercession, with an immediate offer of gift of horses.[72] Inducements of that nature are likely to have been more common during the preceding decade, when royal authority was greater.

All of this, however, was on a tiny scale compared with the financial and commercial enterprises in which Richelieu was to become involved. Not only is the variety of these last impressive, but the size of the sums of money changing hands is such as to require close attention and, if possible, explanation.

It has long been known that François de Richelieu, like his son, took a keen interest in maritime affairs, and particularly in the actual ships of the royal navy. Quite how or when this began is hard to say, but it may well owe something to his participation in the military campaigns against the Huguenot bases of La Rochelle and Brouage. His subsequent activities while *grand prévôt* were not isolated ventures, but required associates and backers, some more anxious to preserve their anonymity than others. They were especially numerous from 1582 to 1586, and owed much to the patronage of the duc de Joyeuse, who would become admiral of France in June 1582. From the very beginning, Richelieu's interest was a mixture of assistance to the crown with the pursuit of private ambitions, and the ventures themselves as much commercial and financial as purely naval.

Maximin Deloche believed that Richelieu's interest stemmed from his being selected by Catherine de' Medici as one of a band of *fidèles*

---

72 Bibliothèque Victor Cousin, *fonds* Richelieu 14, fo. 1, letter to Antoine du Buisson.

to act as cover for her highly-secret plans to singe Philip II's beard after his conquest of Portugal in 1580. This involved sending a fleet and army to occupy the Azores and Brazil in the name of Don Antonio, Prior of Crato, the Portuguese pretender supported by France – plans which were effectively shattered by the defeat of successive expeditions in the Azores in July 1582 and July 1583 respectively.[73] The extent of Richelieu's involvement in either expedition – or indeed in preparatory expeditions in 1579–80 – is extremely difficult to assess, and it is probable that he was no more than a minor participant. Nevertheless, there is reliable evidence that as early as March 1581, he was at least party to discussions about the sending of French naval expedition to the islands.[74] But it is unclear whether his own investment in these disastrous expeditions went any further than taking a hand in lending money to the Portuguese Pretender in May 1582, shortly before the first of them.[75]

There is no doubt, however, that these enterprises alerted him to the possibilities of combining politics and commerce. Despite the setbacks, Don Antonio refused to abandon his ambitions, and there was talk of a new French expedition by September 1583; Henri III played along with such schemes, but never gave them much priority. It was left to men such as Joyeuse, Richelieu, Théodoric Schomberg, the duc d'Elbeuf, and others to organize and finance new ventures. In fact, it was in connection with preparations for a new expedition that the English Ambassador, Stafford, described Richelieu as being 'bukell and thonge' with Guise in December 1583. Richelieu was energetic in organizing the expedition; Stafford believed he was aiming to put a fleet of no fewer than twenty-five ships to sea, and relying on Brest, La Rochelle, Dieppe and other ports to provide ships and victuals.[76] But, from an early point during their preparations, many observers believed that private profit was the main motive of the principals; the project was even nicknamed 'the pretence of Don Antonio', and its destination or its objectives re-

---

73   *Le Père*, pp. 95ff, 191ff. Deloche's principal source is Charles de la Roncière, *Histoire de la marine française*, vol. IV (Paris 1910), pp. 167ff, 'le secret de la reine', as well as documents in his own personal possession which do not appear to have survived. Catherine tried to stake her own personal claim to the throne of Portugal, but largely to embarrass Philip II.

74   *C.S.P. Foreign*, xv, p. 90, Cobham to (?Wilson), 1 April 1581. This report shows Richelieu was anxious to get matters moving, but that Catherine de' Medici was stalling.

75   M.C., XC, 137, 16 May 1582; XC, 138, 17 Oct. 1582, two acts referring to a loan of 60,000 *livres* made to Don Antonio, who handed over a diamond of same value as surety, and which he then 'sold' to Richelieu, a party to the loan, in order to repay his debt. See also *C.S.P. Foreign*, xvII, p. 162, Cobham to Walsingham, 9 March 1583, who asserts that the diamond had been reclaimed by Henri III, who assigned Richelieu payment off the revenues of Brittany, and that Richelieu promptly sold this bond to the duc de Retz for 135,000 *livres*, a very handsome profit indeed for Richelieu, if the story is true.

76   Murdin, *Collection of State Papers*, p. 382, Stafford to Walsingham, 20 Dec. 1583.

mained veiled.[77] The English ambassador wrote that no one believed that either Richelieu or Schomberg, the financiers of the operation, 'would give their money for any purpose but to fill their own purses'.[78] Don Antonio himself confessed in May 1584 to the ambassador that he expected nothing for himself from the projected expedition, and went as far as to cite Richelieu's covetousness and exclusive concern with personal gain at the expense of all else as a prime cause.[79] In any case, the duc d'Anjou's death a month later, in June 1584, altered the political climate in France and killed off the possibility of its becoming anything but a private trading venture.

Long before that date, Richelieu had begun to exploit the commercial possibilities of these developments. The age of crown-sponsored chartered companies, with which the name of his son, the Cardinal, would be so closely associated, had not yet arrived, and it was left to private associations to fill the void. In 1582 Richelieu and a business partner, Hugues Darragon, contracted with a Dieppe captain to fit out and load with specified merchandise three ships, two of which already belonged to them, 'pour faire le traficq' in Ceylon and Peru, and to return with products for French markets.[80] Similar trading expeditions to Guinea, and especially Peru, were undertaken again in 1584 and 1585.[81] How successful they were in making money for their principals is less clear. Richelieu almost certainly had to borrow money or sell shares in ships in order to finance his participation in them, and at least one ship, the *Olonnois*, was wrecked off Brest on its return from Peru in late 1585.[82]

All of this activity was accompanied by constant buying and selling of ships, including some from the royal navy. As an expensive occupation, this was one best practised in the company of others, and we can see clearly enough here the extent to which

77 *C.S.P. Foreign*, XVIII, p. 266, Stafford to Walsingham, 25 Dec. 1583; *ibid.*, p. 419, Francis Nedham to Walsingham, 28 March 1584.
78 *Ibid.*, p. 418, Stafford to same, 28 March 1584.
79 *Ibid.*, p. 493, Stafford to Walsingham, 21 May 1584. From the beginning, English worries centred on the possibility that the ships might be used against English interests in Scotland and in support of Mary Stuart, which explains Stafford's concern about Richelieu's links with her Guise cousins.
80 M.C., LXXVIII, 125, two contracts of 4 March 1582. Richelieu sold a half-share in the two ships, La Perle and La Riche, to Darragon, and they then engaged Captain Pierre Chauvin to mount the operation for them. The contract itemizes the goods that he was to embark before sailing for the Indies from France.
81 M.C., XC, 141, 27 March 1584; XC, 143, 29 March 1585, expedition to Guinea, Brazil and Peru.
82 M.C., XC, 144, 26 Dec. 1585. The vessel, accompanied by a smaller ship, the Marie, was wrecked off the île d'Ouessant. Richelieu's early hopes of recovering his investment as well as his share of the apparently valuable cargo from the captain proved illusory, and he finally ceded all his claims to the captain in return for a mere 1,500 *livres*; XC, 145, 18 April 1586; XC, 146, 18 Sept. 1586.

Richelieu played a full part in the *affairisme* of Henri III's reign. It is
not easy to disentangle speculation involving an immediate turnover
from a more determined pursuit of profit from high-risk trading in
forbidden markets, and no doubt it would be futile to attempt to do
so. The fact is that both options were available to men in Richelieu's
position, thanks to Henri III's willingness to sell or donate ships of
his navy in return for political or financial services. More than once,
indeed, ships which had come into private hands in this way were
then repurchased by the king, with, one suspects, any profit going to
the vendors. For example, in mid-December 1583, Richelieu purchased from the count of Brissac four ships docked at Le Havre – the
Grand Brissac and *Petit Brissac*, the *Pontpierre* and a barque, the *Capre*;
less than a month later, he sold the *Grand Brissac* to Joyeuse, the *Petit
Brissac* to Schomberg, retaining the *Pontpierre* for himself.[83] In mid-
December 1584, the same trio agreed to share out among themselves
the ships (and their equipment) that they had put to sea 'en com-
mun',[84] though on this occasion Richelieu was 'represented' by the
Roberge, one of two ships he had purchased from the duc d'Elbeuf
in September 1583.[85] In May 1585, he sold to Henri III, through
Joyeuse, another ship, the *Grand Biscain*.[86] In general, the purchase,
in whole or in part, of ships from men like Joyeuse or Elbeuf was
part of a combined effort to fit out and finance trading expeditions.
Richelieu himself acknowledged Hugues Darragon and Elbeuf
as equal partners in the trading expeditions of 1582 and 1583
respectively.[87]

It is apparent from the available evidence that at different times
between 1582 and 1586, Richelieu owned, in whole or in part, at
least nine ships, most of which at one time or another were intended
to sail and trade in the Spanish overseas empire. Unfortunately, that
evidence does not enable us to establish the cost to him of his maritime endeavours, nor the profit and loss account of the ensuing
voyages. Some were profitable, but not to the extent of inundating
him with funds, or of becoming his main source of income.[88] On
the other hand, it is likely that a sizeable share of the loans and debts
that he formally acknowledged contracting during these years had to

83 Deloche, *Le Père*, pp. 191–6. Deloche did not know what happened to the *Pontpierre* and
    the *Barque Capre*, but the former was still in Richelieu's possession in 1585: M.C., XC,
    144, 5 Sept. 1585.
84 M.C., XC 142, 19 Dec. 1584.
85 M.C., XC 140, 1 Sept. 1583. This act is not a sale agreement, but a procuration from
    Richelieu to his secretary to take possession of the *Roberge* and a barque named the
    Marguerite.
86 M.C., XC 143, 15 May 1585.
87 M.C., LXXVIII 125, 4 March 1582 (Darragon); XC 141, 27 March 1584 (Elbeuf).
88 Deloche, *Le Père*, p. 108, for such an assertion.

do with purchasing, maintaining and fitting out ships, their crews and cargos.[89]

However, Richelieu's maritime activity and speculation should not be divorced from his other financial ventures. The *affaires du roi* took many forms, and they ought not to be seen as clearly distinct from each other; as Richelieu's own career shows, they represented a sphere in which the well-connected courtier and the professional financier could operate together, and there were few or no obstacles to the activities they might engage in. In September 1582, we find him taking over a contract to impose fines on those who had failed to pay the customary fees owed by those acquiring parts of the royal domain between 1540 and 1572 – a typical example of the kind of expedient the French monarchy regularly resorted to in its search for funds, and one which was always turned over to a financial consortium (*parti*).[90] In January 1583, as a guarantee of repayment of two modest loans totalling 10,141 *livres* (which he promised to repay within six months), he turned over to his creditors 225 blank letters of provision to the value of 30,450 *livres*, for offices of sergeant in the *greniers à sel* of the salt-tax administration in the *généralité* of Tours; the creditors were to dispose of these offices and pay the balance to Sebastien Zamet, who had already been lending Richelieu large sums of money.[91] In March 1584, he claimed he was owed 84,000 *livres* by the crown, and that payment had been pledged to him from the sale of other offices of sergeant of the salt-tax;[92] only a month before, he had mounted a similar operation for another set of modestly-valued offices,[93] collecting cash payments from the men who would subsequently retail the offices. This was a common method of marketing newly-created royal offices, and one that attracted the interest of courtiers.[94] The grant to Richelieu of the letters of provision to the offices suggests that he had been actively involved in finding the ready cash corresponding to the value of the offices in question;[95]

---

89 Numerous traces of this in Richelieu's notarial papers; for example, M.C. XC, 143, 11 March 1585, five separate debts amounting to 24,927 *livres*, contracted in the previous year or so, and owed to various merchants and seamen in and around Brouage seem connected to getting ships ready for such ventures.

90 M.C., XC, 138, 26 Sept. 1582, procuration from Richelieu for enforcement of fines. The original contract dated from 1575.

91 M.C., XC, 139, 9 Jan. 1583. He claimed that he had been given the provisions in lieu of his *gages* and pensions as *grand prévôt*, as well as for other services to the king. *Ibid.*, act of 22 April 1583, stipulating payment to Zamet. The operation involved just over 54,000 *livres* in all, and covered 1527 parishes in the *généralité* of Tours.

92 M.C., XC, 141, 27 March 1584.

93 M.C., XC, 141, 21 and 25 Feb. 1584. The total involved here was 8,000 *livres*, but Richelieu's loan was for just over 3,000 *livres*.

94 The standard account of how offices were disposed of remains Roland Mousnier, *La Vénalité des offices sous Henri IV et Louis XIII* (2 ed., Paris 1971).

95 See A.N. V5 1294 (ii), sale decree of domain rights, 1612.

alternatively, he might simply have been a front man for the financiers bidding for the contract to retail them; another possibility was that it was a form of compensation to him for other services, political or financial. Traces of other deals of this kind have not come to light, but such commerce would explain how Richelieu managed to acquire parts of the royal domain in Poitou at some date in the early 1580s.

By then, the crown's financial problems had become particularly acute; as *affaires extraordinaires* became increasingly numerous and indispensable to the crown, they provided sharp-eyed courtiers and financiers with ample opportunities to respond to the needs of a depleted royal treasury. Between 1583 and 1588 Richelieu was to contract an impressive and constant stream of loans from Zamet, Scipione Sardini and other financiers, mostly Italians like them. The nature of the surviving evidence – formal acts of acknowledgement of these debts – usually makes it impossible to determine the purpose of individual loans, but they were clearly both too numerous and too large to be designed simply to meet ordinary household or other current expenses, especially as Richelieu was simultaneously contracting a plethora of smaller loans from suppliers, merchants and other acquaintances, all of which do seem to relate to this sort of expenditure. The course of this connection can be followed in the accompanying table.

Date of loan	Lender	Size of loan	Date of repayment
March 1583	S. Zamet	285,000	July 1583
Dec. 1583	S. Zamet	120,000	Feb. 1586
March 1585	B. Cenami	33,000	May 1587
Oct. 1585	B. Cenami	33,990	March 1586
Dec. 1585	S. Sardini	16,500	Sept. 1586-July 1587
Dec. 1585	S. Sardini	109,199	May-Sept. 1586 (partial)
Dec. 1585	S. Sardini	9,600	July 1587
Feb. 1586	S. Sardini	36,000	Sept. 1586
Sept. 1586	S. Sardini	100,800	Dec. 1586 (partial)
Nov. 1586	J. Sardini	65,400	May 1587
Dec. 1586	O. Doni	12,000	?
Sept. 1586–Jan. 1588	S. Sardini	231,057	?

Note: The original figures were in *écus*, or fractions of them, and have been rounded up to the nearest *livre*.

Although there is no way of knowing how complete a record this is of Richelieu's financial activities, certain details are eloquent. The very first entry serves to set the tone for what would follow in subsequent years. In March 1583, his secretary acted as his front-man in an enormous loan of 285,000 *livres* to Henri III, to be re-covered from the proceeds of the sale of offices of sergeant in the salt-tax administration; an independent declaration made by Rich-elieu a week later indicated that the money for this operation had been lent to him by Sebastien Zamet, one of the leading financiers of the day.[96] In December of the same year, he acknowledged a sepa-rate debt of 120,000 *livres* to Zamet, and although he did not specify its purpose, the size of the sum and the identity of the lender point towards another loan to the crown. While the loan from Zamet itself was repayable by 1585, it should be noted that Richelieu turned over to Zamet three very recent payment orders (*mandements*) for an equivalent total sum from the *trésorier de l'Epargne* as a guarantee of repayment.[97] Most of the major loans in subsequent years, though they tended to be smaller, followed a similar pattern: Richelieu would formally acknowledge them before his notary, undertake to repay them by a specified date, or in stipulated amounts spread over a period of time, and would surrender payment orders from the treasury as a guarantee. Only occasionally do any of these statements reveal something about what lay behind his borrowings. Acknowl-edging a loan of 37,500 *livres* from Scipione Sardini in January 1587, Richelieu explicitly declared it to be repayable from the proceeds of a tax-contract valued at 390,000 *livres*; we may suppose either that the loan was promptly invested, or that Richelieu had already negotiated a share in the contract on the strength of which he was raising the cash.[98] In late 1588, the treasury paid him 30,000 *livres* owed to him as a consequence of his participation in a loan of 507,000 *livres* to the crown two years before, though it is unclear whether that repres-ented his entire investment in the loan.[99]

Such a pattern raises a crucial question: was Richelieu simply using his position at court to secure favourable payment orders for others at a time of royal penury, or was he an active partner in their finan-cial operations? There was much contemporary criticism of the crown's making payments to individuals whose true identity was concealed by the names of *prête-noms*. Because recourse to secrecy

96   M.C., XC, 139, 14 March 1583, André Richard's declaration that he was Richelieu's *prête-nom* in this contract; *ibid.*, 22 March, Richelieu acknowledges loan of 271,200 *livres* from Zamet.
97   M.C., XC, 140, 23 Dec. 1583.
98   M.C., XC, 147, 25 Jan. 1587.
99   B.N. MS. Fr. 26169, no 2318, *quittance* of 31 Oct. 1588.

was so widespread where the royal finances were concerned, the surviving sources make it difficult to determine who precisely was hiding behind whom. The same document might appear to suggest that Richelieu was acting as a front for those lending him money – securing them financial deals or favourable repayment terms – or, conversely, that they were in turn no more than middle-men acting for others like him, anxious to invest money as discreetly as possible in their tax-farming operations.[100] Whichever may have been the case, there is every reason to assume Richelieu's direct and personal involvement in royal financial affairs, since it is well-known that the leading nobles of the court involved themselves in this way.[101] When in August 1587 Henri III suggested the consolidation of the Paris tax-farms, and the Paris town-hall objected to this, as well as to the proposal that they be handed over to a consortium, it was Richelieu who put the king's case and offered to find a financier willing to make the initial advances of cash.[102] Such an offer would have been unthinkable from someone who had not already acquired experience in such matters, and whose 'capacité' was not known to those concerned.

Despite the difficulties experienced in lifting the veil surrounding Richelieu's financial activities, the figures in the preceding table are far from suggesting a hopelessly escalating level of debt incurred in this sphere of activity. Most of the early recorded loans were repaid by September 1586. The debt of 231,057 *livres* acknowledged in January 1588 consisted of nine different loans contracted since September 1586, and some of it was probably repaid in 1588 or 1589.[103] A new loan of 69,000 *livres* contracted in January 1588 was repaid by March of the same year.[104] Most of the sums that he regularly borrowed in this way seem to have been unsecured on family property, which suggests that they formed a sort of revolving current account; they were accompanied by a solemn promise to repay within a relatively short term (usually six months), and could only have been granted if the lender had a firm and assured working relationship with the borrower. The loans were usually made explicitly 'pour subvenir à ses affaires', and a quick rotation of the capital involved was obviously anticipated. The table shows that this is generally what happened, if not always within the time-span initially agreed. Notwithstanding the court's humiliating retreat

100 For an outstanding discussion of these questions in the age of Louis XIV, see Daniel Dessert, *Argent, pouvoir et société au grand siècle* (Paris 1984). But it is clear that they date from a much earlier period.
101 Boucher, *La Cour de Henri III*, pp. 87–91.
102 Deloche, *Le Père*, pp. 247–8. See *Registre des délibérations du bureau de l'Hôtel de Ville*, IX, pp. 77–8.
103 M.C., XC, 149, 15 Jan. 1588.
104 M.C., XC, 149, act of 30 March 1588 appended to that cited in previous note.

from Paris after the insurrection of May 1588, Richelieu is known to have continued lending small sums – which was probably all he could manage to raise – to Henri III during 1588 and 1589, but all trace of his dealings with his own creditors after May 1588 have disappeared.[105] The upheaval inevitably hit royal and private credit, and Richelieu's account with Sardini, and perhaps others too, must have been in substantial deficit at his death: Sardini and his heirs were among the first to undertake litigation against his estate to recover what was owed to them.[106]

Financial activity on such a scale makes it possible to understand why Richelieu could be in receipt of considerable payment orders or gifts from Henri III, the best known of which, for no less than 354,000 *livres*, dates from around the time of the Cardinal's baptism; others, on a more modest scale, would follow later.[107] But with one fascinating exception, we know virtually nothing about these transactions, or what lies behind them. In April 1585, the *Chambre des Comptes*, the crown's financial watchdog, protested to the king about a gift of 501,000 *livres* plus interest he had made to Richelieu. In particular, the magistrates were concerned about an alleged secret payment of 18,000 *livres* that Richelieu had made on the king's behalf, the details of which he would not reveal. They were also anxious to know if the king had really paid Richelieu 225,000 *livres* for a diamond (possibly the one which became famous as the 'Miroir de Portugal' in the next century), a price which would have made it 30,000 *livres* more valuable than its closest rival in the royal collection! In both cases, the king defended his actions, and the gift was doubtless 'passed' by the *Chambre des Comptes*.[108] But whatever Henri III's reputation may be, it is unlikely that royal generosity on that scale was unconnected to his *grand prévôt*'s activities as a financier. But, towards 1587–8, Richelieu seems, like others in the same position as himself, to have found it increasingly difficult to obtain payment from the receivers-general of royal taxes when he presented his payment orders. It was probably because of such difficulties in obtaining hard cash that he acquired, in March 1587, the public *rentes* (annuities) which formed part of his estate after his death.[109]

105 Bergin, *Richelieu*, p. 19.
106 A.N., V⁵ 1294 (ii), sale decree of seigneurie of Richelieu, 21 Feb. 1621.
107 Deloche, *Le Père*, pp. 238ff.
108 *La Chambre des Comptes de Paris. Pièces justificatives pour servir à l'histoire de ses premiers présidents (1506–1791)*, ed. A.M. de Boislisle (Nogent-le-Rotrou 1873), pp. 167–8. This diamond is doubtless the same as that referred to in n. 75 above. It originally belonged to Don Antonio, the Portuguese pretender, and belonged later to Henriette d'Angleterre and Mazarin. See Daniel Dessert, 'Pouvoir et finance au xviiᵉ siècle: la fortune du cardinal Mazarin', *Revue d'Histoire Moderne et Contemporaine* 23 (1976), pp. 161–81, esp. p. 174.
109 B.N. MS. Nouv. Acq. Fr. 3644, nos. 1149–50, 22 Jan. 1588, for payment of two quarters of *rente* of 9,000 *livres* which he acquired in March 1587.

But there was another, more negative dimension to Richelieu's financial activities. In addition to his current account deficits, he had been accumulating more permanent forms of debt since the late 1570s. He was not alone in this, and his problems in this regard were modest by comparison with the huge debts piled up by noble houses such as Guise, Nevers or Montmorency, whose debts were in some cases public knowledge.[110] But their commitments may not be the most appropriate yardstick by which to measure Richelieu's, and the absence of any table of his assets and debts at his death makes it extremely difficult to measure them against his activities as a financier. Nevertheless, one of the most important and illuminating financial statements that Richelieu ever made was that of March 1584, in which he detailed his commitments to his habitual associate when it came to borrowing money, Hugues Darragon, a man whose role and activities are otherwise obscure. Discharging Darragon from all responsibility, he assumed sole personal liability for debts to the tune of 282,000 *livres*, over 162,000 of which was in the form of capital borrowed from an impressive array of nobles, merchants, royal officials and courtiers, in return for annual rente payments of 13,656 *livres*.[111] He made provision to repay the short-term loans involved, to service or even amortize the *rentes*; as always he could produce payment-orders and IOUs – in this case for no less than 657,000 *livres*, much of which was unlikely ever to materialize. But while some of these debts duly disappeared from his portfolio, he frequently resorted to such onerous methods of borrowing in subsequent years.[112] The individual sums – as low as 2,400 *livres* in capital – might not be excessive by comparison with what we have already seen, but failure to deal with them resulted in a burden of 'structural' debt which, given that Richelieu also failed to pay the annuities regularly, climbed further with each passing year. If he were to die, or was deprived of his other sources of profit and income, his debts would outstrip the family's capacity to service them.

Richelieu was not the only French noble to take a relaxed view of such questions: the royal favour which had enabled him to combine

110 See Robert Harding, *Anatomy of a Power Elite. The Provincial Governors of Early Modern France* (New Haven and London 1978) pp. 143ff; Denis Crouzet, 'Recherches sur la crise de l'aristocratie au xvie siècle: les dettes de la maison de Nevers', *Histoire, Économie, Société* 1 (1982), pp. 7–50.

111 M.C., XC, 141, 27 March 1584. The *rentes* involved up to thirty loans, and the lenders ranged from the widow of Chancellor Michel de l'Hôpital to unnamed minor merchants. I would like to acknowledge the assistance of Robert Descimon in deciphering this long and rebarbative document.

112 Indeed, on the same day as he acknowledged these debts, he empowered Darragon to raise a further 36,000 *livres* in cash against 3,000 *livres* in *rentes*: M.C., XC, 141, 27 March 1584. Similar powers of attorney in order to raise 18,000 *livres* were granted by him in 1587: XC, 148, 6 July 1587.

speculation and duty would protect him from disaster. There is abundant evidence to show that he and his wife lived in considerable comfort in Paris. We do not know how large a household he maintained, nor how lavishly he entertained, but the signs are that he saw no reason to live as a modest *gentilhomme*. The simple fact that he negotiated a price-list for household supplies as early as 1579 indicates at least the intention of imitating the great households, in which such arrangements were standard practice.[113] Accounts settled in subsequent years with suppliers, tailors and other artisans show a willingness to indulge in a range of refined and expensive tastes that were in fashion at the court of Henri III: purchases of marble, expensive tapestries, silk, a great-coat of ermine and gold-braid to be worn perhaps as a knight of the Order of the Holy Ghost, are among the items explicitly mentioned, with substantial bills to suppliers also acknowledged.[114]

Thus, everything we know about the Cardinal's father points to a man who gradually introduced the Richelieu family to the higher levels of court politics and finance, a world of financial dealing and influence-peddling in which he evidently felt entirely at home. Much of the time, he was able to recycle his money and investments, borrowing where necessary, but was usually favoured enough with payment orders to meet his commitments. What spelt trouble for him was the rapid deterioration of the political situation in 1588–9 and, for his family, his sudden death in July 1590. Because of their closeness in time, we shall never be able to weigh the relative importance of these two facts. But there is every likelihood that, had he lived longer and been assured of the goodwill of Henri IV, he would have been in a position to make further, perhaps more modest profits, which would have contained his losses, and staved off his final bankruptcy by enabling him to deal with his creditors from a position of political strength. Not only did his untimely death preclude all this, leaving his widow with a household full of small children whom she would have to raise on her own, but it came at a juncture when there would be no adult male – son, uncle, or other relative – either capable enough or sufficiently well-placed to take charge of the family's affairs for many years. Richelieu's sons had good reason to be ambivalent towards particular features of his legacy, but an attraction to court politics and finance was not one of them.

---

113 M.C., XC, 132, 18 Nov. 1579.
114 M.C., XC, 144, 5 Sept. 1585 (3,240 *livres* for silk); XC, 144, 16 Oct. 1585 (1,080 *livres* for coat); XC, 146, 23 July 1586 (4,800 *livres* for marchandises, silks etc); XC, 146, 21 Sept. 1583 (contract for making of a covered carriage)

V

There remains one further tradition to be added to this collection –
and this is the place the Richelieu family enjoyed in the church before
the Cardinal's time. Because, here, the decisive breakthrough was
only made during the last years of the *grand prévôt*'s life, it can serve
both as a convenient conclusion to our examination of his career, and
as a natural preface to the next stage of the family's history. François
de Richelieu did not confine his attention to the military, financial or
political spheres. Like other courtiers, he was attracted by the advantages offered by the church, advantages rarely so freely distributed as
they were at the court of Henri III.[115] Of course, Richelieu's gains
may seem relatively meagre by comparison with those of the great
families of ecclesiastical dynasts, but they were more extensive than
is generally realized. Perhaps the greatest irony of the Richelieu
family's history – one that François de Richelieu himself could not
have foreseen – is that it was precisely this 'minority' activity which
was to prove so disproportionately valuable to the next generation.

The Richelieu family's record of service or advancement in the
church during the sixteenth century was not remarkable, and scarcely
anything is known about it before the generation of the Cardinal's
grandfather. An important chapter seems to have opened through
the influence of Jacques Le Roy, uncle of the *grand prévôt*'s grandmother Anne Le Roy, and successively abbot of St Florent of Saumur and archbishop of Bourges (d. 1572). It was he who appears to
have encouraged Anne's younger sons to embark on ecclesiastical
careers which eventually enabled them to begin acquiring benefices
in their own right. As we saw, Antoine du Plessis had originally
been destined for the monastic life, but fled his cell to embrace a
turbulent military career instead. Another brother, René, was first a
monk of La Chaise-Dieu, and later abbot *in commendam* of the small
Poitevin abbey of Nueil-sur-l'Autize, near Fontenay-le-Comte. But
he remained an undistinguished figure, and we do not know even
when and where he died. A third brother, Jacques, does at least
emerge from the shadows. He was abbot of the Cistercian abbey of
La Chapelle-aux-Planches from 1551 onwards, prior of the Maison-
Dieu of Parthenay, a minor benefice, and abbot of Ménil in 1584.[116]
He was also briefly dean of the cathedral of Poitiers,[117] and an al-

---

115 See Frederic J. Baumgartner, *Change and Continuity in the French Episcopate* (Durham,
    N.C., 1986), pp. 41ff.
116 M.C., XC, 145, 29 April 1586, for reference to Parthenay priory. This document also
    contains a copy of procuration from Jacques de Plessis, 4 Oct. 1584, which mentions his
    title of abbot of Ménil.
117 This may also have been occurred in the early or mid-1580s, when he was fighting a
    lawsuit over the prebend in the *parlement* of Paris. M.C., XC, 145, 24 April 1586.

moner in the household of Henri II and then of Catherine de' Medici; this last post must have been a sinecure for him since, not being a priest, he cannot have been able to perform many useful functions there.[118] But he would almost certainly have remained as obscure as his brother René had it not been for the favour enjoyed at court by his nephew, the *grand prévôt*. Apart from the murdered Louis II, François had only one brother, Benjamin, who also seems to have become a monk. Unfortunately that is all that is known about him, but it seems quite probable that he was dead by the time François rose to prominence at court.

In both generations of the family, therefore, if there was not an initial dearth of younger sons available for advancement in the church, there was certainly one by the time François was finally in a position to tap the supply of church patronage. Consequently, when in 1584, on the death of René La Salla, bishop of Luçon, Henri III provided yet another token of his esteem for François by granting him the right to 'present' for nomination to Luçon a candidate of his choice, he could only turn to his uncle, Jacques.[119] The latter was still a deacon at the time of his confirmation by Rome; but he neither became a priest nor, so far as is known, ever set foot in Luçon, and died in obscurity in 1592.[120]

The Richelieu family had no distinctive claim to Luçon, on grounds of either geography or tradition, and it may not be too far-fetched to see another case of Joyeuse influence at work here, too. René La Salla was a relative of that family, and his patron, Cardinal Joyeuse, was one of the great benefice-hunters and ecclesiastical power-brokers of the age, a man who would not easily let slip a bishopric on which he had once got his hands.[121] It is not inconceivable that he and his brother, the admiral, paved the way for the royal gift to Richelieu. The practice of 'granting' bishoprics in this way had, it seems, taken off under Charles IX, and although both he and Henri III might make such grants in order to reward loyal servants such as the *grand prévôt*, the beneficiaries were anxious to treat them as more than simple *ad hominem* gifts, and expected them to be repeated when

118 Hanotaux, I, p. 24–5. His source for the information that Jacques was René's successor, *Gallia Christiana in provincias ecclesiasticas distributa* (Paris 1715–1865), vol. II, is frequently inaccurate in its lists of heads of monastic establishments. See also A.D. de la Fontenelle de Vaudoré, *Histoire du monastère et des évêques de Luçon*, 2 vols. (Fontenay-le-Comte 1847), I, p. 333, whose information is the same as Hanotaux's. See n. 125.
119 Louis Delhommeau, *Documents pour l'histoire de l'évêché de Luçon* (Luçon 1971), no. 532, papal indult, 5 Nov. 1586.
120 Fontenelle de Vaudoré, *Histoire des Evêques de Luçon*, I, pp. 333, 338–9.
121 See *Correspondance du nonce Girolamo Ragazzoni 1583–86*, ed. Pierre Blet (Rome 1962), nos. 81, 100, 118, for references to La Salla in connection with the benefices of Paul de Foix, Joyeuse's predecessor as archbishop of Toulouse.

future vacancies occurred. The longer-term consequences for both
royal control of church patronage and the status of noble families
within the church hardly need emphasising.

The importance of Luçon for the future Cardinal should not
obscure the rather tenuous nature of the family's toe-hold in the
church, which his father's early death did nothing to strengthen. It
is still not altogether clear whether François de Richelieu was able to
further influence the disposal of royal ecclesiastical patronage, for
example by securing abbeys *in commendam*, as it was called, for
nominees who would allow him to draw the revenues. But two
isolated references – neither easy to make sense of, and dating from a
few years after his death – suggest he may have had some success in
doing just this. In August 1592, his widow ratified the lease for a
year of the abbey of Absie-en-Gâtine which, she claimed, belonged
to her second son, Alphonse-Louis.[122] It is very unlikely that this
benefice, which was substantial, could have been acquired after her
husband's death. Two years later, Sully recorded the payment of
45,000 *livres* by an *ordonnance de comptant* to Mme de Richelieu as
compensation for the loss of an abbey of St Urbain.[123] There is no
other record of an abbey of that name being held by any member of
the Richelieu family before that date, and the method of reimburse-
ment employed hints at some arrangement for it to be held by a *prête-
nom*. In any case, the fact remains that it had been lost, in or before
1594. Likewise, the abbey of Absie would disappear from sight in
subsequent years, though this may be as a result of dealings over
another abbey by the Cardinal's eldest brother, Henri.[124] And
finally, the abbeys of Nueil-sur-l'Autize, La Chapelle-aux-Planches
and Ménil, held at various times by François de Richelieu's uncles,
did not remain in family hands after their respective deaths.[125]

Despite these losses, we should not exaggerate the immediate
value of the grant of Luçon in 1584. It did not place François de
Richelieu in the same league as the great ecclesiastical brokers of his
time, none of whom would have regarded Luçon very highly. His
son's own later description of Luçon as 'l'évêché le plus crotté de
France' is notorious, but, however harsh it may sound, the reality he
was describing had existed for some considerable time. Luçon and its
temporalities, located uncomfortably close to the great Huguenot
stronghold of La Rochelle, had, like the entire province of Poitou,

122 Martineau, *Richelieu*, p. 66.
123 A.N., A.P. 120, vol. 11, fo. 8v, 1594.
124 See ch. 3, p. 83. The abbey in question was Ile Chauvet, situated in the diocese of
     Luçon.
125 A.N. V⁵ 1227, fo. 66r-v, *lettres d'économat* issued at Tours, 10 March 1593, for the abbey
     of Nueil-sur-l'Autize, vacant since the death of René du Plessis.

suffered heavily since the early years of the religious wars; a considerable portion of the population was Protestant and, confident of the protection of La Rochelle, well entrenched. In such circumstances, and whatever its location, the see of Luçon cannot have been among the most desirable in France, nor its incumbents particularly anxious to reside there. Salla may not be the only bishop before Jacques du Plessis to have been a non-resident straw-man.[126] But if it was not a jewel in the French church's crown, Luçon was not wholly negligible either. Shortly after the king's gift to Richelieu, he arranged a one-year lease of its temporal revenues for the equivalent of 10,000 *livres* net of all charges, though this was to fall to 8,200 *livres* the following year.[127] Such an income was doubtless modest enough in relation to the enormous sums passing through Richelieu's hands at that time, but it was more, for example, than the rental he derived from his landed estates.[128]

The Richelieu family's ecclesiastical traditions before the Cardinal's generation were, therefore, decidedly modest, especially when compared to their military, political and financial records. Rather like the family line itself, they held on a single thread by the 1580s, the elderly bishop of Luçon. Yet the point remains that, by enabling Jacques du Plessis to become bishop, Henri III had thrown them a lifeline for the future more valuable than anyone at the time could have suspected. It strengthened considerably, though it did not create, the incentive to designate at least one younger son from the future Cardinal's generation for a church career from an early age. With the family's other church benefices escaping their grasp, it is not surprising that they attempted to retain Luçon at all costs. With such a slender ecclesiastical heritage, the rising generation's efforts to make its way in the church promised to be neither a spectacular nor a triumphant affair.

126 See Fontenelle de Vaudoré, *Histoire des Evêques de Luçon*, vol. 1, for the author's difficulties in establishing a clear line of succession to Luçon, particularly in the sixteenth century. A.N., M.C., XC, 143, 3 April 1585, lease of Luçon's temporalities by François de Richelieu, in which he refers to one Antoine de Bruière (?) 'cy devant esleu evesque de Lusson', but whose identity remains wholly mysterious.

127 M.C., X.C. 143, contract of 3 April 1585. The lease was to run from 18 April, and the lessee was Gabriel Delamet, alderman (l'ung des pairs) of La Rochelle and, therefore, possibly a Huguenot. Details of the 1586 lease in Delhommeau, *Documents pour l'histoire de Luçon*, no 529.

128 Sorbonne, Bibliothèque Victor Cousin, *fonds* Richelieu, box 22, lease of 19 July 1576 for the equivalent of 6,000 *livres*. This figure probably fell further as a consequence of renewed warfare in Poitou after 1576.

Chapter 2
EARLY YEARS

'L'Enfance d'un prince est toujours, pour ses biographes, un moment d'élection: car c'est là que se noue le pathétique d'une vie . . . bien différente est l'enfance de l'artiste . . . l'artiste naît le jour de son premier chef-d'oeuvre. Jusque-là, il n'est rien. Il entre dans l'histoire alors que l'essentiel de sa vie est déjà joué.'[1]

IT is not uncommon for mystery and uncertainty – and therefore controversy – to surround the early career of major historical figures. As befits a man who made such a profound impression on his contemporaries, this is eminently true of Richelieu. While not all elements of such controversy possess equal importance in the broader sweep of history, learned and often impassioned debate about them has rumbled on for generations. Once he had assumed high office in both church and state, the relative anonymity of his early years appeared, even to his own contemporaries, out of line with the record of his achievements. Eulogists, biographers, novelists and even historians have applied themselves with varying degrees of ingenuity and success to remedying this state of affairs, and to confer a pattern on his early career which would enable it to prefigure the éclat of later developments. The result has all too often been to impose an artificial unity on his career, and to suggest a strong measure of inevitability about his rise to high office in church and state. In some cases, questions tend to be answered before they have been properly asked.

But in the case of Richelieu, the problem of reliable sources is a serious one, and there is, as we saw in connection with the anecdotes about his father's career, a need to treat what passes for 'evidence' with a constructive scepticism. Nothing remotely like Jean Héroard's great diary of the early years of Louis XIII exists for Richelieu. But, then, Louis was born a prince. By contrast, the early biography of his greatest minister fits Thuillier's characterisation of the early life of an artist.[2] Such caveats notwithstanding, even contemporary

---

1 Jacques Thuillier, *Nicolas Poussin* (Paris 1988), p. 25.
2 See Elizabeth Wirth Marvick, *Louis XIII: The Making of a King* (New Haven and London, 1986), for the most systematic use to date of the diary, which also does much to explain the character of Héroard's record-keeping.

anecdotes and edifying tales may have their place in a biographical study, if only for the clues, often quite unintentional, they have left behind for later generations.

It might be thought, for instance, that nothing would be less controversial than the date and place of birth of a future minister, from a well-born and well-connected family, yet since the seventeenth century this question has proved an area of disagreement. Richelieu's baptismal certificate states, simply but with assurance, that he was born on 9 September 1585, and its accuracy has never been seriously challenged. It is the subsequent delay in baptizing him – at the church of St Eustache in Paris in May 1586 – that has fuelled endless debate as to whether he was born in Paris itself or in Poitou. Despite his own later descriptions of himself as a Parisian, a tradition stemming from Mademoiselle de Montpensier and Tallemant des Réaux in the mid-seventeenth century, has been tenaciously defended by those anxious – mainly for reasons of provincial pride – to claim him as a Poitevin born and bred.[3] In the absence of conclusive evidence, the delay in baptizing him raised understandable doubts about Paris as his birthplace, and his own later utterances can be regarded as too vague – he once addressed the aldermen of the city by stating that he was 'parisien comme vous' – to settle the argument. Thanks to some new evidence, the issue can be safely laid to rest. The Richelieu household's normal place of residence was, as we have seen, its Parisian hôtel, not its Poitevin manor-house, and periods of presence in, and absence from, the capital can be detected from records of family business transactions. In the present case, they show quite clearly that the Cardinal's mother was witness to the marriage contract of one of her household in Paris less than four weeks before his birth; she appeared again before the family notary only five weeks after that event.[4] In the light of this, it would have been truly extraordinary – indeed tantamount to a sentence of death – for the grand prévôt to have packed his wife off to Poitou purely in order to give birth to her fourth child on their ancestral lands. And if the newborn was indeed too sickly to be taken to the nearby church of St Eustache

---

3 See Martineau, *Richelieu*, pp. 62–3, for a list of the authorities arguing for Poitou. His own conclusion to the discussion is characteristic of a particular style of advocacy: 'Avec cette naissance à Richelieu, tout s'explique, autrement tout est inexplicable' (p. 63). The arguments for Paris were put by Avenel, 'La Jeunesse de Richelieu' *Revue des Questions Historiques* 6 (1869), pp. 160–1; Hanotaux, *Richelieu*, I, pp. 63–7; and Deloche, *Le Père*, pp. 226–9.

4 M.C. XC, 144, 13 Aug. 1585, for her signature on a marriage contract of one of the *demoiselles* of her household; *ibid.*, 16 Oct. 1585, she pays a bill owed to some tailors by her husband, absent from Paris. This suggests that if anyone was absent from Paris around this time, it was Richelieu's busy father – though he was in the city a few days before the birth of his son: *ibid.*, 5 Sept., two procurations signed by François de Richelieu.

for baptism until May 1586, then his condition would surely have prevented him and his mother from journeying from Poitou to Paris within such a short time after his birth.[5]

That, however, does not dispose of the other difficulty relating to Richelieu's arrival in the world, namely the delay in baptizing him. The latter appears to have nothing to do with his father's absences – usually fairly brief by now – from Paris: his presence there is regularly recorded at the time of Armand's birth and throughout the following nine months. Given that it can no longer be argued that Richelieu was born in Poitou, there remains no real foundation – only a family tradition – for the notion that his baptism may have been delayed because the child was sickly. If the infant Richelieu was, as we are told, too fragile to be taken out of doors to nearby St Eustache, then it would be inconceivable that his parents would not have had him baptized at home. The generally high rates of mortality among infant children in the sixteenth century ensured that parents were anxious to baptize their children without delay. Why, therefore, wait eight months to do so? One can only surmise that Richelieu was less frail at birth than is generally thought, and in no immediate danger. Instead, it is very likely that shortly after his birth there was a private baptismal rite known as *ondoiement*, which is known to have been practised among the royal family and the nobility, and which allowed for a full church baptism at a later date.[6] In the case of Richelieu, it was probably practical difficulties which temporarily frustrated the *grand prévôt*'s determination to put on a proper display for his son's baptism, a display all the more necessary as the two godfathers he had chosen were figures from the high military nobility his father regularly frequented – Armand de Biron, governor of Poitou, and Jean d'Aumont, both marshals of France. The first names given to Armand-Jean du Plessis were equally expressive of his family's affiliations at that juncture. The role of godmother fell to Françoise de Rochechouart.[7]

5   Martineau's arguments for Richelieu's birth in Poitou can be effectively turned on their head: '. . . les difficultés qu'éprouvaient à cette époque les femmes des seigneurs pour faire de longs voyages par suite du mauvais état des routes et du peu de sécurité, qu'offraient les temps de troubles et de désordres qu'on traversait. Leur séjour, par conséquent, presque continuel dans leurs châteaux où elles élévaient leur famille, loin d'une cour dissolue et d'une capitale où l'émeute dominait. Tout cela est de nature à démontrer surabondamment que la naissance du futur cardinal a bien eu lieu à Richelieu, et non à Paris': *Richelieu*, p. 63.
6   For example, the last duc de Montmorency was born in April 1595, but not formally baptized until March 1597 in order to enable Henri IV to be present as a godfather; other members of the family were regularly baptized several months or more after their birth. I owe this information to Dr Joan Davies who is researching into the Montmorency's family's wealth and marriages.
7   Hanotaux, *Richelieu*, I, p. 66, for the text of the baptismal certificate, 5 May 1586.

It is also virtually certain that the first few years of Richelieu's life were spent in the comfortable hôtel of the rue du Bullouer. Between 1585 and May 1588, the court spent more time in Paris than had been the case in the 1570s and early 1580s, and notarial transactions enable us to plot the record of the *grand prévôt*'s presence in Paris until the eve of the Barricades of May 1588.[8] It was, of course, a time of mounting hostility to Henri III's government and, given his functions, the *grand prévôt* would have known in detail about the rebirth of the League after the death of Anjou in December 1584, the mounting public criticism of the régime, and the secret plots the League was organizing against Henri III.[9] Yet it was probably only at the last moment, on the Day of the Barricades itself (13 May 1588), that he and his family hastily decamped from the city, whence he followed Henri III in the direction of Rouen and Chartres, Blois and other towns.[10] François de Richelieu had to remain in personal attendance on Henri III and then, after his assassination, on Henri IV while they laid siege to Paris in 1589 and 1590, but his family was despatched to Poitou. It was probably in mid-1588 that the young Richelieu first set eyes on his 'native' soil south of Chinon in Poitou. This sudden exile from the city and its comforts may or may not have left a distinct mark on an impressionable three-year old, but it should be realized that his was a fate shared by numerous families of nobles and office-holders after May 1588, many of whom feared the visitations of the Leaguers if they stayed behind in Paris; Chartres, Tours and even Bordeaux were among the towns where they took refuge over the next few years. But if Poitou was a refuge from Paris, it was not a refuge from the exactions of civil war. Fighting and pillage took place in the immediate neighbourhood of the Richelieu family lands during subsequent years, especially in 1592.[11]

By the time the last of the religious wars had begun to subside – with Henri IV's adoption of Catholicism in 1593 and his entry into Paris in March 1594 – Richelieu's father was dead, and the family's affairs and future uncertain. But we should avoid making too many assumptions, based on an excessive measure of hindsight, about events after the disappearance of François de Richelieu. When he died suddenly at Gonesse in June 1590, the principal concern of his family was that there was no adult son to take his place, if not as

---

8 Boucher, *La Cour de Henri III*, p. 45, for a graph of the court's movements under Henri III. François de Richelieu's presence in Paris can be gauged from notarial acts bearing his signature in M.C., XC, vols. 144–9.

9 See É. Barnavi, *Le Parti de Dieu: Étude politique et sociale des chefs de la ligue parisienne* (Louvain-Paris 1980), pp. 69ff; Mark Greengrass, *France in the Age of Henry IV* (London 1984), pp. 22–47; Bonney, *The King's Debts*, pp. 23–9.

10 Deloche, *Le Père*, pp. 253ff.

11 Hanotaux, *Richelieu*, I, p. 57.

captain of the king's guards, then at least as head of the family, and no member of the king's entourage. But, apart from common rumours, it was almost certainly too soon for outsiders to know anything definite about the financial affairs of the family. Richelieu's business partners and notaries had themselves endured disruption, uncertainty and a virtual suspension of the normal business and judicial procedures since the events of May 1588. Not until the return of political stability could such matters be dealt with *en connaissance de cause*. Meanwhile, there was nothing to condemn the Richelieu family to perpetual exile in the distant provinces, especially as Henri IV took steps in 1594 to honour certain commitments to them and to indemnify them for certain losses.[12] At that juncture, and before the scale of the *grand prévôt's* debts was fully realized, it looked as though their future was hopeful enough, thanks to royal benevolence. It was not, therefore, quixotic on the part of Mme de Richelieu to return to Paris and resume residence there, not now in the hôtel de Losse in the rue du Bullouer but, according to a notarial deed of June 1595, 'en la maison (. . .) size au carrefour du chevalier du guet' near the Louvre.[13] The address alone says something for her optimism at this time. It seems reasonable to suppose that it was her intention to settle again, with her children, in her native city, yet, as time went by, the true state of her husband's affairs was gradually revealed, creditors began moving in on his estate, and she had little choice but to retreat again to Poitou.

If the chronology as outlined above is substantially correct, it follows that the young Richelieu's longest period of residence in Poitou was between 1588 and 1594, an experience he shared, as we saw, with the children of many other Parisian families. We are assured that his experience of formal education began there under the supervision of the prior of the abbey of St Florent of Saumur, Hardy Guillot.[14] This, in fact, suggests that the boy may well have boarded for much of the time in the abbey itself rather than remaining at home in the family manor. The abbot at this time was none other than Cardinal Joyeuse, but he was an absentee, and the real business of governing this very considerable abbey lay with the prior, who was thus unlikely to have enjoyed sufficient leisure to be private tutor to the Richelieu family. Nothing more than that is known about Armand's early schooling, but the choice of St Florent strongly suggests, whatever changes of direction were to come later,

12 See ch. 1, n. 123.
13 M.C. XCIX, 56, 13 June 1595, agreement between Mme de Richelieu and Simon Belin in respect of a sum of 58,500 *livres* owing to her by virtue of the king's gift of 1590.
14 Hanotaux, *Richelieu*, I, p. 67.

that a career in the church was what the family originally intended for him. The kind of schooling he received between the ages of five and nine or ten, meant that he was ready for life in a 'secondary' college by 1594 or 1595, and it was both logical – and by then actually possible, given his mother's intentions – that he continue his education in Paris. He probably enjoyed the company of his brother Alphonse at college there, while their eldest brother, Henri, joined the court of Henri IV as a page, becoming a *gentilhomme ordinaire* a few years later. Thus, Armand probably enrolled at the college of Navarre around 1595, but how long he remained there is not so certain. Although a college of the university, it was just as much a 'secondary' school, most of whose students simply did their 'humanities', without any expectation or obligation on them to proceed to take a degree.[15] By the later 1590s, it appears that Richelieu's family had decided that he would take up a military career, which makes it even less necessary to think in terms of a long or especially studious first stay at Navarre. He probably finished his course by 1600 at the latest, after which, again according to tradition, he went on to enrol at Antoine de Pluvinel's famous military academy for young nobles anxious to marry military skill and social graces, though there remains the possibility that, for a time, attendance at college and the academy overlapped.

As far as this stage of Richelieu's career is concerned, there are two traditions which merit consideration because both have a bearing on his later activities. The first of them asserts that it was his mother's half-brother, Amador de La Porte, a knight of the Order of Malta, who took charge of the education of Alphonse and Armand.[16] Such an arrangement seems perfectly credible, and would help to explain why there was no difficulty about leaving them in Paris even after his mother and family had returned again to Poitou; throughout this period he would have remained under the care of his uncle, whose means were evidently sufficient to pay both for his studies at Navarre and for the fees at Pluvinel's rather expensive academy.[17] Quite how this uncle, who would prove such a useful auxiliary to the Cardinal in later life, had made his way in the world is still something of a mystery: the early death of François de La Porte had, as we saw, precluded any direct paternal patronage of the kind usually presumed. Born around 1566 and educated at the Paris college of Reims, he entered the order of Malta in 1583, when he probably owed more

15 *Ibid.*, pp. 68–9; Avenel, 'La Jeunesse', pp. 162–4.
16 Hanotaux, *Richelieu*, I, p. 68.
17 *Ibid.*, pp. 73–4; Maurice Dumolin, 'Les Académies parisiennes d'équitation', *Bulletin de la Société Archéologique Historique et Artistique, Le Vieux Papier*, 16 (1925), pp. 417–19.

to François de Richelieu's patronage than to that of his own family.[18] However, we know nothing of the circles in which Amador moved around 1600, and how far these may have been instrumental in furthering the careers of all three Richelieu nephews. Had not fate intervened, Armand might well have followed his uncle into the ranks of the knights of Malta, and distinguished himself in other fields.

There is a second, equally tenacious tradition to the effect that, far from either boarding in college or living with his uncle during these years, Richelieu was reared in the house of Denis Bouthillier, a Paris lawyer and one-time clerk of François de La Porte. There is, needless to say, no more positive evidence for this tradition than for the first, but we can at least safely discard the familiar story that La Porte confided his grandchildren to Bouthillier after François de Richelieu's death.[19] But in the social world of Richelieu's La Porte relatives – that of lawyers and barristers – their Bouthillier acquaintances can never have been far away, and the unmarried *chevalier*, Amador, was doubtless keen to see his nephews frequent boys of their own age. What is not in dispute is that early in his career, Richelieu formed close, abiding, and mutually profitable ties with the Bouthilliers.[20]

All in all, the years after 1595 were ones in which the young Armand's stays in Poitou were probably confined to the admittedly long summer vacations. Much more direct and interesting, if also retrospective, is the evidence for Richelieu's early 'insertion sociale' provided by his early correspondence as bishop of Luçon. His letters to the hitherto anonymous Madame de Bourges reveal a familiarity, respect and confidence that could only have been based on long acquaintance. Jeanne de St Germain was the daughter of Jean de St Germain the elder, a prosperous apothecary whose son, also called Jean, Pierre de l'Estoile numbered among his friends, and whom Estoile complimented on being one of the few honest apothecaries of his acquaintance![21] A few months after Richelieu's birth, in

18 Archives of Order of Malta, vol. 3180, *preuves de noblesse*, 17 Jan. 1584. Some of those giving evidence asserted that he had made the journey to Malta during 1583. The enquiry into his nobility was conducted at the Richelieu residence in Paris.

19 La Porte, as we saw, died in 1572, his son-in-law in 1590; the first grandchild, Françoise, was born around 1578.

20 Avenel, 'La Jeunesse', p. 174. Sébastien Bouthillier, destined, like Richelieu himself, for an ecclesiastical career, may have been closest friend in the family in the early years, and it was he who promoted him a canon of Luçon cathedral as early as 1607; Sébastien's later devotion to him was legendary. His brother, Claude, was no less close to Richelieu. Both brothers were a few years older than the Cardinal. See Orest Ranum, *Richelieu and the Councillors of Louis XIII* (Oxford 1963), p. 34.

21 Pierre de l'Estoile, *Journal pour le règne de Henri IV*, vol. II, ed. A. Martin (Paris 1958), pp. 413, 428–9.

December 1585, Jeanne married François Sauvat, *valet de chambre* to Henri III.[22] They had a daughter, Madeleine, born in 1588, for whom Richelieu would later vainly attempt to find a husband among the Poitevin nobility.[23] Sauvat died within a few years of marrying Jeanne, and, in 1598, she married again, her choice this time being Jacques de Bourges, a man with whom she had previously cohabited.[24] This marriage produced no children. Bourges, who later styled himself an *avocat* at the *parlement* of Paris, was as much an *homme d'affaires* who looked after the business interests of clients as a conventional barrister. Among his principal clients over the years were the La Porte family, especially Charles, *seigneur* de La Meilleraye; he was also, as we shall see, to serve Richelieu in various ways until his death in July 1612.[25] So close was the relationship between the Bourges and Richelieu that he may well have been under their care at some time during his schooling. In any event, the connection is further evidence that his earliest social milieu was not merely Parisian, but 'bourgeois' as well.

None of this should be taken to imply that the young Richelieu was unconscious of his noble rank. The college where he studied, Navarre, was not only one of the largest and best-attended of the many colleges of the university that dotted the Montagne Ste Geneviève, it was also the most aristocratic of them. It is all the more regrettable that a lack of evidence prevents us from doing more than assuming that Richelieu made at least some friendships during his years there among the *jeunesse dorée* of the day. Later chroniclers have generally failed to trace any significant acquaintances back to his stay at Navarre other than some of his long-standing domestic servants – Desbournais, his valet, Mulot, his tutor, and Michel Le Masle, his secretary.[26]

Equally conjectural is the extent to which Richelieu is to be numbered among those tumultuous and high-spirited students of the Latin Quarter whose disturbances made headlines around the turn

22 A.N., M.C., LXXIII, 321, 29 July 1597, *inventaire après décès* of Jean de St Germain, Papers, no. 49, for a reference to the marriage contract. The original has not survived.
23 Avenel, *Lettres*, I, pp. 26, 27, 28, letters to Madame de Bourges, dated by Avenel to 1609. Madeleine married Jean de Fenis, *receveur* of the Paris *maréchaussée*, in early 1610: A.N., M.C., III, 488, marriage contract of 28 Jan. 1610. As Richelieu does not figure among the list of witnesses habitually cited in such contracts, the marriage presumably owed nothing to his efforts.
24 A.N., Y 137, fos. 244–5, 7 Oct. 1598, registration of marriage contract dated 23 June 1598.
25 A.N., S 4073, no. 9, for his will, dated 7 Sept. 1611, and codicils to it. The will contains legacies which refer to La Porte's debts to him; similar references are found in his marriage contract of 1598. His *inventaire*, which would doubtless have revealed much more of interest, has been lost.
26 See Deloche, *Maison de Richelieu*, pp. 103–4.

of the century.[27] But in view of what is known of his character, his strong passions and the military temperament which he later tried so hard to discipline, there is every reason to think of the adolescent who apparently called himself the marquis du Chillou in the opening years of the seventeenth century as tempestuous; the restraint, gravity and haughtiness that characterized the adult Richelieu ought not to be thought of as inherited at birth. For one thing, it is probably to the early 1600s that the allegations of womanizing made later by his critics – some of whom had been close to him in earlier years – can ultimately be traced, and about which vast quantities of ink have subsequently been spilt.[28] But if no evidence at all exists where most writers have looked for it, it seems clear that he was the 'Monsieur de Lusson' who, in 1605, when he had already been nominated bishop, was treated by no less a medical practitioner than Jean de la Rivière, *médecin ordinaire* to Henri IV and a controversial medical figure in Paris, and Théodore Turquet de Mayerne, for what Mayerne diagnosed as 'gonnorhoea inveterata' – and then only after he and a number of other high-society patients had already been given up as hopeless cases by other doctors.[29] Such language in a doctor's private case-book suggests at the very least that the sexual disease that Richelieu was carrying was neither recent nor the result of a chance, unfortunate encounter.

II

But for some time before his encounter with Rivière, the shape of Richelieu's career had been altered drastically, and he had had to bid farewell to the military career for which he was probably temperamentally best suited. The see of Luçon beckoned instead. Like so much in his early career, the entire episode is heavily shrouded in

---

27   Michel Carmona, *Une affaire d'inceste: Julien et Marguerite Ravalet* (Paris 1987), ch. 2, for a graphic if romanticized account.

28   The most virulent attacks came in the many pamphlets of Mathieu de Morgues, who knew him intimately from his time at Luçon. See, for example, his *Très-humble, très véritable et très importante remonstrance au roy* [*c.* 1631], p. 31: 'Il a en sa ieunesse aymé les voluptez, qui luy ont faict faire des choses non seulement indignes de sa profession: mais tout à faict ridicules'. For a tendentious survey of the whole problem, see Louis Batiffol, *Richelieu et les femmes* (Paris 1931).

29   British Library, Sloane MS. 2089, fo. 27v, for a list of the patients, including President Séguier, Mme de Retz, Sébastien Zamet, Leonora Galigai, wife of Concini, and 'M le Cardinal' (indicated as 'Richelieu' in a marginal note); Sloane MS. 2059, fo. 45, 'M de Lusson, 31 maij 1605', with a marginal addition, in the same hand, 'Card de Richelieu'. Hugh Trevor-Roper, *Renaissance Essays* (London 1985), p. 220 and note, was the first to draw attention to this reference, which was repeated by J.H. Elliott, 'Richelieu, l'homme' in *Richelieu et la culture*, ed. R. Mousnier (Paris 1987), p. 191. Having consulted the manuscripts, I see no reason to doubt their veracity, nor to suspect later interpolation.

myth and fable, the legacy of earlier controversies. Because it was to be so fundamental to the rest of his career, even as a politician, it is worth attempting to look again at the political and family context, in which this decisive change of direction occurred.

The Richelieu family connection with Luçon, as we saw, was but one of the many advantages they drew from the favour bestowed by Henri III on the Cardinal's father, and initially its value may not have loomed especially large. It was understood by all parties to such a concession that the real control of the diocese, and especially the right to collect its revenues, lay with the grantee himself rather than with whoever became bishop as a result of his nomination. In canon law, such practices were labelled *confidences*, and were both illegal and sinful. François de Richelieu tried with success to ensure there would be no legal or practical difficulties over Luçon by presenting his uncle, Jacques, for royal and papal approval, while obtaining his power of attorney to deal with all important questions of management and revenue.[30] But, after his death in 1590, it became much less clear what would happen should Bishop Jacques die: would the family be well-placed enough to retain their recent grip on Luçon, and would a new king feel any need to extend favours made by his predecessor? In the event, as we have seen, Henri IV quickly signalled his benevolent intentions towards the family, and there is evidence that they took advantage of this to make their own arrangements to maintain control of Luçon and its revenues. Bishop Jacques seems to have been persuaded shortly before his death in mid-1592 to sign an act of resignation of Luçon in favour of François Hyver, parish priest of St Jean-de-Braye, the Richelieu family parish. This provided a convenient method of retaining the see in the absence of another Richelieu capable of taking the uncle's place and, indeed, was possibly the only way this could have been achieved.[31] Of course, such an act required royal ratification, but it was on the basis of this act of resignation that Henri IV nominated Hyver to Luçon in March 1593, issuing *lettres d'économat* in September 1594 for the temporal and spiritual administration of the diocese until such time as Hyver could obtain the necessary bulls of provision.[32] At the time, these bulls must still have appeared a distant enough prospect: a ban on royal nominees to benefices seeking their pro-

---

30 A.S.V., *fondo* Consistoriale, Acta Miscellanea 53, fo. 321. M.C., XC 143, 3 April 1585, lease of Luçon temporalities by Richelieu on his uncle's behalf.

31 Delhommeau, *Documents pour Luçon*, no. 540, 17 March 1593. See also following note.

32 A.N., V 5 1227, fo. 120r-v, letters of 20 Sept. 1594; registered by *grand conseil*, 22 Dec. 1594. This text states that Luçon was vacant owing to the act of resignation *in favorem* Hyver made by Jacques du Plessis. No independent proof of it has been found, but it was a technique that families were likely to resort to all the more readily in times of political upheaval.

visions in Rome had been in force since 1591 and would not be lifted until 1596, while, for its part, Rome was deeply suspicious of any episcopal nomination made by Henri IV, who in 1593 was still a Huguenot. However, such delays cannot have disturbed the Richelieu family much. From their point of view, the longer the delay the better: Hyver stayed in his parish, as he was meant to, while they and their stewards ran the diocese and collected its revenues.[33] By the end of the 1590s, Armand's eldest brother, Henri, was in control of the Luçon's temporalities, and with every year that passed the day neared when the second son, Alphonse, would be in a position to claim the episcopal title for himself.[34]

The one complicating element in all this was the combative attitude of the cathedral chapter of Luçon, which had not welcomed Jacques du Plessis's nomination in 1584. To the canons, he was another *confidentiaire*, a straw-man put there to do someone else's bidding. François Hyver must have struck them as an even worse nominee than Jacques du Plessis, and his 'appointment' as a mortifying display of contempt for the diocese.[35] More to the point, it meant that the long-standing conflicts between the chapter and the bishop concerning liability for maintenance and long-overdue repairs to the cathedral and episcopal temporalities, which had been severely and frequently damaged during the religious wars, were no nearer than ever to being resolved.[36] Increasingly, this was one of the chapter's principal pre-occupations and, under Jacques du Plessis, no satisfaction had been forthcoming from the Richelieu family. But the chapter was determined to press its case: after Jacques' death, it insisted on regarding the see of Luçon as vacant, and was even prepared, in 1596, to look into the prospect of actually electing a bishop.[37] If they were serious about taking such a step, they had left it too late: Henri IV was now in control of his kingdom, strong enough to block any move to elect bishops, and well disposed to Richelieu family interests. Hyver's claim to Luçon thus held firm, and he finally received his bulls, after a direct appeal from Henri IV, in March 1599.[38]

But in other respects the Luçon chapter proved a tenacious op-

---

33 In 1592, Adam Bajoue, a former underling of François de Richelieu, was administrator of the revenues of Luçon: Martineau, *Le Cardinal de Richelieu*, p. 66, n. 1.

34 Bergin, *Richelieu*, p. 202.

35 *Ibid.*

36 See successive reports on damages since 1560s in B.N., MS. Lat. 17389, fos. 169–73, 175–6, 180–98, 202–132, 234–7.

37 Delhommeau, *Documents pour Luçon*, no. 547, reference to request to canons of Bordeaux cathedral in relation to the chapters' right to elect bishops, 1596.

38 Eubel C. et al., *Hierarchia Catholica medii et recentioris aevi* (Munich, 1898–1958), IV, p. 225; A.S.V., Miscellanea Armarium XII, 145, fo. 114.

ponent. Throughout the 1590s and early 1600s, it went on regarding the see as vacant, and successfully elected its own dean in 1593 against a royal nominee.[39] Later in the decade, it appears to have successfully prevented the Richelieu family from securing a position of canon in the cathedral for Alphonse, even though it was no secret that he was by then the family's candidate for the episcopal mitre.[40] Again, in 1593, the *parlement* of Paris, then resident at Tours, ordered an inspection of the temporalities with a view to assigning responsibility for repairs.[41] There is good reason to presume that the timing of Henri IV's grants – Hyver's nomination in 1593, the *économat* of 1594 – as well as of Hyver's papal provisions in 1599, was designed to frustrate the chapter.[42] But it refused to be put off, and in June 1603 obtained a provisional decree from the *grand conseil* ordering the bishop to devote one-third of his revenue from the diocese to repairs.[43] Clearly, the affairs of Luçon could not be kept discreetly out of the public eye. Conflict might possibly have been muted had Hyver been less blatantly an absentee, unconsecrated caretaker, but we may assume that the Richelieu family was not disposed either to allow him that increment of independence which an episcopal consecration might have provided, or to take the trouble to obtain a suffragan bishop, who would have lacked any claim on the title or revenues of Luçon, but would at least have been capable of conducting the functions of a bishop.

These were the general circumstances which helped precipitate the decision whereby the young Armand-Jean du Plessis would become bishop of Luçon. From his family's point of view, the tactic of using Hyver as a straw-man was not working well: the price had been stiff resistance from the cathedral chapter and a judicial disavowal by a sovereign court. While Alphonse, the second son, had logically been designated as the intended successor – he seems to have been unofficially referred to in the mid-1590s as 'bishop of Luçon' and 'the elected bishop' – sudden changes were not exceptional for the decade, when the real tenure of episcopal sees throughout France was extremely confused.[44] When, therefore, a decision was made around 1602–3 to seek the king's formal approval of Alphonse as bishop of Luçon, it was probably intended mainly as another round in the game of cat and mouse being played with the chapter, since Alphonse,

---

39 Fontenelle de Vaudoré, *Evêques de Luçon*, I, p. 344.
40 *Ibid.*, p. 348.
41 *Ibid.*, p. 341.
42 *Ibid.*, pp. 338–48, 353–4. This is still the most reliable source.
43 *Ibid.*, p. 350; Delhommeau, *Documents pour Luçon*, no. 56.
44 Fontenelle de Vaudoré, *Evêques de Luçon*, p. 354, who writes that the record of a visitation in 1595 stated that 'l'évêque était aux universités, et l'économe en Anjou'.

too, was still a student, and well under the required canonical age for episcopal preferment. Royal approval may even have been given – though at what date we do not know – for Alphonse to be described as an 'evesque nommé', thus leading some historians to include him in the list of bishops of Luçon.[45] But what was entirely unforeseen was Alphonse's apparently sudden decision to break the rules of the game altogether, and to opt instead for the obscurity of a Carthusian cell.[46] Over the centuries, Alphonse has scarcely had a better press than his elder brother, Henri, and his abandonment of family plans for him seemed only to compound numerous perceived defects of character – stubbornness, moodiness, indifference, and so on. However, what has been widely regarded as his precipitate irresponsibility may well be attributable to a very different factor. Alphonse's decision to turn away from the world and become a Carthusian was so sharp and long-lived as to make most explanations of it sound trivial. What evidence there is suggests that his frequentation of the *milieu des dévots* around the turn of the century was more genuine and intense than that of his younger brother, and that the result was some kind of conversion experience, triggered perhaps by the need to choose whether or not to become bishop of Luçon: his 'flight' into austere monasticism and Carthusian contemplation was, if not common, a recognizable product of the intense religious life of the capital around 1600. The Carthusian order, *nunquam reformata quia nunquam reformanda*, was not a painless option for those seeking an easy escape from responsibility.

Given the events of the previous decade, and in view of the Richelieu family's financial and social position, and their ambitions for the rising generation, Alphonse's decision was potentially devastating. Hyver had long since been discredited as a phantom bishop whose absence from Luçon rendered him useless in defending Richelieu family interests. The time had come for change, and we may assume that the lead in forcing a decision was taken by the energetic and well-placed Henri, who was effectively drawing the revenues of Luçon at this time, and who had to face the consequences if litigation with the chapter went against him. It is reasonable to date the decision to press Armand to quit Pluvinel's academy and embark on an ecclesiastical career to the second half of 1603; the verdict of the *grand conseil* in June that year, requiring part of the see's revenues

---

45 *Ibid.*, p. 353, lists him as the 27th bishop of Luçon, but on the next page the author writes: 'on peut se demander si ce personage fut evêque de Luçon'.

46 B.N. MS. Latin 9957, fo. 30, rector's book of the theology faculty for 1600: 'Aphonsus Ludovicus du Plessis nobilis parisiensis episcopus Lucionensis designatus'. His decision to renounce Luçon obviously post-dates this time. See also Maximin Deloche, *Un Frère de Richelieu inconnu* (Paris 1935), pp. 23ff.

to be spent on repairs, probably concentrated the minds of those directly concerned with Luçon. To this day, the exact date of the king's nomination of Armand as bishop is not known, the formal letters being lost, but it presumably came in the months preceding February 1604, when the first recorded mention of it is to be found in the correspondence of the papal nuncio, Del Buffalo, a mention in itself of little significance, but the first hard evidence we have that the family now intended to press on with the uncertain business of turning its youngest son into a fully-fledged bishop.[47]

From the Luçon chapter's point of view, the nomination of yet another Richelieu candidate was but just a further twist in an already long story of evasion and chicanery. Emboldened by the decree of June 1603, it continued to press its demands against the family, and as a result the parties moved towards some sort of negotiated settlement to the dispute in late 1604. It is worth noting that, at this point, the chapter did not know whether Alphonse or Armand was the 'evesque nommé', as it left the name of their interlocutor blank in the power of attorney drafted for the negotiations, preferring to regard the see as vacant; equally, for the purposes of negotiation at least, the family insisted that Hyver was still the titular bishop.[48] But the transaction agreed between the parties after arbitration in December 1604, which was still favourable to the Richelieu family, failed, as we shall see later, to end conflict with the chapter.[49]

III

Armand took no formal part at least in these discussions, all of which were managed by Henri, though he presumably followed them with a keen interest. But once the decision was taken that he would be the next bishop of Luçon, he returned, probably in October 1603, to the studies he had broken off a few years earlier at the College of Navarre. Assuming that he had proceeded no further than the humanities during his earlier sojourn there, he probably had to begin with the philosophy course; only then could he have begun the normally longer course leading to a degree in theology. Given that his was not the only under-age episcopal nomination made by Henri

47 *Correspondance du nonce en France Innocenzo del Buffalo, évêque de Camerino (1601–1604)*, ed. Bernard Barbiche (Rome-Paris, 1964), p. 671, Del Buffalo to Cardinal Aldobrandini, 22 Feb. 1604.

48 Delhommeau, *Documents pour Luçon*, no. 565, procuration from Chapter for negotiations *sede vacante*. Fontenelle de Vaudoré, *Evéques de Luçon*, I, p. 354, for the Chapter's uncertainty.

49 Martineau, *Cardinal de Richelieu*, pp. 132–5, for the text of the transaction, agreed after arbitration by several Paris lawyers.

IV, such a decision may appear surprising; many of his contemporaries among the episcopate, especially those of noble background, felt no compulsion to take university degrees. But it may be that such a course of action was intended to counteract the chapter's attacks on his family's mistreatment of Luçon – at last it would have a properly-qualified bishop. More prosaically, in view of the possibility that provisions from Rome might not be readily granted, the decision could also serve to strengthen the claims of a candidate who in 1603 was only eighteen years of age.

In any case, there is no doubt that Richelieu took his second cycle of study with considerable seriousness. When the nuncio wrote to Rome in support of him in February 1604, he singled out for mention the young cleric's assiduousness in his current studies, though without being more specific than that.[50] The speed with which he completed them over the next few years shows all the signs of the determination and sense of purpose which would become his hallmark in later life. Our knowledge of his years of study between 1603 and 1606 is, as with so much of his early years, based on later testimony, much of it bombastic flattery, so that straightforward facts are hard to come by. There is confusion, too. While much still remains obscure, the following account is based essentially on university records which, if authentic, are not models of clarity.

The most reliable authorities claim that Richelieu began his philosophy studies – a preparatory course for theology – in 1603 at the College of Calvi under Jacques Hennequin, a well-known professor, and then moved back to Navarre where he completed the actual course in 1604.[51] It was a course which normally lasted two years, which in turn would explain why, in July 1605, Richelieu figured for the first time on the rector's list of those seeking testimonials enabling them to take their Arts degree, and why he asked the faculty to grant him the necessary dispensation to defend his philosophy dissertation with a view to taking his M.A.[52] It is not known exactly when he defended his philosophy 'theses', but his earliest biographer, the abbé de Pure, claims that around this time Richelieu offered to hold an open philosophy disputation with all comers, only to be denied

---

50 See n. 47.
51 Michel de Pure, *Vita Eminentissimi Cardinalis Arm. Joan. Plessei Richelii* (Paris 1656), pp. 15–16.
52 B.N. MS. Latin 9957, fo. 82v, 23 June 1605. Charles Jourdain, *Histoire de l'université de Paris au xvi et au xvii siècle* (Paris 1867), p. 42, n. 3. Avenel, 'La Jeunesse', p. 165, n. 4 (quoting Du Plessis d'Argentré): 'respondit (Richelieu) de philosophia in regia Navarra, anno 1604'. This would mean he became an M.A. as early as 1604, which is improbable; D'Argentré offers no proof of his assertion which is contradicted by the records cited by Jourdain. I am much indebted to Laurence Brockliss for his help in deciphering the records of Richelieu's academic progress, though responsibility for the interpretation offered here should not be attributed to him.

permission by the conservative faculty on the grounds that this was 'unusual'. Such bravura would not be out of character for a man already anxious to make an impression – an early example of the desire to *paraître* that critics often levelled at him later – but it is legitimate to wonder whether a similar and better-documented challenge made in 1606 by the future abbé de St Cyran is not here being appropriated by de Pure for his hero.[53]

At any rate, Richelieu did not wait until he took his M.A. before beginning his theology studies, though the master's degree was a formal prerequisite for those wishing to take examinations in theology. According to de Pure, he moved from Navarre to the Sorbonne to begin his theology, but this claim should not be taken too literally.[54] From Richelieu's point of view, the statutes of the university, reformed as recently as 1601, posed serious problems: they required five years of study before a student could complete the first cycle of the theology course.[55] He was not prepared to wait so long, and in July 1606, he again requested a dispensation from the time-limit so that he could be admitted to the *primum cursus* – that is, to the first cycle of examinations leading to the baccalaureate and further degrees – and he duly collected his certificate. It was no doubt a mixture of high rank and academic merit which persuaded the faculty of theology to smooth his progress by issuing the appropriate dispensation at that time.[56] This did not prove an immediate prelude to a public examination, especially as Richelieu would set out for Rome a few months later. When the papacy granted him his provisions to Luçon in December 1606, he was described as a 'bachelor in theology', which although technically inexact was an approximate reflection of his studies to date.[57] On returning from Rome the following summer as a consecrated bishop, he presented yet another – his third – supplication, this time asking the faculty to set down the conditions for his first theology examination; indeed, insofar as his intentions can be gauged from a particularly obscure text, he seems to have wished the faculty to allow him to compress the proceedings to such an extent that the baccalaureate, licentiate and doctoral examinations could follow each other in quick succession. The most important of these was the three-hour examination – known as the *tentativa* – for the bacca-

53 De Pure, *Vita*, p. 16; Jean Orcibal, *Jean Duvergier de Hauranne, abbé de St Cyran, et son temps* (Louvain-Paris 1948), p. 135.

54 De Pure, *Vita*, p. 16.

55 L.W.B. Brockliss, *French Higher Education in the Seventeenth and Eighteenth Centuries. A Cultural History* (Oxford 1987), p. 230, n. 6.

56 De Pure, *Vita*, p. 19, for the petition, taken from the university archives. B.N. MS. Latin 9957, fo. 95, rector's book for June–Dec. 1606.

57 Eubel, *Hierarchia Catholica*, IV, p. 225, Luçon, n. 3; A.S.V., Acta Miscellanea 97, fo. 935.

laureate which, in what again looks like an audacious move, he requested permission to take, while dispensing with the usual requirement of having a president to chair the event. Once again, the faculty was willing to go some of the way to oblige him: they allowed him to undertake the *tentativa*, but were not prepared to let him have everything his own way. He would merely take the bachelor's examination, without a president and in debate with the bachelors 'of the first licence'. This he did at the end of October 1607, defending his first and only 'theological acts' before Hennequin, his master, Flavigny and other bachelors.[58] The faculty's ruling makes it clear that, contrary to legend, he became neither a licentiate nor a doctor of theology.[59] By the same token, it seems reasonable to discount much of the hyperbole which later came to envelop his performance during his Sorbonne examination – it would be difficult to think of any major figure of the century whose *soutenance* was not later described as brilliant or stunning, and as having left both teachers and audience speechless in admiration. No contemporary chronicler refers to Richelieu's theses, let alone to their having won the applause of town and gown. Yet Richelieu was clearly an able and dedicated student: only two days after his defence, he was admitted as a fellow to the Sorbonne, then only a constituent part of the wider faculty of theology.[60]

This is the extent of our knowledge of Richelieu's studies, and it can hardly be described as either enthralling or deeply revealing. But we would probably know even less if Richelieu had not petitioned the Arts and Theology faculties for special privileges and rulings in three successive years. It is more important to note his desire to complete his studies as far as possible, even when external events, which were then directly shaping his career, left him with less than the full time required to take the normal course. When he petitioned in August 1607 to defend his theology theses, he even cited 'the king's wish' as one reason for doing so, a claim which has usually been seen as an expression of the king's patronage and personal interest in the career of a man he is supposed to have addressed as 'mon evesque', but which is probably based on too literal a reading of the Latin text of one of Richelieu's petitions; it was probably no more than Richelieu's application to his own case of the terms of a royal edict of the previous year which laid down a doctorate in theo-

58 De Pure, *Vita*, pp. 42–4. For the debate over whether Richelieu ever completed the examinations for the actual doctorate, see Marvick, *Young Richelieu*, p. 160, n. 93.
59 Lucien Lacroix, *Richelieu à Luçon, sa jeunesse, son épiscopat* (Paris 1890), pp. 62–3, is convinced he took the doctoral examination; Hanotaux, *Richelieu*, I, pp. 85–6, is more cautious, but appears to accept that Richelieu did become a doctor. Both Hanotaux and Lacroix print the relevant passages from the faculty registers, as transmitted by de Pure.
60 Hanotaux, *Richelieu*, I, p. 85.

logy as a qualification for high church office officials.[61] Of course, the concordat of Bologna also required that incoming bishops should have a doctorate from a 'famous university', a stipulation had been more honoured in the breach than in the observance since 1516.

Moreover, an important difference between universities then and since is the often wide gap which separated the course of studies followed from the actual business of taking examinations and degrees, especially among members of the clergy. There were minimum requirements, as we saw in the case of theology in Paris, before examinations could be sat, but exemptions and dispensations were often granted to those displaying sufficient progress or aptitude. On top of that, although professors lectured in the time-honoured and, it appears, rather antiquated fashion, and although individual students were the pupils of particular masters, a great deal of study could (and probably had to) be done independently. For that reason, we should not perhaps attach too much importance to determining who Richelieu's professors were and in what precise ways they may have influenced him intellectually. Private mentors or fellow students may have been more significant influences. Apart from the mention of well-known professors like Hennequin, Flavigny and André du Val, nearly all of the earliest accounts of Richelieu's career refer in a variety of ways to a prolonged period of private study and debate with a doctor from the University of Louvain, an episode which has sometimes been confused or telescoped with a later period of study involving two English divines. Such an episode is in many ways typical of the biographical tradition in which the early accounts of Richelieu's life was written, and it was clearly meant to suggest that this academic experience was more fundamental and more decisive than all the lectures which Richelieu did – or did not – attend at the university. The identity of this intellectual mentor has been much debated, but there is every reason to accept the evidence of de Pure, who identifies him as Philippe Cospeau. Born at Mons in Spanish Flanders in 1571, he had migrated to Paris via Louvain and, even before he became a doctor and full member of the theology faculty, had become an important influence in the university in the opening years of the century.[62] Alphonse de Richelieu, de Pure's main source

---

61 See previous note. The petition was first printed by de Pure, *Vita*, pp. 42–4. For the conditions, see Brockliss, *Higher Education*, p. 5, n. 11.

62 Part of the confusion lies in the description of Richelieu's mentor as a doctor of Louvain. Cospeau had studied there, but had not taken any of its degrees, let alone the doctorate. But his prestige as an ex-pupil of one of Louvain's most famous professors, Justus Lipsius, probably accounts for this ascription. See Émile Jacques, *Philippe Cospeau. Un ami-ennemi de Richelieu 1571–1646* (Paris 1989), ch. 3, for a thorough examination of Cospeau's career at Louvain. Jacques also establishes his family name was Cospeau, not Cospéau or Cospéan.

of information, was himself one of those influenced by Cospeau, and thus well-placed to know about his relations with his younger brother. De Pure's claim that Richelieu shared lodgings with Cospeau around 1604–6 so as to conclude his studies more rapidly seems entirely plausible.[63] Contemporaries later spoke of Richelieu's deference towards, almost fear of, Cospeau – not a character trait we normally associate with the future Cardinal, and which might well be explained by a formative encounter early in his career.[64] Cospeau went on to become a much-respected figure in the French church, and outlived his pupil. Their episcopal careers had more than a passing resemblance, too. In 1606, Cospeau became bishop of Aire in Gascony in a manner which recalls Richelieu's own advancement, though in Cospeau's case it was through the patronage of the formidable duc d'Épernon, in whose gift the see then was, thanks to a concession similar to that made by Henri III to François de Richelieu.[65]

In a wider context, the faculty, and the Sorbonne in particular, were no longer the hot-houses they had been in the last years of the life of Richelieu's father, when they were in the vanguard of opposition to Henri III and Henri IV, and had even gone so far as to pronounce the 'just abdication' of Henri III after the Guise murders in 1588. The doctors who had openly supported the Catholic League had been purged or had gone to ground, and a new generation of academics had taken their place with Henri IV's reform of the university in 1600. Edmond Richer would not become syndic of the theology faculty until 1608, but even before then he had been vigorously defending royal power and crusading for a rejuvenation of gallicanism in all its forms against what he claimed were the excessive claims to superiority, spiritual and temporal, of the papacy. Even pro-papal professors like André du Val had to steer a prudent course to avoid giving offence or arousing criticism.[66] This kind of atmosphere must, if we can judge from his later experience, have been congenial to Richelieu who, under the influence of family tradition, was anxious to marry a career in the church with service to the crown. If it is perhaps not actually true, there is a kind of symbolic truth in the anecdote that, when preparing to defend his theology theses in 1607, Richelieu took the unprecedented step of dedicating them to the king, with an offer of his services, should the king judge him worthy.

---

63 De Pure, *Vita*, p. 18.
64 Jacques, *Philippe Cospeau*, p. 62. Jacques produces no new evidence, but believes Richelieu and Cospeau knew each other from an early date.
65 *Ibid.*, chs. 4–5, for valuable details on his early years in France. See also Orcibal, *St Cyran*, pp. 134–5, for examples of Cospeau's influence.
66 Brockliss, *Higher Education*, pp. 267ff. for a brief survey of these disputes.

For all that he is alleged to have accepted for conventional family reasons the change from a military to an ecclesiastical career, Richelieu undoubtedly developed strong intellectual interests during these years when he returned to the groves of academe. Indeed, had he merely wished to collect a degree for the sake of having one, he might have opted for law rather than theology, as did many bishops at this time: his maternal family background and his acquaintances with the Bouthilliers and others might have pointed him in that direction. Moreover, law degrees required little effort, and could be picked up very quickly, especially outside Paris. By comparison, anyone advancing to the baccalaureate or licentiate, and even more so to the doctorate, in theology, had probably been through the toughest course of study and examination that seventeenth-century French universities had to offer.[67] Richelieu, even when allowance is made for his considerable vanity, was justifiably proud of his academic achievements, and his self-perception throughout his career as a scholarly churchman holds the key to many of his later interests and actions, even in the political sphere.

It would be equally valuable to know with whom Richelieu established significant friendships during his years at the Sorbonne, but there is very little direct evidence upon which to build. The faculty's own registers show that among the future bishops graduating at around the same time as Richelieu himself, were François de Harlay de Champvallon, archbishop of Rouen, his cousin Achille de Harlay de Sancy, who would effectively 'ghost' Richelieu's memoirs, and Léonor d'Etampes, bishop of Chartres and a Richelieu factotum. In a letter of 1616 to Achille de Harlay, Richelieu referred to their 'ancienne cognoissance'.[68] Equally, Richelieu's closeness to Cospeau would certainly have brought him into contact with a large number of the clerics and courtiers who attended his lectures and sermons.[69] More than that, Cospeau's vigourous propagation of a *vera philosophia Christi*, as one of his adherents later described it, would go a long way towards explaining Richelieu's later seriousness of purpose as a bishop and his commitment to the goals of church reform.

IV

Richelieu's immersion in the world of learning was characteristically thorough, and it has been suggested that it may even have served as a

---

67 *Ibid.*, pp. 74, 79–81, 233–4, for the most comprehensive survey to date.
68 *Les Papiers de Richelieu. Empire allemand*, vol. I, ed. Adolf Wild (Paris 1982), p. 11.
69 These names are taken from the rector's book for 1596–1615 in B.N. MS. Latin 9957, fos. 79–116. Léonor d'Etampes's testimony to the influence of Cospeau on his generation, specifically mentioning Achille de Harlay, Alphonse de Richelieu and others, is in A.S.V., Processus consistoriales 34, fos. 497v–99v (1635).

form of self-therapy in his efforts to achieve self-discipline over an unruly nature. But above all, it was stimulated by the prospect of becoming bishop of Luçon. Nominated, as we saw, by the king in late 1603, he began taking orders sometime after that, and was a subdeacon by the time he was approved by Rome three years later. As he stepped into the role initially designed for Alphonse, he doubtless received the two small benefices that his brother had 'inherited' from Jacques du Plessis and which he had had to give up on becoming a Carthusian – the priories of Les Roches and Pommiers-Aigres in the diocese of Tours.[70] Not many clerics stepping into episcopal office in the early seventeenth century were as poorly-endowed as that.

The papacy's delay in confirming Richelieu as bishop has given rise to a number of conflicting views, not to mention dubious anecdotes; it is thus essential to set the record as straight as the surviving sources allow. One of the first requirements on receiving a royal nomination was to see to it that the canonical enquiry *de vita et moribus* required by Rome for the scrutiny of episcopal candidates, was carried out. In Richelieu's case, we know that this was conducted by the papal nuncio, a practice which was not yet the rule. The document itself has been lost, and only a very brief Roman summary of it survives.[71] But it would inevitably have referred, if only because of the standardized questionnaire on which it was based, to the vexed question of Richelieu's age; and while its information was based not on original documents, but on depositions from witnesses, the latter would certainly have alluded to the candidate's age, and at least some of them might have had fairly accurate information on that point. Richelieu himself knew this full well, which is why he – or someone on his behalf – approached the papal nuncio directly in February 1604 about the problem. He revealed to Del Buffalo then that he was 'under twenty' – in reality, he was nearly nineteen – and the nuncio passed this news to Rome, along with the candidate's appeal for favourable treatment by the pope. Cardinal Aldobrandini, the papal secretary of state, confirmed in May 1604 that the request had been passed to Clement VIII.[72] But the cardinal's letter of reply also implies that the curia was still waiting for Richelieu actually to take practical steps to solicit his bulls – an entirely separate matter to

---

70 The original documents in A.S.V., Acta Consistorialia, Miscellanea 97, fo. 935, clearly refer to Les Roches and Pommiers-Aigre, but not to Coussay, as I previously assumed (Bergin, *Richelieu*, p. 202). But Richelieu evidently held Coussay also, which appears to have been virtually a piece of secularized family property.

71 A.S.V., Acta Consistorialia, Miscellanea 97, fo. 935.

72 *Correspondance du nonce Innocenzo del Buffalo*, p. 671, Del Buffalo to Cardinal Aldobrandini, 22 Feb. 1604; *ibid.*, p. 726, Aldobrandini to Nuncio, 31 May 1604.

notifying Rome formally of a royal nomination, and one which the candidate had to initiate himself through the 'expeditionary bankers' and solicitors who handled these matters in the curia. It was not at all uncommon then for candidates to defer doing so for one reason or another; we need but recall the occasional threats made by the French monarchy to dilatory nominees that it would appoint some-one else to their benefices if they did not show more diligence in this regard. It may well be that Henri de Richelieu was hoping to get sufficient backing at court for his brother to obtain his bulls free of charge or at a considerable discount – this being probably the most common reason for delay in seeking bulls of provision in Rome.[73] At any rate, the next known mention of Richelieu's case dates from March 1606 when Cardinal du Perron reported from Rome that the French ambassador had raised the matter of his confirmation with the new Pope Paul V, whose response had been vaguely positive – 'qui luy avoit donné sujet d'en bien espérer'.[74]

Papal reticence is not infrequently difficult to fathom, but in the case of Richelieu and Luçon, the long delay between Richelieu's nomination by Henri IV and his confirmation by Paul V may well have had an additional cause quite unrelated to his age, and arguably more serious than that issue. Armand's title to Luçon was, as we have seen, based firstly on Hyver's act of resignation, duly con-firmed by Henri IV, and explicitly mentioned in the letter of nomi-nation.[75] Although we do not know what other conditions the letters to Rome contained, the terms under which Armand was eventually confirmed in December 1606 leave little doubt that they included financial demands in the form of a pension on behalf of his elder brother, demands of a kind which would have given the papacy good reason to suspect that Armand was merely intended to be his elder's brother *confidentiaire*, as Jacques had earlier been for *his* nephew. The papacy continued to be worried in the early years of the seventeenth century about the extent and persistence of such practices, and was not satisfied with the progress that was being made in eliminating them. It was this which prompted Paul V, in early July 1606, to send a secret brief to Henri IV which was de-signed to persuade laymen controlling benefices through straw-men to return them to proper clerical stewardship in return for a promise

73 Avenel, *Lettres*, VII, p. 422, where Richelieu, in the *Caput apologeticum* written in exile in Avignon in 1618, asserts that Rome did indeed grant him a reduction of 18,000 *livres* for the cost of his bulls of provision. Such a concession would probably not have been made without prior petition and negotiation.

74 Avenel, 'La Jeunesse', p. 166.

75 In proposing candidates to the pope, French kings were required to state the reason why a bishopric was vacant, as is evident from the hundreds of letters to be found in the *Processus consistoriales* series in the Vatican Archives.

that the papacy would be willing to grant them pensions off those benefices and despatch the necessary provisions free of charge.[76] The timing of this move merits attention; it signalled a less severe attitude in Rome, and this change of position may have been instrumental in helping to break the deadlock over Luçon. Equally, it can be seen as contributing to Richelieu's own personal intervention only a few months later: his first 'diplomatic' mission was to Rome, and it was conducted on his own behalf.

By 1606, it is also clear that Richelieu had himself become more directly involved in the affairs of Luçon, although the canons of the chapter were no better disposed to him than they had been to his predecessors, a state of affairs soon to produce yet more conflict: when he insisted that, as an 'évêque nommé', he was entitled to the revenues accruing from the use of the episcopal seal on official acts, the chapter reacted with predictable hostility. The dispute might seem in itself trivial, but arbitration failed to resolve it, and thus further litigation was inevitable. The case went straight to the *parlement* of Paris, where it was judged in June 1606; no less a figure than Cardin Le Bret, then *avocat-général* of the *parlement* and later celebrated for his book on sovereignty and for his service to Richelieu's ministry, made the case for the young Richelieu. But it is ironic – such 'liberty' was to go out of fashion when his client became a minister – that in upholding the validity of Richelieu's case, he should do so only after openly lamenting the times they lived in, and criticizing the behaviour of young 'nominated' bishops who felt free to postpone taking orders because the law enabled them to exercise certain powers of jurisdiction within their dioceses. Victory in the case went to Richelieu, but it was made subject to the condition that he be consecrated within the time-limit set by the royal ordinances.[77] With papal provisions still being withheld from him, it is difficult to see how such a condition could have been enforced, but it probably served to concentrate his attention on the one remaining obstacle to his advancement. At some time in the months following the case, he finally set out for Rome. Further royal letters from Henri IV to his ambassador and to Cardinal Joyeuse followed in early December.[78]

76 A.S.V., Misc. Armarium XLV, Epistolae ad Principes 2, fos. 231–2, 9 July. There is an unsigned and undated copy of a long report, presumably from the nuncio in France, on these problems in A.S.V., *fondo* Borghese III, 127e, fo. 25, and which may well have inspired the Pope's brief to Henri IV. B.N. MS. Fr. 18,002, fos. 191–2, Ambassador Halincourt to Villeroy, 27 June 1606, comments on this decision and its practical consequences.

77 Le Bret, *Decisions de plusieurs questions notables traitées en l'audience du parlement de Paris* (Paris 1630), pp. 569–73. Though Le Bret gives the date of the decree as 19 June 1606, efforts to find the original in the minutes and registers of the parlement have proved fruitless.

78 *Lettres missives de Henri IV*, 9 vols., ed. J. Berger de Xivrey and J. Guadet (Paris 1843–76), VII, pp. 53–5, letters of early Dec. 1606. Marvick, *Young Richelieu*, p. 246, n. 89, is mis-

But before they reached the curia, Richelieu himself had already shown he was his own best ambassador. Very quickly by Roman standards – and as if the curia was merely waiting to be persuaded – he received the long-awaited bulls of provision to Luçon on 18 December 1606, and according to his own later statement, was also remitted 18,000 *livres* from the cost of his provisions.[79] He was allowed to retain his two priories, but the most interesting clause in his provisions, which should be seen in the light of the secret papal brief of July 1606, was the one which specified that a hefty pension of 4,000 *livres* be set aside for his brother, Henri, on condition that there were 3,000 *livres* left over for the bishop.[80] The terms of many a *confidence* can scarcely have differed much from this, and the papacy's willingness to accept such an arrangement sheds its own retrospective light upon the Richelieu family's claim to 'possess' the see of Luçon. A week before his confirmation, Richelieu was granted a separate dispensation from being under the required canonical age of twenty-six years.[81] If the pope actually believed at this point that Richelieu was in his twenty-third rather than in his twenty-second year as was actually the case, this seems a flimsy basis for one of the most long-standing anecdotes about the young bishop's stay in Rome: his deception of the pope about his age, his subsequent confession of the truth once he had been consecrated, the ensuing papal pardon, and, lastly, the alleged papal reaction to the whole episode – 'this man will one day make a great politician, for he is already a great cheat (*furbo*)'.[82] Two popes had been aware for some time that Richelieu was a good deal younger than twenty-six and, in such circumstances, a mistake – however it came about – over a year was surely unimportant. It was only much later and in entirely different circumstances that it would be taken up and used against Richelieu.[83]

But if the exaggerations of the future Cardinal's detractors do not

taken in her attempt to re-date these letters to December 1603 – Halincourt only went to Rome in 1605, and the king's phrase 'J'ay naguères nommé' suggests a considerable lapse of time.

79 Avenel, *Lettres*, VII, p. 422.

80 Eubel, *Hierarchia Catholica*, IV, p. 225.

81 Martin Meurisse, *Histoire des Evêques de Metz* (Metz 1633), pp. 660–1.

82 Mathieu de Morgues, Tallemant des Reaux, Griffet and many others have repeated this anecdote. See the discussion by Avenel, 'La Jeunesse', pp. 169–70.

83 The first occasion was in Rome during the campaign to prevent Richelieu from securing the red hat in 1621. The charge then passed from Richelieu's opponents to the pamphleteers – some of whom, like Mathieu de Morgues, had been close friends of his for many years – who would later give it wider currency. See Antoine Degert, 'Le Chapeau de cardinal de Richelieu', *Revue Historique* 118 (1915), pp. 225–88. In his own apologia of 1618, and before the subject had been raised elsewhere, Richelieu wrote that the pope had confirmed him at the age of twenty-two: Avenel, *Lettres*, VII, p. 422.

merit credence, we can also discount the flattery of the eulogists
who depicted him as dazzling the pope with his learning, even to
the extent of being allowed to take part in the long-running debates
on divine grace – which would later achieve notoriety in the Jansen-
ist affair – then being conducted by the Roman congregation *De
Auxiliis*.[84] Much more trustworthy and revealing are the diplomatic
reports sent by the French ambassador in February 1607 to Henri IV
and his secretary of state for foreign affairs, Villeroy, which quite
unusually for his correspondence contain specific personal details.
After reporting that he had informed Paul V of the king's pleasure at
the 'graces' conceded to Richelieu, Ambassador Halincourt wrote to
Henri IV:

> The pope replied that he was pleased to have done so and that,
> having spoken to the bishop several times since then, he had rec-
> ognized in him a man so full of piety, learning and merit that he
> was happy to have granted them to such a worthy subject (. . .)
> and he wished that your Majesty would be moved to employ his
> services in his profession, for which the pope judges him to be
> perfectly capable. I believe, Sire, that it was my duty to report
> to you that which the good behaviour of the bishop deserves,
> as well as the good opinion the pope and his entire court have
> formed of him.[85]

To Villeroy, his father, the ambassador wrote: 'He is a young man
of much promise, of whom the pope spoke to me several times with
considerable respect and in excellent terms'.[86]

With all the weight of hindsight, there is every temptation to interpret the pope's suggestion of service to the king, even if couched
in conventional terms – 'en sa profession' – as an inspired prediction.
More prosaically, however, it is perhaps not extravagant to suggest
that at a time (early 1607) when French prelates like du Perron and
Joyeuse were busy mediating in Paul V's celebrated quarrel with
Venice, he was more than usually sensitive to the services a promising, intelligent young French bishop could render in both church
and state.[87] Indeed, it is quite likely that Richelieu confided his own
desires to serve the king to the pope during one of the conversations
alluded to by the ambassador.

Whatever confidences were exchanged between him and Paul V,

84 Avenel, 'La Jeunesse', p. 169, n. 2.
85 B.N. MS. Fr. 18,002, fo. 35, to Henri IV, 21 Feb. 1607.
86 *Ibid.*, fo. 54, 21 Feb.
87 See William J. Bouwsma, *Venice and the Defense of Republican Liberty* (Berkeley 1968), pp.
    412–15; David Wootton, *Paolo Sarpi. Between Renaissance and Enlightenment* (Cambridge
    1983), pp. 83–6.

there is no doubt that Richelieu confided a rather different, but no less interesting ambition, to the French ambassador, who passed it on to Villeroy, but not to Henri IV. According to Halincourt, Richelieu told him

> that previously he had aspired to the bishopric of Poitiers, and that the bishop had given him reason to hope he would negotiate with him. I believe Monsieur de Luçon, having spoken to me about it, may still be keen to do so. But as this is a position to which Monsieur de Sully aims to promote one of his people, I advised him not to embark on it without first knowing whether the said M. de Sully would agree. I assured him that you would willingly support him as much as you could, as I humbly beseech you to do.[88]

Richelieu would not have needed lessons in ecclesiastical geography or politics by this stage, and was aware that Poitiers was not only the largest of the three bishoprics in Poitou – both Luçon and Maillezais had been carved out of it in 1317 – but that it enjoyed a sort of un-official 'primacy' over the other two and, in general, much greater prestige in western France as a whole.[89] We shall probably never know what conversations he had had with the then bishop, Godefroy de St Belin, nor the latter's real attitude towards him; negotiations, most of them unsuccessful, for the exchange or resignation of ben-efices were commonplace and incessant in the French church. But this episode leaves no doubt that, from the very outset of his career, Richelieu saw Luçon not primarily as a treasured family heirloom, but as a possible stepping-stone to something better and more de-sirable in the French church. If Richelieu's ambition seems perfectly comprehensible, Sully's was perhaps less that of a royal minister than of a provincial governor anxious to keep his hands on the prin-cipal levers of power in Poitou. Disposing of the see of Poitiers may strike us as a curious ambition for a Huguenot noble, but the signifi-cant point must be that Sully had taken pains to make this known as far away as Rome. In the event, he got his way: only a few months after Richelieu's return to France, he secured the succession rights to Poitiers for a churchman in papal service whom Richelieu almost certainly came to know during his stay in Rome, Henri-Louis de Chasteignier de La Rocheposay, and who duly became bishop on St Belin's death in 1612.[90] It is not known whether Richelieu ever had

88   B.N. MS. Fr. 18,002, fo. 54v, letter of 21 Feb. 1607.
89   Fontenelle de Vaudoré, *Evêques de Luçon*, I, p. 326.
90   B.N., MS. Lat. 18384, pp. 195–6, 30 Sept 1607, *brevet* of coadjutorship for La Roche-posay, then usually referred to as M. d'Abain. See also Maximilien de Bèthune, duc de Sully, *Oeconomies Royales* [ed. Michaud and Poujoulat] (Paris 1837), II, p. 233. I owe this latter reference to the kindness of Bernard Barbiche.

the opportunity of discussing the question with Sully, whose action meant that the first potential avenue to further ecclesiastical advancement for Richelieu was effectively blocked. That, and perhaps later clashes of which nothing is known, may help to explain the enduring frostiness in relations between the two men.

From what we have seen of the ambassador's reports, we can take it for granted that Richelieu's stay in Rome was a pleasant one, not least because he had achieved his objectives so readily. The four or five months he spent there would certainly have given him abundant leisure to visit the city, and admire its churches and works of art. His excellent relations with the ambassador and the good impression he made on the pope's entourage, would have secured for him *entrées* to Rome's best residences, gardens and art-collections, and the opportunity to cultivate the taste for Italian art which he indulged so fully later when he could easily afford the very best Italy had to offer. His artistic interests may indeed have been already well-developed, for at least one source, admittedly from the eighteenth century but with good claims to veracity, asserts that while in Rome he attempted to have tint-drawings made, but that he was frustrated by the inadequate techniques used by the engravers he employed.[91]

Richelieu took his priestly orders in Rome, probably during Lent 1607, and was also consecrated bishop there on 17 April. Shortly afterwards, he took the road back to France. By 2 June, he was back in Fontainebleau to take the oath of fidelity to the king required of bishops, which in turn entitled him to take possession of the temporalities of Luçon. This latter was essentially a legal formality, and could be done by proxy.[92] The next step, obviously, was to translate himself to Luçon itself.

The cumulative effect on Richelieu of returning to academic studies – which, to judge purely by the exemptions he sought, he was anxious to complete as quickly as possible – of conflict with the Luçon chapter, and of securing papal approval as bishop, was a maturing one. Everything happened within a matter of a few years. Adult life and major responsibility came quickly, though not necessarily any earlier than they did for many of his contemporaries. The 'young Richelieu' of childhood and adolescence gave way to a holder of high church office, known and well thought of at court and in

---

91 A.N., O1 1907b, carton 20, fo. 37 (1751). 'Remarques sur l'impression des Estampes en Camaïu et les essais qui en ont été faits et par qui'. I am indebted to Mlle Lizzie Boubli of the Musée du Louvre for this reference, and for her comments upon it and other aspects of Richelieu's career as a patron of the arts.

92 A.N., P 5651 no. 2,555, *lettres de mainlevée*, recording *serment* of 2 June. The letters were registered at Luçon by Sébastien Bouthillier on 26 June. Avenel, 'La Jeunesse', p. 173, used an undated copy of this document, and could not determine when Richelieu took his oath.

Rome. But he had still to prove he was equal to the opportunities that such a social and political 'capital' could provide, and to emerge as an ecclesiastical and political figure in his own right. It is worth noting that the French ambassador in Rome always referred to him as 'the brother of Monsieur de Richelieu', and others did the same during these years. The astonishingly successful pattern of his later career obscures the difficulties facing him at the outset. Richelieu may have been a young bishop, but it is easily forgotten he was not an especially young minister.

Chapter 3
RICHELIEU AND LUÇON

'Richelieu a été un excellent évêque, et l'évêque a préparé le ministre.'[1]

IT may not be immediately obvious why a study of the rise of Richelieu should concern itself, except perhaps in passing, with his career
and activities as a bishop. Surely, it might be objected, they represent
a mere sideline, a distraction from the principal focus of his career –
his obsession with politics and power. But there are a number of
reasons why any view of his career which is too narrowly 'political'
in focus will miss a whole series of activities and attitudes which, if
not directly relevant to the politics of his day, formed the framework
in which his political role developed, and accounts for the manner in
which he himself was perceived by his contemporaries. It is, for
example, important to know how and to what extent he was regarded by contemporaries as a *dévot*. Any answer must lie, in part, in
the activities and associations he built up through his episcopal
career. In turn, these formed the accumulated capital of relations
which, as we shall see, he could – and regularly did – turn to his
advantage in the political sphere. In any event, the notion of a
discrete political 'sphere' is a fiction when one tries to apply it to
early seventeenth-century practice, even though Richelieu's own
political thought would later try to create one with its own rules and
its own ethical code. It is, by the same token, something of a fiction
to devote a chapter specifically to his career as a bishop, since much
of it regularly overlaps with his arrival on the political stage. Indeed,
in several respects, such as the Huguenot question, his role at the
1614 Estates General, and the development of his circle of friends and
clients, his religious and episcopal career runs in tandem with his
political apprenticeship. Nevertheless, it is essential to pursue the
quest for Richelieu the bishop and religious figure, not only for its
own sake, but also to prevent them from becoming neglected, as
they all too often are, in studies of his pre-ministerial career.

When Richelieu returned from Rome in the summer of 1607, he
was in no great hurry to depart from Paris, and to take up office in
Luçon. As we saw, he had yet to complete his studies at the uni-

---

1 Lacroix, *Richelieu à Luçon*, p. 319.

versity, and to be admitted to membership of the Sorbonne. In common with many of his episcopal colleagues, he had also been named an almoner in the king's chapel in 1606, but this appointment was an honorary one, carrying neither formal court duties nor a salary.[2] Nevertheless, the opportunities it offered to appear and perform at court were not to be missed, and Richelieu appears to have preached there at different times in 1607 and again in 1608.[3] But even for bishops who were anxious to take up residence in their dioceses, the business of formal leave-taking of the court (with its opportunities to offer service to important figures there and, perhaps, to secure promises of goodwill in return), of winding up their affairs in Paris, and of making arrangements for legal and administrative representation in the capital, could take months. Given the extent to which episcopal authority and policy depended upon royal support, such care was far from superfluous; the more active the bishop, the more he needed strong royal backing. For whatever reason, Richelieu, who was also ill at various times during 1608 with the migraine headaches that were to afflict him for the rest of his life, postponed his arrival at Luçon until over eighteen months after his return from Rome. For all his subsequent reputation as a man who confronted challenges head-on, this protracted delay suggests a certain hesitation and indecision on his part about directly confronting an arduous and potentially troublesome set of obligations.

In late 1608, Richelieu mustered the strength and courage to leave Paris for his diocese. At Fontenay-le-Comte, in the neighbouring diocese of Maillezais, he was met by a deputation from the Luçon cathedral chapter. They accompanied him on his entry to Luçon itself in late December, which was followed by his solemn induction and an episcopal address, almost certainly the first in living memory, inviting the people of his diocese, whether Catholic or Huguenot, to live in a mutual affection that would be advantageous to themselves and pleasing to the king.[4]

Richelieu was to be bishop of Luçon for a total of just over sixteen years. But after his early years there, his periods of residence became both more episodic and shorter, and had virtually ceased by the second half of 1616, with the exception of the brief period of enforced residence there between his removal from political office in May 1617 and his subsequent exile to Avignon in April 1618. He also set foot there again in 1619, but he never intended it to be more than

---

2 Louis Batiffol, *La Vie intime d'une reine de France au xviie siècle* (Paris 1931), II, p. 49, n. 1.
3 See Marvick, *Louis XIII: The Making of a King*, p. 117; Avenel, *Lettres*, VII, p. 317, Richelieu to du Perron, March 1608, announcing that he could not preach on Easter Sunday 1608.
4 Avenel, *Lettres*, I, pp. 13–15, for the three addresses.

a fleeting visit;[5] in the following year, he sought to have his diocese turned over more officially, but not irreversibly, to his vicar general, Jacques de Flavigny, with the rank of suffragan bishop.[6] But even between 1609 and 1616, he was often absent from Luçon. Within less than eighteen months of his arrival there, he was back in Paris for a sojourn in the capital, and soon announced that he intended doing so annually from then on.[7] He was, so far as we can judge, as good as his word. But even when he was not in Paris, he was not necessarily in Luçon either. He was a willing and regular guest of the bishop of Poitiers, and his favourite residence from about 1611 onwards appears to have been his own priories of Les Roches and especially Coussay, not far from Poitiers, and even closer to the Richelieu family lands. He was ill for much of 1611, and spent the time at Coussay. If his correspondence may serve as a rough guide, it appears that those who wrote to him expected to find him as readily at Coussay as at Luçon. In 1612, his friend the bishop of Orléans finally traced him to Poitiers, having been uncertain of his whereabouts during the previous three months.[8] The most obvious consequence of this pattern of movement was an irregular physical involvement in the affairs of his diocese, though this should not be interpreted as negligence or indifference on his part. His early correspondence with his closest officials shows that he remained a vigilant administrator, and that they were not at liberty to make decisions independently of him. However, few traces of that correspondence survive from after 1615, and there is virtually none at all from the years leading to his final resignation as bishop in May 1623. When his clergy took the decision, potentially with significant political repercussions, to promulgate the decrees of the Council of Trent in Luçon in 1622, it was apparently without his foreknowledge or participation – though he wrote to congratulate them on their initiative.[9] In the case of his seminary, as we shall see, his absence led his chapter and benefice-holders to ignore his directives altogether.[10] The conclusion which emerges from this is obvious -- the larger part of his efforts to recover control of his diocese, to reform its clergy, and to respond to the challenge of Protestantism, were packed into a relatively brief period of intense activity at the beginning of his episcopate.

Of course, Richelieu himself supplied a celebrated reason for his reluctance to reside in Luçon, one that is all the more credible for

5   Ibid., I, p. 625, letter to Sully (late Sept. 1619).
6   B.N. MS. Clairambault 377, fo. 131, undated petition, but filed with 1620 documents.
7   Avenel, Lettres, I, p. 55, letter to Madame de Bourges, 10 June 1610.
8   A.A.E. Mems et docs, France 768, fo. 232, Laubespine to Richelieu, 28 Oct. 1612.
9   Avenel, Lettres, I, p. 751, letter to Luçon Chapter.
10 Lacroix, Richelieu à Luçon, pp. 99–100.

having been made privately – that is, the awful condition of the diocese, and specifically the lack of a proper residence with the minimum standards of comfort and furnishing that a Parisian like him took for granted.[11] For one whose health had already begun to show signs of fragility, the marshlands of lower Poitou represented a serious hazard, and may have been instrumental in bringing about his long illness in 1611. His disgust at the primitive conditions there was genuine, though whether he reflected at all on their causes – Richelieu family neglect as much as Huguenot depredations – must remain a mystery.

At any rate, the mundane problems that arose out of this state of affairs were to obsess him for several years; they form the central thread of his remarkable correspondence with Madame de Bourges. That correspondence, of which only Richelieu's letters have survived, is of an entirely different character to the strained, formal and often excessively deferential letters he found himself writing to public figures, whether of church or of state, during these years. Even though his letters to her were mainly concerned with minor domestic matters – bed-linen, vestments or tableware – they reveal much about his character and ambitions, and also contain elements of humour and self-mockery which historians familiar with his later *gravitas* would find surprising. For example, we can feel his exultant satisfaction at finding for his *maître d'hôtel* a genuine *gentilhomme* who had once served the duc de Montpensier himself (no small satisfaction for a Richelieu!) and who always knew how to receive visitors properly; also his eager anticipation of what a decent set of silver plate would do for his 'noblesse' when inviting guests to his table. But the often playful language in which such sentiments are expressed cannot quite hide the resentment the writer feels, as when, for example, he complains about rented lodgings in Paris and the prohibitive cost of having a *pied à terre* of his own there. When he writes that he is led to believe that people regard him as a 'grand monsieur en ce pays', we can sense his own evident scepticism of such reports, and surmise that his 'noblesse' was not at all as evident around Luçon as he would have liked it to be. Richelieu craved to 'sustain his rank' (*soutenir son rang*), to uphold his family name, and to display his lineage and power to full advantage. This wish to become an *évêque-gentilhomme* was not merely a matter of snobbery, Parisian or otherwise: it also appeared wholly necessary if he was to govern with any degree of success a diocese in which both the Catholic and Huguenot nobility were unruly, and not especially deferential towards their bishop.

11 Avenel, *Lettres*, I, pp. 23–4, letter to Madame de Bourges, April 1610.

In 1609–10, he was particularly anxious to establish a respectable household in order to make his mark as bishop. But it is not clear, for example, that he ever succeeded in finding a proper episcopal residence in Luçon itself. Initially, he preferred rented accommodation to the deserted and devastated bishop's palace, and matters do not appear to have improved much thereafter. When he was obliged by Louis XIII to return to Luçon in late 1617, the cathedral chapter lent him a canon's house and garden adjoining the chapter's own bakery and oven – hardly a distinguished location for a bishop's residence. Confirmation of this unchanged state of affairs came in February 1619, when he made a bequest to the cathedral at Luçon of his altar service and other valuables, all of which were to be found in his episcopal residence, 'qui est sa maison de Coussay'.[12] Evidently, the only solution he found to the problem was to withdraw his residence altogether to the neighbouring diocese of Poitiers.

In this context, one of the strongest complaints Richelieu voiced in his letters to Mme de Bourges, was that he was poverty-stricken (*gueux*).[13] It would be hard to deny that a lack of means curtailed his efforts as a bishop as much as it did those of numerous other contemporaries of his among the episcopate. But here, too, the picture is much less simple than might be concluded from standard descriptions by his biographers and by historians of Luçon, who usually refer to it as being 'among the smallest and poorest dioceses of France'. For one thing, there was no real correlation in the French church between the size of a diocese and the revenues of its bishop. As we saw earlier, the leases of the revenues of Luçon made by Richelieu's father in 1585 amounted to 10,000 *livres*, and in 1587 to 8,200 *livres*. They may have fallen further during the latter phases of the wars, rising again with the return of peace. By 1610, Richelieu himself was in a position to sign a new lease at a significantly higher figure of 13,000 *livres*, one that ran its full nine-year course without any difficulty. Such stability was often elusive, but extremely attractive in the years after the civil wars.[14] Richelieu's see may have lacked many of the minimum requirements of civility, but extreme poverty, it may be suggested, was not one of them. Over thirty years later, in 1641, the general assembly of the clergy recorded over forty bishops as *still* enjoying incomes smaller than was Richelieu's from Luçon in 1610.[15]

If Richelieu's complaint about being poverty-stricken has any genuine foundation, it should be taken as referring to the bishop of

12   B.N., MS. Lat. 18389, fo. 294, donation of 12 Feb. 1619 at Avignon.
13   Avenel, *Lettres*, I, pp. 27, 28.
14   See Bergin, *Richelieu*, p. 231.
15   A.A.E., Mems et Docs, France 841, fos. 1–117.

Luçon, rather than to the see itself. For one thing, he owed his brother, Henri, a pension of 4,000 *livres*, which he seems to have paid until the latter's death in 1619, and this obviously represented a considerable drain on his income. More significantly, few *ancien-régime* bishops depended exclusively – or, in some cases, principally – on the revenues of their bishoprics; they frequently measured success by their ability to attract further royal gifts of abbeys and priories to be held *in commendam*. In this respect, the young bishop of Luçon fared rather badly. Apart from Luçon, the small priories of Pommiers-Aigres and Les Roches were all that remained in family hands after the deaths of his father and great-uncles. Neither priory was especially noteworthy, and together they probably produced little more than 2,000 to 3,000 *livres* in income at most. Given the tendency of generations of biographers to stress the benevolence of Henri IV towards Richelieu, whom he is supposed to have called 'mon évesque', it is his *failure* to reward him with more than the see of Luçon – which was, after all, more of a grant to the Cardinal's family than to Richelieu himself – which is worthy of note, the grant of further benefices being the normal method of showing favour to churchmen and, for a king like Henri IV, a far more neutral method than having to satisfy their eventual political ambitions. Richelieu acquired only one other benefice during Henri's reign, the abbey of Ile Chauvet in the diocese of Luçon, but the king had virtually nothing to do with this, the abbey having been held *en confidence* for several years by Henri de Richelieu, the real architect of the abbey's change of status.[16]

The king's patronage of Richelieu, even in the ecclesiastical sphere, should thus be viewed far more sceptically than has generally been the case. Indeed, we have already seen an example of its limits in Richelieu's inability to secure the coadjutorship of Poitiers in 1607, a failure which did nothing to reconcile him to his fate at Luçon, as he remained on the look-out in subsequent years for something better. A revealing letter, written to him probably between 1609 and 1611 by one of his Parisian agents, Jacques de Bourges, shows that he may even have made overtures to the ageing bishop of Châlons-sur-Marne, Cosme Clausse, whose bishopric was rendered attractive by having a peerage and the right to sit in the *parlement* of Paris attached to it. The same letter also seemed to hint at the possibility of Rich-

16 B.N., MS. Fr. 4328, fo. 64v. The accuracy of this document seems indisputable, as it was a register belonging to a M. Pourcelet, a French 'expeditionary banker' for the Roman curia, and thus involved in the securing and payment of papal provisions for benefices. Pourcelet also notes that Henri de Richelieu used his brother-in-law, du Pont de Courlay, as his *prête-nom* for Ile Chauvet. Although Pourcelet does not mention this, Richelieu probably obtained it around 1608-9.

elieu's negotiating to take the place of the bishop of Béziers as grand almoner to Marie de' Medici, and went on to inform him that the bishop of Carcassonne was resigning as master of the king's chapel.[17] Richelieu's evident inability to follow up any of these possibilities would seem to confirm his relative lack of influence in high places under Henri IV, but it is no less interesting to record that he sought to be kept informed of openings that might suit him. No doubt his own personal history, if not necessarily that of France, would have run along very different lines had he become grand almoner to Marie de' Medici around 1610, nearly a decade before he finally entered her service. It would, among other things, almost certainly have curtailed his activities at Luçon even further. In the event, he found himself wedded to the only bishopric that he would ever hold.

II

There are few signs that, at least in the early years of his episcopate, these difficulties and ambitions blunted Richelieu's determination to become master of his long-abandoned diocese. For all his lamentations about the place, Luçon provided him with the scope for action that suited his temperament so well. As he made perfectly clear to Madame de Bourges in April 1609: 'Je ne manqueray pas d'occupation, je vous asseure, car tout y est tellement ruiné qu'il faut de l'exercice pour le remettre.'[18] The scale of the task is not easy to express, especially when historians disagree even as to the precise size of his diocese, with estimates of the number of parishes varying between 250 and 428. Even if we accept the lower figure, a diocese of that size would still have provided a bishop with a great deal of work and responsibility, and we can safely ignore the oft-repeated description of Luçon as one of the smallest, and by implication most insignificant, of French dioceses. Perhaps more important is the question of how far effective episcopal authority, and therefore the real sphere of a bishop's action, extended. Undoubtedly, generations of episcopal absence and neglect had reduced it considerably, leaving the secular, the collegiate, and the regular clergy with a greatly enhanced sense of autonomy. More specifically, Luçon was a diocese in which a small number of major abbeys wielded considerable authority and power, especially through their rights of patronage to parishes. Some of these abbeys were situated within the diocese, while others were outsiders. Richelieu's early letters show him learning the art of how

17   B.L., Additional MS. 22052, fo. 2. The letter is dated only 'De Paris ceste vigille des roys' (i.e. 5 Jan.).
18   Avenel, *Lettres*, I, p. 23.

to deal with such individuals as the abbots of St Michel en l'Herm, Talmond, Orbestiers and Lieu-Dieu, as well as the abbess of Ste Croix of Poitiers.[19] He found himself dealing with great nobles, as the abbeys in question were in the hands of the comte de Soissons (a prince of the blood), the duc de La Trémouïlle, the duc de Rohan and the ubiquitous Sully, each of whom controlled their abbeys through *prête-noms*. Mme de Ste Croix herself, as a member of the Nassau family, was of comparable social distinction. There was no substitute for prudence and deference in a bishop's dealings with them – St Michel en l'Herm is thought to have controlled up to a hundred benefices in Luçon diocese alone – and this probably constituted Richelieu's first extensive schooling in the arts of diplomacy. Failure to treat such dignitaries correctly could create powerful enemies, while success (always limited) in securing their co-operation depended on a capacity to combine this firmness with tact. If Richelieu's early letters exhibit just these qualities, they also show that deference came more easily to him early in his career than it would subsequently.

Good relations with the clergy of his cathedral chapter were essential to any active reforming bishop. But Counter-Reformation bishops and their chapters were frequently at loggerheads, as the formers' attempts to restore what they considered to be their rightful authority were often strongly resisted. Richelieu had few illusions about the Luçon chapter's attitude to him, as is clear from his very first address to them, in which he alluded to opposition which had emerged even since his appointment, but in which he also promised he would do everything to win their confidence. This was probably a discreet reference to their decision to resume litigation in 1607 because of the Richelieu family's failure to implement their part of the bargain worked out in 1604. It is unlikely that the canons were unduly impressed by Richelieu's rhetoric on this occasion, but he himself had the sense to realize that only a compromise could settle outstanding differences and that it was best to negotiate without further delay. The outcome was the contract signed in early June 1609, in which he agreed to provide one-third of the sums still needed to pay for the restoration of the cathedral buildings, but rejected all further responsibility for their repair and upkeep.[20] Even so, there is good reason to suppose that this effectively removed a long-standing bone of contention, and that the gesture brought

19 *Ibid.*, 1, pp. 29–31, for some examples.
20 B.N., MS. Lat. 18389, fos. 72–5, transaction of 4 June 1609. The Chapter had asked for much more, namely one-third of the bishop's revenue. On the other hand, Richelieu compromised on some other disputes over the Luçon canal and the Chapter's claims to jurisdiction in Luçon and Triaize.

bishop and chapter closer together. Although evidence is very thin,
it appears that Richelieu was able thereafter to draw upon the active
co-operation of some at least of Luçon's canons, and that his appointment of men associated with him to capitular offices reinforced ties
between the parties over the years. Healing the rift with the cathedral
chapter was clearly an important step, but it requires a considerable
ignorance of seventeenth-century realities to believe that in one
stroke of genius he established himself as absolute master of his
chapter, any more than he would later of France. The Luçon
chapter's ability to go its own way outlived his episcopate.

Beyond the great abbeys and the cathedral chapter lay the other
religious orders and the mass of the ordinary clergy. Episcopal
authority was extremely limited in respect of the orders, monastic
and mendicant alike, and the efforts of French bishops to regulate
their preaching and pastoral activities produced celebrated clashes in
Richelieu's own lifetime. It is curious that no specific mention is
made of the orders in his synodal statutes of 1613, and it may be that
he felt he could achieve little that was positive by legislation. On one
point, however, he was wholly typical of his time – in his search for
new religious orders which could assist him to achieve his own
pastoral ambitions and which, because brought in on his personal
invitation, would be more responsive to episcopal wishes than were
older, established orders.

Richelieu's choice of new orders was in every way significant, not
merely for his diocese, but for his own subsequent career. Characteristically, he had scarcely anything to do with those contemplative
orders, especially female, which were at the heart of the intensely
mystical spirituality of French Catholicism in the decades following
the end of the religious wars. His interests at Luçon were more
practical. Within months of the foundation of the French Oratory in
November 1611, Richelieu, apparently the first bishop to do so, had
approached its superior, Pierre de Bérulle, with a view to its establishing some kind of presence at Luçon. Nothing is known about
these initial contacts, but Richelieu's presence in Paris in late 1611
(which would explain the silence of the sources) probably enabled
him to be both quickly and accurately informed about the Oratory's
objectives of reforming and educating the secular clergy. Action
quickly followed, and Richelieu himself, in a letter which has been
assigned to June 1612, revealed that Oratorians, 'qui se doivent
employer en l'instruction des curés', had already been in Luçon for
five or six months.[21] Initially, the Oratory's presence at Luçon was

---

21 Avenel, *Lettres*, I, p. 84, letter to M. de Béthune. This is confirmed by a letter from
    Bérulle to his agent in Rome, Nicolas de Soulfour, 10 Feb. 1613: *Correspondance de
    Bérulle*, I, p. 166.

limited to a few preachers and missionaries, virtual guests of the bishop, and though he had wider plans for them, it would not be until 1616 that they began to take shape.

No less significant was Richelieu's early appreciation of the Capuchins and their activities. They had already embarked on missions in Poitou before he himself arrived in Luçon, and had members resident at both Poitiers and Fontenay-le-Comte; in 1610 a separate 'province' of Touraine was carved out of that of Paris, with no less a personage than Père Joseph (François Le Clerc du Tremblay) becoming its head in 1613. Richelieu lost no time in seeking out the Capuchins to help within his own diocese, inviting them to preach at Luçon itself after Easter 1609.[22] His first contacts with Père Joseph may not have occurred until 1610 or 1611, when both were drawn into the question of the reform of the great Benedictine abbey of Fontevraud near Saumur. However, it took considerably longer to realize his plans for Capuchin establishments within his diocese, as several obstacles had to be negotiated and permissions obtained. Although the first house was only founded in 1616, in the town of Sables d'Olonne, Richelieu was already in correspondence about it three years earlier with Méric de Vic, a councillor of state, who was acting as intermediary between the bishop and the king's council. Not only was Richelieu seeking royal approval for the foundation, but he was evidently hoping for some kind of financial assistance from a hesitant Marie de' Medici. Such high-level contacts might not be part of normal life in a see like Luçon, but when they occur, they convey a direct sense of how extensive a bishop's relations in high places could become. By contrast, much less is known about the Capuchin house founded in the town of Luçon itself in 1619. It was during his enforced residence there in late 1617 that, having already sounded out Père Joseph and Honoré de Champigny, he formally petitioned the Capuchins to found a hospice in the town, on the grounds that such a foundation was subject to much less delay than a full 'convent'.[23] If the house founded in 1619 was in fact a hospice, it would have been a fairly modest affair.

During his years of active residence, Richelieu probably had to be content with a handful of Oratorians and Capuchins who were temporarily assigned to his diocese and who, however highly he might value their skill and devotion, were in no position to achieve miracles among the ordinary clergy or people of Luçon.

There can be no doubt, as his esteem for both the Oratory and the

---

22 Avenel, *Lettres*, I, p. 22, letter to the 'père commissaire des capucins de Fontenay'. Avenel proposed Feb. 1609 as the date of this letter.
23 B.N., MS. Lat. 18389, fo. 293v, letter to Provincial of Touraine, 23 Dec. 1617.

Capuchins shows, that Richelieu's main concern was to improve the
quality of the ordinary, especially the parish clergy; like contemporary Catholic reformers everywhere, he assumed that the religion
of the people as a whole would improve along with the quality of the
clergy. But in the Counter-Reformation church such an improve-
ment usually required greater episcopal control over the clergy,
something which was rarely welcomed with open arms. There were
numerous possible avenues Richelieu could try and he was remarkably quick to attempt most of them. If his effective episcopal action
was too short to judge how successful he was, the record of his
intentions testifies to how closely attuned he was to what active
reformers of the time, both inside and outside France, were
attempting to do.

Shortly after his arrival at Luçon, probably in April 1609, Richelieu held his first diocesan synod. All we know about it is that,
perhaps not surprisingly, it was not fully attended, and that he
imposed fines on some of those absent without good cause.[24] In
keeping with the recommendations of the Council of Trent, he
obviously intended his synods to be regular, probably annual affairs,
though we have no indication as to the specific purposes he expected
them to fulfil beyond assembling the clergy to deliberate on the
affairs of the diocese and their own obligations. One obvious objective was that of producing a new body of diocesan legislation to
reflect contemporary needs and deal with recent problems, especially
among the clergy. What is not clear is how far his synods between
1609 and 1613 were devoted to this legislative task. In any event, it is
indicative of his approach to managing his diocese that he postponed
the synod of 1610 until he could complete the visitation of Luçon's
parishes, after which he would be in a better position to judge what
action really needed to be taken. If he came to Luçon with clear ideas,
even a blueprint perhaps, for its reform, it was evidently one that he
was willing to modify in the light of local conditions.

How many synods met after that of 1610 is not known, but it was
probably out of the accumulated work of successive synods that his
synodal statutes, published in 1613, finally emerged. The overall
object of these statutes was, in Richelieu's own words, to 'regler et
policer nostre dit diocese au mieux que faire se peut'. Despite their
necessarily general tone, they do provide insights into their author's
objectives and preoccupations as a bishop. The *bonne police* he aimed
at naturally began with the clergy, a much wider and more varied
collection of men than is generally imagined. Richelieu's statutes are
thus addressed not merely to parish priests and their curates, but also

24   Lacroix, *Richelieu à Luçon*, p. 86.

to clergy living corporately in chapters, to holders of chaplaincies and other benefices without cure of souls, and even to those who were merely deacons or subdeacons, and who commonly resided for many years in their home parishes and were regarded as part of the 'clergy' in the widest sense. The problems of an early seventeenth-century bishop in disciplining such divergent groups were considerable and could not be solved overnight. Richelieu shared fully the Counter-Reformation emphasis on the dignity of the priestly calling, and insisted that clergy be immediately recognizable, by their dress and deportment. They were not to engage in commercial activities, to frequent taverns, to play cards, or to maintain in their houses any woman 'suspecte pour son âge ou pour sa qualité'; for the same reason, clergy residing in the houses of *gentilshommes* were specifically debarred from acting as receivers, estate agents or solicitors for such families.[25] If some of these strictures suggest information gathered during his visitations, there is even more direct evidence of such influence elsewhere in his ordinances: 'And because, to our great regret, we have seen that several clergy gather together in bands during the fairs and markets in the bigger *bourgs* near their places of residence, such as Marueil, St Hermine, Puybeliard, Châteaunay, Les Esgards, les Herbiers, Thalmond, Montaigu and others, we enjoin the parish priests of these places to be on the look-out and report them to our *official*.'[26] A similar influence of local circumstances can be detected in another decree that within two years of the publication of the ordinances all those who had held benefices for more than three years, or who were subdeacons or deacons, should prepare themselves to receive the appropriate orders.[27]

These statutes also contain directives which would later drive their author to compose his most important pastoral work, the *Instruction du Chrétien*. These required the clergy to perform the *prosne* on Sundays and feast-days, based on the catechism which he had published for that purpose, and to recite the *oraison dominicale*, consisting of the Our Father, the Hail Mary and the Apostles Creed, as well as the Ten Commandments – and in French, so that their parishioners could remember and understand them.[28] To cater effectively for people in larger parishes, he insisted that parish priests must employ and support a curate. But there could be no question of trusting all the clergy indiscriminately: parish priests were to insist that all itinerant preachers present letters of approval from the bishop or his

25 *Ordonnances synodales (1613)*, fos. 80–1, 84v.
26 *Ibid.*, fos. 80v–81r.
27 *Ibid.*, fo. 83.
28 *Ibid.*, fo. 88r. The *prosne* was not quite a sermon, but the reading aloud of a written, devotional text, with perhaps a commentary on it.

grand vicar, while only clergy with explicit approval should be allowed to hear confessions or conduct marriages.[29] Rules were also included for the administration of the sacraments, the care of the sick, and the avoidance of superstitions or magical practices.

Other more episcopal or clerical concerns were present, too, in these statutes. Richelieu ordered his clergy to remind their congregations on successive Sundays that jurisdiction over the affairs of the churchwardens had been reserved to the bishop by a recent royal ordinance. He also encouraged benefice-holders to do all in their power to recover church property lost or alienated during the wars of religion, as another recent royal ordinance allowed them to do on advantageous terms.[30]

Thus, Richelieu's statutes provide at least an indirect commentary on the conditions he encountered in the diocese of Luçon. In general, however, they strongly resemble what other incoming bishops of his generation were trying to do. They were a list of prescriptions, not a record of achievements, and it is no longer possible to accept the dramatic and unqualified comment of an earlier student of his statutes: 'once Richelieu had identified the depth of the evil he faced, he boldly applied the iron that would heal it'.[31] On the contrary, all the evidence suggests that Richelieu himself took a more cautious, realistic view of the task facing him at Luçon.

Richelieu's concern for the pastoral effectiveness of the clergy, and not just their outward appearance and behaviour, is also apparent from the fact that his synodal ordinances appeared alongside a *Briefve et facile instruction pour les confesseurs* published on his orders by Jacques de Flavigny, his grand vicar. It was an instruction, as Flavigny declared to the clergy, that Richelieu judged to be 'necessaire sur tout autre' – proof enough that he had guided Flavigny's pen when composing it. The 1613 ordinances themselves demanded that confessors acquire a copy of this *Instruction* within two months and study it carefully.[32] Here, too, Richelieu was consistent in banning unapproved clergy from hearing confessions. The sacrament was both too serious and too delicate to be administered by any but those with the requisite qualifications. Nor was it a question of mere knowledge, but of psychology and good sense: confessors would have to handle the consciences of inveterate sinners, the timid, the socially diverse, and so on, and positive results demanded an ability to discriminate between cases, to unlock hidden sins, to reassure the

29 *Ibid.*, fos. 91, 86v.
30 *Ibid.*, fos. 91r–v, 94r.
31 Lacroix, *Richelieu à Luçon*, p. 85: 'lorsque Richelieu eut sondé la profondeur du mal, il y porta hardiment le fer qui devait le guérir'.
32 *Ordonnances synodales*, fo. 95v.

faltering, and to judge people's true intentions. He based the entire *Instruction* upon the Ten Commandments and the commandments of the church, which received chapter-by-chapter exposition. In view of the controversies in which Richelieu later became involved, especially over the sacraments and in particular that of penance, with St Cyran and the rigourists, his attitude at the outset of his career should be noted. He regarded true sorrow for sin, called contrition (because based on sorrow for having offended a just and loving God), as superior to attrition (sorrow based on fear of retribution and especially of hell), but he was prepared to accept the latter as sufficient. No doubt, a certain realism, based on his personal experience as a bishop, told him that perfect contrition was beyond all but a tiny few; but he did recommend that the literate classes possess guides to confession and books of devotion to help prepare them to confess properly.[33] As a bishop, however, his primary concern was the mass of the laity, 'les âmes moins sensibles'. In any event, what is perfectly clear from both Flavigny's *Instruction* as well from Richelieu's own *Instruction du Chrétien* is his overriding concern to make sure that those confessing their sins were firmly resolved to mend their ways, and to avoid the circumstances and habits which made them sin. That doubtless seemed a better yardstick for the sacrament's effectiveness than the more elusive notions of contrition or attrition. Neither in 1613 nor in 1618 was Richelieu concerned with disputes which had yet to surface, and which left such a mark on his posthumous *Traité de la perfection du Chrétien*; nor should these later disputes obscure the character of the demands he was making of his own clergy – and laity – in the 1610s.

As observed earlier, Richelieu did not legislate for his diocese in a vacuum or from wholly preconceived ideas. Shortly after his arrival in Luçon, probably after Easter 1609, he also began a personal visitation of his diocese. But for some reason, he failed to complete it that year – a visitation of several hundred parishes, especially if thoroughly conducted, could take a long time. As we saw, it was this visitation that he wished to conclude before holding his 1610 synod.[34] This is the last time that such an activity is mentioned in his papers, though we should not rule out subsequent, perhaps partial visitations which might have become more routine over the years – or been entrusted to his vicars-general. It is particularly regrettable that the records of his visitations have not survived, as they would have provided a practical means of interpreting his early ordinances and synodal decrees, many of which were probably based upon

33 *Ibid.*, fo. 96.
34 Lacroix, *Richelieu à Luçon*, pp. 107–9.

them. In addition, their disappearance deprives the historian of what would have been a fascinating window on to Richelieu's first experience of the exercise of authority.[35]

Richelieu was also at one with contemporary reformers in his desire to go beyond mere synods and visitations, both of which, however much they might be geared towards new, reforming ends, were traditional activities and as such severely limited in their effectiveness. The products of authority, they needed to be supplemented by pastoral and educational initiatives of a newer kind if they were not to remain a dead letter. Richelieu's earliest biographers assert that he preached regularly at Luçon, and there is every reason to believe that he did not limit his oratorical talents to his appearances at court. However, only one sermon by him seems to have survived, that delivered at Luçon on Christmas Day 1608, just after his arrival there. The sermon was based on the biblical text 'the word is made flesh', but the printed version of it is for the most part stilted and obscure, and it only comes to life when its author tries to commend to his audience the virtues of peace – political, domestic, and personal.[36] Richelieu would also, for example, have had ample scope to preach during his visitations, when perhaps his language and message were more attuned to humbler audiences. As his cultivation of the Oratorians and the Capuchins shows, he was a firm believer in the value of preaching. The normal preaching cycles of Advent and Lent appeared to him especially suited 'to rekindling the piety and devotion of souls who had become cold', as he put it on one occasion.[37] Contemporary verdicts on Richelieu's preaching skills varied;[38] but it is more important to note that, in an age when the sight of a bishop in the pulpit was far from common, he was clearly one of a younger generation of French bishops who regarded preaching as a normal part of their duties.

Richelieu could only occasionally hope to reach the mass of his flock through preaching, and if only for that reason, he had to concentrate his efforts and resources upon the clergy of Luçon. The first response, and the one most available to any bishop, to the problem of having an adequate clergy was administrative – to refuse

---

35 See the extensive evidence of visitations which left no written record in the *Répertoire des visites pastorales de la France. Anciens diocèses jusqu'en 1790*, 4 vols. (Paris 1977–86). Among the best of the numerous studies based on such sources are: Louis Pérouas, *Le Diocèse de La Rochelle. Sociologie et pastorale 1648–1724* (Paris 1964); Robert Sauzet, *Les Visites pastorales dans le diocèse de Chartres pendant la première moitié du xviiè siècle* (Rome 1975).

36 A.M.P. Ingold, *Un Sermon inédit de Richelieu (Noël 1608)* (Luçon 1889), pp. 5–16.

37 Avenel, *Lettres*, I, p. 22, letter to Capuchins of Fontenay, 1609. In the preface to the *Briefve et facile instruction*, clergy with difficulties involving confession are recommended to consult the Lent and Advent preachers.

38 Lacroix, *Richelieu à Luçon*, pp. 289ff.

to appoint clergy, especially parish priests, whom he judged incapable of adequately exercising the cure of souls. But in a diocese where he probably held direct rights of appointment to only a minority of livings, this was difficult. Such limited evidence as there is, however, shows that he was determined to remind patrons both of their responsibilities and of his role as bishop. In one instance, he asserted that for those parishes in his personal gift he had instituted the competitive examination, the *concours*, recommended by the Council of Trent.[39] This must rank among the earliest examples of this practice in the French church; and though we have no way of assessing how effective he was in applying it, it should be remembered that when it was subsequently tried by other French bishops, some found it unworkable. As for clergy presented to him by patrons, or those holding claims on parishes by virtue of acts of resignation, his letters suffice to show that he took a direct interest in examining their worthiness. One of his officials referred in a letter to a candidate's having been 'seen and questioned' by Richelieu, and who on formal examination was found to be 'lacking in knowledge'; as a result, the retiring parish priest offered to withdraw the resignation he had made in favour of the candidate, and to leave the choice of a successor to Richelieu himself.[40] Having turned down as incompetent a priest presented to a parish by the abbess of Ste Croix, Richelieu wrote to her suggesting that she allow the living to be filled by *concours*, and that if she were to do so, other patrons would follow her good example.[41] The idea was a clever one, but does not appear to have worked, for around the same time, in what seems like a deliberate exercise in diplomacy, Richelieu declared himself perfectly willing to accept her judgement that one of her chaplains was fit to take up a parish.[42] He also appears to have won some concessions from the comte de Soissons in respect of benefices in his presentation as abbot of St Michel en l'Herm, but it is unclear whether this involved instituting the *concours* for them, too.[43]

Such a policy was obviously designed to warn clerics in search of parishes that they would need to meet certain standards before obtaining episcopal approval. As such, it was an incentive to them to acquire an adequate education before taking orders and, in the longer term, it may well have helped to achieve results. But on its own, it merely passed on responsibility for producing an educated, competent clergy to the clergy themselves – a less than satisfactory

39 Avenel, *Lettres*, I, p. 29.
40 B.L., Additional MS. 22052, fo. 3, J. Chauffour to Richelieu, 10 Dec. 1610.
41 Avenel, *Lettres*, I, pp. 29–30.
42 *Ibid.*, p. 30.
43 *Ibid.*, p. 31.

solution, particularly in the early seventeenth century. Once again, Richelieu proved to be in the vanguard of French efforts to deal with these problems, though, here too, it is difficult to judge the success of his efforts.

Attached to Richelieu's synodal statutes was a little-noticed recommendation, namely that the clergy of several parishes meet weekly in specified towns of the diocese for mutual instruction on the moral and pastoral problems arising out of their ministry.[44] The idea, which may not of itself sound novel or far-reaching, was first tried on a large scale a generation earlier by Borromeo in Milan, in an attempt to raise the standards of the existing clergy. Quite how far Richelieu's recommendation was implemented remains unknown. But it came remarkably early in the reform of the French church, long before the 'ecclesiastical conferences', as these gatherings were called, are thought to have taken root there.[45] Richelieu's objective of weekly meetings was optimistic, perhaps excessively so, as most of the later bishops who valued their educational potential, regarded themselves as fortunate enough if they met once a month for two-thirds of the year.

Much better known as a method of improving the quality of clergy were the seminaries recommended by the Council of Trent. All the evidence is that within a short while of arriving at Luçon, Richelieu had begun to think about founding one in his diocese. The seminary which he founded at Luçon is often credited with being the first of the second-generation of Tridentine seminaries to emerge in France. Here, too, his intentions show how up-to-date he was, but equally it is a subject on which hasty, exaggerated conclusions are best avoided. Richelieu himself was perfectly aware of how risky and complicated such a step could be, and that it was likely to be resisted or ignored by existing clergy and institutions. Writing to him in late 1610, one of his canons who was working on the project with him said that, even if they did not have a 'seminaire de grand appareil' from the outset, they would at least have some sort of college, complete with boarders.[46] Richelieu only made his initial move after extensive consultations. His caution is fully evident from his decision to seek royal letters-patent (which were not legally required) and which were issued in August 1611; they authorized him to found a seminary and – this was the crucial point – to levy a

---

44 *Ordonnances synodales*, fo. 95.
45 See Marc Venard, 'The Influence of Carlo Borromeo on the French Church', in John M. Headley and John B. Tomaro, eds., *San Carlo Borromeo. Catholic Reform and Ecclesiastical Politics in the Second Half of the Sixteenth Century* (Washington 1988), p. 218. Venard asserts that 'without doubt' the conferences were introduced to France by Alain de Solminihac, who was bishop of Cahors from 1636 to 1659.
46 A.D. Lublinskaya, *La France au temps de Richelieu. L'Absolutisme français* (Moscow 1982), doc. no. 20, p. 260, J. Chauffour to Richelieu, 5 Nov. 1610.

tax of 3,000 *livres* for its upkeep on those Luçon benefices worth more than 800 *livres* a year. In Luçon itself, he had to negotiate with his clergy, represented by their syndics, who formally granted him their licence to found a seminary in April 1612. As seminaries were supposed to be diocesan rather than episcopal, founding one required the co-operation of the clergy, who were to be represented in the running of the institution. In anticipation of the syndics' favourable response, Richelieu purchased a private house with his own funds in March 1612, and set it aside for the future teachers and pupils of his seminary. Initially, he relied upon Luçon clergy for the direction of the seminary, overall supervision of which was confided to Antoine Froissard, a canon of the cathedral. But trouble was not long in surfacing in the form of complaints from the benefice-holders subject to the financial levy. The outcome was that Richelieu had to seek a second set of letters-patent in August 1613, which again supported his endeavours, but now extended the tax to all benefice-holders, with the exception of the parish priests. Little is known about what difference this made, but three years later Froissard resigned as superior, a move which opened the way in December 1616, for Richelieu to sign a contract with Bérulle, to turn the seminary over 'in perpetuity' to the Oratory, a few of whose members were already present in Luçon diocese.[47] The modest scale of what Richelieu intended is evident from the clause which stipulated that the Oratory should take in and train 'six or several young men born in the diocese of Luçon and destined for the holy state of the priesthood, and chosen for that purpose by the same priests (i.e. of the Oratory)'.[48] Although the Oratorians were installed in 1617, it is obvious that, even had the contract been fully implemented, the seminary's potential was severely limited; the annual intake envisaged was only a fraction of the total number of clergy, present and future. In the event, opposition and inertia prevented the Oratory and the seminary making even the impact that Richelieu intended. By the later 1610s, he was an absentee bishop, and the Oratorians were left to face local problems largely single-handed. When Richelieu pressed Bérulle to visit Luçon in 1619, the latter was embarrassed that he was unable to find a suitable superior for the seminary.[49] More surprisingly, perhaps, Richelieu himself was unable to have the letters-

---

47 B.N. MS. Lat 18389, fos. 76v–80r. This 'Mémoire à consulter au sujet de l'establisse-
    ment d'un séminaire à Luçon' is in fact a well-documented account of the vicissitudes of
    Richelieu's foundation.

48 A.M.P. Ingold, *L'Oratoire à Luçon* (n.p. n.d.), pp. 4–5, for the text of the contract. The
    original passage runs: 'six ou plusieurs jeunes gens nés dans ledit diocèse de Luçon, voués
    et destinés au saint estat du sacerdoce, et choisis pour cela par les mêmes Pères'.

49 *Correspondance de Bérulle*, II, pp. 33–7, Bérulle to Père Gibieuf, 7 June 1617; Avenel,
    Lettres, I, pp. 603–4, Richelieu to Bérulle, late June 1619. Both men were at that time in
    western France in the entourage of Marie de' Medici.

patent of 1613 registered by the *parlement* of Paris in November 1620, something which would have strengthened his position considerably. The principal reason for this failure was the opposition of the cathedral chapter to the financial levy, in which it no doubt spoke for the benefice-holders generally. The effects of such resistance did not take long to appear, as an absentee bishop could not make his authority felt. Over the next few years, the Oratorians reduced their commitments at Luçon: by 1625, only one of them was left as holder of a cathedral chapter prebend with responsibility to preach and teach.[50] Richelieu's seminary was effectively dead. Whether it had actually achieved anything during its short life is questionable, especially when compared with the difficulties encountered by far better-endowed seminaries founded both then and later.

The seminary question should not be regarded as the only genuine test of the reforming credentials of someone in Richelieu's position, and even less as a basis to damn him for failing to achieve more than he did. But it does serve to illustrate the nature of the problems which beset any bishop attempting innovation at this time, and how circumscribed was his room for manoeuvre. Richelieu was no exception. The significance of his search for royal approval and support in both 1611 and 1613 doubtless derives from an appreciation of the difficulties, but distant royal authority could be often no more effective than episcopal power itself. However close episcopal absolutism may have lain to his heart, it was often wholly impractical in early seventeenth-century dioceses, and only uncritical hagiography can disguise the limited impact of Richelieu's policies as a bishop. Seventeenth-century bishops were far from staking all their hopes on a single institution such as a seminary, and were wholly realistic in not doing so. Seminaries could not produce even limited results in isolation from other initiatives; his own refusal to treat them as a monastic retreat is clear from his requirement that the Oratorians running his seminary should preach, catechize and perform a variety of pastoral tasks.[51] His resort to visitations, synods, new religious orders, and so on, were no less central to his approach towards governing and improving his diocese.

III

Richelieu's experiences as bishop of Luçon, while sharpening his sense of the possible, were far from reducing him to the status of a

50 B.N., MS. Lat. 18389, fos. 76v–80.
51 Hanotaux, *Richelieu*, ii, p. 265, quoting Richelieu's prescriptions of Jan. 1619.

'man of action' ready to throw overboard his earlier labours as a student of theology. Incidental factors, such as periods of ill-health and convalescence, may also have had something to do with his continuing intellectual undertakings, which were not mere substitutes for action. Indeed, it is not too paradoxical to claim that the most extensive evidence of Richelieu the man of action to have survived from these years is of a literary kind. It begins with the publication of a now-lost catechism dating from 1611 or early 1612 – not to be identified with the so-called *Cathéchisme de Luçon*, the name by which his *Instruction du Chrétien* of 1618 is often known – and was followed by the *Briefve et facile instruction pour les confesseurs* of Jacques de Flavigny. Both works were clearly pedagogical treatises, reflecting the immediate, practical priorities of a bishop and an educator rather than a theologian. In them we encounter for the first time two perennial problems long familiar to historians of Richelieu – firstly, the extent to which he personally wrote works published under his name, and secondly, how far he was the actual inspiration for works like the *Briefve et facile instruction*, published under the name of another. As far as the lost catechism and the *Briefve instruction* are concerned, their purpose and format make it entirely possible that Richelieu only supplied the original directives, and perhaps some of the central ideas and format, to those who, like Flavigny, then 'composed' or published them on his behalf.

As we have seen, Richelieu's statutes and other directives placed considerable emphasis upon an educated, at least in the sense of properly instructed, laity. It is, therefore, not far-fetched to regard the *Instruction du Chrétien* as the most comprehensive statement of his approach to what has been called the problem of 'christianising' his flock. Written, or at least completed, in the relative calm and leisure of Avignon, it carries prefatory addresses to both the people and the clergy of Luçon. It has perhaps too often been taken out of its proper context, and been viewed as an academic treatise by a Sorbonne theology graduate. Obviously, it contains numerous theological assumptions, but this is perhaps not the best vantage point from which to examine it; other works like the *Principaux points* of 1617 and the posthumously published *Perfection du Chrétien* are better suited for such analysis, because they are more detached from immediate pastoral considerations.

The *Instruction* is essentially a pedagogical work destined for the education of ordinary Christians, and as such it is not altogether surprising that it later acquired the sobriquet of the *Catéchisme de Luçon*. Although it was not written in the classic, question-and-answer format of a catechism, the appellation doubtless arose from the fact that the work was clearly and systematically divided into sections and lessons for sequential presentation by parish priests from their pulpits to their parishioners during the High Mass on Sundays and feast-days. Richelieu was admirably clear as to his objectives, and quite consciously eschewed discussion of technical points of theology; he included treatments of particular questions in the margins for the benefit of the clergy who would be entrusted with reading out, and elaborating on, the text of the individual chapters, and was anxious to spare their parishioners elaborate, but not essential, theological speculation. It was in the same vein that he even asked parish priests to warn preachers to concentrate more on instructing the people through their sermons than on resolving abstruse or superfluous points of doctrine.[52] Richelieu's technique throughout the *Instruction* is simple, direct and effective: it is to take a phrase or verse of the Creed, and systematically to examine its words, their meaning and implication, with more technical commentary in the margin for the clergy themselves. There are very few learned allusions or quotations from authors ancient or modern; even citations from the Scriptures are kept to a minimum; the text is spare, the prose simple, and the emphasis is on presenting ideas to ordinary people in a form in which they can be grasped. Even so, some of his demonstrations are by no means simple – for example, that on the nature and 'progression' of the Trinity – so quite what parishioners made of some of them during the *prosnes* on Sunday may only be surmised. Much obviously depended, as Richelieu showed he was aware it would, upon the quality of the clergy charged with transmitting his message from the pulpit.

The *Instruction* was constructed around the three requirements of every Christian – what he must believe, what he must do, and the means by which he obtains from God the strength needed both to believe and to do what is necessary for salvation.[53] What he must know is essentially contained in the Apostles' Creed, what he must do is in the Ten Commandments and the commandments of the church, while the means to secure salvation are primarily prayer and the sacraments. Such an approach enables Richelieu to develop more systematically ideas and directives already outlined in his synodal statutes and the *Instruction pour les confesseurs*. His exposition of the commandments follows from the belief that if Christ asked his followers to observe them, it was because he believed it to be possible for them to do so, especially as God's grace was available to assist them. Richelieu even adds that it is in their interest to do so, as

52 *Instruction du chrestien par Révérend Père en Dieu Messire Armand Jean du Plessis Cardinal Duc de Richelieu*, preface to 'messieurs les curez de l'évesché de Luçon', unpaginated. Quotations are from the edition published by Martin Durand in Paris, 1636.
53 *Ibid.*, ch. 1, pp. 4–6.

their salvation is at stake. Although Richelieu's reputation is that of a champion of reasonable Christianity, the modern reader is likely to be struck by the tough line he follows in explaining the demands of the commandments. He may have allowed reasonable exceptions to not working on the Lord's Day, which he does not regard in any case as a kind of sabbath, but, when explaining the fourth commandment, he dwells at least as much on the reciprocal obligations that exist between superiors and subordinates as on the respect due from children to parents; expounding the Seventh, he distributes warnings to *seigneurs*, notaries, benefice-holders, tax-collectors, assessors and so on not to cheat or steal other people's property, and insists that if they do, they are bound to make restitution. If Richelieu makes the commandments central to Christian living, it is because of his confidence in the power of prayer and the sacraments, and especially those of Penance and the Eucharist. Here, too, his subsequent reputation, deriving essentially from comparison with rigourists like St Cyran and the Jansenists, seems at odds with his writings from the 1610s. Unlike the rigourists, he does indeed counsel people to receive Communion regularly, ideally once a month or, if not, at least on the four great feasts of the Christian calendar. But he does not do so in a spirit of bland *insouciance*, and the *Instruction du Chrétien* repeats all his earlier strictures about adequate preparation before taking these sacraments. Since he defines confession as 'a voluntary self-accusation of having committed specific sins', he demands a clear intention to mend one's ways and a thorough examination of conscience beforehand – those confessing once a year only are recommended to devote two hours to doing just that.[54] If Richelieu exaggerates at all here, it is in his obsession with ensuring that both confessors and penitents fulfil to the letter all the conditions required to obtain absolution in the confessional. His ideal confessor was not someone to be approached without trepidation or from whom such absolution could be obtained lightly or cheaply.[55]

The seventeenth-century French church would experience profound disputes over proper religious practices, notably where the sacraments were concerned. In general, it moved slowly to a more rigourist stance than was the case in the decades either side of 1600. If Richelieu's own objections to the precepts of a St Cyran were to bequeath an image of him as championing Christianity 'without tears' – an image which is unconsciously strengthened by his subsequent political career and maxims – then the fact that the *Instruction du chrétien* was widely adopted as a catechism throughout the French

54   *Ibid.*, ch. 26.
55   *Ibid.*, ch. 27.

church suggests, at the very least, that his was a very widely-shared recipe for reform and salvation.

IV

There was one problem that no bishop of Luçon could avoid having to deal with under Henri IV and especially Louis XIII – that of the Huguenots. In the absence of any thorough study, it is difficult to form a satisfactory picture of their presence throughout Poitou. But it is beyond dispute that they remained numerous there and in Richelieu's diocese generally.[56] A report of 1618 claimed that their possession of all Poitou's towns, with the exception of Poitiers and Parthenay, as *places de surêté*, enabled them to dominate the province and ride roughshod over the non-Huguenot population.[57] Sully was governor of the province, and Richelieu had the great fortress of La Rochelle as a neighbour. But this Huguenot superiority was not purely political: one of their leading academies was at Saumur, whose governor, Duplessis-Mornay, 'the Huguenot pope', enjoyed considerable intellectual and political authority. Consequently, local Huguenot congregations and ministers had little reason to keep discreetly out of sight. They were unlikely to welcome a resident bishop at Luçon, and it was virtually impossible for one as keen as was Richelieu to exercise to the full his prerogatives as bishop not to collide with them.

This may seem surprising, given that historians are in the habit of regarding Richelieu as an exception to the general pattern of bitter confessional hatred which characterized relations between Catholics and Huguenots in seventeenth-century France. Such a view is based essentially on the evidence of his treatment of the Huguenots in the 1620s, when he refused to revoke the Edict of Nantes, and from his own later programme for reunion with them, especially as expressed in his posthumously published *Traité qui contient la méthode la plus facile et la plus assurée pour convertir ceux qui sont séparés de l'Église*. But it is not clear that the resulting reputation for eirenicism fits the facts of his early career. If we are to comprehend his role and attitudes, we must examine, with a minimum of hindsight, those early encounters with the Huguenots while bishop of Luçon, whether on the ground or in print.

That Richelieu was aware of the tensions within his diocese is

---

56 See Pierre Dez, *Histoire des protestants et des églises réformées du Poitou* (new edition), vol. 1 (La Rochelle 1936), pp. 231–40, for a brief account of the Huguenot presence around 1600.

57 A.N., TT 262, dossier 8, 'Estat de la religion en Poictou' (Dec. 1618).

evident enough from his inaugural address 'au peuple de Luçon' in December 1608, in which he urged the two religions to live together under the king's peace. But equally, there were, as he would soon discover, practices which he could not accept. Lacroix cites an appeal to Henri IV by Richelieu and his clergy, and a royal edict given in response to them in April 1609, ordering the Huguenots to pay the church tithe for the upkeep of the Catholic clergy.[58] Such speed was remarkable by the standards of the time, and the petition may have been submitted before his actual arrival at Luçon. In the same year, he succeeded in requiring the Huguenots to build their temple in a less provocative part of Luçon than opposite the cathedral, as they had originally planned. He offered them a small monetary inducement to do so, but this did not placate the Huguenot pastor, who complained of harassment and other hostile actions by the bishop.[59] In 1611, he took action to dissuade Huguenot *seigneurs* from preventing benefice-holders from collecting their revenue, on the grounds that to do so constituted intolerable interference in the affairs of another church.[60] In both 1611 and 1613, he appealed to royal officials for action against Huguenots who insisted on burying their own dead in Catholic churches, something which in at least one instance had involved the use of force.[61] Such community disputes were commonplace at this time, and were always likely to degenerate into violence, all the more so as cemeteries in towns like Luçon did not yet 'belong' to either confession. Yet more serious was the fact that Catholic worship had evidently not been restored at all in certain localities either before or during Richelieu's episcopate. Evidence is lacking as to how he dealt with the consequences of this during his early years, but his attempt, in 1621, to obtain royal orders addressed to the governor of Poitou for the restoration of worship in those parts of Luçon 'où jusques icy il n'a point esté remis', gives some idea of how serious the problem was.[62] Some action did follow, but the brief Huguenot revolt of early 1622 made matters worse again for a time, and even after he had resigned as bishop, Richelieu still needed to use his influence to evict the Huguenots from Catholic churches.[63]

58   Lacroix, *Richelieu à Luçon*, p. 122.
59   *Ibid.*, pp. 119–20.
60   Avenel, *Lettres*, I, p. 68, letter to [Monsieur . . .], July 1611.
61   *Ibid.*, I, p. 72, letter to Méric de Vic, 26 Nov. 1611. See Lacroix, *Richelieu à Luçon*, pp. 122–4.
62   Avenel, *Lettres*, VII, p. 497, instruction to Louis de Marillac, July 1621.
63   A.A.E. Mems et docs. France 778, fo. 13, petition from curé of Mouchamp, 19 Jan. 1623, asking for measures to restore worship there, and relating Huguenot abuses during the 1622 revolt. For references to Richelieu's intervention in the ensuing lawsuits over possession of churches, see Dez, *Protestants du Poitou*, I, pp. 269–72.

These facts, scattered over the full span of Richelieu's episcopate, make it quite clear that he was a determined defender of Catholic and clerical interests against what he saw as usurpation by Protestants. To the Huguenots themselves, his public actions spoke louder than the more accommodating sentiments he may have expressed privately to individual members of their church. Such a negative image of him would have been further strengthened by his involvement in attempts to proselytize among their community. Quite how extensive that involvement was is now difficult to say, but it would have seemed to them demonstrated at a general level by his support for the missions of the Oratorians and especially of the Capuchins. But there is also some evidence of direct personal participation, a fact which is hardly surprising in a bishop who modelled himself on Cardinal du Perron, 'le grand convertisseur' of his generation. The Huguenot pastor of Luçon complained in 1609 of his having rebaptized several persons previously baptized in the Huguenot church, activity which points to continuing proselytization of some kind.[64] Richelieu himself wrote at length, probably in 1611, about a failed attempt in which he had been involved, to convert a Huguenot lady during a 'conference' with several Huguenot ministers at Châtellerault.[65] Although this incident took place outside his own diocese, it was, as we shall see, already clear by this time from his political activities that he did not regard the boundaries of his diocese as constituting any barrier to his action.

If it was natural for an admirer of du Perron to embark on personal attempts to convert Huguenots, it was no less so for one who was also a theologian to contemplate wielding the pen against them. The first hint that he was throwing himself into this kind of study dates from October 1612, and comes from no less a source than his good friend, Gabriel de Laubespine, bishop of Orléans and one of the most learned Catholic controversialist writers of his time. Laubespine expressed some surprise at the extent of Richelieu's immersion in the subject, though the tone of his letter suggests that they had perhaps already exchanged ideas on these subjects. Advising him to begin by studying the opinions of their opponents, Laubespine revealed the full measure of his friend's enthusiasm by referring to the 'deux Anglois' that he had engaged to assist him in his studies.[66] Who the English doctors were has never been firmly established. Several writers have seen Richard Smith, whose career was later to be so intertwined with Richelieu's, as one of them, but lacked positive

---

64 Lacroix, *Richelieu à Luçon*, p. 120.
65 Avenel, *Lettres*, I, pp. 78–80, letter to one of the protagonists in this conference.
66 A.A.E., Mems et docs, France 768, fo. 232, Laubespine to Richelieu, 28 Oct. 1612.

evidence for what was a reasonable guess, given that Smith is recorded as having been a member of a group of English catholic divines
who gathered in Paris at the college of Arras between 1612 and
1631, where they engaged in controversial writings against
James I.[67] Some new evidence places the matter beyond all doubt.
Just when Laubespine was writing to Richelieu about his new studies,
Richard Smith was independently confessing to his 'perplexitie' as to
whether he should go to Luçon with Richelieu or remain with his
community at the college of Arras. In the event, Richelieu seems
to have forced his hand, and Smith spent the winter with him at
Coussay.[68] As to the second Englishman employed by Richelieu,
there is some reason to think that he may have been Anthony
Champney, who was an exact contemporary to Richelieu's at the
university, and had been resident in Paris for several years before
joining the Arras community.[69] But whoever it was, his association
with Richelieu was insignificant and short-lived compared to that
of Smith. Unfortunately, we know nothing of how Richelieu discovered such unlikely companions, but we can well imagine an
encounter during his visits to Paris in 1611–12; they may have been
recommended to him by Cardinal du Perron.[70] At any rate, the demands he was to make of Smith were considerable, for although
Richelieu may have attended courses in 'the controversies', as they
were called at the time, during his theology studies in Paris, he was
no expert in that field. In return for his maintenance and, later, an
annuity, Smith was employed to undertake research for, and tutor
Richelieu in, the subject of confessional controversy; he was not
free, if we accept his own statement, to engage in his personal studies
while so employed.[71] Moreover, Smith's initial period of employment
gradually became extended until he became a regular member of

---

67 For the foundation and activities of the English community of the college of Arras, see
A. F. Allison, 'Richard Smith's Gallican Backers and Jesuit Opponents. Part II: Smith at
Paris as Protegé of Richelieu, 1613–c.1642', *Recusant History* 19 (1989), pp. 234–85, esp. pp.
254–9. I am indebted to this author's work on the subject, and also wish to acknowledge
his help in locating Smith's letters.

68 Archives of the Archdiocese of Westminster (hereinafter A. A. W.), series A, vol. 11, no.
181, p. 527, Smith to Thomas More, agent of the English secular clergy in Rome, 15 Oct.
1612.

69 For the members of the Arras community, see Allison (n. 66 above). For information on
Champney, drawn from the archives of the University of Paris, I am once again indebted
to Laurence Brockliss.

70 Avenel, *Lettres*, 1, p. 143, letter of 17 May 1615. The first recommendation probably
occurred during the Estates General.

71 A. A. W., A 13, no. 193, p. 487, Smith to Thomas More, 4 Sept. 1614: 'In the mean time
I staid here in Poitou, and whiles the Bishop is at the States [the Estates-General] I have lead

Richelieu's household.[72] The English community in Paris was initially reluctant to consent to his prolonged absence, but their need for patrons softened these objections somewhat;[73] when, in mid-1613, Richelieu insisted that he would need Smith's services for two to three more years, it required du Perron's personal arbitration to secure their consent.[74] The consequences of Richelieu's association with Smith extended well beyond narrowly academic issues: long before Richelieu would be in a position to secure for Smith the 'bishopric' of the English church in 1624, Smith had made him familiar with the problems, political and theological, of English Catholicism and its responses to the religious policies of James I.[75]

In October 1612, Laubespine wagered that if Richelieu was about to immerse himself in the contemporary religious controversies, it was not 'sans quelque grand dessein et qui doive estre utile à l'église'.[76] While there is no doubting his enthusiasm for such activity, in retrospect, however, the most surprising feature of it was the apparent lack of any immediate intention to publish the fruits of his labours. Of course, it may be that other demands, especially those of politics, interfered with whatever initial plans he may have formulated. In any event, the ample evidence of wide reading during these years would at least help to explain how he was able to assemble quickly, during his period of enforced residence at Coussay in 1617, his *Principaux points de la foy catholique*, a work of middling length which, quite unlike the *Instruction du Chrétien* of the following year, was heavily larded with the apparatus of references to the Scriptures, the Church Fathers, Luther, Calvin, and other Protestant theologians characteristic of such works. Not only the date of its appearance – November 1617 – but the fact that the *Principaux points* was addressed directly to Louis XIII by a recently disgraced minister who was manifestly out to show both his loyalty to the king and his seriousness as a bishop, makes the work symptomatic of the changes that had occurred in his career since he originally embarked on his studies in 1612; inevitably, such a work was as much a political as a religious statement. The additional fact that this, his only contribution to the Catholic-Huguenot polemic of the early seventeenth century, was a hastily-written response to a letter addressed to Louis XIII by the Huguenot ministers of Charenton criticizing a previous attack on

---

72 A. A. W., B 26, Smith to Thomas Rant, 18 Aug. 1624, claiming he had been some thirteen years 'with Richelieu'.

73 A. A. W., A 12, no. 30, Smith to More, 3 Feb. 1613.

74 A. A. W., A 12, no. 125, p. 277, Smith to More, Paris, 2 July 1613; *ibid.*, no. 161, p. 359, to same, Coussay, 9 Sept. 1613.

75 See Alison, 'Richard Smith, Richelieu and the French Marriage', pp. 147–211. Smith also employed Richelieu's good offices in Rome and elsewhere in defence of English Catholic interests: A. A. W., A 12, no. 38, p. 81, Richelieu to Cardinal de La Rochefoucauld, 15 Feb. 1613, *ibid.*, A 15, no. 168, Smith to More, 11 Dec. 1616.

them by the Jesuit Père Arnoux, and not the more considered or systematic statement he might have been expected to produce after several years of study, must partly account for its lack of originality. The format he adopted, in which most chapters begin with a quotation from the Charenton petition and are then followed by chapter-and-verse refutation, also virtually precluded novelty.[77]

But, given the reputation for tolerance which Richelieu has always enjoyed, one often held to be far superior to anything to which his contemporaries could aspire, it is worth paying some attention to its content. In his prefatory address to the king, he went out of his way to deny the ministers' claim that all Catholics hated Huguenots. This was, he argued, a misconception: Catholics loved them very strongly, hence their desire to see them return to the truth and to have that return happen by peaceful persuasion: 'We humbly beseech your Majesty to do good to them, working with all his power to eradicate the error that has taken root in their hearts and to secure their conversion . . . the ways of gentleness I believe to be the most suitable method towards removing error.'[78] The address 'To the reader' which followed, and which stated the purpose of his book, was much less unctuous: 'The Huguenots have every reason to be thankful for our monarchs, and have no grounds for complaining about them as they do; their doctrine is not hated for the reasons they claim, but worthy of hatred for reasons which they conceal; that the Catholic church, its ministers and all those they accuse are innocent of the crimes imputed to them.'

Richelieu's main concern was not so much to defend Arnoux and the Jesuits, towards whom he was already ambivalent, as to counter the Huguenots' claim to be loyal subjects and pillars of the French monarchy, and their assertion that the activities of both the Catholic clergy and the Jesuits were sources of division within the realm. The first fourteen of its nineteen chapters were devoted to rebutting the Charenton ministers' allegations, the remainder 'to examining the reasons why their doctrine should be abhorred by everybody'. He regarded their formal confessions of faith as too inadequate and obscure for this purpose, and resorted to extensive quotation from Luther, Calvin, Beza and other Protestant divines.[79] The argument throughout was as much about politics as religion *per se*, and Rich-

---

77 Deloche, *Autour de la plume*, ch. 4, for the most comprehensive account of the circum-
    stances in which the book was written. My account of its thrust and significance differs
    considerably from his.
78 *Principaux points de la foy de l'église catholique défendus contre l'escrit addressé au Roy par des*
    quatre Ministres de Charenton, preface 'Au roy', unpaginated. I have used the edition
    published in Paris by Denis Moreau in 1618.
79 *Ibid.*, preface 'to the reader', unpaginated.

elieu was in no doubt that the Huguenots bred sedition, overthrew or killed rulers, and revived ancient heresies. The Jesuits, on the contrary, were concerned only with the saving of souls, and sincerely desired peace in the kingdom.[80] His defence of the papacy was no less robust: 'kings would be immortal if their preservation depended on the Popes, who seek their well being, as fathers do for their children'.[81] As for the clergy's stance at the 1614 Estates General, when they blocked the Third Estate's celebrated attempt to enshrine gallican principles in a fundamental law of royal sovereignty, Richelieu was no less expansive and forthright. His riposte to the Huguenot attack on this point was, in fact, taken almost verbatim from du Perron's apologia on that occasion – that the quarrel was a spiritual one, and that the clergy were right to prevent the Estates General from pronouncing on a matter which was *ultra vires*.[82] When, in his final chapters, Richelieu abandoned tit-for-tat polemics, his judgement of the Huguenots was hardly lenient – their religion deserved to be hated because it was schismatic and was a revival of ancient heresies, but no less because it made virtue irrelevant and opened the door to vice.[83] He ended by exposing their teaching, first articulated by Luther, that 'no law made by spiritual or temporal princes could oblige men in conscience'.[84]

Even such a sketchy survey is enough to suggest that Richelieu's work was not that of an original or maverick apostle of tolerance, but rather that of a mainline Catholic bishop; neither the prose nor the tone can have concealed this from contemporaries. It was in no sense a dispassionate analysis of Protestant theology or religious practice, which it rejected out of hand as schism and heresy, and approached simply from the angle of its unacceptable political and moral implications. Consequently it offered little scope for any continuing dialogue.[85] While its tolerance mainly hung on the slender thread of its opening address to Louis XIII, its handling of recent events and controversies can hardly have persuaded Huguenots that new attitudes towards them were emerging from within the episcopal bench.

Richelieu and his friends did as much as they could to promote the *Principaux points*, but the book did not make as much of an impact on contemporary polemics as they hoped; it was certainly much more a

80   *Ibid.*, p. 197.
81   *Ibid.*, p. 180.
82   *Ibid.*, ch. 8.
83   *Ibid.*, chs. 15–18.
84   *Ibid.*, ch. 19.
85   For Richelieu's position in the Catholic-Huguenot polemics of the seventeenth century, see Jacques Solé, *Le Débat entre protestants et catholiques français de 1598 à 1685* (Paris 1985), I, pp. 219–20.

livre de circonstance than his posthumous treatise on the conversion of the Huguenots. The Jesuit Père Coton thanked him for his support and the Sorbonne welcomed it, which gave him great satisfaction.[86] Replies to it were published by at least two Protestant pamphleteers, who bracketed Richelieu with du Perron and other Catholic champions, company which would no doubt have pleased him, but this indicates that Protestants saw no reason to single him out as unusually tolerant or as someone with a distinctive voice worth engaging in the current confessional clamour.[87] His tract was quickly submerged by the political climate which had helped to produce it, and which it did little to quieten. If it had any impact at all, it was to further sharpen existing perceptions of him as a spokesman for the church's increasingly vocal hostility to the Huguenots.

V

The *Principaux points* was written during Richelieu's final period of residence in his diocese. Shortly afterwards, he would experience exile in Avignon, and then embark on his slow return to political life. By then, of course, the obscurity of his early years at Luçon was a thing of the past. That would seem a natural point at which to close this consideration of his episcopal career. But there is much more to that career than ordinances, visitations and books: it also possesses, for want of a better term, a social history which cannot be passed over without missing a crucial dimension of his slow rise to power. Moreover, it should not be forgotten that long after he had left Luçon and become a minister, Richelieu's personal milieu and entourage retained the heavily ecclesiastical character it had acquired during his time as a bishop.

Even a cursory examination of Richelieu's episcopal career shows the importance of the network of relations, friendships and connections made both at the time and later. Often, these links were in no sense political, either in origin or intention, but thanks to his extraordinary skill in moulding his human environment, they would serve him and his career in all sorts of unexpected ways. Equally, the company he sought out and kept enables us to understand better the

---

86 Avenel, *Lettres*, I, pp. 556–7, Richelieu to Flavigny, Nov. 1617; *ibid.*, pp. 557–8, to Jean Suffren, S.J. [Dec. 1617].
87 Deloche, *Autour de la plume*, pp. 148ff. Deloche's view is very different: 'le livre de Richelieu était une victoire, car il restait sans réplique de la part des ministres de Charenton'. This argument from silence seems directly contradicted by the admission that the Huguenot ministers continued their debate with Arnoux and others, devoting only a few lines to Richelieu (p. 149).

kind of face that he showed to the world around him. It is possible to see Richelieu's 'society' as a series of concentric circles, beginning with his own household, and expanding outwards towards more distant figures, both inside and outside the church establishment.

As we saw in the previous chapter, scarcely anything is known about Richelieu's social milieu during his years at Navarre and the Sorbonne, and apart from his professors and a few others like Cospeau, few names of individuals emerge from contemporary sources. Promotion to the status of bishop was bound to change this since, as the case of Richard Smith demonstrates, it created both the need and the capacity to attract a variety of auxiliaries and servants. Not surprisingly, much less is known about the composition of his household than is the case for his years as royal minister.[88] He clearly persuaded some of his earliest servants to leave Paris with him, though how faithfully those who did so represent the Parisian milieu in which he grew up is another thing; his own negative attitudes to Luçon might suggest that not many were ready for that kind of exile. According to tradition, at least three servants from his Paris student days accompanied him to Luçon – his principal secretary and factotum Michel Le Masle, his confessor the Sorbonne doctor Mulot, and his valet Desbournais. All three were to serve him until the end, in roles which were far more indispensable than their modest titles suggest. Others, such as chaplains, secretaries, and even the *maître d'hôtel* whose recruitment caused him such jubilation, came and went, leaving few traces, during his years at Luçon.[89]

But his household is only a small part of the story, and its members would never be allowed to rise beyond their station by a master who had a low opinion of domestic service, at whatever level. Increasingly, as he made his name, the more important and valuable the people who frequented him, the less likely it was that they would be members of the household. A more convincing testimony to his powers of persuasion and attraction is thus provided by the better-known figures who served him at Luçon. Episcopal patronage, even where limited, could obviously be a powerful magnet, and it was common for bishops to bring key officials, often members of their own families, with them to a diocese, rather than rely excessively on local dignitaries. But without members of his own family to draw upon, Richelieu had to look to others to fill key positions. The most obvious example of this is Jacques de Flavigny, one of his Sorbonne professors, who accompanied him to his diocese as his grand vicar.

---

88 See Deloche, *Maison du Cardinal de Richelieu*, for an extensive account; Bergin, *Richelieu*, ch. 2.
89 See Deloche, *Maison du cardinal de Richelieu*, p. 57.

But unquestionably his closest confidant at Luçon was Sébastien Bouthillier, whose unflinching and total confidence in his patron's destiny never faltered, regardless of the setbacks. He had been made a canon of Luçon cathedral, presumably by Richelieu himself, before 1607, and he would later become dean of the chapter in 1614.[90] His manner, personality and affability were to prove enormously valuable to Richelieu, and his premature death in 1625 denied him the rewards his patron would almost certainly have secured for him in the church.[91] Although much less is known of Richelieu's success in Luçon itself with local clergy, it is clear that he persuaded several canons of the cathedral such as the dean, Michel Papin, Antoine Froissard and a few others, to assume important roles in his service. Only Froissard, about whom little is known, was to serve him for the rest of his career, becoming one of his most trusted agents especially where his ecclesiastical interests were concerned.[92]

As we have seen, Richelieu also established relations with both Bérulle and Père Joseph around 1611. While Bérulle would remain in the background until later in the 1610s, relations with the Capuchin were to grow quickly in both intensity and regularity after 1611, aided by the fact that he was provincial of the Touraine Capuchins between 1613 and 1616. Initially, the common ground was probably missionary activity and general pastoral reform, but it soon widened to embrace wider horizons. Both men, for example, played a major part in complicated efforts to reform the abbey of Fontevraud, which led to the foundation, under Père Joseph's supervision, of the Filles du Calvaire.[93] Moreover, because the abbey was governed by Bourbon abbesses, its reform quickly led those involved into the realm of high politics.

Isolated though it might be, Luçon was not an island, and Richelieu's activities, movements and changes of place of residence constantly expanded his range of acquaintances. It was the change of bishop at Poitiers in 1612 which was the major event in the province around this time, and it did much to entice Richelieu away from Luçon. With his experience of Italy and Rome, the cultivated and ambitious new bishop, Chasteignier de la Rocheposay, quickly gathered around him a circle of ecclesiastics, some of them local luminaries. His prompt invitation to Richelieu, whom he obviously knew before then, to join them might well have been penned by

90　A.N., P 565(i), no. 2,555, 26 June 1607, for Bouthillier's registration of Richelieu's oath of fidelity to the king at royal court registry at Luçon; *Gallia Christiana*, II, col. 1419.

91　Lacroix, *Richelieu à Luçon*, pp. 171–81.

92　Bergin, *Richelieu*, p. 52.

93　See Gustave Fagniez, *Le Père Joseph et Richelieu (1577–1638)*, 2 vols. (Paris, 1894), I, esp. ch. 2; Lacroix, *Richelieu à Luçon*, pp. 181–9.

Richelieu to one of his own friends: 'Here you will find mediocre
accommodation, a table that is worse, and extreme goodwill which,
if you please, you will accept to make amends for the rest. I am so
burdened and inebriated by my duties, as I had foreseen, that I do
not know who to blame apart from myself and you to some extent
for having always exposed me to accept this burden.'[94] The invitation, made in July 1612, was one Richelieu seems to have been only
too happy to accept, and may even explain Bishop Laubespine's
ignorance of his whereabouts in subsequent months. But the court
of the bishop of Poitiers was more than a place for agreeable diver-
sion; it was also interested in letters, scholarship, and the religious
controversies of the day. La Rocheposay saw himself as a scholar-
bishop, and published learned theological treatises in later years.
Perhaps the most celebrated of those whom he attracted to Poitiers
around this time was the future abbé de St Cyran, Jean Duvergier de
Hauranne, whose phenomenal learning made him the ideal scholar-
companion for the bishop, filling a role akin to that of Richelieu's
'deux Anglois'. Duvergier's web of acquaintances and relations was
spreading rapidly, and effectively illustrates the range of acquaintances available in the ecclesiastical world. Since his student days in
Paris, he had apparently known Sébastien Bouthillier, who in turn
was also a close friend of La Rocheposay, while Duvergier's original
patron, Bertrand d'Eschaux, bishop of Bayonne and grand almoner
to Marie de' Medici, closely followed the careers of this circle,
Richelieu included. In such circumstances, it was not surprising
that Richelieu should himself have thrown himself into theological
study, bringing Richard Smith with him to Coussay, and even less
so that he and Duvergier should have struck up very close relations.
Their first known meeting dates from 1613, but they may have been
acquainted earlier than that, perhaps even from their student days.
At this point in his career, the future St Cyran was an ambitious
cleric of the kind that appealed to Richelieu. His apologia for La
Rocheposay, who had taken up arms to prevent Condé entering
Poitiers during the troubles in 1614, caused a sensation with its frank
defence of the right of ecclesiastics to resort to the use of arms in case
of necessity.[95] Its broader implications would not have been lost on
someone as worldly-wise as Richelieu. A few years later, it was
Duvergier who would supervise the publication of Richelieu's
Instruction du Chrétien.[96]

94   B.N., MS. fichier Charavay, s.v. La Rocheposay, letter to Richelieu, 11 July 1612.
95   Jean Orcibal, *Jean Duvergier de Hauranne, abbé de Saint Cyran, et son temps* (Louvain-Paris
     1948), pp. 170ff. This great work is still the best study of clerical ambition and mobility
     in the early seventeenth century, as well as of the emergence of the younger generation
     of *dévots*.
96   Orcibal, *Saint Cyran*, p. 482.

Friendships and relations like this loom very large in Richelieu's early career. It was to clergy of the 'second order', as they were called, – men like Duvergier, Bouthillier, Père Joseph and others – rather than to his episcopal colleagues that Richelieu confided his innermost thoughts and ambitions. Life at Luçon and Poitiers was infinitely more relaxed than it would later be at court in the age of Concini and Luynes, and there was much less need for dissembling and secretiveness. Certainly, the closeness and warmth of the relations that Richelieu developed during these years contrasts very strongly with what we know of his later career, when the private man was well hidden behind the studied and glacial exterior he showed to the world around him, so that only a small inner coterie experienced the lighter or more sociable side of his character. As we shall see, Duvergier, Bouthillier, Père Joseph and others went to great lengths to promote Richelieu's career; such devotion can only be explained by the fascination he acquired over them during the early 1610s.[97] It is, of course, equally true that several of these intimate friends of his Luçon years would fall foul of him later, when their knowledge of his early career would make their attacks upon him particularly sharp and damaging.[98]

Richelieu's search for friends and patrons was assiduous, and extended to a wider spectrum of upper clergy and nobility as is clear from his early letters. The strained character of some of them indicates that success was not to be taken for granted. While not an immediate neighbour, Gabriel de Laubespine, bishop of Orléans, seems to have been one of his earliest and closest acquaintances among the episcopate. Their correspondence bears witness to the extent and warmth of their friendship, and the more retiring, scholarly Laubespine supported and applauded the actions of his more ambitious colleague. La Rocheposay of Poitiers seems to have been valued more as a colleague and ally than as an intimate friend, and years later Richelieu would block moves to propose him for the cardinal's hat. From the outset, Richelieu also sought the good graces of his metropolitan, Cardinal Sourdis of Bordeaux, but it is not certain that the adroit mixture of flattery and deference he adopted was hugely successful, any more than it was with the elderly Cardinal de La Rochefoucauld.[99] On the other hand, he would forge much closer links with Sourdis's younger brother, Henri, bishop of the neighbouring see of Maillezais after 1616. His regular visits to

---

97 Abundant evidence for this in Orcibal, *Saint Cyran*, pp. 170ff., 477ff.
98 Mathieu de Morgues was a prime example of this, and became a major source of damning, often wildly exaggerated, accounts of Richelieu's early years. See Deloche, *Maison du Cardinal de Richelieu*, ch. 3.
99 A.A.W., A 12, no. 38, Richelieu to La Rochefoucauld, 15 Feb. 1613, for a good example of these epistles.

Paris from 1610 onwards and his presence at episcopal gatherings served to develop his ecclesiastical network, while his role at the Estates General of 1614 would bring him to the attention of a far wider spectrum of the upper clergy.

If there was one cleric whom Richelieu most wished to impress during these years, it seems to have been Cardinal du Perron. Scholar, preacher, debater, and diplomat, he has often been cited as a role-model consciously chosen by the young Richelieu, but it would be impossible to say whether this choice pre-dated their first encounter. In any event, Richelieu's activities as court preacher in 1607 and 1608 obviously brought him into direct contact with 'the victor of Fontainebleau', who had become head of Henri IV's ecclesiastical household in 1606.[100] Du Perron's later efforts to ensure that Richelieu could retain the services of Richard Smith suggest that these early contacts had been maintained. The older cleric's high regard for Richelieu was enthusiastically conveyed to the latter in 1610 by Sébastien Bouthillier: 'Cardinal du Perron shows his high opinion of you on every possible occasion . . . he said that you should not be numbered among the more junior prelates, that older prelates should step aside in your favour, and that he himself wished to furnish an example of this to the others.'[101] The modern reader has difficulty in taking such ecclesiastical hyperbole seriously, not least because Richelieu himself indulged in it for form's sake with individuals for whom he manifestly had very little regard. In any case, there is no evidence that du Perron himself followed his own advice, least of all when he had the opportunity to do so, especially at the Estates General of 1614.

During the early years of his episcopate, Richelieu also made a number of efforts to act as a director of conscience and consoler of the distressed or bereaved. This led him to compose often long, rather stilted, letters of consolation to a number of individuals, whose names we do not always know, but who included the comtesse de Soissons, Mlle de Senneterre and others.[102] Hindsight, always potentially insidious, might suggest that these letters, like others from the same period, especially to great figures, were employed by Richelieu as a means of bringing himself to their attention. But his own prose and mode of expression make it clear that he was not at home in such a role, particularly in an age which boasted many outstanding practitioners of the art.

Richelieu's search for friends and relations did not end there, nor was it confined to fellow clerics. From the beginning of his episco-

100 See above, p. 102.
101 Richelieu, *Mémoires*, I, pp. 431–4, 16 May 1610.
102 Avenel, *Lettres*, I, p. 48 (Soissons); pp. 49–50 (Senneterre); pp. 75–6 (anonymous).

pate, he corresponded with political figures like Sully, Halincourt, the former ambassador in Rome and son of the powerful Villeroy, Épernon, as well as several others. A bereavement, a return from a foreign mission, or some other event – all proved useful occasions to bring oneself to the attention of important nobles, courtiers or ministers. The degree of success was variable, and Richelieu's own words betray his awareness of acting importunately on several such occasions. Of course, these efforts primarily reflect his desire to *paraître*, to make himself seen and heard, whether in Poitou or in Paris, and as such more detailed consideration of them can be reserved for the following chapter. It should suffice to say here that the ever-widening circles in which he moved – whether physically or through the pen – would serve him well when political and ecclesiastical opportunities began to come his way in and after 1614.

VI

The name of Richelieu has always been inextricably linked with the *dévots* who gave the seventeenth-century French church and religious life some of their most distinctive features. His association with them has usually been viewed in terms of conflict, culminating in his destruction of them as a political force opposed to him and his policies in 1630. It is a mistake to define the relationship in such purely political terms, a habit which has always made it difficult to believe that Richelieu could genuinely be classed as a *dévot* at all. However, it is increasingly clear that even after the clash of 1630, he fully retained many of their fundamental religious and social aspirations. Above all, it would be mistaken to interpret his episcopal career in terms of subsequent political conflicts. When the *dévots* first made their appearance under Henri IV, they were loosely referred to by commentators (and by historians after them) as *milieux* and *cercles*; by the 1620s, however, the talk was of a *parti des dévots* characterized by anti-Huguenot policies at home, and pro-Habsburg attitudes abroad. Clearly, the *dévot* phenomenon changed over time, but even then, political activity was only one, and not the most important, of its manifestations; many, perhaps the great majority of *dévots* had no interest in politics, and continued their religious and professional activities undisturbed long after 1630. Moreover, the chronology of the growth of *dévot* Catholicism is still inadequately understood. Much attention has been devoted to one of its principal vehicles, the secretive *Compagnie du Saint-Sacrement*, founded in the late 1620s;[103]

---

103 The bibliography is enormous, and of very uneven quality. The best studies include Raoul Allier, *La Cabale des dévots* (Paris 1903) and Alfred Rebelliau 'Un Épisode de la vie

more recently attention has been drawn to the networks of devotional confraternities and sodalities which were the more prosaic manifestations of the same religious outlook.[104] Both types of association flourished in the second third of the seventeenth century, and both involved a considerable amount of central direction from Paris. By contrast, the *dévot* movement of the opening decades of the century has, with the exception of its Parisian features, attracted relatively little attention.[105] An important effect of this neglect has been to make it difficult to explain the expansion of *dévot* groups and influence in later decades, and in particular how such influence succeeded in spreading from Paris and other centres over a generation or more. Richelieu's career as bishop of Luçon can be seen as part of an early attempt to establish *dévot* influence in Poitou.

In the first instance, if we bear in mind that the term *dévot* has a highly protean character, there is little difficulty in seeing Richelieu the bishop as a *dévot*. The evidence presented in this chapter should suffice to show how typical he was during his years at Luçon of the younger generation of bishops who set themselves the task of reforming their dioceses, who were open to new ideas and methods, and who legislated, preached and visited their dioceses. Like them, he was not content to 'administer' his diocese in a formal way and from a distance, whether it be Coussay or Poitiers. Of course, it is possible that Richelieu became discouraged at the lack, or at least the slowness, of change within his own diocese, and that as a result he lived there less and less after his early years as a bishop. But the import of this shift ought not to be exaggerated. It is in this connection that his scholarly and polemical pursuits become more rather than less significant. When he arrived in Poitou, there was no escaping the intellectual and pastoral superiority of the Huguenot church, which was exemplified by the Saumur academy and by the calibre of its graduates. Richelieu's association with the bishop of Poitiers and his circle, his use of the Oratory and the Capuchins, and his employment of Richard Smith show that he was part of a determined effort to build up a Catholic counterpart to this Huguenot ascendancy in Poitou. It is less important to determine who was the first to realize

religieuse du xviie siècle: la Compagnie du Saint-Sacrement', *Revue des Deux Mondes*, 16 (1903), pp. 49–82, 540–63: 17 (1903), pp. 103–35. There is also a recent synthesis by Alain Tallon, *La Compagnie du Saint-Sacrement (1629–1667). Spiritualité et société* (Paris 1990).

104 Louis Chatellier, *The Europe of the Devout. The Catholic Reformation and the Formation of a New Society* (Cambridge 1989), is by far the best analysis of this phenomenon.

105 See Jean Dagens, *Bérulle et les origines de la restauration catholique (1575–1611)* (Paris 1952), for the best account of the intellectual and spiritual influences at work after the wars of religion. There is substantial material on the religious life of the capital in René Pillorget, *Paris sous les premiers Bourbons (Nouvelle Histoire de Paris)* (Paris 1988), ch. 11.

the necessity of doing so than to note the concentration of effort and of men engaged in it during the mid-1610s; it is also worth noting that the *Compagnie du Saint-Sacrement* established in Poitiers in the 1640s perpetuated this strongly anti-Protestant stance.[106] Success in this endeavour would serve to raise the prestige of Catholicism throughout the province, and thus assist in the process of internal church reform. By its nature, however, this enterprise could not be confined to individual dioceses, and it was here that the background and associations of men like Richelieu, La Rocheposay and Duvergier de Hauranne proved invaluable in adapting *dévot* influences to provincial circumstances. They moved easily back and forth between Paris and the provinces, transferring ideas and experiences from one to the other – and not always merely from Paris to the provinces – and laying the foundations for the better-known *dévots* of later generations. Even for men without political ambitions, such activities also opened the door to a wider would beyond Luçon and Poitou. To a very considerable extent, Richelieu's earliest political experiences grew directly out of them.

---

106 Tallon, *Compagnie du Saint-Sacrement*, p. 34.

Chapter 4

THE MAKING OF A
POLITICIAN 1607–17

'La plus belle charge de la cour, c'est la faveur.'[1]

THERE can be few political careers on which the weight of hindsight lies so heavily as that of Richelieu. To generations of French political thinkers, writers and historians, he is virtually the incarnation of the French state at a crucial period of its history: his career seems so much a matter of destiny as to lose its historical individuality, and to be largely removed from the realm of the contingent to which ordinary mortals tend to be confined. This conviction is most succinctly expressed in the words of one admiring historian – 'tout ce qu'il a fait, il l'a voulu'. It is as if both history and necessity saw to it that his talents, his 'hautes vues', and superior genius would inevitably find their proper stage. The vexed question of how individual talent or genius could gain recognition, let alone power, in a society like that of early seventeenth-century France, becomes, in such a perspective, subordinate. Yet, if recent historiography has taught us anything about this society, it is how little scope there was for 'outsiders' to make their own way in the social, economic or political world. In all spheres, and *a fortiori* the political, success was dependent upon a firm and broad base of support from family, friends, clients and relations, and advancement took place within certain well-defined institutional settings. The main challenge in any attempt to reconstruct Richelieu's political career must, therefore, be to rely as little as possible on the benefits of hindsight, and to treat him as one political figure among many others, identifying the successive contexts in which he deployed his talent and ambitions without prejudging the consequences of his actions at any stage along the road to power.

The search for the origins, or at least the first manifestation, of political ambition is hard for the historian to forego. It is ironic that in the case of one so supremely 'political' as Richelieu, the search should yield so little. It is quite possible – but entirely unprovable –

---

1 Robert Arnauld d'Andilly, *Journal inédit (1614–1620)*, ed. Achille Halphen (Paris 1857), p. 168. This is referred to hereafter as *Journal d'Arnauld 1614–20*.

that on his return to France in 1607, he was hoping that he would have an opportunity to display his desire to serve the crown, and that he was encouraged to think along these lines by his success in Rome, and by the papal recommendations that had preceeded his arrival at court. Yet, such an assumption immediately raises the question of what opportunities might have been open to him, apart from an 'ordinary' place in the king's ecclesiastical household. This was a very confined arena indeed, and would not have been in any sense political; as we saw, his honorary court almonership merely enabled him to preach occasionally in the royal chapel. Nor could it have escaped his notice that the favour enjoyed by his model, du Perron, though bringing him far greater honours, was not enough to prevent the door to the king's council remaining firmly closed to him. In the short term, Richelieu's ambitions would necessarily have been limited to 'appearing at court'. For many years, his biographers thought they possessed the first expression of his own thinking on this subject in the 'Instructions et maximes que je me suis données pour me conduire à la cour', discovered and published over a century ago.[2] Hanotaux, who argued they had been composed around 1609, was the first to give them wide circulation, but though he later realized they had not been written by Richelieu at all, many studies of Richelieu have continued to cling to them as somehow representative of the 'courtier mind' and, therefore, applicable to Richelieu.[3] The fact is that Richelieu did not really need to indulge in such an exercise, especially at that particular time: he had already appeared at court; he was known to Henri IV, Sully, du Perron and others; and around 1609 at least, he was more concerned to govern his diocese than to haunt the court.

Moreover, it would be equally mistaken to think that Richelieu was pursuing purely individual ambitions from the time he became a bishop. In this respect, the notion that he suddenly became the focus and the bearer of the Richelieu family hopes and ambitions needs serious qualification. Comparison with other noble families whose younger sons became bishops makes it abundantly clear that they were not regarded as the principal vehicle of family aspirations. Richelieu, as we saw, owed his bishopric almost entirely to his eldest brother's efforts; if anyone enjoyed royal goodwill, it was Henri, who by 1607 was a practised courtier, and much better placed than Armand to pursue family interests. Still only in his mid-twenties and yet to marry, Henri held virtually all the reins: he had already been busy salvaging what he could of his father's bankrupt estate, and

2   Edited by Armand Baschet (Paris 1880).
3   Hanotaux, *Richelieu* (2nd ed.), I, pp. 129–32, 551.

would continue to do so until his premature death in 1619. In all this, Armand played scarcely any part, except perhaps that of an occasional counsellor.[4] Henri was the unquestioned head of the family and, when Armand moved to Luçon in 1608, it was this elder brother, closely seconded by his sister Francoise's husband, René de Vignerot, *seigneur* du Pont de Courlay, who was ideally placed at court to assist and promote his career – not the reverse. The fact that the French ambassador in Rome – and others, too – referred to the future Cardinal around 1607 as 'le frère de Monsieur de Richelieu', should make it clear that he had still some way to go before emerging into the limelight. Only when he began to make his way in court politics did the internal balance of the Richelieu family undergo a significant shift.

At the same time, Richelieu's elevation to the episcopate did provide him with opportunities not normally available to many nobles and courtiers. His office was anything but honorific, and though much depended on the character of the incumbent, it carried with it independence as well as authority. Richelieu's own behaviour exemplifies this perfectly: in late 1616, he resisted Concini's suggestion that he resign his bishopric, a step which would have made him wholly dependent on Concini; when he did resign Luçon, it was in 1623, and by then his cardinal's hat more than compensated for the loss of episcopal rank. With relations between church and state – or more precisely between the holders of secular and ecclesiastical authority – still so inextricably intertwined, a bishop in his diocese was inevitably to some extent a political figure, someone on whom the crown counted to maintain 'la paix et repos de nos subjects'. This was perhaps truer in certain parts of France than others, either because of the way some provinces were governed, or because of the political problems they contained. Early-seventeenth century Poitou was not the most peaceful of provinces. It had been deeply involved in, and heavily affected by, the wars of religion. Both the nobility and the towns were divided between Catholic and Huguenot, and existing tensions were exacerbated by the polemics of the Huguenot academy at Saumur and the Jesuits at Poitiers, the promotion of Catholic missions, and so on. We have already seen that, as both reformer and administrator, Richelieu found himself looking for allies and support at court and in the ministry in his efforts to deal with some of the consequences of this state of affairs. However much he might wish to find a role at court, not finding one was far from depriving him of opportunities to display his political talents and his

---

4 *Ibid.*, I, p. 138, n. 1, quoting an unpublished letter from Armand to Henri, 26 Dec. 1611: 'Nous sommes frères, je vous parle à coeur ouvert en ceste qualité'.

readiness to serve the crown; it was a question of finding the conditions in which to exploit them to best advantage.

There are few signs that Richelieu was in any position to serve Henri IV before the king was assassinated in May 1610. That event found the young bishop at Coussay near Richelieu, and it was Sébastien Bouthillier, then temporarily in Paris and acting there as his agent, who recounted to him in great detail the king's death and the rapid installation of Marie de' Medici as regent.[5] Shortly after this, Bouthillier wrote again regretting Richelieu's absence from Paris, and particularly that he could not take the opportunity to deliver a funeral oration, as bishops like Cospeau and Miron of Angers were doing. He felt sure that Richelieu would make the most of an occasion of this kind to distinguish himself.[6] But fear of disorder may well have dissuaded Richelieu from leaving for Paris immediately, though apparently he did write promptly to Marie de' Medici.[7] Other letters from Richelieu, addressed to the king's confessor Père Coton and to Gilles de Souvré, Louis XIII's governor, were delivered by Bouthillier; they drew favourable, if formal, responses from both men.[8] Richelieu's neighbour and brother of the future bishop of Poitiers, Chasteignier de la Rocheposay, wrote to Chancellor Sillery, offering his services to the king and regent, and reporting on assemblies of nobles and movements of troops since the king's assassination.[9] That Richelieu was seriously affected by Henri IV's sudden removal and fearful of a repeat of the disorders of the previous century, is clear from an even more original initiative he took within days of hearing of the king's death – a spontaneous oath of loyalty taken by himself and his clergy and submitted to the regent and the king.[10] Where this idea came from we do not know, any more than we know how he persuaded his clergy to follow his lead. Its strange, exaggerated language suggests a confused mixture of genuine devotion to the crown and a desire to offer his personal services to Marie. But if it was designed to bring its author to the regent's attention, it backfired quite comprehensively. Rather than bring it to Paris himself, Richelieu sent it post haste to his brother, Henri, who was to seek the best opportunity to present it to Marie.

5   Richelieu, *Mémoires*, I, pp. 431–4, 16 May 1610.
6   A.A.E. France 767, fo. 205, 22 May.
7   Marvick, *Young Richelieu*, p. 165.
8   A.A.E. France 767, fo. 205, 22 May. Bouthillier also reported that Henri du Plessis and Pont Courlay had also written to Richelieu.
9   A.A.E. France 767, fo. 206, letter of 23 May 1610.
10 Avenel, *Lettres*, I, pp. 53–4. The three manuscript copies of this oath bear three different dates – 20, 21, 22 May respectively – and a postscript on one of them asks for no place-name to be attached 'as that will be done at both Coussay and Luçon'. From this it seems that Richelieu anticipated the consent of his Chapter and clergy at Luçon.

But no such presentation took place, and a month later, Bouthillier explained that Henri and Pont Courlay both judged it impolitic to present the oath; as Bouthillier had taken pains to ascertain, 'cela n'avoit esté practiqué par personne'.[11] Such actions were evidently embarrassing reminders of the civil wars when oaths of loyalty and union were common; a generation later they seemed to suggest that loyalty to the king was something subjects voluntarily took it upon themselves to proclaim. Precarious though the regency might be, it had no wish to stir up political activity by encouraging subjects, great or small, to band together even for purposes which might in themselves be laudable. When the duc de Vendôme offered a written assurance of his fidelity to Marie de' Medici a few years later, she refused it, replying that 'he could offer no greater assurance than that to which he was obliged by birth'.[12] Richelieu's oath of loyalty was returned to him and to the obscurity of his archives.

This false move was known only to a narrow circle at court, and therefore unlikely to do Richelieu any damage, for within a week or so of receiving Bouthillier's account of its fate, he announced that he would after all set out for Paris. Bouthillier's detailed reports from the capital, especially about the reactions there to the bishop's own *lettres de politesse*, suggest that Richelieu was keen to know how leading clerics and courtiers were disposed towards him, probably in the hope of presenting himself, if not to the regent personally, at least to her entourage. But his intention of visiting Paris every year, which he also announced at this time, should caution against reading any clearly-defined political purpose into his action: the sudden political change enabled his growing restlessness in western Poitou to surface, while a sense of opportunity suggested this might perhaps be the best moment to return to the capital he had left eighteen months earlier.[13]

In the event, Richelieu spent at least five months in Paris from July 1610 until late November or early December. This was his longest stay there before late 1614. He was indeed received by Marie de' Medici, and even presented to her, with the vigorous support of two of her advisers, a petition on behalf of one of his acquaintances.[14] But apart from that, we simply do not know what he was doing in the capital. He would certainly have had leisure enough to observe a political scene already different from that he had known under Henri IV, one in which he would in later years learn to operate. Marie had

11   A.A.E. France 767, fo. 211, letter of 20 June 1610. A letter to the same end from Henri
     de Richelieu has unfortunately not survived.
12   *Journal d'Arnauld 1614–1620*, p. 65. This incident happened in March 1615.
13   Avenel, *Lettres*, I, p. 55, letter to Mme de Bourges, 6 June 1610.
14   *Ibid.*, I, pp. 56–7, letter, dated July 1610 by Avenel, to unknown correspondent.

retained her husband's ministers who, for the time being, remained reasonably united among themselves, though sharing an almost universal detestation of Sully. Princes of the blood like Condé and the comte de Soissons had returned to court, where the increasingly visible power of Marie's favourites, Concini and his wife Leonora Galigaï, were already a source of growing resentment. Indeed, as early as September 1610, the Spanish ambassador compared Concini's position to that of Philip III's favourite (*privado*), the duke of Lerma.[15] The comparison was more apt and unflattering than he may have intended it to be, as the Concinis were still primarily interested in accumulating wealth at the expense of the royal finances; political ambitions would come later. Over the next few years, constantly-shifting alliances would form, dissolve and re-form between combinations of great nobles, ministers and Concini, as each of the parties pressed for advantage or clung to what they possessed. In the circumstances, Richelieu cannot have had many illusions as to the extent to which his services were either needed or welcomed in the summer and autumn of 1610. As we saw, even his search for ecclesiastical preferment around this time, whether at court or in a better bishopric, yielded nothing.[16] When he returned to Luçon for Christmas 1610, he did so empty-handed.

Yet he would be back in Fontainebleau and Paris in altogether more promising circumstances within six months, this time as a result of his role as a religious reformer in Poitou. In early 1611, he was drawn into the affairs of the great abbey of Fontevraud, long subject to rule by Bourbon abbesses. When Eléonore de Bourbon died, her coadjutrix and successor-designate, the reforming Antoinette d'Orléans, refused to accept the vacant office. Years earlier, it had taken a papal order, solicited by Henri IV, to persuade Antoinette to move to Fontevraud from an obscure convent in Toulouse; now, in 1611, she insisted on retreating from Fontevraud, where her efforts at reform were not heartily welcomed, to a smaller, stricter house near Poitiers. It was, it appears, her director of conscience, Père Joseph, who sought Richelieu's help to settle this problem which, because of the individuals concerned, was of direct interest to the court. Between them, they arranged for Antoinette d'Orléans' release and the election of a new abbess, Madame de Lavedan-Bourbon, but this solution required royal approval, and in presenting it successfully at Fontainebleau in early summer 1611, Richelieu enhanced his claim to the attention of the court.[17] Indeed,

15 Quoted in Fernand Hayem, *Le Maréchal d'Ancre et Léonora Galigaï* (Paris 1910), p. 117.
16 See ch. 3, pp. 83–4.
17 Lacroix, *Richelieu à Luçon*, pp. 182ff.

he was by now sufficiently hopeful to take his own advice of the previous year and, earlier lamentations about the cost of living in Paris now forgotten, rented a house in Paris from his old friend, Denis Bouthillier.[18] This time his stay was much shorter – two to three months at most – but he appears to have made more fruitful contact with the regent and some of her advisers. The patents for his seminary were issued and registered by the *parlement* in September 1611.[19] Although he suffered a prolonged bout of ill-health in 1611 lasting perhaps several months, he was now corresponding with important officials in Paris. His illness prevented him from meeting Méric de Vic, an active royal councillor entrusted with pacifying confessional disputes in Poitou in late 1611; from his sick-bed at Coussay, he could only offer him his future assistance, and he specifically regretted missing the opportunity to deal with Huguenot illegalities in Luçon which concerned him as a bishop.[20] If he had not yet found something that could be described as a role, his co-operation was now welcome to the crown, and it was based on his diocese and province rather than Paris.

For a bishop of Richelieu's disposition, there was, of course, much to do and to report upon from western France in the early 1610s. Poitou was a vital strategic province, home to powerful noble families and to leading Huguenots, both among the nobility and in the towns. The important Huguenot assembly of 1611, convened in Saumur under the influence of du Plessis-Mornay, took place in a changing political context, with the crown extremely nervous of the outcome. Sully had been forced out of office, the regency government was cultivating Spain with a view to dynastic marriage alliances, and some of the princes, notably Condé, were willing to play 'the Huguenot card' as part of their own political manoeuvres. But with the Huguenot leaders divided amongst themselves and suspicious of the motives of Condé, Mornay was able to steer the assembly away from adventurism. On the other hand, the crown's ban on assemblies persuaded them to create local organizations in case of trouble later, and ensured they would remain far from sure of their protection under the law.[21]

---

18   M.C., LXXIII, 277, lease contract of 19 June 1611, to come into effect on 24 June. The house was in the rue du Battoir, parish of St Cosme, which Richelieu gave as his address in a contract of 1612 (M.C., XXIII, 244, 15 March 1612) and which was the subject of the refurbishments supervised by Mme de Bourges in subsequent years. The lease was set to run for three years, and it was only when Richelieu settled at court in 1616 that he moved into something much grander, the hôtel d'Estrées.
19   Avenel, *Lettres*, I, pp. 69–70, letter to president Le Coigneux, Sept. 1611.
20   *Ibid.*, I, pp. 72–3, letter of 26 Nov. 1611.
21   J.A. Clarke, *Huguenot Warrior: The Life and Times of Henri de Rohan 1579–1638* (Hague 1966), pp. 33ff.

That Richelieu's activities remained primarily ecclesiastical at this time is no less evident. In late 1611, he tried to secure election as deputy for the ecclesiastical province of Bordeaux to the Assembly of Clergy due to meet in Paris the following spring. In a letter to Cardinal Sourdis, he expressed his willingness to serve if the rumours he had heard to the effect that there was wide support for his candidature were indeed genuine; and he sent off canon Bouthillier to put his case at Bordeaux.[22] Quite what happened there is not known: Richelieu's precipitation in attempting to pre-empt the election may not have been appreciated or he may have withdrawn.[23] At any rate, he was not elected, although Bouthillier was chosen to represent the second-order clergy. The assembly was not a major decennial assembly – that was not due until 1615 – so his non-election was perhaps not a serious reverse; nevertheless, as he himself probably realized, membership of it could have been turned to account when the assembly dealt with ministers. In the event, Richelieu was back in Paris even before the assembly convened there in May 1612. He had an important lawsuit before the *parlement* for the 'conservation du bien de l'Eglise', and that may have been enough to bring him to the capital.[24] Unlike 1611, there is no evidence of any other specific mission, so he may simply have been intent on reminding ministers and patrons of his existence. Again, it is notable that his recorded appearances there were essentially ecclesiastical in nature. Although there is no corroborative evidence, Edmond Richer claimed that Richelieu attended the so-called provincial council of Sens called by du Perron in March 1612 to condemn Richer's strongly gallican tract on political and ecclesiastical power.[25] If he did attend, the occasion would have been embarrassing enough for him: his patron du Perron, who was still *bien en cour*, was deeply hostile to Richer, while Richelieu's own sentiments, at least judging by later evidence, would have been more gallican. If his presence at

22 Avenel, *Lettres*, I, pp. 70–1, letter to Sourdis, 25 Nov. 1611; *ibid.*, pp. 100–2, two undated letters to Sourdis about these elections. Avenel (p. 70, n. 2) confuses the assembly in question with the one which would condemn Richer. See below, n. 25.

23 Sourdis himself, who as a Cardinal did not need to be elected, had to press for permission to attend this assembly, as Marie de Medici evidently preferred to see him active in keeping the peace in Guyenne: B.N., MS. Fr. 6379, fo. 82, Marie to Sourdis, 7 May 1612.

24 Avenel, *Lettres*, I, p. 131, undated letter to Monsieur [. . .] which Avenel tentatively assigned to 1614. The case, about 'une rente qui m'est deue à cause de mon evesché', was settled on 12 March 1612, as appears from a notarized agreement between Richelieu and his opponent of 15 March: M.C. XXIII, 244. The letter should, therefore, be dated early 1612.

25 *Histoire du syndicat d'Edmond Richer, par Edmond Richer lui-même* (Avignon 1753), pp. 89–104. Richelieu's signature does not figure on the assembly's condemnation of Richer's book.

this gathering is mentioned in no other source, it was probably because, like his friend Laubespine, he knew when to keep quiet and to avoid any declaration likely to offend more powerful clergy.[26] Better recorded, if inherently less significant, is the fact that he preached before the king, regent and court in the church of St André des Arts in March 1612 – the only known instance of his preaching in Paris since he became a bishop. He was due to preach again in the Louvre on Easter Sunday, but had to withdraw at short notice.[27] Although his preaching skills elicited no comment from contemporaries, it is clear enough that Richelieu was by now a bishop who moved in increasingly wide circles.

There is every reason to think that Richelieu left Paris in a hurry just before Easter 1612. One of the Huguenot leaders, the duc de Rohan, had just seized control of the important fortress town of St Jean d'Angély, in western Poitou, and it was widely feared his action might ignite a serious rebellion in the region.[28] Richelieu's diocese would have been directly affected, and he probably did not need the court to urge him to return and report on developments there, which is precisely what he did.[29] The earliest evidence of his correspondence with Phélypeaux de Pontchartrain, the secretary of state most concerned with Huguenot and provincial affairs, dates from April 1612. Richelieu's activity was at most indirect, and limited to reporting (optimistically) on his conversations with Mornay, as well as conveying Huguenot unease and fear of fighting other people's battles.[30] Yet the court was reluctant to believe the Huguenots had no secret designs or plans to make trouble. Its suspiciousness made work for Richelieu, yet he could find no evidence of their alleged deviousness. If Richelieu's first report to Phélypeaux affords no distinctive insight into either the Huguenots' attitudes, or his own, another letter written possibly around this time contains the first political statement of interest by him on record: 'For although the present disputes and some unpleasant predictions seem to augur and presage war, I do not think that it can break out quickly, since the means of those who desire it are greatly inferior to their determination. The wise behaviour, affection and fidelity of [the king's] good

---

26 Marvick, *Young Richelieu*, pp. 176–7. There is no doubt that he was in Paris, while the assembly was meeting, as witness the agreement of 15 March.

27 *Ibid.*, pp. 177–8, and n. 72. The source for this is the diary of Louis XIII's Huguenot physician, Jean Héroard. One of Richelieu's propagandists later claimed the king and regent frequently honoured him (i.e. when he preached) with their presence, but there is no independent evidence for this.

28 Clarke, *Huguenot Warrior*, pp. 42ff; Marvick, *Young Richelieu*, p. 178.

29 Such a brief is confirmed by Méric de Vic in his reply to Richelieu's lost letter of 13 May 1612: A.A.E. France 768, fo. 216, 25 Aug. Specifically, Richelieu was to keep an eye on the Huguenot ministers, and to supply their names and opinions.

30 Avenel, *Lettres*, I, pp. 82–4, letter to Pontchartrain. Avenel wrongly gives the date as March 1612, when Richelieu was still in Paris.

servants will preserve us from disturbances at home.'[31] Such a mixture of shrewd realism and wishful thinking reflects an impulsiveness Richelieu would later learn to restrain, but never wholly suppress.

By late 1612, Richelieu was also ready to throw himself into confessional polemic and theological controversy, albeit of an academic kind. As we have seen, his friends imagined this was because he had some 'glorious design' in mind, but Bishop Laubespine seems to have been slightly uneasy, given that Richelieu was a new to such a troublesome discipline.[32] Leaving aside the surprise his decision evinced, the study of the religious controversies was an occupation which corresponded closely to his 'political' role to date, which was focused almost entirely on Huguenot activities and intentions; winning a wider reputation for himself through scholarly endeavours in an age when confessional debate was all the rage was a natural enough road for him to take at this juncture. Replying to one of his letters in late March 1613, de Vic expressed the contemporary perception of Richelieu's position quite accurately: he began by praising him for the 'the care you daily take to augment the Catholic religion', and went on to ask him to act as mediator in a row brewing between the bishop and dean of Poitiers cathedral.[33] Scholarship clearly did not signify withdrawal from active life, but 1613 must rank with 1609 as one of the least documented years of Richelieu's early career. It did, however, witness another visit to Paris, during which he renegotiated the terms of Richard Smith's service to him with Smith's fellow divines of the college of Arras.[34]

In sharp contrast, 1614 has always ranked as something of an *annus mirabilis*, one which opened up unexpected political opportunities. But there is, as we shall see, a great deal of exaggeration as far as Richelieu's role is concerned. In January, the long fuse of aristocratic discontent finally burned out, and one after another the leading princes quit the court to signal their dissatisfaction with Concini and the ministry. A new age of princely 'declarations' began with Condé's scathing attack on the régime's record, and that in turn triggered off an outburst of pamphleteering such as had not been seen since the end of the wars of religion.[35] Individual 'departures' from court had been common enough in previous years, but

---

31 *Ibid.*, I, pp. 86–7, letter to Monsieur du Préau. Arguing from a reference in Richelieu's *Mémoires*, Avenel assigned this to the middle of 1612, but there is little certainty about this connection.

32 A.A.E. France 768, fo. 212, letter of 6 Feb. 1613.

33 A.A.E. France 769, fo. 4, letter of 24 March 1613.

34 A.A.W. A 12, no. 125, p. 277, Smith to Thomas More, Paris 2 July 1613. It was on this occasion that Cardinal du Perron was asked to arbitrate between Richelieu and the English divines.

35 Condé's manifesto is in A.A.E., France 769, fos. 98–143. Much of what follows is taken from Hayden, *France and the Estates General*, ch. 4, 'The revolt of the princes'. See also

the crown, enjoying support from the Guises, Épernon and others, had been strong enough to deal with them. The fact that, talk of 'reform' and the 'public good' notwithstanding, the *grands* had no real common purpose in early 1614, did not lessen the danger their action represented, and the crown's principal concern was to prevent the contagion from spreading to uncommitted nobles and to the Huguenots. It has been claimed that Richelieu travelled to Paris at this time, and received an appointment in the private service of the queen, but there is no evidence for it.[36] Indeed, it is difficult to imagine he would have wished to journey to the capital, let alone been of much use there, now that the leading nobles had repaired to the provinces; Condé, the principal malcontent, had initially gone to Châteauroux in Berry, a province uncomfortably close to Poitou. If the court needed Richelieu's services at all, it was to help hold the line in his own province. What is documented is that he was quick to manifest his loyalty, and that he did so in a way which would presage his political affiliations over the next few years: in February 1614, he addressed a fulsome letter of support and service to Concini, who must have seemed to him, from his earlier experiences of Marie de' Medici's court, to represent the main hope for the continuity and stability of the régime.[37] Over the next few months, he could do little but wait like everyone else while the princes and the crown both raised troops, manoeuvred, and then sat down to negotiate what became, in May 1614, the Treaty of Ste Ménehould, one clause of which incorporated earlier princely demands for an Estates General. But the crisis of royal authority was not as neatly resolved as that. Despite the treaty, the duc de Vendôme, bastard brother of Louis XIII, held out in Brittany, and an attack on Nantes was feared. Further south in Poitou and Guyenne, the crown also feared a spread of sedition. In June, we find one of Richelieu's local correspondents busy spying on a Huguenot assembly at Fontenay, but failing to discover their asssumed 'secret designs'.[38] One of the most celebrated incidents of the year was in June–July 1614, after the signature of the Treaty of Ste Ménehould, when Condé failed in his attempt to enter Poitiers, where Bishop La Rocheposay, arms in hand, repeated his earlier success in frustrating Condé's supporters' plans to seize control.[39] How near Richelieu was to the

Hayden, 'The Uses of Political Pamphlets: The Example of 1614–15 in France', *Canadian Journal of History* 21 (1986), pp. 143–65, for useful observations and data about the propaganda wars. See Denis Richet, 'La Polémique politique en France de 1612 à 1615', in Roger Chartier and Denis Richet, *Représentation et vouloir politiques. Autour des états-généraux de 1614* (Paris 1982), pp. 151–94.
36   Marvick, *Young Richelieu*, p. 185.
37   Avenel, *Lettres*, I, pp. 121ff, letter of 12 Feb. 1614.
38   A.A.E. France 769, fo. 171, letter from Hilaire Goguet, 29 June 1614.

scene of this confrontation is not known, but he was almost certainly in the province at the time. His biographers stress his active support for royal policies throughout this crisis, and draw attention to the instructions he received from ministers to negotiate with potential malcontents and the Huguenots. But a broader perspective shows that he was not unique in this respect. La Rocheposay had received similar instructions in early 1614, while in the vital and much larger province of Guyenne, both resistance to Condé and negotiations to maintain Huguenot quiescence were led by Richelieu's metropolitan, Cardinal Sourdis.[40] Certainly, when compared to the notoriety and seriousness of the Condé-La Rocheposay confrontations – which St Cyran 'immortalized' in his apologia for the bishop[41] – Richelieu's activities seem rather modest.

The crown's pledge to hold an Estates General had to be implemented quickly, as the rebel princes were adamant that it meet before the king attained his majority on 2 October 1614. Given such high stakes, it was no accident that the court's western progress from July to September, designed to secure the return of loyal deputies to the Estates, should have spent so much time in Poitou, with stops at towns like Loudun, Poitiers, Chatellerault and Saumur, at any one of which Richelieu could have easily renewed his contacts with leading royal officials.[42] He had apparently received advance notice of the royal letters convening the Estates General, which were followed, in late June, by an official letter from Sully as governor of Poitou, asking him to ensure the return of deputies known for their loyalty to the crown.[43] Greater encouragement than that he hardly needed, all the more so as his colleague, La Rocheposay, who was not anxious to put his own name forward, ardently championed Richelieu's candidature to represent the clergy of Poitou. That, rather than the mere record of Richelieu's diligent royalism, produced a favourable outcome, where a competition between the two bishops at this juncture might well not have ended to his advantage. This time, there was no need to deal with Sourdis, who was equally busy performing the same function of ensuring favourable results in Guyenne.[44] Letters to Richelieu from La Rocheposay show the

---

39   For Condé's movements, see Henri d'Orléans, duc d'Aumale, *Histoire des princes de Condé*, vol. III (Paris 1886), pp. 28ff. Condé's letter of 11 July to Marie, full of bitter recrimination against La Rocheposay, is at pp. 31–2. See also Clarke, *Huguenot Warrior*, pp. 51–2.

40   Orcibal, *St Cyran*, pp. 177–8, and p. 178, n. 1. (La Rocheposay); Hayden, *France and the Estates General*, p. 65 (Sourdis).

41   See ch. 3, p. 110.

42   Hayden, *France and the Estates General*, pp. 79–80; Marvick, *Young Richelieu*, p. 187, admits there is no record of any such meeting.

43   A.A.E. France 769, fo. 169, letter of 23 June.

44   Hayden, *France and the Estates General*, p. 73.

latter, ably seconded by Duvergier, organizing the detail of the
elections, consulting his clergy, and arranging the meetings of all
three estates of Poitou for mid-August 1614. The only difficulty
arose over whether to elect a second deputy, since the second-order
clergy insisted on being represented.[45] Indeed, so thorough was this
preparatory work, that it seems Richelieu did not bother to turn up
at Poitiers for the elections beginning on 12 August.[46] By comparison, the more serious business of drafting the *cahiers des doléances* was
spread over several weeks. For one so careful as Richelieu to preserve
his papers relating to the Estates General, it is surprising to find no
reference at all to the primary assemblies of the Luçon clergy nor any
trace of their *cahiers*; only that of the clergy of Poitou, which he
probably helped to compile and which he was to present to the
Estates General, has survived among his papers.[47] His mandate was
to demand reforms and defend church interests; his own personal
ambitions were no business of the clergy of Poitou.

In a wider context, the efforts of Richelieu, La Rocheposay and
Sourdis, as well no doubt as of other prelates elsewhere in France,
are evidence that, given disaffection and uncertainty among the
nobility, the crown was forced to rely increasingly on churchmen.
No wonder they – and not just Richelieu – would feel entitled at the
Estates General to assert that they would make the most disinterested
advisers, and that they should be admitted to the council chamber.
This pressure would be further increased by the nature of the issues
raised at the Estates, and the later attempts to implement their
demands.

II

Few of those who have followed the rise of Richelieu have doubted
the importance of the 1614 Estates General to his career, nor the
quality of his performance there. His own later verdict on the assembly itself was, as is well known, scathing: such gatherings were
useless for any purpose save that of finding ways of implementing
decisions made by an enlightened few. But we can assume that no
such thought crosssed his mind when the Estates formally opened in
October 1614 – after rather than before the king's majority had been
declared, and in Paris rather than in Sens, as had originally been

45 Hanotaux, *Richelieu*, I, pp. 148–9, quotes extensively from two unpublished letters.
    These events also demonstrate the 'seniority' of the see of Poitiers, in practice as well as
    in theory, at this time.
46 *Ibid.*, I, 149–50, for La Rocheposay's letter.
47 A.A.E. France 769, fos. 180–90. It is filed alongside with that of the clergy of Angers,
    fos. 191–98.

intended. Equally, the view that 'this assembly has no other claim to fame save that of having counted him among its members', takes little account of the political scene nor of institutional realities, and is unlikely to afford us much insight into either Richelieu's progress or the real part he played in its proceedings.[48]

For several reasons, it is fair to say that Richelieu's role at the Estates General was not especially remarkable and, were it not for the fact that he was chosen by the clergy to address the king at the end of the assembly, he might have attracted no more mention than the bulk of the other bishops in attendance. To begin with, the affairs of the clerical estate were firmly in the hands of older, more experienced clergy, especially cardinals such as Sourdis, du Perron, La Rochefoucauld and Joyeuse; close behind them came senior bishops like Marquemont of Lyon or Miron of Angers. Sourdis, in particular, enjoyed the regent's favour, presiding over the bulk of the sessions, setting the agenda, appointing delegations, and even deciding who should preach during the Sunday services for the assembled Estates. Du Perron's promise of years earlier to give way to younger prelates like Richelieu was now irrelevant in the changed political circumstances. Moreover, room for individual initiative was severely curtailed, as all motions and propositions had first to be supported by the 'gouvernement' to which a deputy belonged; in Richelieu's case, the clerical contingent for the vast 'gouvernement' of the Orléanais appears to have been dominated by the forceful and pro-papal bishop of Angers, Charles Miron. The clergy were quickly cast in the role of mediators between the other estates, partly because of their experience of holding regular assemblies of their own, and the crown was content to put its trust in this established clerical leadership.[49]

The formal records of the debates of the Estates General are distressingly laconic and, even when they are supplemented by diaries and correspondence, there is little sign that Richelieu took a noteworthy part in the great debates that roused the passions of deputies of all orders. From one who was already regarded as effective and articulate, such silence must have been seen as at least partly voluntary. In this context, it is odd that, despite Sourdis's patronage, he did not once preach before the Estates during their eighteen weeks in session, and it was the controversial sermons of his near contemporary Jean-Pierre Camus, bishop of Belley, which attracted most attention.[50]

48 Hanotaux, *Richelieu*, II, p. 13.
49 The fullest and most reliable study of the Estates, based on exhaustive research, is Hayden, *France and the Estates General*, esp. chs. 6–9.
50 See Jean-Pierre Camus, *Homélies des Etats Généraux (1614–1615)*, ed. Jean Descrains (Geneva 1970). Camus's sermons were strong, almost intemperate, attacks upon current

Because of the separate meetings of the three estates and the rows which erupted between them, each one spent much of its time sending delegations to the others to seek support or to settle disputes. Richelieu was one of the many bishops chosen to lead ecclesiastical delegations to both the nobles and the Third Estate but not, significantly, to the court.[51] Even a brief survey of his Estate's record shows that other bishops – including friends like Laubespine, but many lesser-known figures – were much more active in this respect than he was.[52] When truly serious questions arose, it was the senior clergy, cardinals such as du Perron and Sourdis, who took the lead and put the clergy's case to the other estates.[53] That, and Richelieu's silence during major debates, suggests that the clergy regarded him as a useful diplomat but that, when it came to major clashes of a substantive nature, especially over 'receiving' the decrees of the Council of Trent in France, or the Third Estate's attempt to define royal sovereignty in a way that many saw as anti-papal, the clergy preferred Miron or du Perron to defend their position and take a tough line with the other Estates. For example, Richelieu was sent in early November 1614 to persuade the Third Estate to accept the idea that specific matters of major concern to all three Estates should be handled jointly, but his diplomacy failed to dispel their suspicions of the clergy's motives.[54] In the arguments over the *droit annuel* of the office-holders and the article on royal sovereignty, Richelieu's involvement came about only after several other bishops had been employed (especially over the second issue), and was apparently designed to find a compromise or to calm tempers. After several discussions with members of the Third Estate, Richelieu would report back to the clergy in detail and at considerable length, but there is no hint of any personal view on the issues in dispute.[55] In January 1615, he led a deputation to the nobility to persuade the latter to join the clergy in a protest to the crown against action taken by the *parlement* of Paris in the controversy over royal sovereignty and the related question of tyrannicide, but his name does not appear in any record of subsequent dealings on this matter.[56] In no instance

abuses, especially among the clergy, and won him a reputation as something of a firebrand. By comparison, other sermons, and most speeches, delivered during the Estates appear relatively anodyne. See the list of preachers for the duration of the Estates: *ibid.*, p. 81.

51   Hayden, *France and the Estates General*, p. 111.
52   A.N. G 8* 632b. Copy of the *procès-verbal* of the ecclesiastical estate.
53   The history of the clergy's role in the Estates General is well covered by Pierre Blet, *Le Clergé de France et la monarchie* (Rome 1959), I, pt 1.
54   Marvick, *Young Richelieu*, p. 193; Hanotaux, *Richelieu*, II, pp. 21–2.
55   A.N. G 8* 632b, 20 Nov. 1614: '[il] s'est fort étendu et expliqué'. See Blet, *Clergé et monarchie*, I, pp. 33–5, 40ff.
56   A.N. G 8* 632b, 5 Jan. 1615.

does he appear to have become involved in a debate on issues; by confining himself strictly to his brief, he left neither hostages to fortune nor untidy disputes for others to clear up later. We are thus left to speculate on the underlying motives for his behaviour during the Estates. It seems reasonable to assume that he tried to negotiate a safe path through the major confrontations of the assembly. He may have been less than wholly content with the strongly pro-papal assertiveness of some of his fellow bishops, but if he was to retain the goodwill of Sourdis, du Perron and others on whose patronage he depended, he needed to keep such reservations to himself. By giving him mainly diplomatic assignments, the clergy left him in peace.

Hindsight might suggest that while others indulged in controversy Richelieu was playing a different, unrecorded game in the wings, perhaps acting as a discreet, unofficial liaison between the court, individual ministers, and the clergy. That he may have done so cannot be entirely ruled out, but there is no evidence for it. The fact that Henri de Richelieu married Marguerite Guiot in Paris and in considerable privacy in January 1615 while the Estates were in session and without any notable signatures to his marriage contract, forms a striking contrast with Richelieu's subsequent behaviour, and suggests a limited social role for Richelieu at this time.[57] Nor does his name figure anywhere in the despatches of the foreign diplomats who closely followed the Estates, or in the memoirs of the period relating to them. This inevitably raises the question of why he should have been chosen to give the final address to the crown on behalf of the clergy. It should be noted, first of all, that he had narrowly missed being selected to give the opening address in October 1614, and that he would thus have remained a candidate for later selection. More to the point perhaps, his role during the Estates was such that by 23 January 1615, when he was chosen for the task, he could appear, to both the clergy and the other estates, as a deputy who had not been compromised by any of the often angry disputes or the *prises de position* to which they had given rise. Above all, the crown, which had managed to control much of the agenda during the four months the Estates had been in session, would have been happy with such a choice, reducing as it did the risks of embarrassment from a more independently-minded cleric: a Richelieu was certainly preferable to a Camus or a Miron. With the clergy counting strongly on the crown to support their demands, they were anxious to find a spokesman who was obviously *persona grata*. Thus, thanks to a mixture of royal prompting and the patronage of Sourdis and du

---

57 M.C., CVII, 109, marriage contract of 15 Jan. Only Richelieu and Pont Courlay signed on behalf of Henri, who was by then a *mestre de camp* in the Piedmont regiment.

Perron, Richelieu had little difficulty securing the vote. It was thus fitting enough that, when he came to speak publicly, it should have not been in his own name, but as the representative of the clergy.

It was not until a month later, on 23 February, that Richelieu was called on to present the clergy's *cahier* and to deliver his harangue. Before doing so, he asked the clergy to indicate to him the points he should raise in his speech, and he was supplied with a list. As this occurred on the same day that he was to give his address, which lasted over an hour, he may himself have suggested most or all of the thirteen points he was to cover. That in turn may indicate that he simply wanted official sanction for something he had already planned to do on his own initiative, but equally it shows that official approval was essential; it is difficult to imagine a body as experienced and vigilant as the clergy giving that approval, if it were unsure of the outcome. It is obvious that, while he might wish to make as much of this opportunity as possible, Richelieu was bound to follow convention and convey the main thrust of the clergy's grievances.[58]

Because the assembly was an Estates General concerned with the state of the realm, and not an Assembly of Clergy focusing on narrower ecclesiastical issues, there was nothing perverse or 'secular' about Richelieu's raising in his address questions such as the liberality of princes, excessive taxation, or the disastrous effects of the sale of office on both government and the nobility: these, after all, had been hotly debated by the Estates, and the clergy had found themselves drawn into disputes over them between the other two chambers.[59] It was, of course, in his long defence of the rightness of rulers' employing ecclesiastics as councillors that Richelieu was best able to combine a genuine clerical demand in 1614 with his own personal ambition; recent events had persuaded the clergy that gallicans in the *parlement* and in the ranks of royal officialdom generally were hostile to clerics in high political office, and the First Estate was determined, not just in 1614 but later in the decade, to counter this pressure and make its voice heard. Richelieu's exposition of that case was not a 'hijacking' of his mandate for purely personal ends; it was a case that many of his fellow clerical deputies would feel obliged to make.[60] Indeed, much of Richelieu's exposition of it was derived from a speech made earlier during the Estates by du Perron. Moreover, it was followed almost immediately by a

---

58 Richelieu, *Mémoires*, I, pp. 340–65, is the best and most accessible modern text of this speech.

59 Marvick, *Young Richelieu*, pp. 203ff makes much of the secular and 'political' nature of this speech.

60 See Blet, *Clergé et monarchie*, II, p. 416, who argues that Richelieu's arguments could have been those of Archbishop Marquemont or of successive clerical orators of the period.

long appeal to the crown for an official adoption of the decrees of the Council of Trent, a cause even dearer to the hearts of the leaders of the clergy but which, as Richelieu knew well, was not at all popular with royal ministers and leading office-holders.[61] Even his flattery of Marie de' Medici at the end of his address, for all that it might assist his personal advancement, rested on the assumption that a continuation of her rule, though she was no longer regent, was the best guarantee that the clergy's petitions would be answered.

Richelieu was deliberately brief on certain questions because, as he said, other speakers were waiting to follow him. Though the baron de Sénécey and Robert Miron, presidents of the Second and Third Estate respectively, delivered shorter addresses, they covered many of the same issues as Richelieu and, Miron in particular, demanded far more extensive reforms.[62] All three wanted to see the Estates remain in session while the *cahiers* were being examined by the council. But the crown was already preoccupied with other problems, and was anxious to send the deputies home. Richelieu could take comfort from the favourable reaction to his speech, especially from the clergy and, in common with several other speakers and preachers at the Estates before him, he quickly arranged to have it printed and circulated as widely as possible. He was duly complimented by many who either heard his speech or read the text of it, and this gratified him, although it may have been less important to him than were the friends and contacts he made during the Estates General itself.[63]

The 'failure' of Richelieu's bid for Marie de' Medici's personal favour in early 1615, and the subsequent 'retreat' of the 'disappointed' political bishop to his residence at Coussay is firmly established in the folklore that envelops his career. The facts do not warrant such a conclusion. Though eligible, Richelieu chose not to attend the Assembly of Clergy which met almost immediately after the Estates General between May and August 1615. He may have concluded there was little point in his doing so, or he may have feared further

---

61   See Blet, *Clergé et monarchie*, I, pt. I, ch. 4, for the best account of this issue at the Estates General. See also Joseph Bergin, *Cardinal de La Rochefoucauld. Leadership and Reform in the French Church* (New Haven and London 1987), pp. 51–4.

62   See Bonney, *The King's Debts.* pp. 81–4, for the claim that the '*cahier* of the third estate was the most far-reaching criticism of financial mismanagement since the manifestos of the Catholic League, and greatly exceeded them in the penetration of its analysis and the detailed proposals for change . . . [it] influenced all moves towards financial reform until 1630' (p. 84).

63   One of those to congratulate him was his brother, the Carthusian Alphonse: A.A.E. France 770, fo. 41, letter of 29 May 1615. The bishop of Nantes and the future bishop of Chartres seem to be among those with whom Richelieu became friendly during the Estates: *ibid.*, fo. 43, letter of 21 June. Nantes also reported on events during the Assembly of Clergy.

unwelcome confrontations with the crown. His decision was not extraordinary: this Assembly of Clergy was much smaller than the recent First Estate, and several more senior prelates, such as Sourdis and Marquemont of Lyon, also returned to their dioceses at the same time as he did.[64]

If Richelieu genuinely expected his address to produce an immediate political result, it would have been a triumph of ambition over realism. By the time the deputies finally dispersed, in late March 1615, further political trouble involving Condé, the *parlement* and the office-holders, was brewing. The crown's failure to respond to the issues and demands made by the Estates themselves would soon become a new weapon in the hand of critics and rebels. Marie de' Medici was far more concerned with concluding the Spanish marriages which the Estates had supported, and of which Richelieu himself had approved in his address. Villeroy was restored to favour after a brief retreat to his estates and, despite continuing enmity between him and Chancellor Sillery, there was no obvious prospect of new faces, episcopal or otherwise, being brought into office.[65] In the circumstances, to have stayed on at court would have made Richelieu merely another absentee bishop among many. As it was, he quickly returned to the Poitiers ecclesiastical milieu, and to the studies begun in 1612 and interrupted by the events of the previous year.[66]

Within weeks of returning to Poitou, Richelieu was to resume the kind of role that he had been playing since 1612 – that of a loyalist bishop acting as the eyes and ears of the court in a potentially troublesome region.[67] A new revolt by Condé and the duc de Bouillon, protesting against the Spanish marriages and demanding the enactment of reforms proposed by the *parlement* and Estates General, began as early as May 1615. When negotiations collapsed in late July, the crown warned the towns, as it had in early 1614, to be vigilant, while Condé called for armed support. Yet, despite support from the Huguenots under Bouillon, Rohan and La Force, Condé could not prevent the court from proceeding, heavily protected by the duc de Guise's army, to Bordeaux and Bidassoa to seal the

---

64 Blet, *Clergé et monarchie*, I, pp. 125ff.

65 For a concise account of events after the Estates General, see Hayden, *France and the Estates General*, pp. 166–71.

66 A.A.W. A 14, no. 83, p. 275, Richard Smith to Thomas More, 21 April 1615, announcing Richelieu had already returned to Coussay. The deputies had been dismissed on 24 March, and Smith's letter suggests that Richelieu had been back at Coussay for sometime before 21 April. Smith also added that Richelieu's return came 'too soone for me' and had obliged him to interrupt his personal studies.

67 See his letter to Marie de' Medici on the movements of the princes in Avenel, *Lettres*, VIII, p. 9, 6 Nov. 1615.

Spanish marriages. Its prolonged halt at Poitiers during late August and much of September 1615 enabled Richelieu to effect another discreet entrée, but this time with something tangible in prospect.[68] In late July, one of his most influential mentors, Bishop Bertrand ʾd'Eschaux of Bayonne, grand almoner to Louis XIII, had written to him urging him to let his name go forward for the grand almonership to the king's bride, Anne of Austria, whose household was then being formed. This was not the first time the matter had been discussed by them, yet Eschaux still remained uncertain about whether Richelieu really desired such 'domestic' employment. Indeed, after more than one change of mind, the office had already been virtually given to their mutual friend, Bishop Laubespine of Orléans, but at the last minute Marie de' Medici had insisted on overturning the decision and withdrawing the *brevet* appointing him.[69] Richelieu seems to have known about all this, but we do not have his reply to Eschaux's renewed prompting. His behaviour – asking Eschaux, for example, to enquire into the state of Laubespine's affairs at court – suggests that, while desiring preferment, he feared he might be treated like Laubespine, and confined himself to an oblique expression of interest in the event of another embarrassing result. Nevertheless, when he called on the court at Poitiers, it seems that he received an oral promise of the grand almonership, perhaps from Marie de' Medici herself, and this commitment must have seemed reasonably firm, as he did not feel it necessary to accompany the court to the south-west. Instead, he relied upon Eschaux and Duvergier, to keep him informed of the court's doings, which both of them did.[70] Likewise, a steady flow of letters from other correspondents in late 1615 kept him abreast of the confused military and political situation, notably on the movements of the princes and leading nobles in the west and south-west.[71] He himself passed on these 'intelligences' to the queen mother. His appointment as grand almoner to the new queen of France was formally confirmed at

---

68 *Ibid.*, I, pp. 148–50, Richelieu to Marie de' Medici about illness of her daughter at Poitiers, August 1615. Avenel wrongly assigned this letter to July 1615.

69 A.A.E. France 770, fo. 50, letter of 30 July 1615. This version of events is confirmed by Francois de Malherbe: *Oeuvres*, ed. A. Regnier, 5 vols. (Paris 1862–9), III, p. 514, letter to Peiresc, 10 Aug. 1615.

70 Orcibal, *St Cyran*, p. 480, nn. 1–2, for extracts from Duvergier's letters. 'Si vous ne m'eussiez expressément commandé de vous écrire des nouvelles, je n'eusse pas pris la hardiesse de vous en écrire: tant il y a de l'incertitude en tout ce qu'on raconte' (n. 1). One of these detailed letters is in B.V.C., fonds Richelieu 14, fos. 7–8, 10 Nov. 1615.

71 See, for example, the six letters of one La Vacherie written during Sept.–Oct. 1616 in A.A.E. France 770, fos. 61–6. Richelieu's brother, Henri, was serving as a *mestre de camp* in the royal army facing Condé, and also kept him informed of events. See the letter from him in Hanotaux, *Richelieu*, II, pp. 95–6.

Bordeaux in November 1615 and, because it was a newly-created office, he received it without having to open his purse.[72]

For the time being, this new position did not produce any great effect. Although it gave him a modest toehold at court, immediate residence there was not obligatory. In some respects, the appointment may be regarded as something of a consolation prize: Richelieu was apparently not considered at all for the grand almonership to Marie de' Medici herself, vacant on the withdrawal of Cardinal Bonzi in the same year. Nor, despite its wide currency, is there any foundation for the view that he became Marie's *secrétaire des commandements* at this point, a post which, for all its ostensibly 'private' character, was extremely difficult to secure, and presupposed a measure of personal familiarity and confidence that Richelieu simply did not yet enjoy.[73] Either of these posts would, of course, have drawn him far more deeply into court life.

The court itself again halted briefly at Poitiers on its return from the south-west in January 1616, and from there moved to Tours and Blois, where it stayed until early May. Condé might not have been able to prevent the Spanish marriages, but the levy of a Huguenot army now raised the prospect of a wider and more dangerous second-phase rebellion. As before, negotiations with Condé and his supporters seemed a lesser risk than military escalation. The talks, which began in mid-February at Loudun, close to Richelieu's own residence, were not concluded until early May.[74] But with Villeroy still in charge of affairs, there was little prospect of an outsider like Richelieu enjoying even a walk-on part, and none of his former correspondents present at Loudun, such as de Vic and Pontchartrain, were in a hurry to make use of his services. But it is possible that he was kept informed of what was happening by Père Joseph, who was one of those playing the role of mediator.[75] For their part, Richelieu and his brother were reduced to protesting about the depradations to family property by the armies of the rebel princes.[76] The bishop, doubtless reluctantly, kept out of sight, only sending one of his secretaries to court to judge the lie of the land and, in particular, to

72 Avenel, *Lettres*, VIII, p. 9, letter to Marie de Medici, 6 Nov. 1615.
73 Bergin, *Richelieu*, p. 71.
74 Aumale, *Histoire des princes de Condé*, III, pp. 61ff. For a chronicle of the conference of Loudun, *Journal d'Arnauld 1614–20*, pp. 141ff. The papers and acts of the conference are published in L. Bouchitté, ed., *Négociations, lettres et pièces relatives à la conférence de Loudun* (Paris 1862).
75 See Fagniez, *Le Père Joseph et Richelieu*, I, pp. 70–3. For Nevers' role, *Journal d'Arnauld 1614–20*, p. 129.
76 Avenel, *Lettres*, I, pp. 163–4, 167, 168–9, letters to comte de Sault and duc de Nevers, Jan.–Feb. 1616. Some of these letters may have been written by Henri de Richelieu, not by Armand.

investigate rumours of an 'exchange' of some kind involving Richelieu; the matter was evidently so sensitive that the other party could only be described as the 'colosse froid en marbre'.[77] Nothing came of this enigmatic mission, whatever it was, but, when the court finally returned to Paris in May 1616, Richelieu was quick enough to follow it and, for reasons we shall see presently, he was probably made a councillor of state shortly afterwards.[78]

Richelieu may have played no part in the Treaty of Loudun, but within six months its political consequences would have a decisive impact on his career. Extensive concessions were made to Condé, to a number of his supporters, and to Huguenot leaders such as Rohan. Richelieu himself would later regard these concessions as a scandalous instance of political blackmail by irresponsible *grands*.[79] Nevertheless, the treaty, like so many attempts at reconciliation before and after 1616, was far from achieving its objectives; by seeming to reward rebellion and by redistributing governorships, pensions and other favours, it served to sharpen the resentment of the disappointed, whet the appetites of others, and increase mutual suspicion all round. Despite his gains, which included the promise of a significant role in council, Condé himself continued to be extremely suspicious of the court's motives, and showed no hurry to leave his new governorship of Berry, thereby creating further anxiety about his real intentions.[80] It was as one of several envoys despatched by Marie de' Medici to reassure the prince, to dissuade him from further thought of revolt, and to confirm the offer to him of the presidency of the council of finance, that Richelieu gained his first major opportunity to practice the kind of mediation that (however much he might later deplore the political instability which made it necessary) would play such a central part in his political career in coming years. He made the most of his opportunity when it came in June 1616, having already corresponded with Condé about his grievances before leaving court.[81] He succeeded partially because he was in a position to make some further concessions to him, one of which, ironically, was to make amends for events at Poitiers in 1614, and to allow the

77   *Ibid.*, I, pp. 164–6, letter to Charpentier, early Feb. 1616.
78   No trace has ever been found of the *brevet* appointing him a councillor, but it probably preceded his mission to Condé in late June 1616.
79   Bonney, *The King's Debts*, pp. 87–8, for the concessions; Joel Cornette, 'Fiction et réalité de l'état baroque', in Henri Mechoulan, ed., *L'Etat baroque* (Paris 1985), pp. 65–70 (n. 68), for a graphic, tabulated presentation of the contents of the secret articles of the treaty. See also Richelieu, *Mémoires*, II, pp. 8–13.
80   Aumale, *Histoire des princes de Condé*, III, pp. 69–71.
81   London, P(ublic) R(ecord) O(ffice), S(tate) P(apers) 78 (France) (hereafter P.R.O. SP) vol. 65, fo. 230, Thomas Edmondes, English ambassador, to Sir Ralph Winwood, Secretary of State, 21 June 1616. Avenel, *Lettres*, VII, pp. 319–20, Richelieu to Condé, 4 June 1616.

supporters of the prince – who had clearly not forgotten the insult –
to return to their offices there.[82] While Richelieu was now advancing
his career by placating Condé, his colleague La Rocheposay, who
had borne the brunt of Condé's anger, felt sufficiently threatened by
the outcome of his diplomacy to offer his resignation as bishop of
Poitiers to Marie de' Medici.[83]

Condé himself finally returned to court in late July 1616. By
then, there had been several important ministerial changes. Whatever his immediate ambitions, this was a significant development
from Richelieu's point of view. Apart from the fall of Sully in 1611,
the ministry had proved itself remarkably adept at survival, and it
was only in 1616 that it finally became a direct victim of the political
upheavals of the regency. Among other things, the Loudun agreement called for changes in the king's council, and these began almost
immediately after Loudun. Concini, too, was anxious to make
changes: he had not participated in the Loudun negotiations, and was
aggrieved at having to surrender his governorship of Picardy for the
lieutenance générale of Normandy. In mid-May, Chancellor Sillery
lost the seals to Guillaume du Vair, while Claude Barbin, who had
been intendant of Marie de' Medici's personal household, became
contrôleur-général des finances, and effectively deprived Jeannin of the
management of the royal finances. Both Marie and Concini were
especially anxious to be rid of Villeroy, whose disgrace – and that of
Puysieux, who held the *survivance* to his secretaryship of state – was
first mooted in June, but was only completed, after much wrangling,
in mid-August.[84] Since neither Villeroy nor Puysieux would resign
the secretaryship without substantial compensation, the new incumbent, Claude Mangot, a protegé of Léonora Galigaï, exercised its
functions by simple commission.[85] Though he became a councillor
of state during this time – probably before his mission to Condé –
there was as yet no hint of any major political advancement for
Richelieu, least of all to secretary of state. Indeed, one of the objects
of his encounter with Condé was to secure the prince's approval

---

82   For the background to this mission, see Aumale, *Histoire des princes de Condé*, III,
     pp. 69–73. For the mutual suspicions of the princes after Loudun and Richelieu's
     mission, duc d'Estrées, *Mémoires*, ed. Paul Bonnefon (Paris 1910) pp. 134–7. Richelieu's
     own later account is in his *Mémoires*, II, pp. 29ff.

83   B.N. MS. Clairambault 368, fo. 417, La Rocheposay to Pontchartrain, 30 Sept. 1616.
     His resignation, made during the summer of 1616, had been returned to him after the
     arrest of Condé on 1 Sept., which presumably ended La Rocheposay's immediate fears
     of revenge by the prince's local supporters.

84   P.R.O., SP 78/65, fos. 221–3, 229, 235–7, letters from Edmondes to Winwood, June-
     July 1616.

85   *Journal d'Arnauld 1614–20*, pp. 173–6 (June), 185 (Aug.).

of the promotion of Mangot and the removal of Villeroy and Puysieux.[86]

The new ministry was inexperienced, unknown, and too beholden to Concini to possess any genuine authority, so that when Condé finally took his seat in council in late July 1616, he quickly became the dominant force in government. Strangely, now that he had achieved what he had been fighting for since early 1614, the prince does not appear to have had any clear idea of what to do with his new power, though his triumph was too short-lived for us to be sure of his intentions. But the possibility that he might build up a governing faction around him – all commentators agree that his 'crédit' grew very rapidly at this time – must have appeared real enough.[87] While it is impossible to plot with any confidence Richelieu's own leanings during these months of uncertainty, his efforts to cultivate Condé in June and July 1616, went beyond merely acting as Marie de' Medici's emissary and suggest an attempt to hedge his bets, in the hope of benefiting from the prince's goodwill should he engineer a further redistribution of offices.

As many anticipated, the wheel of fortune had not ceased to turn. Condé's dominance, which logically presupposed Concini's loss of power, made him just as exposed as his adversary to the hostility of even those who had until recently supported him. More seriously, he did not have the ministers in his pocket and still lacked solid and broad-based support in court and in government; his fellow *grands* were suspicious of anyone aiming to claim overall power for himself. Indeed, while he was supposedly master of the council, Condé was simultaneously party to talk of eliminating Concini and even of removing Marie de' Medici from power altogether. But on 1 September 1616, he was arrested and imprisoned in the Bastille in a swift and bloodless coup which restored Concini and his wife to favour, and enabled them to tighten their grip on government.[88] An immediate ministerial reshuffle was unnecessary, since the main ministers, Barbin and Mangot, were clients of Marie and the Con-

---

86 P.R.O., SP 78/65, fo. 230, Edmondes to Winwood, 21 June 1616. Condé's reply was not very positive: he 'wished that care might be taken not to discontent so ancient a servant as Monsieur de Villeroy was'.

87 Estrées, *Mémoires*, pp. 134ff., for a good account of the factional intrigues of the summer of 1616.

88 It has sometimes been asserted that Richelieu was one of those who advised the queen mother to arrest Condé, but there is no evidence that he did so. At the time, most of the odium for this action was directed against Sully who, during a visit to court, was thought to have advised Marie de' Medici to take such action: P.R.O., SP 78/66, fos. 47–9, James Hay, Earl of Carlisle and Edmondes, to Winwood, 1 Sept 1616; *ibid.*, fo. 65, Carlisle and Edmondes to Winwood, 6 Sept 1616.

cinis. Indeed, throughout these months, Barbin seems to have been the key ministerial and political figure, trusted by Marie de' Medici, courted by Condé and Concini, and possessed of energy and courage. Only du Vair turned out to be a mistaken choice – he was both too little of a politician and too well-disposed to the *grands* to suit either Marie or Concini. Thus, when the time came – sudden ministerial disgrace being the exception rather than the rule at this juncture – to remove the seals from him, only limited ministerial changes were necessary. On 25 November, Mangot vacated his secretaryship to take the seals, while his former post – still tenable as a commission – went to Richelieu.[89] This time, according to Arnauld d'Andilly, the actual distribution of posts was swift and unannounced: apparently neither Mangot nor Richelieu knew what was planned until they were summoned to the king's cabinet.[90]

III

Writing years later at Richelieu's own request, the future maréchal d'Estrées described his appointment in 1616 as that of 'un homme singulier et si rare qu'il sembloit qu'en l'état présent des affaires de France, ce ministre avoit été plutôt donné du ciel que choisi par les hommes'.[91] The rest of Estrées' encomium was even more effusive, and was to be echoed by many other commentators. The historian can hardly be satisfied by such explanatory sleight of hand, the effect of which was to conceal the real facts of the Cardinal's first elevation, and is entitled to look for less celestial reasons for Richelieu's claim to ministerial rank in November 1616.

For all the efforts of Estreés and others to mystify the record, Richelieu was obviously 'choisi par les hommes'. In the short-term, there can be no doubt that he had successfully brought himself to the attention of those who mattered at court, especially in the aftermath of the Treaty of Loudun, at a time when disgraces and reshuffles created unusually favourable opportunities for advancement. By contrast, the memory of his oratory at the Estates General was an irrelevance. The mission to Condé was the first tangible proof of his success, and the mission itself, although only partially successful, added to his reputation as a political operator. Months later, in October 1616, he was chosen to win back another disaffected *grand*, the duc de Nevers, but this time a solution was quite beyond him,

89 *Journal d'Arnauld 1614–20*, pp. 242–3.
90 *Ibid.*, pp. 241–2.
91 Estrées, *Mémoires*, p. 155.

and insincere promises replaced positive results.[92] Nevertheless, the mission reflected the council's perception of his talent for diplomacy, and it comes as no great surprise that, despite his lack of success with Nevers, he was chosen within a matter of weeks to travel to Spain as extraordinary ambassador. We can only speculate how different his career might have been had he left for Madrid in November 1616.

In the intervening months, however, Richelieu had emerged as more than another useful or talented diplomat. The kind of political capital he had been accumulating emboldened him to set his sights higher than an embassy. Charting his progress is difficult without forcing too much of a pattern on his and others' behaviour at this juncture. The first hint of advancement comes with his success in winning a still unclear position in the service of Marie de' Medici. The real significance of the promotion of Barbin and Mangot in the summer of 1616 cannot have been lost on him, and convinced him of the value of personal service to the queen mother. During September and October 1616, his correspondence shows him acting virtually as one of the queen mother's intendants, even interceding for old servants anxious to preserve their position in her service, or attempting to find the means of meeting some of her personal financial commitments.[93] Such activities may well have been in- formal, as there is no trace of any written commission. Whatever the arrangement was, it was bound to bring Richelieu into regular contact with those who mattered at court and in the ministry.

The nature and extent of Richelieu's relations with Louis XIII himself before and during his first ministry are virtually impossible to gauge. As a busy secretary of state, he would regularly attend on Louis who, by April 1617 had developed a strong dislike of his imperious manner; this response ought not perhaps to be viewed too exclusively, as it formed part of the king's general loathing of those who, like Richelieu, were leading figures in the final phase of the Concini régime.[94] Richelieu's political apprenticeship was thus served against a background of kingly absence or dislike.

Moreover, it does not seem that Richelieu's service to Marie de' Medici was on its own the decisive factor in his ministerial promo- tion. Certainly, she was playing a much more active role in govern- ment at this time than she is usually credited with, but when it came to applying political pressure, the real influence was exercised by others; it is probably fair to say that Richelieu's record meant that she

92 *Journal d'Arnauld 1614–20*, pp. 213–14. P.R.O., SP 78/66, fos. 117–18, Edmondes to Winwood, 19 Oct. 1616.
93 Avenel, *Lettres*, I, pp. 177–8, letter to M. Barentin, late Sept. 1616; *ibid.*, pp. 178–80, letters to Potier de Blancmesnil and his son, Potier de Novion (Oct. 1616).
94 See A. Lloyd Moote, *Louis XIII, the Just* (Berkeley, Calif., 1989), pp. 89–92.

was not opposed to ministerial office for him when his name was put
forward. Again, Richelieu's correspondence leaves a clear enough
trail. As we saw, he had offered his services to Concini as early as
February 1614, and probably continued to do so right up to his
appointment as a minister. Particularly obsequious letters, written
shortly before and after his elevation, show how far he was prepared
to go in acknowledging himself as Concini's *créature*, one who owed
everything to his 'maker'.[95] At the same time, however, Concini's
numerous changes of mood and losses of nerve in 1615–16 also
heightened Richelieu's awareness that it was his wife Léonora who
was the more resolute and purposeful personality. When he began to
court her favour it is impossible to say. It was alleged during her trial
in 1617 that she had secured the grand almonership for him and this,
given Léonora's close attention to matters of patronage and Marie de'
Medici's vacillation, seems entirely plausible.[96] At any rate, during
the second half of 1616, Richelieu's letters increasingly show his
appreciation of her importance – something which can be seen not
merely in those he addressed to her personally, but also in his comments scattered through letters written to others.[97] Embarking on
his mission to Condé in June 1616, he made it clear that it had her full
support.[98] When he was finally appointed secretary of state, he experienced no difficulty in acknowledging his overriding debt to both
Concinis.[99]

Richelieu's relations before November 1616 with other ministers
and councillors of state are even more uncertain and elusive, subject
as they were to later reinterpretation by many of those concerned,
himself included. But as an important element in the post-regency
régime, they contributed over the years to making him known and
acceptable to those close to the throne. Even so, it required care and
application on his part, and it was not a simple progress. Some of his
earliest mentors parted with him subsequently: Méric de Vic, who
was among the first to enable him to serve the ministry, gradually
became a determined adversary; Pontchartrain, too, had cooled
towards him by the time of the Loudun negotiations. By that point,
as we saw, the sheer precariousness of ministers' tenure of office
made actual incumbents understandably nervous of potential challengers, and there is no sign that the Brûlarts, father and son, or
Villeroy himself were ever anything but hostile or indifferent to

95   Avenel, *Lettres*, I, 183–6, letter probably written before 20 Nov. 1616; *ibid.*, 194–5, letter
     of 29 Nov.
96   Hayem, *Le Maréchal d'Ancre et Léonora Galigaï*, p. 309.
97   Avenel, *Lettres*, I, p. 176, letter of Sept. 1616; *ibid.*, p. 186, letter of Nov. 1616.
98   *Ibid.*, VII, p. 320, letter to Condé, 4 June 1616.
99   *Ibid.*, I, p. 195, letter of 29 Nov. 1616.

Richelieu. He seems to have fared better, on the other hand, with newer figures such as Barbin and Mangot, like him servants of Marie and the Concinis, and also seeking greater things. Though Richelieu's subsequent attitude to him would be ambiguous, it was Barbin who probably did most to persuade Concini and Marie during the summer and autumn of 1616 that Richelieu should, to use his own language, be 'employed', and eventually given Villeroy's secretaryship in late November.

But there is also a wider and longer-term perspective on Richelieu's first elevation, one which it is much more difficult to convey satisfactorily. As we have seen, he had always been assiduous in cultivating powerful figures, and his early correspondence is replete with evidence of it. Yet we should be wary of thinking he was always successful. There is no sign that great nobles such as Soissons, Longueville, Sully or Épernon paid much attention at all to him in his early years. Indeed, this 'neglect' of him underlines once again the importance of Richelieu's episcopal rank and his indebtedness to the patronage of his fellow clergy. It was they rather than the court whom he impressed most in 1614–15, and their support thereafter, especially in the highly clerical entourage of Marie de' Medici, proved vital to him. To the examples already cited, we may add another, albeit an untypical one. Surprisingly, in view of their later inseparability, Richelieu and Père Joseph went their different ways in 1614, with the Capuchin drawing close, personally and even politically, to Nevers and even Condé: Nevers supported his plans for a crusade and a *milice chrétienne*, while his elder brother was a member of Condé's household. By 1616, this had the unexpected effect of enabling Père Joseph to play a discreet but effective part in clearing the way for Richelieu's successive missions to negotiate with Condé and Nevers.[100] But as the example of Père Joseph unmistakably shows, even those of Richelieu's clerical friends who are usually seen as being under his spell, enjoyed influence independently of him at this juncture; few of them owed either their influence or their careers to him, and we should not rush to conclude that they constituted the kind of clientèle associated with his later years, when its members would find themselves far more dependent on him.

Beyond that, we have surprisingly little hard information about Richelieu's personal and social rather than specifically political connections at court. Perhaps for that reason, many names have been suggested over the years as having played crucial parts in bringing him to the attention of Marie de' Medici and her entourage. The most

100   See Fagniez, *Le Père Joseph et Richelieu*, I, p. 75.

commonly adumbrated has been that of Madame de Guercheville, lady-in-waiting to Marie, but it has to be said there is no evidence for her influence – or for the others – apart from the hagiographical tradition itself. But for obvious reasons, one figure ought to be singled out – Richelieu's brother, Henri. His prolonged difficulties with their father's estate and creditors, makes the legend of his being one of the *dix-sept seigneurs* who set the tone at court extremely implausible, and this may be another case of his being confused with someone else. Nevertheless, Henri was a man with connections of his own and, it is clear, ready access to Marie de' Medici herself. Richelieu's reliance on him in the matter of presenting his oath of loyalty to Marie de' Medici in May 1610 was no accident, any more, for instance, than is the fact that she sent Henri on a mission to the duke of Lorraine in 1610. Later he became a *mestre de camp* in the Piedmont regiment and, as we saw, served in that capacity against Condé in 1615. When Bishop Eschaux wrote to Richelieu in July 1615 about the grand almonership to Anne of Austria, he made a point of stressing that Henri fully agreed with him in judging the post to be in the bishop of Luçon's best interests. It is impossible to know how far Henri had developed any specific ambitions of his own before his brother's rise, but if he did, it seems probable that they were focused on a rise through the military hierarchy. To most of the *noblesse militaire* before 1616, the name 'Richelieu' signified Henri rather than his episcopal brother. Henri's social circle is not well known, but his close friendship with the sons of the great financier Zamet – creditor and associate of his father – and his marriage to the widow of a senior parlementaire, give some small idea of the store of social relations whom he could call upon to assist Armand.[101]

When we shift our attention away from the circles of patronage and clientage in which Richelieu moved, and ask what kind of political image he presented in late 1616, the picture is equally unclear. Of course, this exercise is itself somewhat artificial, as a neat separation of patronage and political commitment cannot be sustained in this period. A self-confessed *créature* like Richelieu had little opportunity to define his own political profile independently of his patrons. Hitherto, his support of actual royal authority as exercised by Marie de' Medici had been his broadest principled position. The detail of such a position is another matter, though it did mean a strong aversion for aristocratic and Huguenot *frondes* of all kinds. An interesting but far from infallible yardstick are the foreign ambassadors who, as soon as he was appointed, were anxious to take the

---

101   Sébastien Zamet became bishop of Langres in 1615; his brother Jean, baron de Murat, followed a military career. In his will, Henri de Richelieu left a few bequests to Jean Zamet 'affin de se souvenir de moy': A.N., M.C., CVII, 113, testament of 24 Dec. 1618.

measure of the man with whom they would now have to deal. The Venetians were not all reassured, reporting home that he was obviously pro-Spanish; his grand almonership and regular visits to the Spanish ambassador even convinced them that he was a pensioner of the king of Spain.[102] The English ambassador, the experienced Thomas Edmondes, thought the appointment to be an outright triumph for the Spanish and papal factions at court, and characterized Richelieu as 'by faction Spanish and a great Brouillon'.[103] The Spanish ambassador could hardly have been more enthusiastic: Richelieu, he wrote, professed to be his personal friend, and he could think of no one in France who was better intentioned towards the interests of the Spanish crown.[104] The newly-arrived papal nuncio, Bentivoglio, regarded the entry of a bishop into the king's council as an unreserved blessing, and obviously assumed strongly pro-papal sentiments in him.[105] Richelieu's own sensitivity about his reputation emerges clearly from a conversation he had with Edmondes only days after his appointment. According to Edmondes, 'the bishop laboured earnestly to persuade me, not to believe that he is anyway Spanish affected; or notwithstanding the character, which he beareth of a priest, that he will be any whit the more partial in the execution of his charge against those of the Religion (Huguenots); but protested contrariwise, that he would give better proof of his integrity and indifference, than other of his predecessors had done'.[106] Richelieu's own statements apart, there is no worthwhile evidence of his opinions, not least because scarcely any contemporary commentators – pamphleteers, diarists or others – ever mentioned him or his doings before late 1616. To all but a tiny milieu, France's newest secretary of state was a minor, even unknown figure in a similarly obscure ministry.[107]

IV

When the Venetian ambassadors reported the ministerial changes of November 1616, they claimed that Mangot's secretaryship had first been offered to Barbin, and that he had declined it on the grounds

---

102 Lacroix, *Richelieu à Luçon*, p. 248, n. 1, letter of 29 Nov. 1616.
103 P.R.O., SP 78/66, fos. 156v–57r, letter to Winwood, 27 Nov. 1626.
104 Letter of 28 Nov. 1616, quoted by Avenel, *Lettres*, I, p. 192. It should be noted that the Spanish ambassador was *mayordomo* to Anne of Austria, and Richelieu her grand almoner, thus facilitating regular contact between the two men.
105 *La Nunziatura di Francia di Guido di Bentivoglio*, ed. Luigi Steffani (Florence 1863–70), I, p. 14.
106 Thomas Birch, *An Historical View of the Negotiations between the Courts of England, France and Brussels from the Year 1592 until 1617* (London 1749), p. 400, letter to Secretary Winwood, 30 Nov 1616.
107 See Orcibal, *Saint Cyran*, pp. 482–3; Deloche, *Autour de la plume*, p. 106.

that his financial post was more remunerative and involved less work.[108] On the other hand, as an office the secretaryship was potentially the more durable of the two, at least if its incumbent had the opportunity to purchase the actual title to it. For that reason, it appears that Mangot, who had been negotiating to purchase Villeroy's interest, was none too pleased to have to accept the less secure keepership of the seals instead.[109] Richelieu, for his part, did not pursue Mangot's negotiations, and his resources would not have allowed him to offer anything in the order of the 400,000 *livres* Villeroy was apparently asking. But there is no doubt that he was stepping into an onerous position. Despite a reference in his letters of appointment to his exercising his charge either separately or jointly with Villeroy, no such co-operation was envisaged and the real objective was to exclude Villeroy altogether. Not only did Richelieu have to serve his turn as secretary to the king, but he was also taking over the foreign affairs portfolio which had for decades been the jealously guarded private fief of Villeroy. Like Villeroy, he was also given responsibility for military affairs.[110] What could not be guaranteed was that he would exercise Villeroy's extensive influence in all areas of government, such influence being the fruit of long tenure and personal connections, not a simple matter of institutionalized divisions of labour among ministers. However, that Richelieu was keen to exploit all the possible advantages is evident from his success in securing precedence rights in council, by virtue of his episcopal rank, over his fellow secretaries of state. It was hardly the most tactful of moves, especially as he was the most junior of them, but one which was characteristic of a status-obsessed age; moreover, it was one he would repeat, albeit at a higher level, on entering the council as a cardinal in 1624.[111] His emoluments, while less than what he would enjoy at the height of his power, were substantial and commensurate with his new responsibilities.[112]

Richelieu was fortunate enough to find that France's foreign relations in late 1616 were in a healthier condition than her internal affairs. This has often been obscured by the bad press that the regency of Marie de' Medici has generally had over its conduct of foreign affairs, behind which often lurks an implicit negative comparison with the more assertive policies associated with Henri IV or

108 Lacroix, *Richelieu à Luçon*, p. 248, n. 1, letter of 29 Nov. 1616.
109 *Journal d'Arnauld 1614–20*, pp. 242.
110 See Hélène Michaud, 'Aux origines de secrétariat d'état à la guerre: les règlements de 1617–1619', *Revue d'Histoire Moderne et Contemporaine* 19 (1972), pp. 389–413, esp. pp. 391–2.
111 See Hanotaux, *Richelieu*, II, pp. 132–3. This privilege was revoked, doubtless at the demand of the other secretaries, after his fall in 1617.
112 Bergin, *Richelieu*, p. 73.

Richelieu's own later ministry. If the regency did swap the policy of Henri IV's later years – allegedly of standing up to Habsburg pretensions – for one of conciliation towards Spain, it was out of recognition of changed political circumstances. The powers of a regency were held to be as circumscribed in foreign affairs as they were domestically: great initiatives or involvement in foreign wars were to be postponed until the monarch came of age and could make his own decisions. Moreover, with the growth of internal dissent, it was becoming more difficult to carry through an active or controversial foreign policy. In the event, even the Spanish marriages, which involved no formal treaty or alliance with Spain, were opposed by Condé and other princes, and were regarded by the Huguenots as a threat to their position. If nothing else had come of it, the protracted affair of the marriages at least dissuaded the Spaniards from fanning the flames of internal dissension in France at a particularly sensitive time; the Spanish marriages proved most valuable in French domestic politics before they actually took place. Elsewhere Villeroy, who needed no lessons in the connections between foreign and domestic affairs, discreetly directed his efforts abroad towards resolving the Cleves-Jülich dispute in north-west Germany (by the treaty of Xanten, November 1614) and the Savoy-Spain conflict over Montferrat in northern Italy (by the Treaty of Asti, June 1615). But by mid-1615, his influence began to wane, and domestic affairs, culminating in the conflict over the Spanish marriages and the Loudun negotiations, claimed much of his attention. Richelieu's immediate predecessor, Mangot, held office for little more than three months, and is generally thought to have had little understanding of his duties, even to the extent of leaving ambassadors' letters unanswered. This seems less than fair to him, and Richelieu himself would later be accused of being too distracted to give foreign affairs his full attention, a charge which he admitted was well-founded.[113] The real problem was not the action or inaction of the secretary of state, but the ministerial instability which gave rise to a protracted row over the secretaryship itself, involving Mangot, Villeroy and Puysieux, during which Villeroy refused to discharge his duties or to allow Mangot to do so.[114]

If much ink has been spilt over the claim made in the *Testament*

---

113 Steffani, *Nunziatura di Bentivoglio*, I, p. 126, letter to Borghese, 28 Feb. 1617, relaying Monteleone's complaint about his distraction; for Richelieu's own admission, see Adolf Wild ed., *Papiers de Richelieu. Empire allemand*, vol. I. (Paris 1982), pp. 47–9, letter to Baugy in Prague, 10 April 1617. Four letters had remained unanswered.

114 P.R.O., SP 78/65, fo. 232, Edmondes to Winwood, 21 June 1616, *ibid.*, fos. 235–7, same to same, 3 July; vol. 66, fo. 2, same to same, 22 July; *ibid.*, fos. 29–33, same to same, 10 Aug.

Politique that, on taking office in 1624, Richelieu set the abasement of the Habsburgs as one of his overriding objectives, there is no hint at all of any such idea in 1616–17. Insofar as he developed a general objective while in office, it was that of ending conflicts and restoring peace throughout western Europe. However, one feature of his first ministry is firmly in keeping with his later record – a preoccupation with the affairs, not so much of the empire, but of Northern Italy. French mediation had helped produce the treaty of Asti of June 1615, by which Savoy and Spain were to disengage and disarm, while the rival claims to the disputed duchy of Montferrat – which, sandwiched between Spanish Milan and Savoy, was obviously important to each party – were being examined. The French had an interest in securing and supporting allies in Italy, but Savoy was a troublesome and unpredictable partner, all too likely to drag France into its quarrels. Another traditional ally, Venice, was also frequently at odds with the Spaniards, whose control of Milan was a constant source of worry. In 1615–16, the Venetians were also embroiled in a war with the Uskoks across the Adriatic, one in which their enemies were supported by another Habsburg, Archduke Ferdinand of Styria. Meanwhile, hostilities had resumed between Savoy and Spain, with Lesdiguières, the Huguenot governor of Dauphiné, leading a French force across the Alps to support Savoy without so much as bothering to secure royal approval. In late December 1616, Richelieu relaunched Mangot's earlier attempts to unscramble and terminate these disputes, and proposed to do so by persuading the different parties to send plenipotentiaries to Paris. France would offer its mediation, and a negotiated settlement would enhance its prestige. But apart from the question as to whether a single effort to resolve the disputes was well conceived and feasible, he soon found to his cost that the interested parties were singularly lacking in faith in France's ability to achieve results. The Venetians, whose goodwill he was perhaps most anxious to win, were the first to disappoint him. They probably already had strong doubts about the strength of the Concini régime, and consequently the permanency of its foreign policy. Whether Richelieu realized it or not, these doubts were fully confirmed for them when he himself refused, out of evident fear of offending the Spaniards, to grant them permission to move troops they had recruited abroad through the Swiss valleys controlled by the Grisons, France's allies. His efforts were consequently shattered when the Venetians, without warning, simply asked for the negotiations for a settlement of their dispute to be transferred to the court of Madrid.[115] When this news reached him, Richelieu would claim

115   The best account of these matters, as of French policy generally in this period, remains
        Victor-Lucien Tapié, *La Politique étrangère de la France et le début de la guerre de trente ans*

that France was indifferent to where or how negotiations were conducted, so long as the outcome was a return to peace; but behind the
increasingly philosophical tone of his correspondence with France's
ambassadors in Turin and Venice, there is no doubt about his bitterness at having been so comprehensively rebuffed by the Venetians. And when Savoy followed suit and opted for papal mediation
in its dispute with Spain, Richelieu's chances of rebuilding French
standing in northern Italy promptly folded.[116] It was not the last
time he would experience how difficult it was for France to deal with
the intractable conflicting interests of a strategically vital part of
Europe and to extract either advantage or prestige from them.[117]

Within the empire, Richelieu simply followed Villeroy's objective
of ensuring that the imperial title passed to Archduke Ferdinand of
Styria, largely on the grounds that, with direct heirs of his own,
Ferdinand's succession would prevent the Spanish Habsburgs from
pressing their branch's claims to the title in the future. As the Habsburgs moved to agree among themselves on this outcome, Richelieu's principal concern was to ensure that France's interests were
not damaged by Madrid's attempts to secure unacceptable territorial
'compensation' for accepting Ferdinand's succession – the Tyrol, for
example, or Alsace. In late 1616 and early 1617, there was little else
French diplomacy could do, and the European conflagration ignited
by the imperial succession crisis had origins which at this point no
French minister could anticipate or master.[118]

One chapter from Richelieu's tenure as foreign minister has always
attracted considerable attention, though not always for reasons
relating to the immediate context of the events in question. Confessional divisions among the German princes had worsened some
years earlier to the point where Catholic and Protestant unions had
been founded in 1608–9: this was a new situation to which French
diplomacy, with its traditions of cultivating princely allies and defending their 'liberties', had to adjust. In early January 1617, Henri
de Schomberg was despatched on a mission to the German princes,
especially the Electors, with a view to explaining and justifying
French foreign and especially domestic policy since 1610. There was

---

(1616–1621) (Paris 1934), ch. 1. He rectifies the account given in Hanotaux, *Richelieu*, 11,
    pp. 141–55, 177–84.
116   Avenel, *Lettres*, VII, pp. 345–6, Louis XIII to Brûlart de Léon, French ambassador to
    Venice, 7/8 Feb. 1617.
117   See J.H. Elliott, *Richelieu and Olivares* (Cambridge 1984), esp. ch. 4. William F. Church,
    Richelieu and Reason of State (Princeton 1972), part ii.
118   Wild, *Papiers de Richelieu. Empire allemand*, vol. 1, letters 1–33 cover the period of
    Richelieu's tenure of office. They include letters written to his predecessor, Mangot, and
    thus convey a sense of the continuity of policy. There are only five letters in all to the
    French resident at the court in Prague, Baugy, for the entire period of Richelieu's tenure
    of office, and few of them do more than repeat existing objectives.

a good deal to explain, as Richelieu was not the first to appreciate: the duc de Nevers had been on his way to Germany to defend the Spanish marriages ('sur le sujet du mariage du Roy') when Condé was arrested but, failing to secure an explanation of the arrest, Nevers promptly exchanged the role of emissary for that of malcontent.[119] Richelieu and his fellow ministers may thus have been reviving that earlier mission, but on a larger scale, when they sent extraordinary ambassadors to the Dutch and the English for the same purpose. For his part, Schomberg was to reassure the German princes and imperial cities on his itinerary that the Spanish marriages had not turned France into a handmaiden of either Madrid or the papacy, but that she retained her freedom of choice, and would therefore remain faithful to her allies and past policies. Richelieu himself must have been particularly sensitive to the need for such reassurance, if only because of foreign scepticism of a régime with a reputedly pro-Spanish bishop as foreign minister. Above all, Schomberg was to convince his hosts that the arrest of Condé and the treatment of the Huguenots were not what they were portrayed to be abroad: the king was determined to treat all his subjects even-handedly, and rebellion had to be treated as such, however much some might attempt to give it a religious colouring. Historians anxious to depict the early Richelieu as a champion of *raison d'état* have understandably seized upon this kind of language. Richelieu's concerns were not philosophical or strategic, but worryingly practical – in essence he was determined to ensure that French rebels, especially Huguenots, would not be supported by foreign, particularly Calvinist, princes, as had so often been the case in the past. Not for the last time, he used his carefully-filed records of the enormous sums of money distributed to the *grands* since 1610 as an argument in defence of royal policy – to discredit their claims of ill-treatment at home, and to explain France's difficulty in paying its debts to its neighbours![120] His appreciation of the importance of using French diplomacy to win the propaganda war on this question is also evident from the regular letters on internal affairs that he despatched to French ambassadors in Prague, Turin and elsewhere.[121] France's eastern 'frontiers' were so many avenues for the passage of foreign mercenary armies, the recruitment of which its

119 *Journal d'Arnauld 1614–20*, pp. 213–14. The arrest of Condé obviously made Nevers's mission virtually impossible, hence his letter to the king – 'assez hardie', according to Arnauld. Many of the papers and instructions concerning Nevers's mission are edited in E. Griselle, *Louis XIII et Richelieu* (Paris 1911), pp. 219ff.

120 Avenel, *Lettres*, I, pp. 208–35.

121 *Papiers de Richelieu. Empire allemand*, vol. I, pp. 27, 40, for mention of separate letters to Baugy. See also references in n. 135 below.

neighbours might be either unable or unwilling to prevent. With Huguenot *grands* like Bouillon holding Sedan as an independent principality and having powerful relatives abroad, internal trouble with the *grands* quickly assumed international dimensions. Richelieu was anxious to deny them access to such dangerous facilities, which might in turn deter the crown from taking military action to defend its authority.[122]

In the event, however, Schomberg was unable to convince his hosts with such arguments. The Calvinist Palatinate, whose attitude was of crucial significance, let it be known in suitably diplomatic code that its benevolence would depend on how the crown behaved at home, and that in the case of action against the likes of Bouillon and the Huguenots, it might not be able to prevent them from obtaining assistance. With little to offer his sceptical hosts, Schomberg's mission petered out inconclusively. Richelieu did not hesitate, however, to enlist him as a recruiting agent for German mercenaries at the height of the offensive against the *grands* in February 1617, but left him without instructions as to how he should wind up his efforts at diplomacy.[123]

Thus Richelieu's conduct of foreign affairs, when not actually subservient to domestic priorities, shows few signs of the superior vision habitually ascribed to him. In fairness to him, it should be said that, apart from his other cares, he received virtually no help from Villeroy, and was reduced to asking the ambassadors for copies of their instructions and for reports on negotiations in progress. Relations with them may not have been helped by his own first circular letter to them, which was not a model of tact. Because no evidence has survived that would enlighten us on his views of French foreign relations prior to his first taste of ministerial responsibility, we must perforce interpret both him and them by the record of his few months in office. These were, of course, too short for categorical conclusions to be drawn, but the evidence of his willingness to follow earlier leads, to leave a good deal to the initiative of individual diplomats, as well as the instances where he was outwitted by others more experienced than himself, all suggest that he still had a long way to go in learning the reality of European power-politics. French diplomats abroad did not waste much energy deploring his fall from power, and seemed happy enough to welcome back Villeroy and Puysieux in May 1617, while they in turn found that there were few significant changes with which they had to deal. But in the

---

122 The fullest account of Schomberg's mission is Tapié, *Politique étrangère*, pp. 51ff.
123 Avenel, *Lettres*, I, pp. 300–1, king to Schomberg, 15 Feb. 1617. The best account is in Tapié, *Politique étrangère*, pp. 59–60. He argues that Richelieu may not have realized the contradiction between Schomberg's two assignments.

context of Richelieu's political career as a whole, the experiences of 1616–17 were no doubt formative. However briefly, they obliged him to weigh foreign and domestic priorities together, to appreciate the connections between them, and, although there were as yet no conflicts on the scale he would encounter in the 1620s, to formulate some general rules of thumb on how to deal with France's neighbours. He would make mistakes during his second ministry but his preoccupation with foreign affairs and close attention to the changing map of Europe was perhaps the outstanding legacy of his first experience of office.

V

It will be clear by now that Richelieu, even had he wished to do so, could not have confined his attention to foreign questions. Not only was departmental specialization still too embryonic for that, but all secretaries of state bore internal administrative responsibilities. In addition, his own portfolio included the 'ordinaire et extraordinaire des guerres', with specific charge of the *taillon*, or military tax.[124] He was, therefore, effectively minister for war, and to critics of the last Concini ministry the confiding of such a responsibility to a bishop seemed the ultimate incongruity.

By the time Richelieu took office in late November 1616, the arrest of Condé had had time to bear its fruits. To contemporaries, 'the arrest . . . and the ministerial reshuffle which followed, marked the apogee of the Concini's power and influence.'[125] Whatever the merits of its individual members, the ministry was viewed as Concini's creation, an impression enhanced by the sacking of du Vair (which made room for Richelieu), while in subsequent months continuing rumours of yet more ministerial changes further reduced its credibility and reputation.[126] Even the populace of Paris signalled its opinion of Concini's power by ransacking and then demolishing his residence in the Faubourg Saint Germain in September 1616. Most of the great nobles had promptly absconded from Paris after Condé's arrest, some out of fear that a wider purge of opposition was intended. Mayenne, Bouillon, Vendôme, and others gathered at Soissons, where for a time they were joined even by the duc de

124   B.V.C. fonds Richelieu 14, fo. 10, Richelieu to *trésoriers de France* at Lyon, 26 Dec. 1616, asking them to send statements of the value of the tax for 1617.
125   Bonney, *The King's Debts*, p. 89.
126   P.R.O., SP 78/67, fo. 74, John Woodforde, secretary of English ambassador, to Winwood, 15 April 1617. For similar reports by the Venetian ambassadors, see Hanotaux, *Richelieu*, II, p. 129, n. 1.

Guise, whose habitual loyalty to Marie de' Medici had been rudely shaken by Condé's fate. The *drôle de guerre* that followed was more a series of 'incidents' reminiscent of 1614, with individual nobles trying to raise troops, strengthen garrisons, and surprise particular towns and citadels, yet it was sufficient to prolong the political malaise. However, princely unity proved elusive, and Marie de' Medici's promise, in early October, to observe the terms of Loudun, enabled several *grands* to discard the posture of open resistance and to return discreetly to court.[127] Richelieu's own mission to Nevers in October 1616 was one of many attempts to take the pressure off the crown; his failure was itself of no great consequence, as the maverick duke remained for the time being an isolated figure. Writing to two of France's ambassadors at Christmas 1616, Richelieu expressed personal and ministerial optimism about the situation at home: Guise, Épernon and others were loyal to the crown, Nevers and the malcontents were weak and isolated, and the armies the crown was organizing would have little difficulty in dealing with them. Either the princes recognized where their duty lay, or the king would compel them to do so *par raison d'état*.[128]

Such optimism may have been designed for foreign consumption and to give credibility to French diplomacy, but was it justified? Like the Fronde years of mid-century, the mid-1610s were characterized by sudden swings in the political pendulum. As later, one thing above all ensured continuing political unrest – the refusal of the princes, whatever their mutual jealousies and recriminations, to accept the supremacy of Concini at court and over the government.[129] Richelieu would have been naive to believe that there were no clouds in the sky in late 1616, but he may have been fortified in his belief that the recruitment of two, and then three royal armies, would give the crown a decisive advantage over the rebels. In the first days of 1617, the papal nuncio reported intense discussions and plans for war, but it is hard to be sure if a decision to use all necessary force to reassert royal authority was taken at this time, even in principle; as on previous occasions, the original intention may well have been merely to mount a show of force in order to nudge the princes back into line before negotiating with them.[130]

In the event, the crown's military preparations produced a reac-

---

127 *Journal d'Arnauld 1614–20*, pp. 194ff, offers the best evidence of the circumstances and consequences of Condé's arrest.
128 Avenel, *Lettres*, I, p. 202, letter to Philippe de Béthune, 25 Dec. 1616; *ibid.*, VII, pp. 326–7, letter to Tresnel, ambassador in Rome, 23 Dec. 1616.
129 For a useful comparison of the two periods of upheaval, see R.J. Bonney, 'Cardinal Mazarin and the Great Nobility during the Fronde', *English Historical Review* 96 (1981), pp. 818–33.
130 Steffani, *Nunziatura di Bentivoglio*, I, pp. 37–9, letter of 17 Jan.

tion, which then propelled it into actually using the military forces it had been raising. Bouillon launched his manifesto of rebellion on 6 January 1617, to be followed a few weeks later by Nevers, Mayenne, and Vendôme. As in previous years, a war of manifestos and declarations preceded the fighting itself, with each side heaping opprobrium on the other and justifying its line of action; by now, the princes were well used to attacking the abuse of power by foreign adventurers, the maladministration of the finances, the failure to respond to the major demands of the Estates General, and for good measure, the replacement of the old ministers by men without honour or integrity.[131] The crown raised the stakes by responding directly to these successive challenges, and between January and March 1617, several royal declarations against the princes were registered by the *parlement* of Paris.

The crown also published its own counter-manifestos and replies to those of the rebels, duly signed by the king. This option, which committed the prestige and reputation of the king more directly than hitherto, may well have been inspired by Richelieu. At any rate, it was he, as secretary of state, who counter-signed them and, more importantly, it was he who composed them. It was the first time that he engaged in an activity with which he was to be associated, both directly and indirectly, for the rest of his life – pamphleteering. No doubt, his episcopal career and his studies in religious controversy equipped him for political polemic; even if the subject matter was different, the techniques and language were very similar. It is likely, though it has never been conclusively proved, that the king's open letter of 17 January 1617 in reply to Mayenne's manifesto was Richelieu's work. Its tone was pugnacious, and its unyielding defence of royal justice, clemency and authority showed little inclination to recognize political circumstances for what they were.[132] Much the same message is conveyed at far greater length, and in a more abrasive and relentlessly interrogatory mode, in the most significant of his compositions during his ministry, the *Declaration du roy sur le subject des nouveaux remuemens de son royaume*, put together in three days in mid-February 1617. Its function as an instrument of policy, and not as an attempt at persuasion, was underscored by its uncompromising defence of the behaviour of Concini and Marie de' Medici: the crown was blameless, its conduct and authority beyond criticism by subjects, however great. The *grands* had no grounds for complaint, as kings were completely free to reward whomsoever they saw fit.[133] Richelieu himself acknowledged the purpose of the dec-

131 Bonney, *The King's Debts*, pp. 89–90.
132 Avenel, *Lettres*, I, pp. 255–8, 17 Jan. 1617.
133 *Ibid.*, I, pp. 301–16, 18 Feb. 1617.

laration when reporting its reception in council to Concini: he modestly claimed that although it was 'mal digérée comme venant d'une mauvaise main', it was thought by the council to contain enough material to have some impact on public opinion.[134]

By February 1617, the ministry, with Richelieu acting as its most visible spokesman, was committed to wielding the sword as much as the pen. But his own role was not confined to proving how mighty the pen could be. His duties as secretary for war pressed heavily on him, as he acknowledged in his dealings with France's ambassadors abroad.[135] His correspondence leaves no doubt whatever about the energy with which he tried to ensure that the three royal armies operating under the comte d'Auvergne, the maréchal de Montigny and the duc de Guise, should be brought up to full strength, adequately supplied and paid and, above all, that they should move vigorously against the rebels, especially at Soissons, as well as in Champagne and the Nivernais, the principal centres of resistance. Letters and instructions rained down on commanders and officials, sometimes several a day to the same person; the surviving texts, often hasty, repetitive and obscure, testify to Richelieu's frenetic activity. It is a pattern of activity which bears an uncanny resemblance to that ascribed to the Cardinal's client-minister of war, Sublet des Noyers, during the late 1630s.[136]

But if that later parallel is anything to go by, it raises problems of interpretation. Although, by the 1630s there was a separate department of war, Sublet's real power as minister was very limited; his role was subordinate and did not enable him to take significant military or financial decisions.[137] Obviously, we cannot simply assume the same applies to Richelieu himself in early 1617, but the parallel should remind us that there is a serious risk of document-induced illusion where his first ministry is concerned. As the only member of the Concini ministry to recover from political disgrace, his voluminous correspondence can easily give the impression that he virtually ran the government in early 1617. But financial issues were as acute and as crucial as those of a purely logistical or military nature. New expedients had to be found to raise money, and council records show heavy borrowing at this time.[138] All of this was pri-

---

134 *Ibid.*, I, pp. 316–17, letter of 22 Feb. 1617.
135 For example, he only replied to Béthune's letters of 7, 18, 19, 22 March on 8 April: *ibid.*, I, p. 501. See also *ibid.*, VII, p. 344, letter to ambassador to Venice, 7 Feb. 1617.
136 See Orest Ranum, *Richelieu and the Councillors of Louis XIII* (Oxford 1963), pp. 100–19.
137 See David Parrott, 'The Administration of the French Army during the Ministry of Cardinal Richelieu' (Oxford D.Phil thesis, 1985), esp. pp. 77–9. I am grateful to Dr Parrott for permission to consult his excellent thesis.
138 Bonney, *The King's Debts*, p. 90.

marily Barbin's responsibility, and although Richelieu was personally in charge of the military tax, the *taillon*, everything that is known about French wartime finance indicates that his activities were dependent upon the financial measures dictated by Barbin. According to one reliable commentator, another forgotten member of the ministerial team, Mangot, made an impressive début as keeper of the seals; his co-operation in smoothing the passage of new fiscal edicts was indispensable.[139] But while Mangot later lost Barbin's esteem, Richelieu was shrewd enough to realize that a close alliance with Barbin was the best way to strengthen his position, even vis-à-vis Concini.[140]

More importantly, of the numerous problems faced by Richelieu, that of dealing with the military commanders and persuading them to step up their military operations, evidently proved the most difficult to handle. He could only cajole, flatter and try to motivate men of superior social rank, over whose own political views he had no control. He seems to have had most success with Montigny's southern army, because he managed to secure a senior position of *maréchal de camp* in it for his brother, Henri, who then served as his most reliable channel of communication with Montigny himself.[141] But the power to command and coerce was not his to exercise, so that he had to utilize the king's name and signature as extensively as possible; 'the service of the king' is the phrase that recurs most often in his relations with military commanders. Despite the inevitable difficulties, that language, and the efforts that underpinned it, slowly began to produce results as the royal armies inched forward to an apparently inevitable military triumph.

But the principal political problem in early 1617 was not that of the determination and resourcefulness of the ministry – which struck observers and astonished the rebel *grands* – but the growing divorce between the rhetoric of 'the service of the king' and political reality. The nearer the crown came to subduing the rebels in March–April, the more obvious it became that the fruits of triumph would be reaped exclusively by Concini – a prospect which even supporters of the crown found unpleasant. The papal nuncio, hardly a friend of rebellion, reported with all too evident sympathy the widespread

---

139 *Journal d'Arnauld 1614–20*, pp. 249, 252. Richelieu himself concurred with Arnauld's judgement in his *Caput apologeticum*: Avenel, *Lettres*, VII, p. 422, 'Mangot, excellent pour le sceau'.

140 Steffani, *Nunziatura di Bentivoglio*, I, pp. 147–50, letter of 14 March 1617; P.R.O, SP 78/66, fo. 74, Woodforde to Winwood, 15 April.

141 For one example of this, see Avenel, *Lettres*, I, pp. 347–8, Richelieu to Montigny: 'Mon frère vous aura maintenant fait sçavoir particulièrement la volonté du roy'. See also *Journal d'Arnauld 1614–20*, p. 271. The previous holder of this post withdrew to his estates on being superseeded by Henri de Richelieu.

feeling that the princes, for all their egoism, were not guilty of the charges laid against them in Richelieu's pamphlets.[142] Even commanders of the royal armies such as Guise were suspected of not really wanting a military solution to the political crisis, and there were even rumours in February–March 1617 of a third party of *grands* not in revolt, but hostile to Concini.[143] Symptomatic of this uncertainty was the fact that plans to have the young Louis XIII join his armies or travel to Reims were first postponed and then abandoned altogether, allegedly out of fear that he might himself take the opportunity to either use his armies or even join the rebels to end Concini's dominance![144] Richelieu's own behaviour echoes these developments in a curious fashion. In late January, he briefly and privately expressed his doubts about the manner, but not the rightness, of the crown's behaviour, but such doubts gave way to greater resolution and confidence in a military solution in the ensuing weeks.[145] By late March, when he was again finding time to devote his attention to foreign affairs, he briefed the English ambassador's secretary in great detail: with obvious satisfaction, he claimed that within a month the three royal armies would have a combined strength in excess of 30,000 men, with further reinforcements stationed in Liège and elsewhere, and that abundant financial resources were also available.[146] With Nevers and some of the *grands* beginning to seek negotiated terms, victory seemed only a matter of time; success would enhance royal power, and silence the critics of a ministry which had proved its worth.

No appraisal of Richelieu's months in office can avoid the question of Concini's power and how he fitted into it. Once again, those involved – and Richelieu in particular – were not anxious to advertise their relations with the favourite after his bloody demise. Although much was subsequently made of the power Concini wielded, no satisfactory account of that power and how he exercised it has yet appeared. Certainly, his political style does not resemble that of Luynes, Richelieu or Mazarin when they acquired equivalent influence in government. During the period of his greatest influence,

---

142 Steffani, *Nunziatura di Bentivoglio*, I, pp. 40–9 (at p. 43), 27 Jan. 1617; *ibid.*, pp. 105–6, 4 Feb.

143 Steffani, *Nunziatura di Bentivoglio*, I, p. 129, letter of 28 Feb.; *ibid.*, p. 159, 25 March.

144 P.R.O., SP 78/67, fos. 65–7, Woodforde to Edmondes, 13 March 1617; *ibid.*, fo. 73, same to Winwood, 15 March, surmising that the king desired 'to franchise himselfe'. See also Marvick, *Louis XIII*, pp. 189ff.

145 Steffani, *Nunziatura di Bentivoglio*, I, p. 74, letter of 1 Feb. 1617; *ibid.*, I, p. 132, 28 Feb.; *ibid.*, I, p. 150, 14 March.

146 B.L. Stowe MS. 176, fos. 74–77, John Woodforde to Edmondes, 22 March 1617. Woodforde subsequently tried to verify what Richelieu had told him, and concluded that his claims were accurate.

he spent most of his time in Normandy, of which he became lieu-
tenant-general after the Treaty of Loudun, and where he also obtained town governorships which he was intent on strengthening.
His search for a power base outside the court, first in Picardy and
then in Normandy, fuelled the existing loathing and suspicion of
him among the political class, setting a pattern for future favourites
and ministers to imitate, and for their opponents to castigate. His
brief visits to court do not seem to coincide with policy changes or
initiatives, with the exception of the early months of 1617 when the
offensive against the princes was being orchestrated.[147] Thus, it is
possible that ministers actually had some latitude in handling day-to-
day matters, with Marie de' Medici taking overall responsibility for
government decisions. Moreover, there is no sign that Concini
intervened in foreign affairs, so that Richelieu probably enjoyed
considerable freedom of movement there. On the other hand, as
Concini's principal exigencies were financial, Barbin and Mangot
were almost certainly subject to more direct and intense pressure
from him. However, unlike Barbin, Richelieu did not have a long
history of personal service to Concini, so he probably had to make a
much greater show of his devotion, both immediately before and
during his ministry, thereby leaving embarrassing ammunition for
his critics. In the complex and subtle connections between favour,
dependency and influence, Richelieu was more of an outsider who
clearly enjoyed less influence in government than did a Concini-
dependent such as Barbin.[148]

But Concini was also imperious and hypersensitive, and Richelieu
found it prudent as well as necessary to keep him informed of events
at frequent intervals between February and April 1617, despatching
a regular stream of letters to him in Normandy. Indeed, after Concini's death, some of Richelieu's letters were cited as evidence of the
favourite's excessive power, and of how abject the ministry had been
– to which an exasperated Richelieu could only attempt to reply by
asking since when had 'civilities' become criminal.[149] Yet it is clear
from their correspondence, and especially from one of Concini's
often-cited outbursts, that Richelieu found it increasingly difficult

---

147 Steffani, *Nunziatura di Bentivoglio*, I, p. 43, letter of 27 Jan. 1617; *ibid.*, pp. 72–6, letter of
     1 Feb. 1617, in which the Nuncio describes Concini as more resolute than any of the
     ministers he had previously spoken to: decisive action was a matter of life or death; *ibid.*,
     I, pp. 166–7, letter of 28 March.
148 *Ibid.*, I, p. 74, for the Nuncio's interesting comparison of Barbin's favour and Richelieu's
     independence, which Bentivoglio also attributed to Richelieu's noble birth, merit and
     office.
149 *Ibid.*, I, p. 352, letter of 5 July 1617.

to deal with his demands and behaviour.[150] Concini's pressure on Richelieu in November 1616 to resign his see of Luçon in return for other benefices has been mentioned earlier. Whether Concini tried to make that a condition of his entry into the ministry is unclear, but Richelieu was initially willing enough to oblige him.[151] It was only when the most astute Barbin pointed out that this was designed to make him more dependent on Concini's favour that he eventually declined to do so.[152] It was perhaps as a lesser concession in that direction that Richelieu resigned his grand almonership to Anne of Austria in early 1617, the proceeds of which helped him arrange the marriage of his sister, Nicole, to the marquis de Brézé, later that year.[153] Likewise, Concini's demands for money and his recruitment of troops, especially in Liège, for his own unspecified purposes, complicated Richelieu's efforts to co-ordinate the war effort; here too, he was reduced to using letters bearing Louis XIII's signature to elicit Concini's co-operation.[154] The pressure was obviously considerable, and it led to a partial loss of nerve in the weeks immediately before Concini's assassination. The evidence for this is indirect. Both Richelieu and Barbin seem to have asked Marie de' Medici to be allowed to resign office, while another source simply affirms that she made Richelieu promise to continue in office.[155] Only a matter of days before Concini's murder, Richelieu made independent overtures to Louis XIII's confidant, Luynes, offering to keep the king informed of anything that came his way.[156] But the thinking behind this move was essentially prudential – rather like his overtures to Condé the previous summer – and designed to secure insurance in the case either of dismissal by Concini or of another loss of favour by Concini himself. The English ambassador's secretary, who reported the common rumour that Richelieu's discontent arose from the fact that Concini 'did of late somewhat imperiously check him for a dispatche he had made contrary to his liking', nevertheless concluded

---

150 Richelieu, *Mémoires*, ii, pp. 168–9.
151 B.L. MS. Stowe 176, fo. 70, Edmondes to Winwood, 10 Dec. 1616. Richelieu himself referred to actual negotiations over benefices involving père Coton, the king's confessor, in a later letter: Avenel, *Lettres*, i, pp. 677, letter to M de Sceaux (1621).
152 Richelieu, *Mémoires*, ii, p. 112.
153 Bergin, *Richelieu*, p. 33.
154 Avenel, *Lettres*, i, pp. 398–9, king to Concini, 14 March 1617; *ibid.*, p. 447, 25 March.
155 Louis Batiffol, 'Le Coup d'état du 24 avril 1617', *Revue Historique* 97 (1908), pp. 43 (n. 5), 44 (n. 1), quoting the best contemporary account of Concini's assassination, the *Relation exacte de tout ce qui s'est passé à la mort du maréchal d'Ancre*.
156 Steffani, *Nunziatura di Bentivoglio*, i, p. 194–5, letter from Bentivoglio to Borghese, 25 April 1617, relating Richelieu's own efforts to withdraw during the previous two weeks. Batiffol, 'Le Coup d'état du 24 avril 1617', pp. 65–6, esp. p. 66, n. 1; Richelieu, *Mémoires*, ii, pp. 166–7, 169–70.

that 'there is little doubt made but that they will easily make up this breache again'.[157] There is no sign in all this that Richelieu feared or suspected anything as drastic as the events of 24 April 1617. When the blow fell, it would find him quite unprepared, and would leave the ministry, its policies and its individual members ruined and discredited.

157   P.R.O., SP 78/67, fo. 80, Woodforde to Winwood, 20 April 1617.

Chapter 5
THE ARTS OF SURVIVAL

'The frame of this country which heretofore, like one of those huge massive poligonall bodyes described by the Geometricians, on what syde soever it fell, found means to keepe it selfe upright, and to subsist, hath received so little alteration by these late motions, that it seems only to have returned to its former base.'[1]

ON the morning of Concini's assassination, Richelieu was visiting a Sorbonne rector's residence, and was, by his own admission, dumbfounded by the suddenness of the event.[2] He was aware of the king's resentment against his mother and her favourites – that was no secret – but he simply did not believe either he or his entourage would be capable of such drastic political surgery. Like his fellow ministers, Richelieu immediately tried to make his way to the Louvre rather than lie low, as yet unwilling or incapable of grasping the significance of what had happened, and confident that his services would still be required. He was certainly in no mood to act upon the rector's parting recommendation – to meditate on the vagaries of fortune. It took the more experienced and more realistic Barbin to disabuse him: when they met and Richelieu ventured that the elimination of Concini had saved them all from further trouble, Barbin retorted, 'Hè, Monsieur, you are deceiving yourself if you do not see that the consequences of this will rebound on us'.[3] And when Richelieu finally entered the Louvre itself, he was subjected to a more celebrated and hostile outburst from the king: 'Now at last, Luçon, I am free of your tyranny (. . .) be off, get yourself out of here!' It took a few discreet words from Luynes, to whom Richelieu somehow managed to speak in the general confusion – Louis XIII was then standing on a billiard table! – for the king to moderate his language, if not his hostility, and to concede that he might remain, considering he was a bishop and a councillor of state. In the semi-hysterical atmosphere of the crowded Louvre, this was in itself no small achievement. Accounts differ as to whether Louis XIII also

---

1 Sir Edward Herbert to Sir Robert Naunton, Paris, 29 Sept. 1620: P.R.O. 30/53/3, fos. 104–5.
2 Richelieu, *Mémoires*, II, p. 183.
3 *Journal d'Arnauld 1614–20*, p. 293.

declared that Richelieu's secretaryship of state was to revert to Villeroy, or simply told him to repair to the council meeting then in progress. At any rate, when he did enter the council chamber, Villeroy and Châteauneuf quickly made it plain to him that he was no longer welcome there.[4] Here was a first manifestation of the tenacious ministerial opposition which bedevilled Richelieu's career until his return to office seven years later. In such circumstances, it was not obvious to whom he could turn next: Marie de' Medici was being held incommunicado, and he was no longer grand almoner to Anne of Austria.[5]

These well-rehearsed biographical details should not disguise the seriousness of the political changes which Concini's assassination set in motion. For over a generation, the Italian's fate would be repeatedly recalled in order to frighten ministers whose power and wealth were regarded as excessive. The need to rid France of the queen mother's favourite had obsessed and dominated those around the king to the exclusion of almost everything else, so that it is not clear to what extent detailed plans for a new régime had been laid. Whatever skills he might subsequently develop, Luynes was probably incapable of conceiving the outlines of a new régime beyond securing favour for himself and his own. It is one of the many paradoxes of a period rich in them that the only member of Luynes's kitchen-cabinet capable of planning not just the coup against Concini but its aftermath, was Barbin's principal subordinate in the finance ministry, Guichard Déageant.[6] Politically as well as administratively the short-term transition was greatly facilitated by the decision to recall the old ministers – Villeroy, Sillery and his son Puysieux, Jeannin and du Vair – not least because their dismissal had figured prominently among the *gravamina* of the rebellious princes. Above all, the civil war halted abruptly when news reached the rival

---

4 The most comprehensive critical study of the coup is still Batiffol, 'Le Coup d'état du 24 avril 1617', *Revue Historique* 95 (1907), pp. 292–308, 97 (1908), pp. 27–77, 264–86. For Louis XIII's attitude to Richelieu, see pp. 270–1. For Richelieu's reception in council, see *Journal d'Arnauld 1614–20*, p. 291; P.R.O., SP 78/67, fos. 81–2, Woodforde to Winwood, 24 April 1617. See also the lively reconstruction in Marvick, *Louis XIII*, chs. 13–14.

5 The papal nuncio, who promptly agreed to assist Richelieu at this juncture, thought he would willingly accept the post of French ambassador in Rome, but concluded that the new ministry would probably want a man of its own choosing in such a prestigious post: Steffani, *Nunziatura di Bentivoglio*, I, pp. 203–4, letter of 26 April 1617.

6 Pontchartrain, Paul Phélypeaux, seigneur de, *Mémoires* (ed. Petitot) (Paris 1822), p. 235; Fontenay-Mareuil, François Duval, marquis de, *Mémoires* (ed. Petitot) (Paris 1826), pp. 382–3. Déageant's own account of these and subsequent events is to be found in his *Mémoires envoyés à Monsieur le Cardinal de Richelieu contenant plusieurs choses particulières et remarquables arrivées depuis les dernières années du roi Henri IV jusqu'au commencement du ministère du cardinal de Richelieu* (Paris 1756); it needs, as the title suggests, to be treated with caution.

forces that Concini and his régime were no more. As the armies began to melt away, promptly undoing Richelieu's labours of several months, the rebel princes and their followers began returning to court; there the king welcomed them as friends and defenders of his state, and duly amnestied them. Only Condé was excluded from this exercise in largesse and, despite short-lived talk of his release, remained incarcerated until late 1619.[7] Soon it was being said that the court had never been so well-attended, especially by the great aristocracy, many of whom were no doubt doubly reassured by the manner of Concini's fall.[8] Faction and civil strife seemed unfortunate nightmares from a discredited and discarded past.

In these propitious circumstances, the problem of what to do with Marie de' Medici could only seem less formidable. In her case, there seems to have been no suggestion of either a political trial or exile abroad. Internal exile had always seemed the only acceptable method of removing her from the political stage, but the practical details and conditions for this do not appear to have been fully decided upon.[9] The nine days which she spent confined to her quarters in the Louvre, while the king obstinately refused either to see or negotiate directly with her, created a peculiar kind of political vacuum which proved to be yet another of those oblique opportunities for Richelieu to offer his services as a go-between, an offer Luynes was happy enough to accept. Richelieu had been among the first to receive permission to visit her, and this enabled him to interpret and relay her wishes.[10] However, it was not Luynes but Déageant, soon to become an *intendant des finances* with considerable political influence, who dealt directly with Richelieu and Marie.

Thus, as the initial violence of the coup subsided and more restrained counsels began to prevail, Richelieu was able to negotiate a series of conditions for Marie's demotion and departure which, if they did not assuage her bitterness, at least spared her the full ignominy that might otherwise have befallen her.[11] In so doing, Richelieu also managed to apply the brakes, for the time being, to his own fall from grace. Indeed, by any measurement of the retri-

---

7 Steffani, *Nunziatura di Bentivoglio*, I, pp. 192–5, letters of 25 April 1617. See also Batiffol, 'Coup d'état', pp. 271–2; Moote, *Louis XIII*, pp. 98ff. For speculation about Condé's release, see Steffani, *Nunziatura di Bentivoglio*, I, pp. 202–3, 276, 303.
8 *Journal d'Arnauld 1614–20*, pp. 305–6; P.R.O., SP 78/67, fo. 126, Edmondes to Winwood, 12 June 1617.
9 Steffani, *Nunziatura di Bentivoglio*, I, pp. 198–201, letter of 26 April 1617.
10 *Journal d'Arnauld 1614–20*, p. 284.
11 Steffani, *Nunziatura di Bentivoglio*, I, pp. 210–11, letter of 9 May 1617; P.R.O., SP 78/67, fo. 95v, Woodforde to Winwood, 5 May 1617, explicitly mentions Richelieu's involvement in delicate negotiations as to how Marie would address her son when taking leave of him on departing to Blois. See Batiffol, 'Coup d'état', pp. 281–3; Chevallier, *Louis XIII*, p. 171.

bution visited upon the Concini régime, he escaped lightly. Barbin was pursued remorselessly, although his subsequent trial and eventual banishment were long delayed.[12] Mangot, once he had surrendered the seals without protest, was left in relative peace. Richelieu alone managed to find a part to play which kept him on stage. But it was one for which there might be a high price to pay, and it may be doubted whether, in his desire to keep a foot on the political ladder, he realized this as speedily or as fully as he later claimed. Luynes's willingness to accept him as mediator between the king and his mother was based on Richelieu's readiness to manage her affairs and report back to him on her and her entourage, just as he had previously offered to do, while a minister, in respect of Concini. That offer was now acceptable in the new and much-changed circumstances. In return, Richelieu believed he had secured a promise from Déageant – and perhaps from Luynes also – that they would defend him at court against rumours and intrigues concerning him and his actions.[13] No one would do more to discredit Luynes both among their contemporaries and for posterity than Richelieu, which makes it especially ironic that he owed his escape from complete disgrace to the new favourite, who clearly felt (and would later say so) that he had earned the right to his gratitude and co-operation.

By the time the queen mother's party left Paris for Blois on 3 May 1617, Richelieu may well have found the time to reflect upon the unpredictability of fortune. Yet he had not emerged from the crisis as empty-handed as had his erstwhile colleagues. Although France had experienced considerable turmoil in the preceding years, there was no real precedent for what was now unfolding – a disgraced queen mother living in internal exile, while retaining all her offices, pensions, jointure in lands and royal demesne, as well as the important provincial governorship of Normandy. It remained to be seen how far she could be persuaded to accept her present condition and allow the king a free hand to govern as he saw fit, or whether she would use what power she still retained to fight her way back to court and government. The rhetoric of royal absolutism, so liberally used by Richelieu himself when in office, placed such exclusive emphasis on the powers of kingship that it offered few answers to one of the major practical headaches facing the French monarchy – the political role of the royal family. Thus, much more than the pro-

---

12 *Journal d'Arnauld 1614–20*, pp. 293–4.
13 Avenel, *Lettres*, VII, pp. 397–8, letter to Déageant, (late June 1617): 'Si je n'eusse pensé estre garenty de l'envie et de la rage par l'appuy que vous scaves, je ne me fusse jamais embarqué au vaisseau où je suis. Ayant comme je vous ay dict, avant que de partir, bien prévu toutes les difficultés et les obstacles qui se sont rencontrez et rencontrent en l'affaire dont il est question . . .'

spects of the bishop of Luçon hung on the outcome of this fresh and unscripted departure in French politics. The new titles of president of the queen mother's council, keeper of her seal, and *intendant* of her affairs which Richelieu would shortly assume were a thin disguise for a role that promised to be neither glorious nor without risk.[14]

II

Richelieu's first major exercise in the art of political survival had, in the short term, enabled him to extricate himself from political catastrophe far better than anyone could have anticipated. His firm belief in his own innocence had prevented any immediate loss of nerve. Had it not done so, he might have been arrested as the new powers seem to have initially intended or, at best, been exiled to his diocese.[15] But his was still no more than a case of 'so far, so good'. The real test was yet to come, and he would soon have the opportunity to realize that he had only fashioned a poisoned chalice for himself. Removed from the king's entourage, member of a court-in-exile at Blois, that boasted its full complement of intriguers and pretenders to his role as chief minister to a fallen ruler, Richelieu's efforts to keep all sides happy, while promoting his own indispensability, soon ran into trouble and alienated most of those who dealt with him. It may seem odd that, despite his success with Luynes and his new position, Richelieu proved unable to dominate the queen mother's court, or enjoy her full confidence. Her entourage was relatively small, dominated by women and ecclesiastics. Many of the latter were, like Marie herself, Florentines, or at least Italians. However, it was not so much men like Bishop Hurault of Chartres, or Cardinal Bonzi and his nephew, the coadjutor-bishop of Béziers, who posed the main threat to Richelieu, but lesser figures like the abbés Tantucci and Rucellaï, men of more obscure background and motivation who, like the Bonzis, had for many years moved in the circles around the Concinis and the queen mother. Rucellaï had been tipped for ministerial office towards the end of the Concini régime, and his ambition made him the natural adversary of Richelieu.[16] Tantucci played a devious game of his own, regularly shuttling between Marie and Luynes, Blois and Paris, as did the Bonzis and several others.[17] None of them operated under Richelieu's direct

14 *Ibid.*, VII, p. 386, Richelieu to Luynes, *c.* 10 May 1617.
15 Steffani, *Nunziatura di Bentivoglio*, I, p. 272, letter of 4 June 1617.
16 *Ibid.*, I, pp. 230–1, letter of 16 May 1617. The nuncio's correspondence for the rest of the year is full of accounts of Rucellaï's strange behaviour.
17 Their letters to Richelieu during the summer of 1617 are scattered throughout A.A.E. France 771.

instructions and, indeed, he was not powerful enough to control either their movements or their actions.

For his part, Richelieu realized that a rapid reconciliation between Louis XIII and the queen mother was impossible, and that to insist upon one would be impolitic: it would only exasperate the king and alienate Luynes, whose own position would be vulnerable in the event of a reconciliation. He concluded that a more patient line had to be followed, and argued with Luynes and Déageant that the court should facilitate this – and so ensure there would be no untoward explosion – by offering Marie satisfaction on matters of minor or purely personal interest.[18] Equally, he insisted that she had no desire to stand in the way of Louis and Luynes governing as they saw fit, but would do her best to satisfy the new favourite.

But all this left Richelieu vulnerable to the charge that he was lukewarm in defending Marie's cause, and more concerned with his own interests. Her resentment at what she regarded as mistreatment was not difficult to exploit, and courtiers like Rucellaï and Tantucci tried to capitalize on her exasperation. She has generally been seen as lethargic while actually in power, especially after the Estates General of 1614, but once ejected from it she recovered much of her energy; respect for what she saw as her rights as the king's mother, and her search for reparation of the wrongs inflicted upon her acted as a focus and gave her a greater sense of purpose.[19] The vexed question of Richelieu's complex relations with Louis XIII during his long second ministry has always exercised historians, but less attention has been given to his relations with Marie, which were in their own way no less troublesome. Both in 1617 and later, he had considerable difficulty in harnessing her ambitions and resentments in a coherent fashion, and was, therefore, perennially suspected of pursuing objectives of his own at the expense of her interests.

Richelieu's behaviour during the hectic few weeks of the Blois interlude, as reflected in his correspondence, shows him in a very unfamiliar light indeed. As he wrestled with the contradictions of the position in which he found himself, he became more shrill and paranoid than at almost any other time in his career. At first, when he arrived in Blois, he confidently reported to Luynes that everything was in order, that the queen mother was anxious to render every service, and that he himself could scarcely believe how com-

18 Avenel, *Lettres*, VII, pp. 388–9, letter to Luynes; *ibid.*, p. 390, to same, 12 May.
19 See, for example, Marvick, *Louis XIII*, p. 123; J. Russell Major, *Representative Government in Early Modern France* (New Haven and London, 1980), p. 397. There are dissenters from this negative view of her: see, for example, Hayden, *France and the Estates General*. But there is general agreement that her interest in the routine of government was limited, and that she was extremely sensitive about her rank and rights.

pletely she had put recent events and humiliations behind her; despite the intrigues of others against him, Richelieu insisted that her confidence in him had only grown.[20] Ten days later, he claimed that a direct appeal from Rucellaï to Marie de' Medici for his dismissal had only served to shatter the abbé's intrigues and to reinforce that confidence.[21] This temporary victory secured his formal appointment, with the court's approval, as keeper of Marie's seal and president of her council.[22]

This optimism was premature and was designed primarily to reassure the court that Richelieu was fulfilling his part of the bargain struck after the coup against Concini. But as he attempted to draw Louis XIII, Luynes, and, Déageant, into his confidence, with a view to underwriting his actions as Marie's 'guardian', the more they began to back away in suspicion of his motives and ambitions. The English ambassador even reported that the court was unhappy with what appeared to be Richelieu's growing 'empire' over the queen mother, fearing the uses to which it might be put.[23] Within days of his arrival, Déageant was already alluding to the two issues that would prove to be the bishop's downfall – the persistent rumours of intrigue and subversive plotting in Marie's entourage, and her own complaints that Richelieu and Villesavin, her principal secretary, were only there to spy on her.[24] In subsequent letters, the first complaint was reiterated, with Déageant stating bluntly that as Richelieu was now in charge of Marie's affairs, he would also be held responsible for the behaviour of her followers.[25] Yet even Richelieu's regular reports on Marie's court and entourage were themselves regarded with a jaundiced eye: someone prepared to go so far must surely have deeper motives and must, despite his repeated protestations of loyalty and service to the king and Luynes, probably be involved in the suspicious comings and goings reported from Blois. Richelieu's own increasingly agitated letters abound with references to a wide assortment of unnamed 'envieux' and 'ennemis' in both Blois and Paris, and with desperate pleas for support and goodwill. By early June, he was lamenting to Déageant that he was 'le plus malheureux des hommes, sans l'avoir mérité';[26] a week later, he complained to Luynes, whose letters to him rarely

20 Avenel, *Lettres*, VII, p. 927, letters to Luynes and Déageant, 8 May.
21 *Ibid.*, VII, pp. 391–4, letter to Déageant, 18 May.
22 B.N., MS. 500 Colbert 91, fo. 112, *brevet* of 19 May.
23 P.R.O., SP 78/67, fo. 131v, Edmondes to Winwood, 12 June 1617.
24 A.A.E. France 771, fo. 112, Déageant to Richelieu, 10 May, referring to reports of intrigues: 'Je ne vous tairray point qu'a toutes heures l'on a les oreilles battues . . .'; *ibid.*, fos. 118–19, same to same, 15 May.
25 *Ibid.*, fo. 123, Déageant to Richelieu, 19 May.
26 Avenel, *Lettres*, VII, pp. 397–8, letter of early June.

ventured beyond polite formulae, 'je suis combattu de toutes parts'.[27]
Even the Assembly of Clergy, then in session, was rumoured to
have been critical of him.[28]

A month of having to deal with conflicting pressures finally took
its toll. Richelieu's sudden departure from Blois to his priory of
Coussay on 11 June remains as shrouded in mystery and controversy
as it was at the time. He was tipped off by his brother of a decision
taken in the king's council to disgrace him, and he chose to leave of
his own volition rather than wait and suffer the indignity of further
disgrace.[29] The tip-off turned out to be a false alarm, which led some
historians to conclude that it had been deliberately engineered by
Richelieu, but it had been an open secret during previous weeks that
the court was anxious to remove him from Blois.[30] Indeed, there is
independent evidence that shortly before Richelieu's withdrawal,
Louis XIII had tried, but failed, to persuade Marie to dispense with
his services.[31] In later years, Richelieu would become a master of the
finely-timed threat or 'request' to retire from office, but in 1617 he
was still a subordinate political actor whose position was one of
weakness, not strength. As far as we can judge his intentions from
the confused and insincere statements of all those concerned, he
seems to have wished to force the hand of both Marie and Luynes,
and to elicit firm expressions of support from them. Subsequent
frantic efforts, including his own, to portray his departure as just a
brief period of leave taken with Marie's permission – an elaborate
fiction which she, in her anxiety to secure his return, duly supported
– proved as unavailing as they were disingenuous. Richelieu did not
respond to Marie's repeated entreaties to return post-haste to Blois,
hoping no doubt that if Louis or Luynes instructed him to do so, his
hand would be enormously strengthened and his detractors con-

---

27 *Ibid.*, VII, pp. 399–400, letter of 8/9 June.
28 A.A.E. France 771, fo. 125, Déageant to Richelieu, 24 May. Richelieu refused to believe
    the entire assembly could be against him.
29 *Ibid.*, fo. 117, Henri de Richelieu to Armand, 14 June; Griselle, *Louis XIII et Richelieu*,
    pp. 212–13, same to same, 27 June.
30 Steffani, *Nunziatura di Bentivoglio*, I, pp. 223, 250, letters of 16 and 23 May respectively.
    It was the loss of the original letter warning Richelieu which led Hanotaux to suspect
    that Richelieu and his brother between them fabricated a convenient excuse for his sud-
    den departure from Blois. This interpretation seems excessively Machiavellian, even by
    the standards of the time. See Hanotaux, *Richelieu*, II, pp. 219–20.
31 P.R.O., SP 78/67, fos. 130–1, Edmondes to Winwood, 12 June 1617: 'The Bishop of
    Lusson is the person that doth now absolutely governe the queen mother, where with
    the king was so much displeased, as he was once taking order to have removed him from
    thence, but I understand that the said resolution is now suspended upon the queen's
    earnest suite.' B.N. MS. Baluze 323, fo. 3, 'extrait' from Marie's reply to king's letter.
    Her reply was dated 8 June, three days before Richelieu's abrupt departure from Blois.
    The full text of neither of these two letters seems to have survived, but the English
    ambassador's report lends force to this interpretations of events.

founded.[32] But no such instruction was forthcoming: on the contrary, by leaving so precipitately, he had manoeuvred himself into a position where it could only prove easier to dispense with him altogether. Within days, his departure from Blois was sealed by a royal letter which, heavily laced with irony, applauded his decision to return to his diocese and his flock, and bade him not to move from there without express royal permission.[33] He could do little but accept his sentence, promising to 'observe religiously what the king wished'.[34] Marie de' Medici continued to protest vehemently, but her pleas, in which she increasingly gave vent to her antipathy to Luynes, were resented by the court, which persisted in ignoring them.[35]

For his part, Richelieu took his cue from the royal missive and quickly decided upon his immediate priorities: had not the king enjoined him to devote himself to his diocese, so that his flock 'should obey both God's commands and mine (i.e. the king's)'? Trying as best he could to close this most recent chapter in his history, Richelieu concluded a letter to Louis, in late June 1617, with the claim that he was currently occupied 'parmy mes livres aux divertissemens et fonctions de ma profession'.[36] His choice of words here is hardly fortuitous, and indicates a clear preference for his library at Coussay over the marshlands of Luçon. Indeed, within a month or so of leaving Blois, he was presented with an opportunity not only to bring to fruition his earlier studies of the confessional controversies, but to defend and enhance his reputation by doing so, thus extending his circle of friends and supporters. In mid-July 1617, the Huguenot ministers of Charenton published their reply to the court sermons of the Jesuit Père Arnoux attacking their beliefs; they did so in a work addressed directly to the king, a tactic which gave sufficient offence for legal action to be initiated against the ministers.[37] Alleging that their work was doing considerable damage in his own province of

---

32 See Richelieu's letters to Luynes in Avenel, *Lettres*, VII, pp. 407–10; the letters of Tantucci and Bonzi in A.A.E. France 771, fos. 131, 132, and the extracts from those of Marie de' Medici published in Avenel, *Lettres*, VII, pp. 403–5.

33 Avenel, *Lettres*, I, p. 541, n. 1, letter of 15 June; Richelieu, *Mémoires*, II, p. 247.

34 Avenel, *Lettres*, VII, pp. 410–11, letter to Louis XIII, 18 June. Richelieu's brother reported that the letter was well received by the royal council: Griselle, *Louis XIII et Richelieu*, pp. 212–13, letter of 27 June.

35 See selections from her letters to Louis XIII and Luynes in Avenel, *Lettres*, VII, pp. 401–7. To Louis XIII, she wrote: 'Ne me faictes des affronts que j'aimerois mieux mourir que de les endurer'(p. 403). To Luynes: 'cela me faict croire qu'on ne se mesfie de luy, mais de moy' (*ibid.*).

36 *Ibid.*, I, pp. 541–3, late June 1617.

37 *Journal d'Arnauld 1614–20*, p. 310, 12 July 1617; Steffani, *Nunziatura di Bentivogiio*, I, pp. 361–3, 366, 389, 392, letters of 19 and 25 July; Richelieu, *Mémoires*, II, pp. 254–5, for Richelieu's own account.

Poitou, Richelieu quickly resolved to reply to them.[38] But, even if this 'damage' was genuine, Richelieu was enough of an opportunist to hope to benefit from being able, like them, to address his work directly to the king. By his own account, it took him six weeks to write the *Principaux points de la foy catholique*; it was an occupation which he was anxious to make known in both political and ecclesiastical circles.[39] Throughout the book run the twin themes of obedience to kings as God's anointed, and of the catholic church's steadfast commitment to that doctrine. Richelieu's subsequent efforts to circulate his book as widely as possible, and the reception it received from fellow-ecclesiastics, doubtless bolstered his claim to be entirely absorbed by his role as a scholar-bishop.[40] Apart from that, however, its impact seems to have been relatively limited. As a defence of the Jesuits, it was not as fulsome and wholehearted as it needed to be – Richelieu was after all a Sorbonne man – in order to win their full and powerful endorsement.[41] Its other objective, that of contributing to his political rehabilitation, proved equally elusive.

However much Richelieu might insist upon the ecclesiastical and intellectual nature of his current activities, he could not put his recent past out of his mind. He clearly kept his political antennae fully extended after his exile from Blois; various members of Marie's household, as well as his brother and his brother-in-law, both still at court, kept him informed of events, and passed on rumours or gossip.[42] Marie herself soon softened her irritation with him and his brother after his departure, and he eventually replied to her letters.[43] His own correspondence again took on the characteristics of his early letters from Luçon – exaggerated expressions of deference and gratitude to a wide range of people who had written to him, or even spoken well of him to others.[44] But more than anything else he was preoccupied with the damage to his reputation that he perceived was being done by continuing innuendo and rumour. Still convinced that his record was patent evidence of his devotion to the crown – 'I

38 Avenel, *Lettres*, VII, p. 414, letter to du Vair, Oct. 1617.
39 *Ibid.*, VII, pp. 412–14, letter to Père Joseph. See previous note.
40 *Ibid.*, I, pp. 556–7, to Jacques de Flavigny, Nov. 1617; *ibid.*, p. 607, to Nicolas Coëffetau; *ibid.*, p. 608, to M. de Guron. Avenel assigns the letters to Coëffetau and Guron to 1619, but they clearly refer to his book and the 'ennemis de l'église', and thus probably date from late 1617. For episcopal reactions to the book, see Griselle, *Louis XIII et Richelieu*, pp. 375–7, Sébastien Bouthillier to St Cyran, 4 Feb. 1618.
41 Deloche, *Autour de la plume de Richelieu*, pp. 142ff.
42 This ample correspondence is in A.A.E. France 771, fos. 152–82.
43 B.V.C. Fonds Richelieu 14, fo. 47, Cardinal Bonzi to Richelieu, Blois, 15 June 1617, conveying the queen mother's anger against Henri, and pleading with Richelieu to return to Blois. Griselle, *Louis XIII et Richelieu*, pp. 165–6, undated letter to Marie, but probably June–July 1617.
44 Avenel, *Lettres*, I, pp. 544–5, 548–51, for several letters to mostly anonymous correspondents.

served the king in obeying the queen mother's commands' – it mattered a great deal to him that this was understood and accepted. Only two weeks after being confined to Coussay, he addressed to Louis XIII the first of several acts of self-defence which he was to pen over the next few months. 'I protest before God, Sire, that although I cannot prevent people from defaming me, I shall ensure they have no grounds for doing so . . . On leaving office, Your Majesty did me the honour of recognizing me for what I am – a man genuinely zealous for your service and one anxious to merit, in accordance with my condition, a reputation without blemish.'[45] But Luynes proved as cool as ever to his overtures, while the queen mother's own requests for Richelieu's return to her service were flatly rejected by the crown.[46] Nevertheless, in September 1617, Richelieu decided to follow advice given him by his brother and attempted, rather belatedly, to regain the goodwill of the powerful Déageant; it is equally interesting to note that he requested Père Joseph, whom he had not seen for eighteen months but whom he knew to be in touch with Déageant, to act as his intermediary in this.[47] By October, he was sufficiently encouraged by the results to feel that the time was right for a another direct approach to Louis XIII.[48] In doing so, he may have reminded the king of his promise, apparently conveyed to Père Joseph, to permit him to return soon to Marie de' Medici's service.[49] Not only did this vigourous lobbying, with its tactless recalling of promises made concerning him, irritate the king, Luynes and the ministers, and fail completely to achieve its end, but it brought down on him in late October a further humiliation – a new sentence of exile, this time from Coussay to Luçon itself.[50] Once again, Richelieu's response combined acceptance of the king's command with a stubborn restatement of his innocence.[51]

45 *Ibid.*, I, pp. 541–3, late June 1617.
46 P.R.O., SP 78/67, fos. 178v–79r, Edmondes to Winwood, 10 Sept. 1617; Steffani, *Nunziatura di Bentivoglio*, I, p. 395, letter of 2 Aug. 1617; pp. 499–500, 14 Sept.; p. 525, 27 Sept.
47 Avenel, *Lettres*, VII, pp. 412–14. His brother's advice was conveyed in a letter from Tantucci: A.A.E. France 771, fo. 158, 13 July. See his earlier letter to Luynes in Avenel, *Lettres*, VII, pp. 411–12.
48 Fagniez, *Le Père Joseph et Richelieu*, I, pp. 78–9, quoting Père Joseph's letter to Cardinal Borghese, in which he claimed, mistakenly as it turned out, that his mediation had been successful.
49 Steffani, *Nunziatura di Bentivoglio*, I, pp. 499–500, letter of 14 Sept., mentions the promise given to Marie de' Medici that Richelieu would be recalled within two months. The actual form taken by Richelieu's approach to the king is not known, but his letter of 2 Nov. probably repeats the substance of that approach. See n. 51.
50 B.N. MS. Clairambault 372, fo. 271, minute of royal letter, 26 Oct. 1617; Steffani, Nunziatura di Bentivoglio, II, pp. 66–7, letter of 8 Nov.
51 Griselle, *Louis XIII et Richelieu*, pp. 181–3, letter to Louis XIII, 2 Nov. 1617. Griselle, using the original of this letter among Pontchartrain's papers, corrects Avenel's

But the casual remark he made in his covering letter to Pontchartrain is no less revealing: before retiring to Luçon, he would have to remove his remaining belongings from Blois. It was his way of admitting that his hopes of a return there had now effectively been dashed.[52]

It was not, therefore, until November 1617 that Richelieu actually set foot in Luçon itself, where he remained until April 1618, living, as we saw, in temporary lodgings provided by the canons of his cathedral. He had not neglected the affairs of his diocese while at Coussay. In late September he was making arrangements for Bérulle's Oratory to send a preacher to Luçon for Advent and Lent.[53] We have also noted that his contract with Bérulle for the establishment of his seminary awaited implementation, and that he approached the Capuchins to found a hospice in the town of Luçon.[54] But these few cases apart, we know little of Richelieu's pastoral activities in late November 1617.

In any case, Luynes's régime had by that date even less reason than before to listen to Richelieu's protests of innocence and honourable conduct. His departure from Blois had not produced any unpleasant consequences and, despite rumours of continuing 'menées et intrigues', the fate of Marie de' Medici was not a central consideration for the rest of that year; no knight errant had as yet emerged from among the aristocracy to rescue her from her disgrace. If the court kept a close eye on Marie and her circle, it was essentially to prevent a coalition of malcontents from forming around her; its worst fear was that, for all their mutual enmity, a tactical alliance between Marie and Condé – negotiated by Richelieu, for example – might constitute a serious threat to Luynes's emerging régime before it had become fully established.[55] Luynes, who had married Marie de Montbazon – who as the duchesse de Chevreuse would prove to be one of Richelieu's most implacable enemies – was still busy consolidating his position as favourite, and gradually filling the void left by Concini.[56] By the autumn of 1617, the decision had been taken to hold an Assembly of Notables which would advise on how to implement the principal demands of the Estates General of 1614, deal with the serious deterioration of the royal finances since that

---

suggested date of Sept. 1617. Avenel's text was based on an undated minute: see *Lettres*, I, pp. 551–3.

52 Griselle, *Louis XIII et Richelieu*, pp. 183–4, letter of 2 Nov.
53 A.A.E. France 771, fo. 179, Charles Gérault to Richelieu, 23 Sept. 1617.
54 See pp. 85–6, 95–6.
55 For recurrences of these fears, see Steffani, *Nunziatura di Bentivoglio*, I, pp. 381–2, 19 July 1617; *ibid.*, II, 277, 14 March 1618.
56 Moote, *Louis XIII*, pp. 102–4.

date, and to help win acceptance for the new political dispensation.[57] The court left Paris in mid-November, and remained at Rouen while the assembly deliberated there throughout December 1617. While both the court and the notables converged on Rouen, Richelieu was in Luçon arranging for the marriage of his sister Nicole to Urbain de Brézé, a future governor of Anjou and marshal of France, but at the time, despite his undoubted noble lineage, little more than heir to an impressively long list of family debts.[58] The anonymity of the marriage, 'sans cérémonies aucunes', contrasts sharply with those of Luynes and his brothers around the same time, and provides its own eloquent testimony of Richelieu's loss of favour.[59]

III

Yet worse was in store for Richelieu, and by mid-April 1618 he would be obliged to 'vider le royaume' and depart for a more painful exile in the papal enclave of Avignon. His own subsequent account asserts he was not surprised at the order when it came, given the moral turpitude of those governing France at the time. Less rhetorically, he attributed the decision as Luynes's response to obscure manoeuvres involving several leading nobles – Rohan, Montbazon, Épernon and Bellegarde – and a plan allegedly devised by the imprisoned Barbin to secure the return to court of Marie de' Medici, by then closely watched and confined at Blois![60] Richelieu's own influence at Blois had probably reached its lowest point, all the more so as, in a tactic that Louis XIII and Richelieu himself would later repeat several times in the households of Anne of Austria and Gaston d'Orléans, the personnel of Marie's household had been reduced, changed or suborned in varying degrees by Luynes.[61] In early 1618, she was primarily concerned with the fate of Barbin, then facing trial, though both she and Richelieu still seemed to hope that the latter's return to her service was a serious possibility.[62] At any rate,

57 See Bonney, *The King's Debts*, pp. 96–8.
58 Bergin, *Richelieu*, p. 33.
59 Avenel, *Lettres*, I, pp. 554–5, Richelieu to Henri de Richelieu, undated. Avenel assigns the letter to Oct. 1618, but it should be late Nov.
60 Richelieu, *Mémoires*, II p. 279; Steffani, *Nunziatura di Bentivoglio*, II, pp. 253–4, letter of 26 Feb. 1618, referring to close military surveillance of Blois.
61 Louis Batiffol, *Louis XIII a vingt ans* (Paris 1910), pp. 322–3. As early as August 1617, the court refused Richelieu's candidate for a secretaryship in Marie's service, and was even less ready to allow his sister, Nicole, to enter the queen mother's household: Steffani, *Nunziatura di Bentivoglio*, I, p. 395, letter of 2 Aug. 1617. Freedom to choose her own household would be one of Marie's principal demands after her escape from Blois in 1619.
62 Steffani, *Nunziatura di Bentivoglio*, II, p. 348, letter of 25 April 1618.

an abrupt halt was called in February 1618 to the manoeuvres concerning Marie de' Medici's future. Essentially, Luynes was still unready to allow a royal reconciliation, and Louis XIII feared the effects of his mother's return to court.[63] In fact, this murky episode, in which reality, rumour, and innuendo were so closely intertwined as to make an objective assessment difficult, enabled Luynes to conduct a sweep against those who were critical of his aggrandizement, of the continuing exclusion of the *grands* from government, and of financial retrenchments at court – all a microcosm of the conflicts to come in 1619 and 1620.[64] As a result, he further tightened his control of Marie's household, placing her under closer surveillance; and by moving Mayenne to the governorship of Guyenne, he secured that of the Ile-de-France for himself. Less wilful and erratic than Concini, he had gradually accumulated offices and wealth which outstripped those of his predecessor.[65]

His protestations that he was a busy ecclesiastic notwithstanding, Richelieu had allowed his hopes of rehabilitation to surface again in late 1617 and early 1618. But by then his reputation was such that he had to contend with a factor which virtually enjoyed an independent existence of its own, and which would continue to dog him in subsequent years – the court's almost automatic assumption that he was either the guiding hand behind intrigues involving Marie de' Medici and potential malcontents, or that he was at least aware of them. In September 1617, the English ambassador echoed the common opinion at court that Richelieu was a 'great *brouillon*'.[66] At any rate, he embarked on another campaign of self-defence in late 1617 and early 1618, a campaign in which he enlisted an old patron, Bertrand d'Eschaux, to try to change the king's opinion of him, as well as Montbazon, Luynes's father-in-law, to defend him against calumny and rumour.[67] But he had singularly little success. On the contrary, the first sign of renewed trouble for him was the decision, taken in February 1618, to exile Henri de Richelieu and Pont-Courlay to their estates: it was no secret that they handled Armand's affairs in Paris, keeping him informed of events.[68] When this did not suffice,

---

63 Batiffol, *Louis XIII a vingt ans*, pp. 336–8.
64 See *Journal d'Arnauld 1614–20*, pp. 358ff., for a chronicle of the events of March-April 1618; Pontchartrain, *Mémoires*, pp. 260–1; Steffani, *Nunziatura di Bentivoglio*, II, pp. 295–6, 29 March 1618.
65 The comings and goings between Blois and the court can be partially followed in *Journal d'Arnauld 1614–20*, pp. 348–9, 358–9. For the exchange of governorships, see Bonney, *The King's Debts*, p. 94, n. 3.
66 P.R.O., SP 78/67, fos. 178v–79r, letter of 10 Sept. 1617.
67 Avenel, *Lettres*, I, pp. 558–61, two letters to Eschaux, late 1617, early 1618; *ibid.*, 561–3, to Montbazon. He also expressed his bitterness at the attacks against him to his brother, Henri: *ibid.*, I, pp. 563–4.
68 *Journal d'Arnauld 1614–20*, p. 361.

and Luynes extended his purge of the opposition, all three of them were ordered, on 7 April, to depart to Avignon, where they arrived a month later.[69] Indeed, Richelieu had yet again presented the crown with an easy excuse to move against him when, in another of his exasperated protests against the rumours circulating about him, he asked the king to assign him a place of residence – he even suggested the Bastille in the first draft of his letter, but on second thoughts, crossed it out! – where he would be safe from unfounded allegations.[70] The crown was only too ready to oblige him, though not before it, too, had second thoughts about the place of exile: Avignon was preferred to Rome, as it was feared he would be too 'free' in Rome. Two days before the order to depart was given, news arrived in Paris that Henri de Gondi, the rather colourless bishop of Paris, had been made a cardinal; six months later, in response to growing pressure from the clergy for a seat in council for one of theirs, he would even assume the nominal 'presidency' of the king's council.[71] Richelieu's career and ambitions could not but seem matters of merely historical interest, especially as others seemed about to reap the rewards of the demand for a clerical role in government which he had so forcefully put at the Estates-General.

If Richelieu's political 'traversée du désert' actually began with his successive 'retraites' at Coussay and Luçon, where he could at least recover an earlier sense of purpose as scholar and bishop, its full severity only hit him during his exile in Avignon. In more recent French history, such experiences have often enabled their protagonists to take stock of their career and beliefs. In Richelieu's case, the distance he had fallen in the twelve months since April 1617 would have been fully and painfully borne in upon him. Given the normal fate of disgraced royal ministers, particularly those of an execrated régime, there was little ground for hope, and few illusions left to cling to which might veil the disgrace that had progressively befallen him. Like Marie de' Medici's own fate, there was no telling how long his exile might be, nor how it would end. To a considerable extent, Richelieu had been the victim of his own repeated efforts to vindicate himself. Shortly after his departure from Blois, Tantucci had written to him: 'nous nous sommes fait le mal à nous mesmes'.[72] Richelieu may not have reflected then upon such a casual remark, coming as it did from someone he distrusted, but in his eagerness to protest his innocence and secure his recall, he not only

69 Griselle, *Louis XIII et Richelieu*, pp. 185–6, Richelieu to Louis XIII, 11 April 1618. The royal order was issued on 7 April.
70 Avenel, *Lettres*, I, pp. 564–5, letter to Louis XIII, early 1618; *ibid.*, VII, p. 415.
71 *Journal d'Arnauld 1614–20*, p. 359, 5 April 1618.
72 Quoted in Avenel, *Lettres*, VII, p. 406.

succeeded in exasperating the court, but on nearly every occasion unwittingly compounded his own difficulties. Deloche suggested that the immediate cause of Richelieu's banishment in 1618 was his authorship of a tract defending the queen mother; though this case remains unproven, his failure to grasp the court's abhorrence of attempts to justify or rehabilitate the regency and the régime of Concini is indisputable.[73] The Richelieu of subsequent years was less impulsive and 'naïve'; by then his ability, even determination, to temporize and disregard the past show that he had indeed learned some of the lessons of his experiences between the fall of Concini and his exile to Avignon.

All the evidence, thin on the ground though it is, suggests that he, Henri, and Pont-Courlay lived extremely discreetly while at Avignon. The fact that they were fully aware throughout their stay there that they were kept under constant surveillance by Pontchartrain would have obliged them to act with discretion, while heightening their sense of isolation and danger.[74] Even the papal vice-legate there, the future nuncio to France, Guidi di Bagno, seems to have kept his relations with Richelieu to a minimum, and only to have dealt with him privately. Much as the papacy might deplore the removal of bishops from their dioceses and, in this case, their exile to papal territory without any prior consultation, Rome was in no mood to jeopardize its relations with the French court by a show of support or protection for Richelieu. Indeed, its principal fear was that his presence might draw Avignon, and through it the papacy, into French factional intrigues.[75] The archbishop of Lyon, who was French ambassador in Rome, confessed, in language which reiterated the widely-held view of Richelieu, that he feared Avignon would be just as convenient as Toulouse, Rennes or Aix 'pour les pratiques et menez (sic)' of the bishop of Luçon.[76]

It has also been suggested that Richelieu verged on the suicidal while at Avignon. But bad as his circumstances might be, it is doubtful whether he was ever quite as depressed as that – even in Avignon. Obviously, the sudden release from the constant tension and strain of the previous two years had an effect on his highly-strung temperament. But here, too, his first instinct, however futile it might

---

73 Deloche, *Autour de la plume de Richelieu*, ch. 5.
74 See a series of letters to Louis XIII and especially Pontchartrain from those involved in the surveillance, in Griselle, *Louis XIII et Richelieu*, pp. 190–9.
75 Georg Lutz, *Kardinal Giovanni Francesco Guidi di Bagno. Politik und Religion im Zeitalter Richelieus und Urbans VIII* (Tübingen 1971), pp. 15–16; Lacroix, *Richelieu à Luçon*, pp. 238–40. See Steffani, *Nunziatura di Bentivoglio*, II, pp. 427–8, Cardinal Borghese to nuncio, 30 May 1618, for Rome's displeasure and cautious reaction.
76 B.N. MS. Fr. 18012, fo. 205v, Denis Simon de Marquemont to Puysieux, secretary of state, 17 May 1618.

appear, was to fight back and defend himself. The strange, cryptic *Caput Apologeticum*, which he dictated in short bursts to his secretaries, was just such an exercise in self-justification. It shows some signs of having been conceived in case he was drawn into the forthcoming trial of Barbin. In it, he refused to accept he was just another victim of the political game, and ranged over his entire career, from the moment he was nominated to Luçon, before returning, as always, to his services – and those of his family – to the crown before and during his period of ministerial office.[77] No completed version of this apologia has ever been found, and it may be that the growing bleakness of his position dissuaded him from completing what promised to be a waste of effort. But he did throw himself into other, less apologetic intellectual activities. At Christmas 1618, when writing to ask the king to assign him yet another place of exile, he tried to reassure him about his intentions by announcing his wish to compose an answer to the Huguenot replies to his *Principaux Points*.[78] Nothing ever came of this, but by that date he had probably finished writing his most substantial work, the *Instruction du chrétien*. In its own way, this, too, bears witness to a growing resignation and discouragement, most notably in the plea, reiterated at the end of each chapter, that the parishioners of Luçon pray for their bishop.

There were other, more personal reasons, too, for his unhappy state of mind, ones which did not relate to past events or politics. His brother, Henri, lost both his wife and her infant son within two months of each other in late 1618. Such family tragedies only seemed to compound the Richelieus' sense of desolation and even to presage the extinction of the family name altogether. Given Richelieu's acute sense of family history and reputation, the effect of such a blow was enormous, surpassed only by the loss of Henri himself the following year. In Henri's own case, the deaths of his wife and son led to a will in which he left virtually his entire estate to different religious orders.[79] No such extreme dispositions from Armand's pen have come to light, but his despondency emerges from the 'spiritual testament' which he addressed two months later, in February 1619, to the cathedral canons of Luçon. Facing up to the prospect of death without seeing Luçon again, he appears in a more sympathetic light than usual during these difficult years, not least when he expressed spiritual convictions of an intensity which would not surface again until the latter years of his life.[80]

---

77 Avenel, *Lettres*, VII, pp. 416–22.
78 Griselle, *Louis XIII et Richelieu*, pp. 204–5, letter of 20 Dec. Richelieu's letter to Pontchartrain of the same date (*ibid.*, pp. 205–6) refers to a book 'qu'on imprima à la Rochelle contre moy'.
79 Bergin, *Richelieu*, p. 35, for the terms and significance of the will.
80 Avenel, *Lettres*, VII, pp. 424–6, 8 Feb. 1619.

IV

It is ironic that as Richelieu's despondency should have reached its nadir in early February 1619, events were already in train which would directly bring about his rehabilitation although he was certainly unaware of this. On 27 January, the duc d'Épernon had left his stronghold at Metz, where he had been living in semi-disgrace, for Angoulême in his governorship of Aunis and Saintonge where, according to carefully laid plans, he was joined in early March by Marie de' Medici, who fled from Blois on 22 February.[81] She had not received the 'petits contentements' that Richelieu had recommended when at Blois, while the snubs and tight surveillance she had to endure rendered her viscerally distrustful of Luynes.[82] Within days of leaving Blois, the first of several letters addressed to Louis XIII reached the court, justifying her escape to a free and safe place of residence from where she would inform the king in due course of her ideas for necessary reforms of government; it was soon followed by others in the same vein.[83] In Paris, after much initial uncertainty about the scale of aristocratic support for Marie, counsels of peace prevailed.[84] Once the decision had been made to distinguish the position of Marie, presumed innocent because 'abducted' against her will, from that of Épernon and his associates, the way was open, in principle, for negotiations to begin with Marie.[85] Richelieu was by now alone in Avignon, since Henri and Pont-Courlay, after several fruitless requests, had been allowed to return to Paris for personal reasons.[86] It is not possible to be sure whose idea it was to suggest to the king and Luynes that they recall Richelieu at this juncture, but we can discount as unnecessary flattery the notion that it was Richelieu himself, somehow well informed of these events

81 Guillaume Girard, *Histoire de la vie du duc d'Épernon* (Paris 1655), pp. 312–24, for the most detailed and circumstantial account of these events. Girard, an eye-witness to many of the events he writes about, entered the service of Épernon, as one of his secretaries, in mid-1619. Though obviously partisan, his account is of considerable value in providing a perspective which differs from that usually inspired by Richelieu's memoirs.

82 Most notably the signed declaration extracted from her under oath in November 1618 that she would renounce all associations inside and outside the kingdom; that she would inform the king of plots against him; and that she would not insist on returning to court against his will: *Négociation commencée au mois de mars de l'année 1619 avec la reine mère Marie de' Medicis par M le comte de Béthune et continuée conjointement avec M le cardinal de La Rochefoucauld* (Paris 1673), pp. 78–80, 3 Nov. 1618. It was a step which Luynes later regretted: Pontchartrain, *Mémoires*, pp. 267–8.

83 *Négociation avec la reine mère*, pp. 11–13, letter of 23 Feb.

84 Pontchartrain, *Mémoires*, pp. 275, 277–8.

85 Steffani, *Nunziatura di Bentivoglio*, II, pp. 202–5, 216–19, letters of 27 Feb. 1619.

86 Griselle, *Louis XIII et Richelieu*, pp. 170–2, 200–8, for several petitions from Richelieu, his brother and Pont Courlay, that they be allowed to return home for a brief period. Richelieu's own requests were ignored.

at Avignon, who did so. In fact, his recall had already been briefly mooted only weeks earlier during one of the periodic alerts over the queen mother's behaviour at Blois.[87] Richelieu himself subsequently attributed the decision to the influence of his clerical friends Sébastien Bouthillier and Père Joseph, who succeeded in persuading Déageant, still Luynes's confidant, that sending him to Angoulême would be a worthwhile move.[88] The Capuchin's involvement seems to be corroborated by the fact that the royal letter bidding Richelieu to join the queen mother was taken to Avignon by Père Joseph's brother. On 7 March, two weeks after Marie's nighttime escape from Blois, Richelieu eagerly began his journey across central France.[89]

Yet the unspecified mission upon which he now embarked, and the circumstances surrounding it, were very different from those of May 1617 when he rode off with the queen mother to Blois. Her most recent 'departure', effected under the patronage of the feared and dangerous Épernon, had come close to – and might yet – detonate a civil war reminiscent of those of her own regency. She had promptly appealed to the leading nobles to assist her in voicing her complaints which, she insisted, concerned the *bien de l'Estat*, and not simply her private grievances or interests. Though nearly all excused themselves and adopted a wait-and-see attitude, there was no certainty that magnates like Montmorency or Bouillon would not join her, given their unpredictable alignments and realignments during previous years, as well as their current attitudes towards Luynes's régime.[90] Furthermore, Marie's court at Angoulême was itself different from the one Richelieu had left in May 1617. With civil war a real possibility, a delicate balance of power obtained there, the leading protagonists being Rucellaï, the brains behind Marie's escape, and Épernon, whose military resources seemed no less crucial to the whole enterprise.[91] Lesser figures such as Phélypeaux de Villesavin and Chanteloube, were as ill-disposed to Richelieu as ever, for none of them had forgotten his record during Marie's sojourn at Blois. While others had taken serious risks in accompany-

---

87   Steffani, *Nunziatura di Bentivoglio*, III, pp. 197–8, letter of 13 Feb. 1619.
88   Richelieu, *Mémoires*, II, pp. 334–5.
89   Avenel, *Lettres*, VII, pp. 426–7, letter to king, 10 March. Richelieu was arrested by the governor of Lyon, who, unaware of his mission, suspected him of being involved in a conspiracy centred on Marie!
90   *Négociation avec la reine mère*, pp. 17–19, 22–3, 57–9, 62–75, 96–101, for the queen's numerous appeals and the responses to them. For the court's fears, see Pontchartrain, *Mémoires*, pp. 275–6, 284–5. Girard, *Vie d'Épernon*, p. 335, claimed that many potential supporters of Marie in Picardy and Champagne followed Bouillon's lead.
91   Girard, *Vie d'Épernon*, pp. 298–310, for Rucellaï's negotiations with Bouillon, Épernon and others. At this stage, Girard himself was still in the service of Rucellaï.

ing the queen mother to Angoulême and had as a result seen themselves branded by the court as traitors, Richelieu was now being sent
there by Luynes, and the intentions which lay behind his mission
were not such as to inspire much confidence among those already
there. Some kind of clash was inevitable, one that was bound to
overlap with, and be complicated by, the nature and outcome of the
quarrel with Louis XIII and Luynes.

By the time Richelieu reached Angoulême, there had already been
intensive contacts between the queen mother and the king. Sébastien
Bouthillier and her personal confessor, the Jesuit Jean Suffren, had
been among the first to visit her, followed by a full scale 'embassy'
led by Philippe de Béthune and Bérulle. Béthune arrived a week
before Richelieu but, empowered only to ascertain what kind of
'secure place of residence' she sought, and to promise her every
satisfaction if only she would disown Épernon, his mission had
made little headway.[92] This was hardly surprising: Marie went out
of her way to defend Épernon, and was still refusing to be drawn
on the question of a safe place of residence, while Béthune had no
authority to table any concrete proposals.[93]

Richelieu thus made his entry at a moment of stalemate, but his
own subsequent account, which portrays him as turning the tables
on his opponents at the first meeting of Marie's council is, in the light
of subsequent events, too dramatic to be genuinely convincing.[94]
While he sensibly seems to have waited until summoned to submit
his own ideas of what course of action should be taken, he lost no
time in seeking to establish a political base, without which no argument over policy could be won. His first call was to Épernon who,
pleased to have an ally against Rucellaï, offered him his considerable
patronage.[95] This tactical alliance was not a vote for military confrontation, for Épernon too wanted peace rather than have to face
Louis XIII and Luynes alone, but it naturally precluded Richelieu's
advising a course of action inimical to Épernon's interests, as Rucellaï,
the champion of Marie's early return to court, was already coun-

92   *Négociation avec la reine mère*, pp. 3–7, instruction to Béthune, 5 March; *ibid.*, p. 26, for
     the additional 'secret' instruction concerning Épernon, 8 March. See also Michel Hous-
     saye, *Le Père de Bérulle et l'Oratoire de Jésus 1611–1625* (Paris 1874), pp. 256–70; *Journal
     d'Arnauld 1614–20*, p. 414.
93   *Négociation avec la reine mère*, pp. 26–34, for Béthune's first report from Angoulême, 21
     March.
94   Richelieu, *Mémoires*, II, pp. 341–3; Fontenay-Mareuil, *Mémoires*, pp. 442–3. Hanotaux,
     Richelieu, II, pp. 285–7, accepts this triumphalist version of events.
95   Girard, *Vie d'Épernon*, p. 339–40. This account is, of course, partisan, asserting that
     Richelieu, arriving at Angoulême when peace was ready to be signed, contributed little
     to solving the political crisis. In his memoirs, Richelieu makes no mention of Épernon's
     assistance, preferring to lump him together with his other enemies at Angoulême
     (Richelieu, *Mémoires*, II, p. 339).

selling.[96] These constraints are evident enough in what seems to be the first, and one of the few surviving, memoranda from Richelieu to Marie at this time. In it, he acknowledged the diversity of advice on offer to her, and then argued in passably convoluted language that he thought she would be best advised, in the short term, to pursue her stated objective of a 'safe and free place of residence' of which she would be mistress. At the same time, he stressed that her control of the latter should be exercised in such a way as not to compromise the longer-term objective of a reconciliation with the king and a return to court. He did not believe that the time was yet right for return, given past and present mistrust; only time could heal the wounds inflicted on her since 1617.[97] But he also warned her that her natural desire to retain and protect her servants should not induce her to act in a way which might prolong faction and intrigue. He concluded by suggesting that were she to be persecuted in the future, despite living irreproachably in her chosen place of residence, public opinion would be on her side, and assured her that he would himself be one of those who would then argue that the government of France was being sacrificed to private interests, and would support the 'search for remedies to prevent the ruin of the king and the country'.[98] Such cautiously-phrased advice can hardly have come as a complete revelation to Marie, while its menacing final point about future, if unspecified, action were there to be any 'persecution', seemed to offer hope to those in Marie's court who advocated action rather than negotiation.

But Richelieu's ability to sketch out a plan of action was not, as we shall see, the same as having things all his own way, even when the time came for serious negotiations with Louis and Luynes. Marie de' Medici remained subject to other influences, some of which were at least as powerful as the bishop of Luçon's logic. Béthune's early despatches only mention Richelieu as one member among several of the queen mother's council, and the well-informed nuncio wrote in April that Rucellaï was still Marie's confidant and secretary.[99] This would help to explain why, in late March and early April, further open letters to Louis XIII kept up her protests against the way France was being governed, and reiterated the acute need for reforms which

96 Girard, *Vie d'Épernon*, pp. 338–9.
97 An immediate return to the court, which Louis XIII and Luynes strongly desired, would have involved abandoning Épernon, something Marie was unwilling to contemplate. Richelieu's advice took account of this difficulty.
98 Avenel, *Lettres*, I, pp. 581–3, undated memorandum for presentation to Marie by one of her secretaries, Lecomte.
99 *Négociation avec la reine mère*, p. 109, letter of 31 March 1619; Steffani, *Nunziatura di Bentivoglio*, III, p. 277, letter of 10 April. Bérulle, who had returned briefly from Angoulême, was probably Bentivoglio's source of information.

she would reveal when she felt safe enough to do so. Indeed, for a short time and despite Marie's caution, at least two manifestos were drafted at Angoulême, one of which Béthune persuaded her to disown once he saw its contents. This, the more moderate of the two documents, demanded a full-scale reform and restructuring of the king's council, more vigilant control of financial administration, and stronger measures to prevent favourites from acquiring excessive wealth and power.[100] The second manifesto was a far more vitriolic attack on the Luynes régime, providing a long list of its mistakes and abuses, from its unworthy treatment of the queen mother to its handling of royal finances and governorships, so that it has been described as 'renewing past criticism of Concini against the new favourite' and effectively 'turned the tables on him'.[101] Neither critique circulated widely or for long, nor did either attract much comment or attention in 1619. Louis XIII, however, was not at all reassured by Marie's behaviour, and his truculent replies reflect anger at the queen's attempts to conduct political debate in public, with all its attendant risks.[102] In the *dialogue des sourds* then developing, each side resorted to the fiction that the other was unable to speak its mind truthfully: for Marie, Louis was in thrall to Luynes and his cabal, while the king firmly maintained that she was Épernon's hostage, and that the negotiations were being used to whip up support for her cause among the *grands*. At one point, Louis sharply reminded Marie of the lessons of recent history, lessons she could not ignore:

> Have you forgotten that this alleged 'reformation of the state' has been the tocsin which twice ignited rebellion and devastated my kingdom during your regency, and are you in conscience ignorant of the fact that my state, having recently emerged from such calamities, was never more glorious and contented than when you left Blois, and that your retreat to a dangerous place has begun to change people's opinions?

This last point was to prove only too accurate a prophecy of what would happen in the coming year. And while Marie refused to abandon Epernon and those around her, there was even less chance

100 *Négociation av·c la reine mère*, pp. 112–16, 'Escrit signé de la Reyne Mère du roy en forme de manifeste'; *ibid*., pp. 111–12, for Béthune's (undated) rebuke to her at a time when she was refusing to divulge to him her ideas on reform.
101 *Extrait des raisons et plainctes de la Reyne mère du Roy* (n.p., n.d.). See Bonney, *The King's Debts*, p. 100.
102 *Négociation avec la reine mère*, pp. 31–2, Béthune to Louis XIII, 21 March. Béthune had rebuked the queen mother for her appeals to the *grands* to assist her. The king scolded Béthune in turn for not listening to the queen mother's ideas, thus giving her a pretext for publishing them: *ibid*., pp. 47–9, letter of 27 March.

of Louis XIII's being party to her criticism of those around him, Luynes in particular, whom he fully and publicly protected from her barbs. As he reminded her: 'a sovereign authority which does not protect the good makes itself odious even to the bad'.[103]

The crown had, in any case, taken measures in case there was a wider revolt. Some of the queen mother's potential supporters were quickly approached and prevailed upon to remain loyal.[104] Another move was initially no more than a threat but, in the wider context of contemporary politics, a particularly interesting one: immediately after Marie's flight, well-publicized moves to rehabilitate Condé, the most important victim of the régime of Marie and Concini, with a view to his actual release from Vincennes, were set in motion; although they were then suspended until October 1619, they mollified his powerful relatives and allies and, not for the last time, demonstrated his value as a political counterweight to the queen mother.[105] In contrast, Épernon, who had been one of the pillars of Marie's regency, now found himself having to bear the brunt of royal criticism for 'abducting' the queen mother, a treasonable offence which led to his being deprived of his offices and pensions.[106] But above all, the crown was taking no military chances, and spared neither money nor effort in raising adequate forces.[107] Schomberg in the governorship of Limousin and Mayenne in that of Guyenne took firm action to prevent any show of armed support for Marie, with Schomberg effectively blockading Épernon in Angoulême. Such measures, combined with a policy of waiting to see if Marie's propaganda enlisted as yet undeclared supporters, enabled the crown to conclude that the revolt had been effectively contained; without serious support from the *grands*, her criticisms of the regime would lack real menace.[108] The crown decided, in early April, to offer concessions, but it was only when Cardinal La Rochefoucauld and Béthune brought these to Angoulême later that month that the log-jam began to break, and eventually led to one of the strangest 'treaties' in French history, that of Angoulême, the very chronology

---

103   Griselle, 'Louis XIII et sa mère', *Revue Historique* 105 (1910), pp. 302–31; 106 (1911), pp. 83–100, 295–308, at vol. 105, pp. 309–15, letter of 8 April 1619.

104   Fontenay-Mareuil, *Mémoires*, p. 437.

105   Steffani, *Nunziatura di Bentivoglio*, III, pp. 219–20, letter of 27 Feb., a few days after news arrived of Marie's departure. *Journal d'Arnauld 1614–20*, pp. 413–14, 416, entries for 21 March, 8 April 1619. Since the fall of Concini, when his release was first seriously considered, it was realized that he could be 'used' against the queen mother His release was delayed in 1619 for fear of provoking a complete break with her.

106   This threat was repeated in Louis XIII's letters to Marie: see Griselle, 'Louis XIII et sa mère', pp. 308, 312, 313–14.

107   Pontchartrain, *Mémoires*, p. 275.

108   Bonney, *The King's Debts*, pp. 99–100.

of which varies from one historian to another.[109] Given Marie's demands for a safe place of residence, and the king's often repeated pledge to ensure her freedom of movement, the queen mother was offered the governorship of Anjou in exchange for that of Normandy, with the town governorships of Angers, Chinon and Ponts de Cé astride the Loire added for good measure.[110] Following established ritual in such affairs, a veil would be drawn over events since her flight from Blois, her supporters would benefit from an amnesty, recovering both offices and pensions, she would regain full control of her household, and the debts she had incurred would be paid by the royal treasury.

The offer quickly produced general heads of agreement, which the indefatigable Bérulle took to Paris for royal approval, and which he strongly recommended by emphasising the queen mother's genuine desire for peace.[111] But the court took a very different view when Bérulle also revealed that, despite agreeing to make peace, Marie was holding out for more than was on the table. She found the governorships of Anjou and of the towns included with it insufficient compensation for Normandy, and demanded in addition to them either Luynes's fortified town of Amboise, with its stone bridge across the Loire, or the governorship of Nantes. It was a condition which sharply revived the court's doubts about her stated willingness to live within terms set for her by the king, and indicated that she was subject to contradictory pressures from her entourage. The council concluded that such a concession would be widely seen as a sign of weakness and a tacit admission that revolt paid greater dividends than loyalty.[112] Bérulle returned to Angoulême in early May 1619 with royal agreement to the basic terms of the treaty, but with a flat refusal of the demand for Amboise or Nantes. Despite the king's refusal, Marie proclaimed peace anyway and even celebrated it with a solemn *Te Deum* in Angoulême cathedral. The culmination of this confused series of moves, which betray haste and ineptitude rather than Machiavellian cunning, was that La Rochefoucauld and Béthune formally signed the articles of the treaty on 12 May, and then instructed Mayenne and Schomberg to withdraw their forces from around Angoulême. At court, there was dismay and disbelief that such action should have been taken without prior consulta-

109   See the remarks about it in Tapié, *Politique étrangère*, p. 328.
110   *Négociation avec la reine mère*, pp. 188–94, instructions for La Rochefoucauld, dated 8 April 1619; Griselle, 'Louis XIII et sa mère', pp. 316–17, Louis XIII to queen mother, n.d.
111   *Journal d'Arnauld 1614–20*, p. 419.
112   B.N., MS. Fr. 15699, fos. 374–83, instructions to La Rochefoucauld and Béthune, 11 May.

tion.[113] The immediate military pressure on Marie had been lifted, in return for which she had only given oral assurances of wanting peace; she had not signed any of the public declarations required of her which were judged essential to terminating local exactions and troop movements, and, worse still, she had even allowed herself the luxury of a few days reflection before giving a final answer as to whether she would indeed agree to exchange Normandy for Anjou.[114]

It would take much of the summer of 1619 to deal with the consequences of these misunderstandings – as well as of others that would arise out of them – before the meeting that was supposed to seal Marie's reconciliation with Louis XIII could take place. The part played by Richelieu in these negotiations is far less clear than is generally believed, and his intentions and tactics were as subject to suspicion as those of the other leading *dramatis personae*. That he came to play a significant role is beyond doubt, yet we should not jump to the conclusion that, like some masterly puppeteer, he obliged both the queen mother and the court to play the game by his rules. The fact is that for much of the time between March and June 1619, he figures only indirectly in the otherwise voluminous sources for the negotiations, and it is from often cursory references that we have to deduce his contribution, without being able to document it with any precision.

From the outset, Richelieu supported a negotiated solution, but one which involved the search for a secure political base for the queen mother, rather than a trusting return to court. Yet, despite that, it remains unclear whether he was immediately empowered by Marie to undertake negotiations on her part; as we saw, neither Béthune nor the nuncio mention him at all in the initial period following his arrival at Angoulême. But with or without a formal mandate from Marie, he enjoyed several clear advantages from the outset. Unlike Épernon or Rucellaï, he was in no way compromised by involvement in the escape from Blois; while the court held the first two responsible for the crisis, and thus refused to formally negotiate with them, Richelieu was burdened only with the court's

---

113 *Journal d'Arnauld 1614–20*, pp. 420–2. B.N., MS. Fr. 15699, fos. 384v, 388–91, Louis XIII to La Rochefoucauld, 13 and 16 May, expressing his unhappiness with the outcome, especially over the instructions given to Mayenne before a binding agreement had been reached with Marie or the court's prior approval sought. See also *Correspondance de Bérulle*, II, p. 24–5, Cardinal de Retz to Bérulle, 15 May, for another expression of the court's reaction. The royal envoys were, however, also under instructions to conclude a speedy agreement, and they may have been too ready to take Marie's response as a sufficient proof of that.

114 B.N., MS. Fr. 15699, fos. 374–79v, for details of the court's requirements in the king's instructions to La Rochefoucauld, 11 May 1619. They were repeated to La Rochefoucauld on 16 May: *ibid.*, fos. 388–91.

earlier suspicions of him. Another advantage was that, Béthune apart, the intermediaries employed during the ensuing negotiations were ecclesiastics, virtually all of whom Richelieu knew, and who for their part doubtless found it natural – and easier – to deal with him than with others in Marie's entourage. Several of them had personally supported negotiation from the outset, and were enlisted as intermediaries because they were thought to be agreeable to Marie and Épernon.[115] While these facts did not of themselves guarantee easy or successful diplomacy, they greatly served to smooth Richelieu's return to active political life. Bérulle, though less high-ranking than either Béthune or La Rochefoucauld, was the real *fil conducteur* of the negotiations from beginning to end. Close to Luynes, yet trusted by Marie de' Medici, he accepted that Richelieu was anxious for a firm peace settlement, and did much to reassure the court about his attitude.[116] Soon, Richelieu found himself in correspondence with the Jesuits, Arnoux and Suffren, confessors to Louis and Marie respectively, and both ardent protagonists of a speedy reconciliation.[117] And as negotiations progressed, the circle of those who looked to him as crucial to a successful outcome widened still further. Rarely has an ecclesiastical milieu been so visibly at the forefront of the political scene: reconciling Louis XIII and Marie de' Medici became a major *dévot* 'cause', and Richelieu was ideally placed to take full advantage of it. With their assistance, the task of convincing the court it had been wise to bring him back, while still retaining the goodwill of the queen mother, was rendered less hazardous.

While it is difficult to itemize Richelieu's specific contribution to the negotiations leading to the 'treaty' of 12 May, he was certainly vital, despite changes of mood by Marie and those around her, in ensuring that a deal would be negotiated with the court. He was not averse to striking the hardest bargain possible, as is evident from the record of the discussion of the governorships of Nantes and Angers. Equally, he was flexible enough to lower his sights when Louis XIII refused to improve his original offer, convincing Marie to accept peace rather than break off talks and risk all on war. By the time the 'treaty' of Angoulême became public, in mid-May 1619, he was being praised in most quarters for steering the queen mother towards an agreement. By then, the nuncio, while remarking that Richelieu had 'his own measure of hotheadedness' (*la sua parte di*

115 The best source here is the nuncio's correspondence in Steffani, *Nunziatura di Bentivoglio.*
     Bentivoglio followed the negotiations closely, and though he did not wish to encourage
     formal papal mediation, was in close touch with ministers and influential courtiers.
116 Houssaye, *Bérulle et l'Oratoire*, ch. 8, esp. pp. 260ff., for an ample, if rather pious, ac-
     count of Bérulle's activities.
117 Avenel, *Lettres*, I, pp. 593–6, Richelieu to Jean Arnoux, April 1619.

caldo in testa), was in no doubt that he was the one to support against Rucellaï.[118] Luynes, Cardinal de Retz and even the imprisoned Condé now regarded him as a man they could address directly, and his reputation was to grow strongly throughout the summer of 1619.[119] But this change of fortune was not just a consequence of successful diplomacy. Eulogists and correspondents alike were also recognizing in Richelieu a man who had emerged during these months as much more than a diplomat. By the summer of 1619, he was also being variously referred to as the queen mother's own 'favori' and 'tout puissant dans son esprit'.

V

At the same time as Richelieu struggled to secure the initiative in the negotiations with Louis XIII's emissaries, he also kept his attention firmly fixed on political realities around him. The remark he made in later life, to the effect that he found it easier to master the battle-fields of Europe than the king's study, could also be applied to Marie de' Medici's court at Angoulême. But if we are seeking evidence of how far he had learned from previous experience and mistakes, it is to be found in his determination to establish himself as undisputed master of the queen mother's affairs. He now understood fully the need to build up a political clientèle which would leave him less vulnerable to changes of fortune in future and, over the next few years, he managed to intertwine his own affairs and those of the queen mother so comprehensively as to render their individual fortunes inseparable in the eyes of contemporaries. Indeed, as Marie gradually regained much of her earlier influence in government, her affairs increasingly became affairs of state. This less visible dimension of Richelieu's activity in and after 1619 presages his later record as royal minister. His experiences since 1617 taught him not to rely simply on his service or his achievements – let alone on gratitude from any quarter. The credit for making peace with the court in May 1619 was from the beginning as fragile as the peace itself, all the more so as it gave rise to prolonged bickering and suspicion. Richelieu's identification with Marie de' Medici after this date owes at least as much to his personal domination of her affairs, political

---

118 Steffani, *Nunziatura di Bentivoglio*, III, pp. 317–19, letter of 9 May. By that date, Bentivoglio had had the time to confer with Bérulle, who was making his second return visit to court, about conditions at Angoulême.

119 A.A.E., Mems. et docs., France 772, fo. 102, Condé to Richelieu, 24 June 1619; Avenel, *Lettres*, I, pp. 462–3, Richelieu to Luynes, 19 June 1619. See Hanotaux, *Richelieu*, II, p. 290.

and private, as to his 'political' standing *per se*. Just as he would seek, after 1624, to consolidate his position and his power through marriage alliances, the acquisition of governorships, the exercise of patronage, and the accumulation of wealth, so from 1619 onwards he would seek to strengthen his existing position under Marie de' Medici's patronage.

In this respect, Épernon's early patronage of Richelieu at Angoulême was of crucial importance, and should not be obscured by their bitter enmity of later years. The duke's support certainly smoothed Richelieu's return to Marie's good graces, and the bishop, in his turn, took great care not to cross Épernon during the ensuing months. There is little reason to doubt the word of Épernon's biographer – who was present at Angoulême – that it was he who persuaded Marie to make Richelieu president of her council and to confide to him her seal and the post of *surintendant* of her household shortly after his arrival: that is, to entrust to him the general direction of her affairs.[120] The nominal presidency and chancellorship still remained in the hands of the aged Potier de Blancmesnil, and indeed sometime later in 1619 Marie actually prevented Richelieu from acquiring Blancmesnil's offices outright.[121] But this refusal was made more out of loyalty to an old servant than from any intention of limiting Richelieu's power. The reality of the changes is clear enough from the fact that by May–June 1619, provincial officials and agents handling the queen mother affairs knew that it was to Richelieu, not Blancmesnil, that they should direct their letters and enquiries.[122] More than anyone else, he reaped the full benefit of the clause in the Treaty of Angoulême guaranteeing Marie's right to dispose of her own household and its offices. Nor was he content to carve out a place for himself alone – he needed allies in Marie's entourage, and could not afford to leave influential enemies in position there. He quickly gathered around him at Angoulême as many relatives, in-laws, and close friends as he could, all of whom would help to consolidate his power, and who would not have to wait long before enjoying the rewards of his patronage. A formal roll call of Marie's officials for the following year or so hides the extent of the upheaval within her household and of Richelieu's ruthless elimination of rivals there. Phélypeaux de Villesavin, who had been one of his adversaries at Blois, was disgraced, and his key post of Marie's *sec-*

120 Girard, *Vie d'Épernon*, p. 340.
121 Avenel, *Lettres*, I, pp. 642–4, letters to Florent d'Argouges, Marie's treasurer, and to Antoine Potier, sieur de Sceaux, undated but obviously from 1619.
122 See, for example, A.A.E., Mems. et docs., France 772, fos. 93, 95–6, letters of 10 and 16 June respectively from officials in Haute and Basse Marche on questions concerning the royal domain there, which formed part of Marie's dower rights. In some of these letters, Richelieu is actually addressed as Marie's chancellor.

rétaire des commandements given to Claude Bouthillier, friend and loyal servant of Richelieu.[123] Through Bouthillier and some new members of Marie's council, Richelieu was easily able to control the administration of her affairs.[124] Others, such as Bishop Hurault, Marie's *grand aumônier*, and the Bonzis, while not actually dismissed, were unceremoniously marginalized during 1619. Hurault kept his post until his death in May 1621, when Richelieu took it for himself; meanwhile, his control of the queen mother's religious and ecclesiastical interests was assured by the appointment of Sébastien Bouthillier as her *premier aumônier*.[125] With little choice but to retire to his diocese, Bishop Bonzi was reduced to asking Richelieu for permission to visit Marie and take formal leave of her on his return to Béziers.[126] The queen mother's household had, as we saw, been considerably reduced since the 1617 coup, with many of her officials and servants judging it better to distance themselves from her.[127] Now in 1619, as they woke up to the sudden political changes, they began to pen embarrassed apologias to Richelieu, who replied to several of them in some of the frostiest letters to emanate from his pen.[128] Indeed, with Marie's political fortunes reviving, numerous other offers of service began to flood in, leaving Richelieu, to whom most were addressed, with both the enviable task of whom to select, and the opportunity of peopling her expanding court and household with individuals largely beholden to his good offices. In August 1619, a Monsieur de Barentin wrote to remind him of Marie's earlier promise to appoint him her *procureur-général*, but he seems to have had no response, let alone satisfaction;[129] a year later, the office was confided to Bérulle's brother, Jean.[130] Not all of these begging letters emanated from the lowly or the obscure, as a number of figures closely associated with the careers of both Marie de' Medici and

123 Bergin, *Richelieu*, p. 73.
124 Marie's council had been dominated by the Potier family led by Blancmesnil. In 1619, Denis Bouthillier de Rancé and Nicolas Lecomte, both close to Richelieu, became members. The future *surintendant des finances*, Claude de Bullion, was already a member whose connections with Richelieu date from at least 1619, if not before. The council's membership tripled between 1619 and 1625. See Batiffol, *La Vie intime d'une reine de France au xvii siècle*, I, pp. 190–1.
125 Avenel, *Lettres*, I, pp. 616–17, Richelieu to Philippe Hurault, Aug. 1617; A.A.E., Mems. et docs., France 772, fo. 145, Hurault to Richelieu, 24 Oct. 1619; Avenel, *Lettres*, I, pp. 636–7, Richelieu to Hurault (late Oct. 1619), referring to two earlier letters from Hurault.
126 A.A.E., Mems. et docs., France 772, fo. 129, letter to Richelieu, 11 Sept 1619.
127 Batiffol, *Louis XIII a vingt ans*, pp. 322–3.
128 Numerous letters in this vein in A.A.E., Mems. et docs., France 772, fos. 100–1, 111–13, 125, 131. For some of Richelieu's replies, see Avenel, *Lettres*, I, p. 595, to vicomte Sardini; *ibid.*, pp. 636–7, to Hurault; A.A.E., Mems. et docs., France 772, fo. 238, to Monsieur [. . .].
129 A.A.E., Mems. et docs., France 772, fo. 118, 20 Aug. 1619.
130 Griselle, *État de la maison de Louis XIII* (Paris 1912) p. 68, n. 2678.

Richelieu began to appear again in mid-1619. The Marillac brothers, Louis and Michel, were actively involved in Marie's installation in the governorship of Anjou, with Michel being appointed *intendant* of the province for that specific purpose, and Louis assuming military responsibilities. By October 1619, the duc de Bellegarde, governor of Burgundy, was among those seeking ways of actively assisting Marie.[131] Her court and her affairs were becoming a kind of state within the state.

The principal victims of these changes, political and 'domestic', were Rucellaï and his circle, whose relations with Richelieu rapidly degenerated as they realized that his earlier warning to Marie de' Medici against the factious among her servants was no idle threat. Rucellaï himself was naturally bitter at the prospect that the benefits of his diplomacy, which had set the queen mother free, would be reaped by someone else. But although Marie declared she could neither suffer his presumption nor take his advice, and Rucellaï himself announced his intention of leaving Angoulême soon after Richelieu's arrival there, he could not be disposed of as easily as others, and obviously continued to enjoy some influence there.[132] Our sources are laconic on this point, but Rucellaï clearly managed to intervene in some way in the negotiations with Luynes, who may have even welcomed a measure of confusion in Marie's counsels, and Rucellaï was intelligent enough to exploit the ambiguities of each side's position. At one point, he angrily rejected as contemptible a pay-off of 90,000 *livres* suggested by Marie on Richelieu's advice.[133] But it was in the weeks following the Treaty of Angoulême that any semblance of a truce between the supporters of Richelieu and Rucellaï broke down. Rucellaï's position had weakened considerably by then, even to the point where an angry letter from Marie to Louis XIII, which briefly revived the king's doubts as to her peaceful intentions, could be successfully passed off by her as yet another of Rucellaï's 'aberrations'.[134] But the main reason for the breakdown appears to have been Richelieu's determination to exploit the treaty's terms to the full and, in particular, to distribute the governorships granted to Marie to his own clients; this was bound to exacerbate relations with those who were faced with the prospect

---

131 A.A.E., Mems. et docs., France 772, fos. 140–1, 151, letters to Richelieu, 16 Oct. and 10 Nov. 1619 respectively.

132 Steffani, *Nunziatura di Bentivoglio*, III, p. 277, letter of 10 April 1619: 'egli è il confidente, il segretario, l'uomo di stato'.

133 Girard, *Vie d'Épernon*, p. 340; Richelieu, *Mémoires*, II, pp. 359–60; *Journal d'Arnauld 1614–20*, p. 437. Both Arnauld and Richelieu claim Rucellaï neither accepted nor rejected the offer.

134 *Journal d'Arnauld 1614–20*, pp. 425–7. See the king's reply in Griselle, 'Louis XIII et sa mère', pp. 322–5, 31 May.

of receiving no tangible reward for their services since the escape from Blois.[135] In particular, the marquis of Mosny, a close friend of Rucellaï, was angered by the choice of Henri de Richelieu as governor of Angers, and left for court at the end of June.[136] Worse was soon to follow. The marquis de Thémines, captain of the queen mother's guards, was another associate of Rucellaï who was unhappy with the aggrandizement of the Richelieu circle. After several incidents and abortive duels between various members of the two parties in early July, Thémines and Henri de Richelieu drew their swords during a chance encounter in an Angoulême street, on 8 July, and in the ensuing tussle Henri was mortally wounded.[137]

The death of his elder brother was a severe blow, politically and personally, to Richelieu. His private sense of loss remains palpable, not just in his contemporary letters, but even in his later account of the event.[138] Although Henri de Richelieu was a childless widower, his brother continued to regard the future of the Richelieu line as lying with him. If his death now focused the family's destiny wholly on Armand, it also left him with responsibility for the estates of both his father and brother, each of which involved large debts, difficult lawsuits and numerous creditors.[139] On his own admission, Richelieu was briefly tempted to abandon politics after his brother's death, but when Bérulle took his confession at its face value and pressed him to return to his diocese, he found his advice was resented.[140] Political retirement quickly lost its appeal for Richelieu: a few months later, François de Sales reported him as saying 'qu'*enfin* il se rangeroit à mon parti, pour ne penser plus qu'à Dieu et au salut des ames', but the bishop of Geneva evidently set less store by this promise than had Bérulle before him.[141]

135 Fontenay-Mareuil, *Mémoires*, pp. 444–5. See the comment of Épernon's biographer on the Richelieu faction's power: 'rien ne se donnoit qu'à leurs prières, et seuls ils avaient la disposition de toute la Maison': Girard, *Vie d'Épernon*, p. 341.

136 *Journal d'Arnauld 1614–20*, pp. 430–1, for his arrival at court. Mosny is quoted as saying 'que M. de Richelieu n'avoit rien, ni par naissance, ni par courage, ni par fidélité, qu le deust faire préférer à luy (i.e. Mosny)'.

137 Girard, *Vie d'Épernon*, p. 341. Girard was an eye witness to the event. Both Girard and Arnauld (*Journal 1614–20*, pp. 435–7) contradict Richelieu's claims (*Mémoires*, II, pp. 362–4) that Bérulle, who was also passing by, had the time to confess and administer the last rites to Henri.

138 Avenel, *Lettres*, I, pp. 603–6, 614–16 letters to various individuals who had offered their condolences to Richelieu; *ibid.*, VII, p. 467, letter to Luynes, 29 July; Richelieu, *Mémoires*, II, p. 364.

139 A.A.E., Mems. et docs., France 772, fo. 106, letter from Adumeau, Henri's *homme d'affaires*, to Richelieu, 19 July 1619, offering his services and explaining steps taken to protect Henri's property against his creditors since his death. For a more detailed treatment of this problem, see Bergin, *Richelieu*, pp. 34–40.

140 Houssaye, *Bérulle et l'Oratoire*, pp. 290–1.

141 *Oeuvres de Saint François de Sales* (Annecy edition), vol. XIX (Lyon 1914), p. 37, letter to Jeanne de Chantal, 5–19 Oct. 1619.

In political terms, too, Henri's death was a greater loss to Richelieu at the time than is often realized, robbing him of a trusted and resourceful figure whose military career was on the verge of producing political dividends. As one observer somewhat rhetorically, but accurately, put it: 'how many positions [*charges*] did we not see fall vacant as a result of this loss, for what could the dead man, had he lived longer, not have aspired to from the infinite power of his brother?'[142] In 1619, Richelieu's 'lay' clientèle was still limited, and probably less blindly devoted than he would have liked, so he could not afford any thinning of their ranks. Nevertheless, ill wind that it was, the death of Henri de Richelieu did strengthen his brother's hand politically. It finally obliged Rucellaï as well as Thémines to leave Angoulême, 'in such a manner', as Déageant put it, 'that the field of battle was left entirely to M. d'Espernon and M. de Luçon'.[143] Thémines's captaincy of Marie's guards was promptly awarded to Richelieu's brother-in-law, Brézé, while the governorship of Angers was assigned to his uncle, Amador de La Porte. Nothing was being left to chance, and the political methods exhibited by Richelieu as Louis XIII's minister were already being perfected.

Richelieu's concern to secure the Angevin governorships for his clients was a logical extension of his search for a power base while still at Angoulême. Wider questions, such as that of Marie de' Medici's return to court, did not distract him in particular from seeking to build a provincial power base which might act as a counterweight to Luynes and his supporters. We do not know who first suggested that Marie exchange the governorship of Normandy for that of Anjou, but it was an idea which Richelieu was bound to find attractive – 'estant Angevins, ce seroit gouverner en nostre pays'.[144] But his preferences, and those of the queen mother's entourage generally, were not founded solely on provincial patriotism. The demand that the provincial governorship of Anjou be supplemented by those of Angers, Chinon and Ponts de Cé was founded on their strategic value as bridgeheads across the Loire. It is clear that before such a demand was formulated, there had been extensive discussion at Angoulême. In a long memorandum on the relative merits of the governorship of Angers versus that of Nantes, Richelieu – if, as seems probable, he composed the 'discours et raisons' on the subject preserved among his papers – allowed his imagination to run freely

142 Girard, *Vie d'Épernon*, p. 341.
143 Letter from Guichard Déageant to the Marquis de Coeuvres, 28 July 1619, quoted in *Rapports et notices sur l'édition des Mémoires* du Cardinal de Richelieu, II, p. 183, n. 1. See also Marie de' Medici's judgement of Rucellaï in Avenel, *Lettres*, VII, pp. 465–6, letter to anonymous correspondent, early July 1619.
144 Avenel, *Lettres*, I, p. 592.

ahead of present political realities. By the same token, it shows the extent to which he was a product of the political arithmetic of the age of Concini and Luynes. Rarely has the 'places de sûreté' frame of mind, so often associated with the Huguenots, been so fully laid out nor in such detail. The comparison between Angers and Nantes – highly favourable to the latter – is comprehensive to a fault, and some of the reflections on, for example, the facility offered by Nantes for contacts both abroad and in Brittany reveal a ruthless streak which did not recoil from the prospect of foreign assistance in case of later conflicts.[145] The determined pursuit of provincial governorships and similar *places fortes* by Concini and Luynes attracted intense interest and criticism, and raised questions about their intentions as well, of course, as sharpening the appetite of those who opposed them for a share of the spoils. In the end, Marie de' Medici and Richelieu had to be content with Anjou, and the lesser town governorships of Angers, Chinon and Ponts de Cé. It was doubtless for the same reasons that they wanted Nantes that it was denied to them. Richelieu himself acquired no formal title to any of these governorships, but his strategy was clearly divined by at least one contemporary, who commented that Richelieu 'knew that whoever was master of these places would also be master of the queen mother's fortune . . . and he did not wish to be subject to anyone else'.[146] Much of the summer and autumn of 1619 was spent in establishing and consolidating his grip on the province, and involved an impressive list of further demands made of the crown in Marie de' Medici's name.[147] Although dilatory in its responses to demands, the court did not seriously stand in their way: it was, after all, preferable to see the province in Richelieu's hands than in those of the far more dangerous and powerful Épernon.

VI

As we saw, the conditions in which the Treaty of Angoulême was negotiated were confused. Some of the crucial concessions to Marie de' Medici, like the governorships, were not strictly part of it at all, but a matter of private undertakings. For these reasons alone, further negotiation was unavoidable, but progress was not helped by con-

145 *Ibid.*, 1, pp. 587–93.
146 Fontenay-Mareuil, *Mémoires*, p. 445.
147 A.A.E., Mems. et docs., France 772, fos. 115, 189–92, for those put to Montbazon and others, July–August 1619. Avenel, *Lettres*, 1, pp. 626–9, Richelieu to Amador de La Porte, Sept. 1619.

tinuing mutual distrust. With Louis XIII and his court successively resident at Amboise, Blois and Tours between May and September 1619, there was increased communication, if not understanding, between the two sides. A constant stream of negotiators and messengers, including Bérulle, Béthune, Père Joseph and others, shuttled busily between the court and Angoulême for several months, in an effort to reassure the queen mother, to allay her suspicions of the court's unwillingness to honour its promises to her and, above all, to hasten her consent to a meeting with Louis XIII.[148] But her decision to remain in Angoulême and her reluctance to come to court also reflected the interests of her supporters, notably Épernon, as is clear from her demands for formal assurances that they be favourably treated;[149] without that, she repeatedly argued, her return to court would be desertion, and would, in turn, leave her a virtual prisoner in a hostile environment.[150] Marie's personal obstinacy was too genuine to be ignored, and at Angoulême there had, from the outset, been parties for and against her return to court. In 1617–18, the court feared the political dangers of the queen mother's returning there to reclaim a share of power; in 1619, it was her reluctance to return which created nervousness and suspicion. Richelieu was consequently obliged to perform a careful balancing-act in the negotiations and, on this issue at least, those who regarded him as all-powerful at Marie's court were somewhat hasty in their judgements. Although the departure of Rucellaï and his allies strengthened his political position considerably, it also had the effect of leaving him and Marie with fewer alibis when the court increased its pressure on her to meet Louis XIII. Certainly, it is noticeable that both scrutiny and suspicion of his motives began to grow during this period, obliging him to hedge his preferences with many qualifications. For example, when his uncle, La Porte, went to court in early July to take his oath as governor of Angers, Richelieu instructed him to remain as tight-lipped as possible and that, if pressed on the question of Marie's return to court, he should say it was a good idea but that the decision should come from the queen mother herself.[151] A month later, the nuncio reported that her excuses seemed increasingly strange and frivolous, and his conversations led him to believe the

---

148 See Houssaye, *Bérulle et l'Oratoire*, pp. 280ff; E. Griselle, *Profils de jésuites au xviiè siècle* (Paris 1911), chs. 3–4, on Arnoux and Suffren.
149 *Correspondance de Bérulle*, II, pp. 51, 55–6, Retz to Bérulle, c. 25 July and 21 Aug. 1619 respectively, for clear illustration of this stumbling-block to reconciliation.
150 Avenel, *Lettres*, VII, p. 930, queen mother to Prince Thomas of Savoy, July 1619; *ibid.*, pp. 468–9, to Louis XIII, Aug. 1619; Steffani, *Nunziatura di Bentivoglio*, III, p. 421, letter of 30 July :'ella non vuol venire ad essere menata in trionfo a Parigi'.
151 Avenel, *Lettres*, I, pp. 463–4.

delay was part of Richelieu's efforts to 'dominate the queen more completely'.[152] Rumours even began circulating that he was conspiring with Luynes and Déageant to prevent a royal reconciliation.[153]

Nevertheless, the intensive diplomacy of the summer of 1619 did gradually resolve many of the outstanding difficulties, even if it did not generate significant reserves of confidence between the two sides. Marie definitively accepted the governorships offered by Louis XIII in late May, and was free to install new governors in them by early July.[154] By then, the amnesty for her followers had also been registered by the *parlement* of Paris. In mid-August the duc de Montbazon accepted a long list of conditions and demands presented by the queen mother, most of them financial in character or relating to the Anjou governorships.[155] Despite this, Marie continued to demand further assurances of Luynes's goodwill, going so far as require formal guarantors of the Angoulême treaty.[156] Meanwhile, both through letters and his clerical confidants, Richelieu had been trying to impress on Luynes the need to win the queen mother's good graces, without which paper agreements would be worthless.[157] Finally, after Montbazon's 'embassy' and the concessions of mid-August, Richelieu judged the time had come to break the stalemate and, with the continuing assistance of Suffren, Bérulle and Père Joseph, engineered a direct appeal to Marie by the king's confessor, Arnoux, urging her to return to court.[158] Couched in terms of religion, conscience, and respect for promises already made, Arnoux's intervention had the desired effect.[159] Once it became clear that Marie had at last decided to meet Louis XIII, it was

---

152 For the court's impatience with the queen mother's behaviour, see *Correspondance de Bérulle*, II, pp. 49–50, Luynes to Bérulle, 17 July; *ibid.*, pp. 50–2, Retz to Bérulle, *c.* 25 July. Also Steffani, *Nunziatura di Bentivoglio*, III, 399–400, letter of 16 July; *ibid.*, pp. 420–3, letter of 30 July. The phrase Bentivoglio used was 'per posseder più la Regina'.

153 Steffani, *Nunziatura di Bentivoglio*, III, pp. 434–7, letter of 14 Aug.; *ibid.*, III, p. 455, 25 Aug.: 'per suo proprio interesse'.

154 A.A.E., Mems. et docs., France 772, fo. 104, *brevets* for governorships, 2 July. See Eusèbe Pavie, *La Guerre entre Louis XIII et Marie de Médicis* (Angers 1899), pp. 28–9.

155 A.A.E., Mems. et docs., France 772, fo. 115–17, promises signed by Montbazon, 16 Aug.; Avenel, *Lettres*, VII, pp. 468–9, Marie to Louis XIII, *c.* 16 Aug.

156 Steffani, *Nunziatura di Bentivoglio*, III, pp. 444–5, letter of 17 Aug.; *ibid.*, 448, 453, letters of 25 Aug. Among others, she wanted Prince Thomas of Savoy and the duc de Mayenne as guarantors, but neither they nor the court welcomed such an idea: in the last resort, only the king could honour his own promises.

157 Avenel, *Lettres*, VII, pp. 466–7, letter of 29 July; *ibid.*, pp. 471–2, letter of late Aug. But letters were less effective than intermediaries such as Bérulle or Père Joseph.

158 *Ibid.*, VII, pp. 469–71, letter to Arnoux, along with suggested points for his letter to Marie, Aug. 1619. Arnoux was, in effect, acting as a kind of guarantor of the treaty in his capacity as guardian of the consciences of both Louis XIII and Luynes, to both of whom he was confessor.

159 A.A.E., Mems. et docs., France 772, fos. 121–2, letter of 22 Aug.

Richelieu who was sent ahead to court to make the necessary arrangements to put an end to the long running dispute.[160]

For all its profusion of ceremony, embraces, and promises, the long-delayed reunion of king and queen at Couzières near Tours was not the lasting *rapprochement* that had been hoped for, and soon the two courts began to go their separate ways.[161] For the same reason, it was not the triumph that a mediator like Richelieu might have expected, though he himself had been well received at court. He left Tours as empty-handed as his patron. It has often been claimed that he had spun out the negotiations during the preceding months in order to demonstrate his indispensability to the court, and especially to secure the promise of a cardinal's hat as the reward of his goodwill. It would be entirely in character for him to aspire to such a prize, but the difficulty lies in proving what effect such an ambition might have had on his behaviour during 1619. Certainly, the detailed demands over money, garrisons and offices put to the crown in the queen mother's name bear his stamp, and to that extent he can be seen as taking advantage of his position; but such concerns were those of a man and a 'party' more interested in deeds than in promises. Equally, Richelieu may have hoped for the promise of a cardinal's hat by the time the royal reconciliation finally occurred. But there is no evidence to support the view that this was a *sine qua non* of his co-operation.[162] The traditional belief that he received such a promise, either at the time of the Angoulême treaty or while at court in September 1619, is thus without foundation.[163] It is surely more significant that, just before her meeting with Louis XIII, Marie de' Medici made it clear that it was Épernon's son, Archbishop La Valette of Toulouse, who was her choice for the purple.[164] La Valette had, of course, been officially recommended to Rome a few years earlier, but had been struck off the king's list as a result of his active part in the escape from Blois; his reinstatement was part of the queen

160 Griselle, 'Louis XIII et sa mère', p. 331, Louis XIII to Marie, n.d. (early Sept. 1619).

161 *Journal d'Arnauld 1614–20*, pp. 447–8; Steffani, *Nunziatura di Bentivoglio*, III, pp. 486–8, letter of 7 Sept 1619.

162 The papal nuncio, whose business it was to keep a close eye on French demands for new cardinals, and who had been quick to report his suspicion that Richelieu was aiming for the red hat in early 1617 (Steffani, *Nunziatura di Bentivoglio*, I, p. 156, letter of 14 March 1617), makes no mention of similar ambitions in mid-1619.

163 Avenel, *Lettres*, I, pp. 618–20, mistakenly dates the king's letters recommending both La Valette and Richelieu to Sept. 1619. See also Avenel, 'L'Evêque de Luçon et le connétable de Luynes', *Revue des Questions Historiques* 9 (1870), pp. 110–11; Hanotaux, *Richelieu*, II, p. 306 (who is equivocal); Degert, 'Le Chapeau de cardinal de Richelieu', pp. 230–1.

164 *Journal d'Arnauld 1614–20*, p. 443, 18 Aug. 1619. In early 1618, La Valette had been passed over in favour of the Cardinal de Retz, to the considerable annoyance of Épernon: *ibid.*, pp. 359–60. For the archbishop's role in preparing Marie's escape from Blois, see Girard, *Vie d'Épernon*, pp. 304ff.

mother's insistence on restoring Épernon and her other allies to their offices and perquisites.[165] There is little sign that Richelieu had any part in Marie's decision, which shows clearly that his influence was not enough to displace the Épernons from their perch and that, in the last resort, Épernon *père* still weighed more heavily in her political calculations than did the bishop of Luçon. Moreover, Louis XIII promptly endorsed Marie's choice in late August, and officially proposed La Valette to Rome a month later.[166] Richelieu himself reluctantly accepted that there was little he could do to alter these decisions, and in his rather gauche attempt to offer his congratulations to La Valette, he reveals himself as a man who knew his turn had not yet come.[167]

VII

The royal meeting at Couzières terminated the first act of the so-called 'war of the mother and son'. Though there had been scarcely any bloodshed, the 'war' was not without consequences. Not only did it divert the crown's attention from foreign issues, but it also blew it off course in other respects, too; with Villeroy dead and Jeannin resigning in September 1619, the idea that France was still being governed according to the sage maxims of Henri IV retained little credibility. Above all, the war badly damaged financial policy, forcing the crown to abandon Jeannin's efforts at retrenchment and reform. The Treaty of Angoulême may have cost the crown less than that of Loudun which Richelieu had so strongly excoriated when in office, but in 1619 expenditure reached record levels.[168] Buying out Anjou and the other governorships, and underwriting Marie de' Medici's personal debts since her flight from Blois, cost the exchequer nearly 2.5 million *livres*.[169] More serious still, the events of 1619 indicated that, despite the limited number of Marie de' Medici's committed supporters, the honeymoon period enjoyed by the post-Concini régime was over, while the ensuing half-

165 Steffani, *Nunziatura di Bentivoglio*, III, p. 486, letter of 3 Sept. 1619. Bentivoglio had earlier predicted that if Épernon were restored to the king's good grace, his son would be reinstated as a French candidate for promotion as cardinal: *ibid.*, III, p. 409, letter of 30 July.

166 Steffani, *Nunziatura di Bentivoglio*, III, pp. 464–6, letter of 28 Aug., but the royal promise was only fully confirmed when the king wrote to Rome the following month to recommend him. See Avenel, *Lettres*, I, p. 635, Marie de' Medici to Luynes.

167 Quoted in Hanotaux, *Richelieu*, II, p. 310.

168 Bonney, *The King's Debts*, p. 99; Françoise Bayard, *Le Monde des financiers au xviie siècle* (Paris 1988), pp. 29, 33 (tables).

169 *Journal d'Arnauld 1614–20*, pp. 429–30. Fontenay-Mareuil, *Mémoires*, p. 444.

reconciliation with Louis XIII left the door ajar for critics of the
régime to voice their complaints – for precisely that 'altération des
esprits' which Louis XIII had predicted early in the year.

For their part, Marie de' Medici and Richelieu could not but conclude from their sojourn at Couzières and Tours that neither Louis
XIII nor Luynes was particularly eager to offer her the role beside
the king which, as queen mother, she regarded as her right.[170] But,
while the king was probably even more determined than his favourite not to allow her the seat in council which this implied, he could
not be blamed directly for the continuing impasse.[171] So elaborate
fictions continued to dominate relations between the two sides – on
the one hand, the king's *bon naturel* and filial respect, on the other
Marie's consuming desire to serve the king and his state. Criticism
and complaint had thus to be concentrated on third parties who
seemed bent on wrecking, for their own selfish ends, the harmony
which should obtain between two well-intentioned individuals. For
Marie and her entourage, Luynes was the obvious source of their
woes, as he insidiously exercised the base arts of a favourite to poison
the king's mind. Richelieu's own memoirs are the *locus classicus* of
this view of contemporary politics, though he does refer to 'les
favoris' rather than exclusively to Luynes; nowhere does he attach
any blame either to Louis XIII or his ministers, whose distrust of
him was more tenacious than that of the less consistent Luynes.[172]
To the king and the court, the trouble at Angoulême and, later, at
Angers, sprang from the *brouillons* and intriguers who tried to mani-
pulate a well-intentioned queen mother. In due course, Richelieu's
own *Mémoires* would perpetuate a vision of contemporary history
based upon such foundations.

While Louis XIII returned to Paris in late September 1619, Marie's
court-in-exile settled at Angers, encountering difficulties which
gave Richelieu his first real experience of local power outside the
ecclesiastical sphere, and which occupied him for some time.[173] But
this was only one of several reasons why the flow of letters and
emissaries between Angers and the court continued unabated during
late 1619 and early 1620. While the court plied the queen mother

---

170 Fontenay-Mareuil, *Mémoires*, p. 449; Batiffol, *Louis XIII a vingt ans*, p. 363.
171 B.N., MS. Nouv(elles) acq(uisitions) fr(ançaises) (hereafter B.N., MS. Nouv. acq. fr.)
     3538, fos. 2–4, Bassompierre to comte de Tillières, his brother-in-law and ambassador
     in London, 2 Oct. 1619.
172 For examples of this, see Griselle, 'Louis XIII et sa mère', pp. 90–2, queen mother to
     Louis XIII, 7 Dec. 1619; Richelieu, *Mémoires*, III, pp. 2, 6, 10–12. Richelieu claims that
     even the ministers were ill-treated by Luynes.
173 Avenel, *Lettres*, I, pp. 620–3, letter to Marillac (Sept. 1619); *ibid.*, I, pp. 627–9, notes for
     a letter to Amador de La Porte (late Sept. 1619). There were disturbances in the town,
     which the officials of the courts seemed unwilling to repress.

with items of information and requests for her advice, Richelieu tried to persuade Luynes that unless he convinced Marie of his good-will by appropriate action, her suspicions of ill-intent would remain, preventing her from being reunited with Louis XIII.[174] As before, her demands for satisfaction, the honouring of promises already made, particularly at Angoulême, and for a broader show of good-will towards her, tended to become questions of confidence, while perceived footdragging by the crown – for example, over the payment of her debts and the treatment of her supporters – reinforced the predisposition to interpret royal decisions in a negative light.[175] The climate of trust, always fragile, deteriorated still further during late 1619. Richelieu claimed later that personal slights kept Marie in a state of resentment: the appointment of a new governor for Gaston d'Orléans, like the marriage of her daughter earlier that year, was decided without consulting her.[176] But it was the release of Condé, delayed until mid-October, which had a much greater effect. Marie had previously insisted that the release, to which she did not object in principle, be postponed until after her own reconciliation with Louis XIII.[177] But it was the subsequent royal declaration publicly absolving Condé from all blame and attributing his incarceration to the abuse of power in 1616, which reopened old wounds, and led to a new war of words between Marie and Louis in December 1619.[178] Indeed, Marie went on to demand a second declaration declaring *her* to be no less innocent than Condé, but even now, in the early months of 1620, neither Louis XIII nor Luynes could bring themselves to give her that final discharge for her record as regent which, by removing a persistent source of grievance, might have closed a still-painful chapter of recent political history.[179]

Of course, the Condé affair was about much more than personalities or past politics. Viewed from another angle, it was part of the rapid increase in the power of Luynes which, because it had begun

174　Avenel, *Lettres*, VII, pp. 473–7, two letters of Dec. 1619.
175　*Ibid.*, VII, pp. 479–81, memorandum of 26 Jan. 1620.
176　Richelieu, *Mémoires*, II, pp. 392–5. Batiffol, *Louis XIII a vingt ans*, pp. 457–8, rebuts such charges, and argues that Marie's actual behaviour was the opposite of what her subsequent claims of mistreatment allege.
177　*Négociation avec la reine mère*, pp. 177–9, Béthune to Luynes, 12 April 1619; pp. 179–80, Luynes's reply, 16 April, postponing Condé's release as part of his efforts to negotiate a settlement with the queen mother.
178　Avenel, *Lettres*, VII, pp. 473–5, Richelieu to Luynes, 2 Dec. 1619. See Griselle, 'Louis XIII et sa mère', pp. 89–93, for the exchange of royal letters; Aumale, *Histoire des princes de Condé*, III, pp. 104ff.
179　Avenel, *Lettres*, VII, p. 480, 'mémoire donné à M de Brantes', 26 Jan 1620, for the queen mother's demand; Griselle, 'Louis XIII et sa mère', pp. 97–8, Louis XIII's reply, 26 Feb. See also Steffani, *Nunziatura di Bentivoglio*, IV, pp. 100–10, letter of 29 Jan 1620. Frequent reports on the effects of the Condé declaration can be found in Bentivoglio's despatches for Dec. 1619 and Jan. 1620.

to move into a highly-visible phase, increasingly antagonized the
political élite and provided willing recruits to the queen mother's
second revolt.[180] It was in August 1619 that Luynes became a duke
and peer, and this was followed soon afterwards by the elevation of
his brothers Cadenet and Brantes; after hugely profitable marriages,
they became dukes of Chaulnes and Luxembourg respectively. During the year, Cadenet also became a marshal of France, *intendant des
finances* and a minister; another relative, Modène, entered the council
in January 1620.[181] Louis XIII's inability to refuse Luynes anything
seemed only to increase with time, and thus to threaten the existing
political balance, the most blatant example of this occurring when
Marie de' Medici finally surrendered the governorship of Normandy
in mid-1619. Luynes initially attempted to trade it for the governorship of Provence, his native province, and then of Brittany, but
failed to acquire either.[182] However, a complex series of exchanges
did soon follow, with Normandy itself going to Longueville, Luynes's own governorship of the Ile-de-France to Montbazon, his
father-in-law, while Luynes himself picked up Picardy (the subject
of so much trouble under Concini) from Longueville, who had held
it since 1616. Exchanges of provincial governorships were not unheard of, but it was the crown's readiness to allow Luynes, like
Concini before him, to supplement his with important town fortresses like those of Amiens, Soissons, Boulgone, and Calais, which
was regarded as particularly unacceptable.[183] Other governorships
and favours, paid for by an obliging monarch, would follow later,
culminating in Luynes's appointment as constable of France and
keeper of the seals in 1621.[184]

But, as Richelieu's own behaviour would later show, such frenetic
personal and family aggrandizement could not be divorced from
broader political developments: it ultimately needed to repose on
sure political foundations, and the events of 1619 had already revealed potentially troublesome cracks in them. In releasing Condé
and publicly wiping his political slate clean, Luynes's régime finally
decided to play the Condé card for all it was worth.[185] Luynes was
anxious not only to prevent the prince from becoming a focus of
further discontent or from teaming up with malcontents like Bouillon
– or even, despite their enmity, with the queen mother herself – but

180   Fontenay-Mareuil, *Mémoires*, p. 452.
181   *Journal d'Arnauld 1614–20*, pp. 445–6; Fontenay-Mareuil, *Mémoires*, pp. 468–9; Pont-
      chartrain, *Mémoires*, p. 294; *Journal d'Arnauld 1620*, ed E. Halphen (Paris 1888), p. 5.
182   Pontchartrain, *Mémoires*, p. 287.
183   Bonney, *The King's Debts*, p. 94; *Journal d'Arnauld 1614–20*, p. 440.
184   Chevallier, *Louis XIII*, pp. 200–2, for a convenient account of Luynes's progress.
185   See Steffani, *Nunziatura di Bentivoglio*, III, pp. 511–12, letter of 13 Sept. 1619; *ibid.*, III,
      pp. 533–4, letter of 22 Sept. Also Pavie, *Guerre de Louis XIII et Marie de' Medicis*, pp. 55ff.

also, by treating him on such favourable terms, to attach him firmly to Luynes's own interests and policies. By comparison, annoying Marie de' Medici must have seemed the lesser evil. Indeed, in the early months of 1620, the Luynes-Condé alliance seemed to carry all before it, and probably did more than anything else to dissuade the queen mother from settling her differences with the court.[186] Luynes's use of Condé to buttress his power constituted a lesson which would not be lost on Richelieu. However much he might deplore the damage it did to both Marie de' Medici's interests in 1620 and to his own personal ambitions during the early 1620s, he would several years later seize the opportunity to strike a similar bargain with the prince, one which considerably strengthened his hold on office.[187]

It is, consequently, not difficult to understand why the queen mother and her supporters felt that a deliberate attempt was being made to keep them in a weak and isolated position. Contradictory views have long been current as to the part played by Richelieu in the second act of the 'war of the mother and son', and in particular over the extent of his responsibility for the gradual drift towards armed confrontation. His reception at Tours, where he had been vouchsafed a number of confidences and half-promises, seems to have rekindled his optimism, and to have motivated him in subsequent months to work actively for the queen mother's return to court.[188] By November 1619, he was convinced he had persuaded her to do so, but his timing proved awry, and the Condé affair, with all the recriminations that followed it, extinguished those immediate hopes.[189] Consequently, his influence became considerably less decisive by the last days of 1619 than it had been a few months before. Indeed, after the semi-failure at Couzières, his continuing advocacy of Marie's return to court reduced his room for manoeuvre, while, at Angers, opponents of Richelieu's policy of accommodation did not find it hard to uncover signs of the court's bad faith. Others in Marie's entourage now seemed to speak the kind of language to which she was predisposed to listen: that a return would leave her isolated and humiliated in a hostile environment, and that she should remain instead at Angers and from there try to rally those who were disenchanted with Luynes's ascendancy. Richelieu himself singled

---

186 Steffani, *Nunziatura di Bentivoglio*, IV, pp. 74–7, letters of 17 Jan. 1620.
187 See Aumale, *Histoire des princes de Condé*, III, pp. 173ff. The circumstances of this rapprochement have yet to be fully investigated.
188 Steffani, *Nunziatura di Bentivoglio*, IV, p. 30, letter of 18 Dec. 1619. Retz had told Bentivoglio that the court was satisfied with Richelieu, of whose advice to the queen mother it approved.
189 Avenel, *Lettres*, I, pp. 637–8, letters to Retz and Arnoux (early Nov).

out Chanteloube, the governor of Chinon, as his most influential opponent in Marie's circle in late 1619, and as the main source of this kind of advice.[190] It is notoriously difficult to pinpoint this shift in attitudes at Angers, and it is best to regard it as a gradual development; there is no evidence for the view that the queen mother began plotting a second war against her son immediately after the meetings at Tours.[191] Nor should we regard Richelieu himself as a reliable witness to what went on in late 1619 and early 1620. The brief account in his *Mémoires* is a masterpiece of reticence, and skilfully draws a veil over the lengthy struggle for influence to which it so tantalisingly alludes:

> These reasons [i.e. against a return to court] were not without plausibility, and did not lack supporters; they were defended by the *grands*, who hoped to take advantage of public divisions, and by my own enemies who hoped in this way to grab the confidence of my mistress. As a result, I was obliged, out of considerations of prudence, to accept their ideas and, as wise pilots do, to give in to the storm . . . One is often obliged to follow views of which one least approves.[192]

At the very least, such an admission of opportunism suggests that Richelieu's original arguments carried less and less weight, and that certain members of the nobility were using their influence to tilt the balance the other way. Yet it should not come as a complete surprise that he rallied to the other point of view. The argument that he had every interest in bringing the queen mother back to court – where he would himself be correspondingly more powerful – rather than vegetating in provincial exile, is only partially convincing. A return to court on Luynes's terms had little attraction for either of them, especially if Condé enjoyed significant influence and supported Luynes; were Richelieu and Marie to find themselves obliged to return there, the chances of turning the tables on their opponents

---

190   Richelieu, *Mémoires*, II, pp. 390–1. Chanteloube abandoned his governorship in 1621 in order to join Bérulle's Oratory. After the Day of the Dupes, he followed Marie de' Medici into exile, and became one of Richelieu's most determined pamphleteer-adversaries. Pavie, *Guerre de Louis XIII et Marie de' Medicis*, pp. 95–101, follows Richelieu's interpretation of events.

191   Fontenay-Mareuil, *Mémoires*, p. 452; Pavie, *Guerre de Louis XIII et Marie de' Medicis*, pp. 49–50.

192   Richelieu, *Mémoires*, II, p. 391. 'Ces raisons, qui ne manquoient pas d'apparence, n'eurent pas faute d'appui; elles furent soutenues des grands, qui espéroient profiter des divisions publiques, et de mes ennemis, qui pensoient, par ce moyen, de dérober la confiance de ma maitresse, si bien que je fus, par prudence, contraint de revenir à leurs pensées, et, à l'imitation des sages pilotes, de céder à la tempête . . . on est souvent obligé de suivre les opinions qu'on approuve le moins.'

once back at court must have seemed minimal.[193] In any case, Richelieu knew perfectly well that he still had no political future independently of Marie de' Medici and that, given the enemies he had made among her entourage, he could hardly expect to make yet another comeback. Thus, however genuinely he may have disapproved of a military confrontation with the crown, the last thing he was prepared to do was tamely to surrender the direction of Marie's affairs to someone else; his determination not to do so led him into manoeuvres and compromises which would later give rise to accusations of treachery from friend and foe alike.

VIII

If, unlike 1619, fighting actually occurred in 1620, it was only after much indecisiveness and uncertainty on both sides. Once again, dissensions at court, where Condé's growing influence (the fruit of his alliance with Luynes whose power was already sufficiently resented by many) exacerbated traditional rivalries among the great aristocratic houses, triggering a new round of defections of leading nobles, reminiscent of the early 1610s.[194] In many cases, the roles had altered sharply since 1619: the first to leave court, in late March 1620, and retire to his governorship was Mayenne, Marie de' Medici's most redoubtable opponent the previous year.[195] Although the *grands'* discontent had intrinsically little to do with her predicament, Mayenne and the duc de Retz signed solemn promises within days of leaving court to support her in return for her full protection and a promise that she would not negotiate or settle independently of them. Over the next few months, similar 'indentures' and promises, oral as well as written, were also made by leading nobles such as the ducs de Roannez, Rohan, Montmorency, and Coligny de Châtillon, as well as by lesser figures.[196] But support for Marie among the *grands* was much wider than that, and some of those who made no such solemn promise to her were potentially even more

---

193 Hanotaux, *Richelieu*, II, p. 319. The nuncio opined that she was more likely to end up in Vincennes than in the council: Steffani, *Nunziatura di Bentivoglio*, IV, 69–70, letter of 2 Jan. 1620.

194 For regular, often biting, comments on the resentment against Luynes and Condé, see Steffani, *Nunziatura di Bentivoglio*, IV, pp. 69–70, 74–5, 77, 152, 194, letters of Jan.-early April 1620. See also Pavie, *Guerre de Louis XIII et Marie de' Medicis*, p. 112ff. for a tableau of aristocratic discontent in 1620.

195 *Journal d'Arnauld 1620*, p. 11.

196 A.A.E., Mems. et docs., France 773, fos. 38, 43–4, 49. Batiffol, *Louis XIII a vingt ans*, p. 371, n. 5 (Montmorency). An important feature of these promises was that the loyalty they required was exclusive even of the service of the king.

powerful allies – princes of the blood such as the Soissons; Henri IV's natural offspring, the Vendômes; the ducs de Longueville, Épernon, Brissac and many others. Whatever their individual motives, such a league was an ominous prospect, especially when compared to the dismal failure of Marie's appeals for support a year earlier. Between April and July 1620, much of northern, western, and south-western France seemed to slip from the crown's control, providing the potential for one of the most formidable malcontent revolts since the time of Henri III.[197]

While such support was welcome at Angers, where fruitless negotiation with emissaries from the court had virtually become a way of life, it is not clear whether the queen mother and her advisers quite knew how to master it and exploit it to the full. Insofar as a coherent response did evolve, it was one which envisaged further negotiation from a position of increased political and military strength. For its part, the crown was scarcely more decisive in its approach to the crisis. While Condé was bellicose and vengeful, anxious to prove he was the crown's most zealous champion, Luynes and the ministers feared civil war, not only for its own intrinsic dangers, but because it might reduce their political influence to the advantage of Condé and those who favoured military solutions to the political crisis.[198]

While bringing civil war a step nearer, the immediate effect of the defections of Mayenne, Retz and others was to give a fresh impetus to negotiations between the two sides, and this could not fail to bring Richelieu back into the limelight. His own subsequent claims to have had little influence in the queen mother's counsels at crucial points in late 1619 and 1620 were no doubt intended to refute accusations that he played his part in propelling her into military confrontation with the crown, but they have also created a smokescreen around his activities generally at this time.[199] Not only did the court not share that view of his position, but the highly circumstantial accounts in his *Mémoires* – compiled from his own papers – of Marie's discussions with, and point-by-point responses to, a succession of royal emissaries during the first half of 1620, suggest anything but a man reduced to 'faire l'antichambre'. Thus, when Montbazon was sent by Luynes on another of his missions to Angers in mid-April 1620, he was instructed to pin the blame for the strange behaviour of the queen mother squarely on Richelieu, and to make it clear that any failure to achieve agreement would be attributed to him. Riche-

197 See J. Russell Major, 'The Revolt of 1620. A Study of the ties of fidelity', *French Historical Studies* 14 (1986), pp. 391–408; Hanotaux, *Richelieu*, II, pp. 331–3.
198 *Journal d'Arnauld 1620*, p. 18; Steffani, *Nunziatura di Bentivoglio*, IV, pp. 220–1, letter of 6 May 1620. See Hanotaux, *Richelieu*, II, pp. 336–8.
199 Richelieu, *Mémoires*, III, pp. 48, 73–4.

lieu, he continued, had already missed several opportunities to demonstrate her good faith. The intention behind language such as this may have been to frighten him into a more conciliatory line or to make him exert himself more energetically, but – especially when we note that it was rounded off with an accusatory 'car chascun sçait qu'elle est sa puissance' – it would hardly have been used about someone of no consequence or influence.[200] Luynes repeated the same refrain in June, and a month later, when Louis XIII was already subjugating rebel Normandy, Richelieu was actually denounced by name by the king for his role in bringing the conflict to a head.[201] However, the Montbazon mission failed to produce the hoped-for capitulation: on the contrary, if we can believe his later account, Richelieu took it as evidence of the court's weakness and uncertainty, and its effect was to strengthen the determination to remain at Angers and demand the full implementation of the terms of the treaty of Angoulême.[202] Moreover, although the threat of war might endanger his eminence as the queen mother's principal adviser, it also revived the peace lobby of the previous year which, as we saw, contained a large complement of clerics like himself – Arnoux, Suffren, Bérulle, Sébastien Bouthillier, Père Joseph, Archbishop Jean du Perron of Sens, and Cardinals de Retz and de La Rochefoucauld. In fact, those who wished for a peaceful solution to the current crisis could not but look to Richelieu, the bishop and the diplomat, not because he held the key to war or peace, but because he was quite simply one of the few political actors in a position and endowed with the necessary skill to engineer a peaceful compromise.[203]

There is other evidence, too, that throughout the months leading up to the *drôlerie* at Ponts de Cé, Richelieu continued to manage the queen mother's financial and political affairs. Before and after April 1620, when the *grands* began defecting to her side, her treasurer, Florent d'Argouges, remained in Paris, harrying ministers into paying the monies owed to her since 1619 and raising new loans. It is clear from his regular correspondence that it was to Richelieu that he referred difficulties, and it was Richelieu who he asked for

200 A.A.E., Mems. et docs., France 773, fos. 172–4; *Journal d'Arnauld 1620*, p. 12.
201 A.A.E., Mems. et docs., France 773, fo. 54, Luynes to Richelieu, 19 June; *Mémoires de Mathieu Molé*, ed. A. Champollion-Figeac (Paris 1855–7), I, pp. 237–44 (at p. 241), for the royal declaration.
202 Richelieu, *Mémoires*, III, p. 17; Steffani, *Nunziatura di Bentivoglio*, IV, pp. 206–7, letter of 22 April 1620.
203 The most active of these men during early 1620 was du Perron of Sens. For his letters to Richelieu: A.A.E., Mems, et docs., France 773, fos. 23, 45, 48, 55–6, 60. See Steffani, *Nunziatura di Bentivoglio*, IV, pp. 220–1, letter of 6 May, on du Perron's value as a mediator.

decisions.[204] At the same time, d'Argouges provided Richelieu with a useful link to both ministers and leading financial officials. Moreover, Richelieu clearly maintained his own lines of communication between Paris and Angers, doubtless so as to retain some freedom of action, and not to find himself wholly dependent upon information and intermediaries of whom he could not be entirely certain. As so often, the role of principal *homme de confiance* again fell to Sébastien Bouthillier, who also worked closely with d'Argouges.[205] Michel de Marillac, *intendant* of Anjou, also served as an intermediary when in Paris.[206] Richelieu's own discretion notwithstanding, it is thus impossible to believe that the *pourparlers* with the discontented *grands*, which extended over several months and which in some cases led to the making and signing of formal promises, were not conducted by him through the medium of trusted agents in Paris and elsewhere.[207] Nor did he confine his efforts to organizing an anti-Luynes coalition. Even if his preferred objective was a negotiated compromise, the impending trial of strength was one which required military preparedness. Raising troops might be largely a matter for the *grands*, but the necessary commissions and instructions had to be approved by Marie de' Medici and issued through her chancery.[208] In his subsequent account of the events of 1620, Michel de Marillac, one of Richelieu's closest collaborators at Angers, would not hesitate to attribute to him overall responsibility for the efforts to raise money and troops – efforts which involved seizing crown revenues and other 'voies de fait', but which by July 1620 had produced a war chest of over 2.3 million *livres* and a paper-strength army of over 50,000 men.[209] Indeed, it was for his part in ordering the seizure of royal tax-receipts that Louis XIII denounced Richelieu in July 1620.

204 A.A.E., Mems. et docs., France 773, fos. 2, 10, 41–2, 46–7, 51–2, 62, for d'Argouges's letters to Richelieu between Jan. and July 1620.

205 His correspondence with Richelieu has not survived, but his activities are mentioned by Richelieu's other correspondents. See A.A.E., Mems. et docs., France 773, fo. 10, d'Argouges to Richelieu, 10 Feb. 1620; fo. 15, Michel de Marillac to Richelieu, 21 Feb.; fo. 23, du Perron de Sens to Richelieu, 28 Feb.; fo. 42, d'Argouges to Richelieu, undated; fo. 45, du Perron to Richelieu, 6 May. Richelieu, *Mémoires*, III, p. 4. See Batiffol, *Louis XIII a vingt ans*, p. 369, n. 2, undated letter from Richelieu to Bouthillier.

206 See his letters to Richelieu in A.A.E., Mems. et docs., France 773, fos. 11–13, 13, 36–37, Feb.–April 1620.

207 The Soissons were rumoured in May 1620 to be in touch with Angers, yet they only fled Paris on 30 June: see Steffani, *Nunziatura di Bentivoglio*, IV, pp. 240–1, letter of 20 May.

208 *Journal d'Arnauld 1620*, p. 36, for the arrest of agents carrying large numbers of blank commissions from Marie de' Medici. See Puysieux's correspondence about these commissions in A.A.E., Mems. et docs., France 773, fos. 70–1. A draft of a commission is in *ibid.*, fo. 79v.

209 See Pavie, *Guerre de Louis XIII et Marie de' Medicis*, pp. 148–9, 159, for extracts from Marillac's account.

Finally, it is likely that, through Louis de Marillac, he was in a position to exercise more influence in military matters than he was prepared, either then or later, to admit.[210]

The problem with the 1620 revolt was not that Marie de' Medici lacked supporters, military forces or money; it lay in the failure to achieve any effective unity of purpose and action. The scathing account in Richelieu's *Mémoires* of the quarrels and maverick behaviour of the *grands* may betray an apologetic purpose, but it scarcely conceals his frustration at his inability to weld them into a working coalition, especially where military matters were concerned.[211] But beyond that, as the former patron of Concini the queen mother was not ideally placed to act as the focus of principled opposition to the Luynes régime. Yet, in view of what we have seen of Richelieu's efforts against the *grands* in early 1617 and his subsequent propaganda against Luynes, the Brûlarts, and La Vieuville, it is perhaps surprising that a more sustained propaganda assault was not mounted against Luynes in 1619–20. Marie de' Medici consistently claimed during 1619 that she had important suggestions to make for the good of the state, but then obstinately refused all invitations to reveal them in negotiations.[212] In July 1620, she allowed the reprinting of the 1619 manifesto demanding conciliar and financial reform and, above all, specific measures to curb the ambitions of favourites.[213] This time, however, she sought to broaden its appeal by sending it to the *parlements* and, by praising the magistrates' zeal for the good of the state, to draw them into the conflict on her side.[214] It is tempting to discern Richelieu's hand in all this. Although he evidently approved of the manifesto, he can hardly be credited with the authorship of an unrevised text which had first been composed before his arrival at Angoulême.[215] On the other hand, the move to enlist the *parlements* and exploit their discontent in mid-1620 is indicative of his political style. However, nothing came of that ploy: the crown quickly settled its dispute with the office-holders over the *droit annuel*, and the *parlements* simply refused to receive the queen

210 Hanotaux, *Richelieu*, II, p. 331.
211 Richelieu, *Mémoires*, III, pp. 45–7, 69–73, 81.
212 Griselle, 'Louis XIII et sa mère', pp. 295–6, Louis XIII to Marie de' Medici, undated (but early 1620?), reproaching her for her evasiveness in this respect.
213 The document is generally known as the *Manifeste d'Angers*, but the text is identical with that of Angoulême.
214 Avenel, *Lettres*, VII, pp. 485–6, letter of *c*. 20 July 1620.
215 For Richelieu's own summary of the manifesto, see *Mémoires*, III, pp. 58–61; for that of 1619 and Béthune's reference to it, see *Négociation avec la reine mère*, pp. 111–12 (undated letter, but probably late March); pp. 112–16 (manifesto). Deloche, *Autour de la plume*, pp. 208–12, develops some characteristically elaborate arguments on why the manifesto could only have been written by Richelieu.

mother's letters.[216] Equally intriguing is Richelieu's own later admission that a second manifesto, couched in far more virulent language and directly attacking the wide-ranging abuses of the Luynes régime, particularly for its treatment of the queen mother, was also drafted in July 1620; in fact, though he does not allude to its content, this document was probably the *Extraict des raisons et plaintes de la Reyne mère*, also produced the previous year at Angoulême. According to Richelieu's later account it was only against considerable opposition that he and Marillac convinced the queen mother that it should not be circulated, let alone sent to the king, on the grounds that its 'liberty and bitterness required more power than we then possessed if it were to be upheld'. Above all, he concluded that such a public complaint would render any agreement impossible.[217] Although we may well suspect the accuracy of this account, in which he dissociates himself from the *enragés* of Angers, the admission is a revealing one. His attitude is further illustrated by the history of another tract, the *Vérités chrestiennes* which, in its unyielding defence of the queen mother, constantly accused 'the favourites' of deceiving Louis XIII.[218] Its directness and language make it virtually certain that Richelieu was its author, but he was prudent enough to allow it to be ascribed to his confidant, Mathieu de Morgues. Richelieu may have found it advisable to fall in with the preparations for war, and even to play an obscure double game, but there were serious limits to his willingness to widen criticism of the régime at this crucial juncture and, consequently, to gamble all on the fortunes of war. It would not be the last time he would demonstrate his reluctance to be tied to firm partisan commitments.

If we accept that Richelieu trimmed his sails during the run-up to the revolt of 1620, so, too, did Luynes. As the *grands* began defecting, he tried to staunch the loss of support for the régime and himself by deciding to bring Guise, Nevers and Bellegarde into the council, and by contracting a marriage alliance with Lesdiguières.[219] He also continued to hope that negotiations with the queen mother would bring results. Between April and June, belated efforts were made to implement certain clauses (especially financial) of the Treaty of Angoulême; to those were added offers of new concessions to the

---

216 *Journal d'Arnauld 1620*, p. 34; A.A.E., Mems. et docs., France 773, fo. 72, letter to Puysieux, 28 July 1620.
217 Richelieu, *Mémoires*, III, pp. 61–2. The French text runs: 'sa liberté et aigreur avoient besoin d'une puissance plus grande que la nôtre pour être soutenue'.
218 *Vérités chrestiennes au roy très-chrestien* (Paris 1620).
219 *Journal d'Arnauld 1620*, pp. 17, 19, 32. Pavie, *Guerre de Louis XIII et Marie de' Medicis*, pp. 177–83. Fontenay-Mareuil, *Mémoires*, pp. 468–9. Arnauld claims that opposition forced Luynes to defer the entry of Guise and the others into council, which in turn angered them.

queen mother, including the governorship of Nantes, and even what was taken to be a vague hint of a cardinal's hat for Richelieu himself.[220] Strong as the temptation to accept must have been, the balance among Marie's support had by then tilted sufficiently towards confrontation that a limited agreement – which would have excluded most of the *grands*, as well as those who had served her in 1619 – was politically too risky: it was as much out of necessity as of choice that Marie and Richelieu stood by her supporters.[221] For his part, Louis XIII was increasingly influenced by the assertive and combative Condé, whose enthusiasm for the defence of royal authority embraced the queen mother's supporters and the Huguenots alike. The departure of the Soissons from the court in early July, and the activities of Longueville and others in Normandy and the western provinces, revealed how serious the challenge to royal authority had now become, while Rohan's support for the queen mother raised the even more serious prospect of Huguenot participation in the revolt. This latter appalled the papal nuncio and the *dévot* peace lobby, and ensured that there would not be a complete break with the queen mother: on the same day as the king set out for Normandy at the head of a small force, Archbishop du Perron led an impressive delegation to Angers in the hope of finding a compromise that would avert civil war.[222] While the king and his army pacified Normandy and then headed south towards Angers, Richelieu and the queen mother were engaged in increasingly frantic efforts to avoid a military collision. Even as the king's forces began scattering the rebels at Ponts de Cé on 7 August, the negotiators were en route for Angers with peace terms actually agreed by Louis XIII!

IX

Despite its impressive roll-call of participants and its geographical extension, the revolt of 1620 ended in an inglorious rout at the hands

---

220 Especially during the three 'embassies' of Monsieur de Blainville to Angers in May–June 1620: A.A.E., Mems. et docs., France 773, fos. 211–13, for details of proposals and negotiations. For Richelieu's letters to Blainville, see Avenel, *Lettres*, VII, pp. 483–5, 21 May and end of May respectively. See also *Journal d'Arnauld 1620*, pp. 15–16, 18; Richelieu, *Mémoires*, III, pp. 27ff.

221 Pavie, *Guerre de Louis XIII et Marie de' Medicis*, pp. 209–11.

222 Griselle, 'Louis XIII et sa mère', pp. 303–4, Louis XIII to Marie de' Medici, 6 July 1620. Its other members were Jeannin, Montbazon, and Bellegarde; Bérulle was added later. The queen mother had complained that the court had in the past only sent emissaries who were all Luynes men, and not independent enough of him to inspire confidence. A.A.E., Mems. et docs., France 773, fo. 61, Luynes to Richelieu, 7 July 1620. See *Journal d'Arnauld 1620*, pp. 20–1; Steffani, *Nunziatura di Bentivoglio*, IV, p. 318, letter of 9 July.

of a régime which for long seemed unwilling to take decisive action, and which later suffered lasting discredit at the hands of the vanquished. Most versions of the revolt regard Richelieu as the one participant who was lucid and rational enough to weigh and calculate the odds, and who knew just how to snatch victory from the jaws of defeat. In reality, he appears to have believed as little as everyone else that there would be a clash of arms. When he did face the prospect that events would be decided in this manner, his tone was one of powerless resignation: such an eventuality inspired no elation in him whatever.[223] The 'harangue' which he allegedly delivered to Marie a month before the battle at the Ponts de Cé, exhorting her to examine her conscience as to the wisdom of espousing the cause of the *grands*, and of opposing the power of a king who was God's anointed, was essentially designed to deflect royal criticism of his intentions and behaviour.[224] If, in the immediate aftermath of defeat, Richelieu was able to resume with the court negotiations which had never been formally broken off, it was not because such transparent manoeuvering on his part coerced or deceived anyone, but essentially because Louis XIII and Luynes had themselves learned something from the discord of the previous three years. A combination of military success and the appearance of other political problems (the Huguenots and Béarn in particular) enabled them to be more lucid and magnanimous than in the past, and to realize that a full reconciliation with Marie de' Medici was the only way to prevent her from remaining a natural rallying point for the discontented nobility.[225] The rare and grudging tribute to Luynes on this issue in Richelieu's *Mémoires* can be regarded as the best evidence of such an interpretation.[226] In such circumstances, Richelieu's skill lay in keeping his nerve, reading the intentions behind the court's generous post-victory gestures, and then resuming the task of seeking the 'tempéraments' necessary for an agreement. The 'treaty of Angers' which was finalized within a few days of the queen mother's defeat, was essentially an updated version of the Treaty of Angoulême which, after all the prevarication of the previous year or more,

223 Avenel, *Lettres*, I, p. 653, letter to Archbishop La Valette, 2 Aug. 1620.
224 Richelieu, *Mémoires*, III, pp. 39–44, for summary of the 'harangue.' See Deloche, *Autour de la plume*, pp. 204–8, for the suggestion that Richelieu neither composed nor delivered it to Marie de' Medici at all, but that it was published in Paris under his name by Père Joseph.
225 Griselle, 'Louis XIII et sa mère', pp. 304–5.
226 Richelieu, *Mémoires*, III, p. 85: 'En quoi il faut dire, à l'honneur du sieur de Luynes, que la façon avec laquelle il se porta en cette action fut du tout dissemblable à lui-même, ne se prévalant pas injustement en cette occasion de l'avantage qu'il avoit, ains offrant les mêmes conditions que peu de jours auparavant il avoit faites.'

was now to be honoured in full by the crown. The queen mother and those who had supported her would be declared innocent, and, with a few exceptions, restored to their offices and pensions.[227]

The crown's generosity was not confined to such broad, general terms. Since the failed reconciliation of the previous year, it had become increasingly clear that account needed to be taken of Richelieu's own personal 'interests'. His career prospects might still be dependent on the queen mother, but advancement and recognition of his services were anything but mere footnotes to the political agenda. As we saw, Luynes's overtures to Marie de' Medici in April–May 1620 had singled him out quite deliberately, alternately blaming him or promising him rewards for his co-operation. Within a few days of the Treaty of Angers, he had secured the kind of reward that all parties assumed mattered most to him – the king undertook to adopt him as a French candidate for the red hat.[228] Little is known about the circumstances in which this promise was extracted from Louis XIII, but both Richelieu and Marie de' Medici were anxious to secure it as quickly as possible, while the victorious king remained in a generous mood. On 22 August 1620, the first of many royal letters recommending his candidature were despatched to Rome; a week later, Richelieu even managed to have Sébastien Bouthillier sent there for that purpose as a royal emissary.[229]

But as we shall see, even this long hoped-for move was not to prove an undiluted triumph. Suspicion among the queen mother's entourage of Richelieu's motives and behaviour had been intense, and he might not have survived at all at Angers had the leaders of the rebel cause been more united or more ruthless. In particular, the haste with which the flag of surrender was raised after the Ponts de Cé skirmish, when the bulk of Marie's forces and support were intact, and escape towards the south-west was still possible, reinforced the earlier suspicion of Richelieu's collusion with Luynes, and of his readiness to negotiate a solution which would advance his own ambitions at the expense of others.[230] This was hardly surprising, given both the inescapable ambivalence of any revolt claiming to

---

227 A.A.E., Mems. et docs., France 773, fos. 100–6, for the main articles and addenda which make up the 'treaty' of Angers. There is a synopsis of the terms in Pavie, *Guerre de Louis XIII et Marie de' Medicis*, pp. 579–80.

228 Avenel, *Lettres*, I, p. 655, Louis XIII to Paul V, 29 Aug. 1620.

229 B.N. MS. Fr. 3722, fo. 5; Avenel, *Lettres*, I, p. 655, Louis XIII to pope, 29 Aug., for Bouthillier's mission.

230 The version of events in Richelieu's *Mémoires*, III, p. 84, appears to be at variance with the facts. He claims that it was he who argued for a retreat south of the Loire, where the queen mother still possessed fresh troops and powerful supporters, but that it was the pusillanimous comtesse de Soissons and others which dissuaded Marie from doing so.

defend the 'true' interests of the monarchy, and Richelieu's unwillingness to let the *grands* dictate the course of opposition to Luynes.
But while he rightly calculated he could afford to ignore the recriminations of the queen mother's supporters – the Treaty of Angers,
after all, declared them innocent and restored them to their positions
– Richelieu was, for all his later claims to the contrary, too eager to
overlook the deeply-rooted distrust of him at court, from the king
downwards. Not only was Richelieu promised the red hat after
Ponts de Cé, but Luynes, with his Mazarin-like fondness for *com-
binazioni*, offered to marry his nephew to Richelieu's favourite niece,
the future duchesse d'Aiguillon, and thereby seal their political reconciliation. Richelieu, whatever his *Mémoires* may assert, made no
more than a token show of resistance. In the euphoria of reconciliation, the practice of dynastic politics between the leading families –
'l'union des favoris' as one commentator aptly labelled it – promised
to open up further avenues of advancement to him and, with the
queen mother's return to court now imminent, to render promises
already made all the more secure.[231]

By August 1620, Richelieu had come through the three toughest
and most formative years of his career to date. What he had learned
during them were essentially the arts of political survival, of which
he would remain a great master until the end. He had carried his
political apprenticeship to a point where even those who mistrusted
him most could not but respect – and in some cases, fear – his skills
as a political operator. It was these, not the statesmanship or the
'hautes vues' with which he is often credited, which enabled him
to cope with disgrace and emerge with enhanced credit from the
turmoil of 1619–20. Only when he once again became a minister
would he have to confront comparable difficulties, albeit this time
from the other side of the political fence. There was a considerable
difference between the relatively unknown bishop of April 1617 and
the would-be cardinal of August 1620, a difference that is readily
recognizable in the political commentaries of the time. Of course,
Richelieu was still largely the prisoner of his ambition, and of factional politics; the reconciliation of August 1620 took longer to
achieve in practice than most observers predicted then, and it could
not erase the memory, especially as far as Louis XIII was concerned,
of Richelieu's involvement in a rebel cause. Heavily dependent on
the promises and the goodwill of an unsympathetic king and his
ministers, he remained politically vulnerable. The coming years

---

231 Fontenay-Mareuil, *Mémoires*, pp. 448–9; Richelieu, *Mémoires*, III, pp. 89–92, for Riche-
     lieu's retrospective and disdainful account of the background to the marriage, and his
     own alleged lack of enthusiasm.

would be a stern test of his patience, not his most obvious quality; he was no longer quite so young, and his health was showing growing signs of fragility. For all the prescience that is usually ascribed to him, he can hardly have imagined how long his further advance would be delayed.

Chapter 6
GAMES OF PATIENCE

'C'est une grande gloire au roy d'avoir des ministres si puissans.'[1]

WHEN Guillaume du Vair sought and obtained his provisions as bishop of Lisieux in 1617, one surprised observer wagered that he would probably aim to become a cardinal, in order, 'to cover himself against future stormes'.[2] Though it was rumoured at the time that the king supported the candidature of his keeper of the seals, the matter was apparently taken no further. Even if there was no substance to the rumour, it would have made considerable sense for du Vair to aspire to the cardinalate, particularly in an age of unstable ministerial tenure. Ecclesiastical politicians still enjoyed considerable advantages over their lay colleagues, not least when it came to losing favour, or fighting off efforts to ruin them. Nor was du Vair alone in realizing that cardinals were better placed than other clerics to cover themselves in such storms. In Spain, the fall of the detested favourite, Lerma, in 1618, was cushioned by his entry into the college of cardinals. On the other hand, the arrest and imprisonment, also in 1618, of Cardinal Khlesl, minister to Emperor Mathias, was evidence that cardinals were not a law unto themselves, but could be treated harshly by rulers who were sufficiently determined.[3] Richelieu himself would later discover that his 'princely' rank in the church would not prevent numerous attempts to unseat, or even assassinate him. But between the two extremes represented by Lerma and Khlesl, the rank of cardinal offered an array of positive opportunities in the affairs of both church and state – at court, in the council, in the curia, and so on.

Within France, since the death of Henri IV there had been growing pressure from the church for a greater voice in government and the council, and Richelieu himself, in his Estates General speech, was only one of many ecclesiastics to press that case. His brief period as

---

1 Avenel, *Lettres*, I, pp. 731–2, Richelieu to *commandeur* Sillery, 28 Sept. 1622.
2 P.R.O. SP 78/67, fo. 186r–v, Thomas Edmondes to Ralph Winwood, 10 Aug. 1617. Edmondes' surprise was due to du Vair's well-known stoicism and scepticism on religious questions.
3 J.H. Elliott, *The Count-Duke of Olivares* (New Haven and London, 1986), pp. 35–6; R.J.W. Evans, *The Making of the Habsburg Monarchy* (Oxford 1979), p. 65.

secretary of state showed that such preferment did not have to be reserved exclusively for cardinals. However, ideas as to what constituted a proper political role for churchmen had been changing since the previous century. Partly because of its peculiar circumstances, and also because it included the war portfolio, Richelieu's secretaryship appeared to many at the time to be especially inappropriate for a bishop;[4] he was the last French bishop to occupy such a position during the *ancien régime*. By contrast, a seat in the king's council, or even the presidency of it, was regarded as eminently suitable for leading church figures. Prizes like these were necessarily more elusive, and generally proved less accessible to 'mere' bishops than to their hierarchical superiors, cardinals. Moreover, because promotion to the cardinalate was itself such a 'political' matter, divorced from even ecclesiastical concerns, success in obtaining a red hat was always likely to draw cardinals that much closer to the centre of the political circle. When Chancellor Sillery suggested in 1622 that the tradition of cardinals residing in Rome ought to be revived, he did concede that the king might retain one of their members to serve as an 'ordinary' member of his council.[5] None of this should be construed to mean that the king of France was constantly besieged by a clamour of cardinals demanding entry to his council, but rather that the ambition to enjoy a place in council was one that cardinals could afford to entertain.

In Richelieu's case, that ambition was no secret; the papal nuncio had first hinted at it in March 1617, when Richelieu's ministerial position, which the papacy itself had strongly welcomed, briefly gave him good reason to aspire to a red hat.[6] Since his fall, other names had been put forward but, by 1620, only one of them, the first Cardinal de Retz, had been successful; the fact that he had also become president of the council in the meantime only served to underscore the continuing political value of being a cardinal. But Retz's status as a candidate for promotion was in sharp contrast to that of Richelieu, and his route to the cardinalate was the more conventional one: his candidature was in no sense a political 'pay-off', and his political advancement only really began *after* his promotion to cardinal. Because Richelieu's candidature was so obviously a pay-off, it was naturally vulnerable to whatever reservations and recriminations might surface after the initial decision had been taken. For that reason, it was probable that Richelieu would have as much

---

4 See Michaud, 'Aux origines du secrétariat d'état à la guerre', p. 403, for reference to criticism of Richelieu by members of the French upper clergy 'qui jugeoient cet employ peu convenable à sa profession'.
5 A.A.E., Mems. et docs., France 777, fo. 101, letter to Puysieux, 6 Sept. 1622.
6 Steffani, *Nunziatura di Bentivoglio*, I, p. 156, letter of 14 March 1617.

to fear from obstacles placed across his path as from competition
with other candidates.

II

The king's acceptance of Richelieu's candidature in August 1620, and
the tortuous events of the two years that followed before he finally
became a cardinal in September 1622, constitute a vital stage in his
career, both as churchman and as political figure; it was also intimately connected to the evolving balance of power around the
throne. As we shall see, for all his disclaimers at the time, it is clear
that Richelieu attached the utmost importance to satisfying this
ambition, and it made perfect sense for him not to commit himself to
actions or policies which might jeopardize it. Once he had secured
the red hat, he could raise his head again more assertively: as an
ecclesiastical *grand*, he was the equal of his lay counterparts, to
whom he no longer needed to bow or defer. The two years it took
him to become a cardinal constituted an experience which, if less
formative than those of 1617 to 1620, tested certain qualities and
shaped new ones. Far less in control of events and more dependent
on the goodwill of others than he would have wished, Richelieu
would have to moderate his impulsiveness and learn to dissimulate
to good effect. Indeed, at times, even some of those closest to him
were to complain of his apparent stoicism and lethargy in pursuing
his own interests.[7]

The complex history of how Richelieu became a cardinal has all
too often been interpreted in unnecessarily narrow, moralizing
terms, particularly by his biographers, most of whom have been
content to follow the canon enshrined in his *Mémoires*. The king's
initial approval of his candidature is viewed as a deserved triumph
for Richelieu and as the rightful recognition of his superior abilities,
while the subsequent opposition to him is regarded as petty and
spiteful. The effect has been to create a one-dimensional perspective,
which largely discounts contemporary political realities. A credible
account must acknowledge this wider framework – which, in turn,
should not overlook the conventions of ecclesiastical politics. One
fact that should be borne in mind is that Richelieu's candidature
arose towards the end of the long pontificate of Paul V and in the
early months of that of Gregory XV, and that each of them was

---

7 Such complaints were most frequently made by Sébastien Bouthillier in Rome. His
   letters to Richelieu and Claude Bouthillier are in A.A.E., *Correspondance politique*, Rome,
   vols. 23, 28.

governed by considerations which had little to do with either him or French politics. Nor were the two years he was made to wait especially long by contemporary standards; it had, after all, taken a good deal longer for him to gain confirmation as bishop of Luçon.

Richelieu's adoption as a candidate for the college of cardinals occurred at the expense of Archbishop Marquemont of Lyon, a career official and diplomat who had been listed since 1619 and who enjoyed the strong support of ministers such as Chancellor Sillery and Puysieux, sole secretary for foreign affairs since Villeroy's death.[8] As permutations of this kind were common enough, Marquemont's supporters did not suddenly feel compelled to switch their support to his rival, all the more so as political animosities between them and Richelieu were no secret; if they were patient and resourceful enough, there was more than a reasonable chance that the king might be persuaded to change his mind about Richelieu, and reinstate their preferred candidate.[9] Furthermore, Richelieu was listed alongside Épernon's son, La Valette, whose candidature, as we saw, went back several years before 1620. The listing of two candidates was a traditional way of opening the bidding for red hats in Rome; by increasing pressure on the papacy, it gave the king room for diplomatic and political manoeuvre, and did not commit him more than he wished to either candidate. It was only if – or when – he was pressed by the papacy that the king would have to indicate which of the candidates had his preference, but he could do this in the semi-privacy of diplomatic communications, and preferences could be reversed depending on circumstances. More important than all these considerations was the fact that, in 1620, neither La Valette nor Richelieu was a genuine king's candidate – both were manifestly protégés of Marie de' Medici, and Louis's simultaneous acceptance of both of them was an act of sudden generosity towards her which left him and the ministry without a candidate they could call their own. By so obviously appearing to reward disobedience rather than loyalty, the king's erstwhile opponents rather than his supporters, this was bound to evoke dismay and envy at court.[10] As so often, the affair was to be further complicated by other, related rivalries. For example, the long-serving papal nuncio, Bentivoglio, also aspired to promotion, but

8 See Cécile Pozzo di Borgo, 'Denis Simon de Marquemont, archévêque de Lyon et cardinal (1572–1616). La carrière d'un prélat diplomate au début du xviie siècle', *Archivum Historiae Pontificiae* 15 (1977), p. 285.

9 See E. Griselle, 'Un cardinalat différé', *Documents d'Histoire* 2 (1911), pp. 527–43.

10 In April 1624, Louis XIII complained to the papal nuncio that Retz, La Valette and Richelieu had all been made cardinals on the initiative of people other than himself: A.S.V., Nunz. Fr. 401, fo. 59, Bernardino Spada to Cardinal Francesco Barberini, 18 April 1624.

given the perennial uncertainty about the intentions of an ageing pope and his entourage, he hoped to strengthen his case by obtaining the formal support of the king of France. His successor, Corsini, would do precisely the same in 1622. The nuncios consequently viewed both La Valette and Richelieu as rivals, and their correspondence provides highly-coloured accounts of their respective promotions.

In August 1620, all of this was still in the future. At that juncture, Louis XIII did not need to make known whether or not he ranked Richelieu above La Valette. For their part, as if not quite believing their good fortune, both Richelieu and Marie de' Medici were anxious to exploit the king's gesture as swiftly as possible; haste seemed essential, as they feared, not without reason, that if they missed out on a possible creation of new cardinals expected during the 'ember days' of early September 1620, there might not be another opportunity for some considerable time.[11] A special envoy, Chasant, was therefore despatched with all speed to Rome to notify the pope of the king's choice of candidates. Richelieu also took the unusual step, as we have seen, not simply of sending his own confidant, Sébastien Bouthillier, to Rome, but of ensuring that his mission had formal royal accreditation, too.[12] It was this sense of urgency on the part of Richelieu and Marie which obliged the king and his ministers to think hard about the concession that had just been made to La Valette and Richelieu. Though Louis XIII's personal views on the question were conveyed by ministers who already had a strong anti-Richelieu bias of their own, there is every reason to believe that he found it abhorrent that Richelieu might be so rapidly rewarded with a red hat for his role in the recent opposition to him. Although La Valette's nomination had again been suspended during the 1620 revolt, his behaviour had been more restrained than in 1619, and both the continuing political uncertainty and the impending clash with the Huguenots over Béarn made it more politic than ever to conciliate his powerful father.[13] Accordingly, Chasant was secretly instructed to say, if pressed by the pope, that the king would prefer to see La Valette promoted before Richelieu, whose case was not to be regarded as an urgent priority. However, the alarm soon passed, and no new cardinals were created in September 1620. But although neither Richelieu, Marie de' Medici nor Bouthillier was aware of the crown's real intentions, these were now known to the papal entourage and the papal nuncio. Bentivoglio was to be fully apprised of

---

11 Degert, 'Chapeau de Richelieu', p. 233.
12 Avenel, *Lettres*, I, p. 655, Louis XIII to Paul V, 29 Aug. 1620.
13 Degert, 'Chapeau de Richelieu', p. 245. Épernon had remained with his forces to the south of the Loire during the military revolt of July-Aug. 1620, and his political stance remained unclear for some time thereafter.

them during a round of visits to ministers in early September 1620, and was only too happy to emphasise how widely held such views were at court. Even before being taken into the ministers' confidence, he had perceived the strength and the range of opposition to Richelieu.[14] Puysieux duly confirmed to him that Richelieu's candidature had been agreed to in order to please the queen mother, and made it clear that the king was reluctant to undertake the efforts that would be needed to reward him.[15] Luynes, having proposed a marriage alliance to Richelieu, seemed less categorical but, with the recent revolt still fresh in his mind, he agreed it was too early to judge how Richelieu would behave; rapid promotion would make him too independent and powerful too quickly, and his being obliged to wait might well provide some guarantees of good behaviour.[16] Once informed of these attitudes, Rome was under no real pressure to act, and had little difficulty in playing its normal game of procrastination. The effect of successive royal letters to the pope in support of La Valette and Richelieu, all pointing out that the king was acting expressly in response to the queen mother's requests, was, perhaps intentionally, to create the impression that the king himself had little interest in the outcome. At any rate, it was not long before Sébastien Bouthillier was warning Richelieu that Marie's interests, past or future, were the wrong basis for a campaign of persuasion in Rome.[17] Finally, as allegations began to circulate in Rome about Richelieu's own past behaviour, it is not surprising that neither Bouthillier nor the French ambassador, who was also kept in the dark on the court's real intentions, could make any progress.[18]

Historians are familiar enough with Richelieu's subsequent complaints about the machinations of the cabal opposed to him. However, it would be a mistake to assume that either he or Marie de' Medici was idle during the latter months of 1620; on the contrary, they exerted themselves considerably, even excessively, during their stays at court. Bentivoglio reported in caustic terms their suggestion, made just as Louis XIII was about to march off to Béarn to restore Catholicism there, that he should threaten to withdraw his ambassador from Rome if Richelieu was not promoted cardinal.[19] They

14 Steffani, *Nunziatura di Bentivoglio*, IV, pp. 392–3, letter of 26 Aug. 1620.
15 *Ibid.*, IV, pp. 408–10, letter of 6 Sept. 1620.
16 *Ibid.*, IV, pp. 414–18, letter of 6 Sept. 1620.
17 B.N., MS. Fr. 3722, fos. 2, 4–6. A.A.E., Rome 23, fos. 490–1, letter to Claude Bouthillier, 21 Oct. 1620. He specifically warned against using hints of further faction within France if the queen mother was not given satisfaction. Unfortunately, the two long letters he wrote to Richelieu at this time have not come to light.
18 A.A.E., Rome 23, fo. 492v, Bishop Laubespine to Richelieu, 12 Nov. 1620.
19 Steffani, *Nunziatura di Bentivoglio*, IV, pp. 448–9, letter to Rome, 21 Oct. 1620; pp. 449–50, Puysieux to Bentivoglio, 14 Oct. 1620; Batiffol, *Louis XIII a vingt ans*, pp. 604–5.

tried to exercise sustained, if less dramatic, pressure once the king
had returned to Paris in November. Moreover, circumstances
seemed particularly favourable by that time: the Combalet-Pont-
Courlay marriage was finally arranged and celebrated in considerable
pomp at the Louvre in late November, all of which made Luynes
veer towards Richelieu, whose candidature he now openly and
strongly supported.[20] New royal letters were sent to the pope, and
Richelieu himself pressed the ambassador and the former nuncio,
Cardinal Ubaldini, to intervene strongly on his behalf in Rome.[21]
But Luynes's defection notwithstanding, the remaining opposition
proved solid enough and, with willing papal co-operation, managed
to blunt the impact of Luynes's pressing intercession on Richelieu's
behalf; even Arnoux was reported to have bound Louis XIII in
conscience not to allow Richelieu to be promoted.[22] If this indeed
suggests a vigilant cabal, it has to be said that, even though embroidered by the nuncio, the pressure from Richelieu and the queen
mother lacked subtlety, and as a result was badly received at both
courts. But, with both Bouthillier and the French ambassador, the
marquis de Coeuvres, busy in Rome, Richelieu's opponents were
taking no chances on the outcome.[23] In particular, Épernon realized
fully that the queen mother had thrown all her weight behind Richelieu, to whom he complained bitterly in early November 1620 of
his – and the queen mother's – ingratitude.[24] Simultaneously, he
warned his son, La Valette, to keep his guard up, and to be careful as
to whom he should have dealings with: 'Keep an eye on things in
Rome, as I know for certain that Monsieur de Luçon will hinder you
as much as he can, irrespective of his demeanour and pleasing words
towards you. You can talk to Monsieur de Luynes in order to avoid
untoward events. I have been informed that you can safely find out
what is happening from the nuncio.'[25] Such vigilance, which suggests that Épernon and his son were more successful than Marie
de' Medici's camp in turning La Valette into some sort of 'king's
candidate', contributed to their success: when Paul V created his
final crop of cardinals in early January 1621, La Valette, as well as
the nuncio Bentivoglio, were in the list, while Richelieu was not.
Louis XIII and the court put on a deliberate show of disappoint-

---

20 Steffani, *Nunziatura di Bentivoglio*, IV, pp. 495–6, 503–4, 510, letters of 12, 17, and 30
    Dec. 1620; pp. 519, 524–5, 9 and 15 Jan. 1621 respectively.
21 Avenel, *Lettres*, I, pp. 661–4, letters of early Dec. 1620.
22 Steffani, *Nunziatura di Bentivoglio*, IV, p. 519, letter of 9 Jan. 1621.
23 See Avenel, *Lettres*, I, pp. 661–4, letters from Louis XIII to Paul V and to Cardinal
    Borghese, and from Richelieu to Coeuvres and Cardinal Ubaldini, 4 Dec. 1620.
24 *Ibid.*, I, p. 659, letter of 2 Nov. 1620.
25 Letter of 22 Nov. 1620, quoted by Lacroix, *Richelieu à Luçon*, p. 249.

ment at Richelieu's rejection, but in reality there was considerable satisfaction at the outcome.[26]

The failure of Richelieu's first bid for the red hat was not due simply to personal causes. The fact is that neither he nor his patron had succeeded in obtaining much political leverage after the Treaty of Angers. On the contrary, it was Luynes, by moving so swiftly to end the armed confrontation between Louis and his mother, who had regained the initiative; the partial eclipse which he had experienced during the revolt was undone, and none of the attacks that would be mounted against him between then and his death in December 1621 were to do much damage to his position as royal mentor; there was no effective opposition to his becoming successively constable of France and keeper of the seals in 1621. Though the military campaigns of 1620 and especially 1621 would take their toll of ministers and councillors of state, as well as raise doubts about the wisdom of the anti-Huguenot policy itself, there was little to threaten the new political stability of the court and the ministry. For the same reason, there was no pressing need to make substantial political gestures towards either Marie de' Medici or Richelieu. Her efforts at Brissac and Poitiers, in August–September 1620, to obtain a place for herself in council proved fruitless, and so long as that was denied her she would remain disenchanted with the court. Moreover, as the Béarn expedition was taking shape during these same months, she was in an uncomfortable, defensive position: though she and *dévots* of all hues were anxious to see Catholicism restored there, she had opposed 'innovation' in Béarn, and had consorted with Huguenot magnates like Rohan, during the recent revolt. During the major anti-Huguenot offensive of 1621, she would consistently claim to desire the success of the king's arms, but continued to proclaim her 'affection' for Rohan and his brother, Soubise.[27] Another general feature of these years should also be noted at this point. Considering how much talk there had been since 1619 about the conditions and circumstances of the queen mother's return to court, it is ironic that, just when she finally agreed to return there on Louis XIII's terms, the court itself should be facing the prospect of near-disappearance for much of the next two and a half years. Between July 1620 and January 1623, Louis XIII and his court resided for no more than eight months in or around Paris, and most of that was between November 1620 and late April 1621; the rest of the time, it was on the move, and was often reduced to the condition of

---

26 *Journal d'Arnauld 1621*, ed. E. Halphen (Paris 1891), p. 6.
27 Avenel, *Lettres*, VII, p. 500, Richelieu to Archbishop du Perron, 23/24 July 1621; *ibid.*, pp. 504–6, Richelieu to Luynes, (Aug. 1621).

an uncomfortable military camp. 'Normal', sedentary court life only resumed in early 1623. The disruption was more than merely a social nuisance: an important consequence of this pattern of movement was that political decisions were often consciously postponed until the king could return from campaign or, as when ministerial vacancies arose, that the opportunity to lobby for replacements was limited largely to those accompanying him on campaign. Throughout these years neither Richelieu nor Marie de' Medici accompanied the court for very long during its annual peregrinations; the task of rebuilding their political credit and pressing their claims to high office was thus rendered much more difficult – and prolonged – by physical separation from the court. For Richelieu himself, this repeated disruption was an added incentive to concentrate upon obtaining the red hat.

III

In January 1621, Richelieu seems to have taken the news that he had been passed over by Paul V more stoically than his recent pressure or his later anti-Luynes animus would suggest.[28] However real his disappointment might have been, it was at least possible to believe that the way would henceforth be clearer now that the Épernon clan had been satisfied. Moreover, Paul V himself died within weeks of La Valette's promotion, raising the hope that a new papacy might view his case in a more favourable light. But new popes habitually waited some time before creating cardinals proposed to them by Catholic rulers, being initially more concerned to promote relatives and close friends with a view to establishing their pontificate on a firm footing. This is what Gregory XV duly did in April and July 1621, after which he appeared reluctant to be rushed into a new round of promotions.[29] However, the deaths of Cardinals Bonzi and Guise in the summer of 1621 reduced the number of French cardinals to just four, which, in turn, increased the pressure to fill the growing number of vacancies in the college of cardinals sooner rather than later, and for replacements for Bonzi and Guise to be chosen from among the ranks of the French episcopate. But, while such accidents could not but revive the hopes of one in Richelieu's position, they created an obvious dilemma for the French crown: could the case for such replacements be pressed home without handing a victory to the queen mother's favourite? Luynes had abandoned his short-lived

28 Degert, 'Chapeau de Richelieu', p. 257.
29 *Ibid.*, pp. 260–3.

support for Richelieu as early as January 1621 and returned to his earlier position, having no doubt measured the strength of the resistance to his candidature in both Paris and Rome.[30] Moreover, the very secrecy of the earlier opposition to Richelieu – the extent of which he was still not aware – itself generated a kind of conspiracy from which those involved found it difficult to extricate themselves. In November 1621, the nuncio Corsini was duly let into the secret of Luynes's continuing opposition – or rather indifference – to Richelieu's candidature.[31] By then, Archbishop Marquemont had been reinstated as an official French candidate, and he was not without supporters.[32] Luynes himself died the following month, but even without him there was still determined opposition to Richelieu's promotion. Indeed, with Louis XIII, Condé and several other leading figures either hostile, indifferent or lukewarm, the Brûlarts – Sillery, Puysieux and the *commandeur* de Sillery, brother of the Chancellor and incoming ambassador in Rome – were now arguably better placed than ever to block him.

It would require signficant political realignments at court before such barriers could come down. But there were few signs of that throughout 1621. Marie de' Medici's growing *mauvaise humeur* at her lack of influence created renewed tension, and fuelled suspicion of both her and Richelieu, especially when she decided to quit the court altogether in July 1621 and to remain in Anjou for the remainder of the anti-Huguenot campaign.[33] Very soon, there were allegations that she was fortifying Angers again, that she was in touch with the Huguenots, and that she was even forming a *tiers parti* opposed to Luynes.[34] Needless to say, none of this served Richelieu's interests, and he fully realized it. In retrospect, it was a risk that was inherent in his chosen tactic of subordinating his career and ambitions to the satisfaction of her interests – while letting it be understood that his personal interests were, of course, an integral part of hers! This approach was designed to add weight to his personal claims to preferment but it was always unlikely to bring results in a climate of political tension, and it was also vulnerable to his patron's unpredictable outbursts and diplomatic obtuseness. If we can judge from the surviving fragments of his correspondence rather than from the

---

30 Steffani, *Nunziatura di Bentivoglio*, IV, pp. 535–6, letter to Borghese, 19 Jan. 1621.
31 Degert, 'Chapeau de Richelieu', p. 267.
32 B.N., MS. Fr. 3722, fo. 9, Louis XIII to Gregory XV, Dec. 1621. This letter, which recommends Richelieu before Marquemont, makes it clear that Marquemont had been reinstated before that date.
33 Batiffol, *Louis XIII à vingt ans*, pp. 380–1. Incidents during the court's progress westwards towards Nantes and St Jean d'Angély reinforced her suspicions of a deliberate attempt to snub her and keep her apart from Louis XIII.
34 Hanotaux, *Richelieu*, II, pp. 492–4.

waspish account in his *Mémoires*, Richelieu was a model of restraint and diplomacy during the 1621 military campaign. He despatched Louis de Marillac to court in early July 1621 in order to dispel the rising suspicions of the queen mother's intentions, and his presence there throughout the ensuing military campaigns enabled him to act as an effective intermediary.[35] Richelieu's own correspondence with friends like Archbishop du Perron and Marillac also show his anxiety not to alienate Luynes, his chagrin at continuing misunderstandings (which he was even willing to attribute to negligence rather than malice), and his efforts to fend off accusations that he and the queen mother were undermining Louis XIII's policies.[36] In his dealings with Luynes over benefices and other matters, he showed a surprising alacrity to defer to him and to propose alternatives, as well as to express gratitude for Luynes's goodwill.[37] In general, Richelieu was more sensitive than his patron to the extent to which both of them were enmeshed in the web of royal patronage, of which Luynes was an accomplished master.[38] It comes as no great surprise that it was during 1621 that Sébastien Bouthillier complained most strongly about Richelieu's failure to press his claim to a red hat vigorously enough.[39] On that subject, Richelieu's correspondence with Luynes and the court shows a studied detachment; the impetuous pressure of the previous year was not repeated, and he merely implied that success in Rome would certainly come if the court were to demonstrate its intentions and goodwill.[40] Interestingly, it was in August 1621 that Richelieu received an astonishingly frank, and possibly unsolicited, battery of counsels as to how he should behave from the pamphleteer Fancan, who had by then followed his brother, Vincent Langlois, into his immediate circle.[41] Among other things, Fancan

---

35   Avenel, *Lettres*, VII, pp. 494–8, instruction for Marillac, July 1621. A.A.E., Mems. et docs., France 775, fos. 55–79, for Marillac's letters to Richelieu, early July to late Nov. 1621.

36   Avenel, *Lettres*, VII, pp. 509–13, instruction for des Roches, 22 Oct. 1621. The central theme of his letters to du Perron is the need to achieve genuine understanding between the queen mother, Louis XIII and Luynes: A.A.E., Mems. et docs., France 775, fos. 21–6, du Perron's letters to Richelieu, May to late Aug. 1621. Richelieu's own letters make identical points: Avenel, *Lettres*, VII, p. 493 (to Arnoux, 10 July), pp. 500–2 (to du Perron, 27 July), pp. 504–6 (to Luynes, Aug. 1621).

37   Avenel, *Lettres*, VII, pp. 509–10, to Des Roches, Oct. 1621. There is a favourable judgement of Luynes in another letter to an anonymous correspondent: *ibid.*, pp. 514–15 (late 1621?).

38   Luynes's frequent letters to Richelieu also served to keep communications open between the two courts: A.A.E., Mems. et docs., France 775, fos. 1–18.

39   Degert, 'Chapeau de Richelieu', p. 263.

40   Avenel, *Lettres*, I, pp. 690–1, letter to Luynes (no date); VII, pp. 509–14 (at pp. 510–11), instruction to Des Roches, *c.* 10 July 1621.

41   See Léon Geley, *Fancan et la politique de Richelieu de 1617 à 1627* (Paris 1884); Gustave Fagniez, 'Fancan et Richelieu', *Revue Historique* 107 (1911), pp. 59–78, 310–22; 108 (1911), pp. 75–87.

recommended that Richelieu and Marie de' Medici abstain from all intervention in political matters, and that they live as virtually private persons henceforth; Richelieu should demand nothing for himself from the court, but concentrate on obtaining every satisfaction for his patron. In particular, Fancan also recommended that since he had had no success in Rome, he should recall Sébastien Bouthillier, and declare he had no further interest in becoming a cardinal.[42] For the most part, this advice fits closely with Richelieu's actual behaviour at the time, but it would probably be mistaken to regard his behaviour as a mere application of Fancan's maxims. There was, in any case, at least one counsel which he was manifestly unwilling to follow: much as he might profess to leave the matter of his red hat to the court, he had no intention of publicly renouncing his ambition to become a cardinal. It was not the last time Fancan was to misjudge a man to whom a cardinal's hat represented far more than the satisfaction of simple personal vanity.

The death of Luynes a few months later, in December 1621, was bound to alter the political landscape, but it was not a foregone conclusion that change would necessarily turn to the advantage of Richelieu and his patron. Luynes, however one judges his overall political record, used the power he derived from the king's favour in the cause of moderation and compromise. It was that more than anything else which had kept together the coalition of forces which dominated French politics in previous years and, if his power and enrichment created hostility, his political style helped to contain it. Moreover, Louis XIII's declaration immediately after Luynes's death that he would not take another favourite, while well-intentioned and laudable, had as its immediate effect the opposite of what he intended: it generated considerable uncertainty as to what precise form the government would take henceforth.[43] From the point of view of Richelieu and Marie de' Medici, it at least held out the prospect of a fuller reconciliation than had proved possible while Luynes lived, all the more so as Louis XIII was prompt to assure his mother of his goodwill.[44] For that reason, Richelieu and Marie lost no time in sending the trusted Louis de Marillac back to the king immediately after Luynes's death, with the task of reporting on changes and pressing their claims on him. But Marillac's initial hopes quickly

42 Avenel, *Lettres*, I, pp. 685–9. Avenel attributed this advice to Père Joseph, but Fagniez argues convincingly for Fancan: *Le Père Joseph et Richelieu*, I, p. 99.

43 A.A.E., Mems. et docs., France 775, fo. 84v, Marillac to Richelieu, 29 Dec. 1621; fo. 88r, same to same, 29 Dec. See also Moote, *Louis XIII*, p. 106; Berthold Zeller, *Richelieu et les ministres de Louis XIII, de 1621 à 1624* (Paris 1880), p. 6, quoting the Venetian ambassador. See, for the comparison with 1661, Daniel Dessert, *Louis XIV prend le pouvoir: naissance d'un mythe?* (Brussels 1989).

44 Zeller, *Richelieu et les ministres*, p. 7.

faded as he came to realize that none of the existing ministerial interests wished to make room for them.[45] A loose coalition between Schomberg, Condé and Cardinal Retz – which enabled Schomberg to become the leading minister until his disgrace in early 1623 – quickly formed after Luynes's death in order to counter the influence of the Brûlarts, and promptly obtained the keepership of the seals for Méric de Vic, an erstwhile mentor of Richelieu.[46] Thus, for all Richelieu's hopes and Marillac's diligence among the royal entourage, the omens had become distinctly less favourable for 'outsiders' such as the bishop of Luçon by the time the king returned to Paris in late January 1622. Marie de' Medici despatched Richelieu to intercept Louis XIII at Orléans where, by his own account, he ventured to suggest to him that while 'the wisest princes had always guided the ship [of state] themselves, they had employed good pilots to help them to navigate'.[47] Unfortunately, there is no independent evidence that he actually had the temerity to lecture the king in this fashion, using language which clearly hinted at his own, and not just his patron's, navigational skills.[48] If he really did speak in these terms, it brought him no reward at all, and probably confirmed Louis XIII's antipathy towards him. Indeed, it may also have helped to circumscribe what the king was prepared to offer his mother: when, only a week later, she finally captured that elusive place in council, it came with some unambiguous restrictions – she would attend on certain occasions rather than as an 'ordinary' member, Richelieu would remain excluded, and she would not make him privy to the king's business.[49] In their different ways, Marie and Richelieu were still hindering as much as helping their respective political comebacks.

The course and cohesion of the post-Luynes regime was also bound to be tested by dilemmas over policy, both at home and abroad. Although numerous Huguenot towns had been recovered and protestant autonomy notably reduced in 1620 and especially 1621, it was the failure to capture Montauban which attracted adverse comment, damaging the king's reputation and raising doubts about the wisdom of the anti-Huguenot policies.[50] As we saw, the queen

45 Marillac's first reports are in A.A.E., Mems. et docs., France 775, fos. 83–6 and fos. 88–9, 29 Dec. 1621.
46 Journal d'Arnauld 1621, p. 104.
47 A.A.E., Mems. et docs., France 775, fos. 132–3, Marillac to Richelieu, 19–20 Jan. 1622; vol. 776, fo. 7, Sillery to Puysieux, 19 Jan., for proof of the reality of this mission. See also Batiffol, Louis XIII a vingt ans, p. 609, n. 3.
48 Richelieu, Mémoires, III, pp. 207–9, for a synopsis of his words to Louis XIII. See also Zeller, Richelieu et les ministres, p. 10.
49 Journal d'Arnauld 1622, ed. E. Halphen (Paris 1898) p. 13.
50 Bonney, The King's Debts, pp. 106–7; A.D. Lublinskaya, French Absolutism, The Crucial Phase 1620–1629 (Cambridge 1968), pp. 193–4.

mother and Richelieu were suspected of not supporting the campaign, and even after Luynes's death, they were still having to defend themselves against such accusations.[51] Moreover, the chances of a rapid or significant shift in policy were sharply reduced by the Huguenot revolt led by Soubise in January 1622: within a mere two months of returning to Paris, Louis XIII was again preparing to set off on the campaign trail in western France. However, if we are to believe Richelieu's *Mémoires*, there were indeed policy debates in council in early 1622. His account of them is somewhat oblique and less full than those of other contemporary incidents – for example, his own speech to Louis XIII at Orléans. At any rate, he claimed he advised Marie to urge the king to look objectively at the dangers and the real value of further anti-Huguenot campaigns and, also, to consider the need to press the Spaniards to honour the Treaty of Madrid (April 1621) by which they had promised to evacuate the Valtelline passes that they had occupied since 1620.[52] But, according to Richelieu, her advice was not welcome, and Condé persuaded the king to ignore it.[53] The Treaty of Madrid still seemed to satisfy French demands, and allowed the crown to resume its anti-Huguenot option with a clear conscience.

In any event, a change of priorities would not have been a simple matter, even without Soubise's revolt, as anti-Huguenot policies remained inseparably tied up with the political influence of Condé and his ministerial allies. Despite the *orages* it sometimes entailed, the prince's support had been invaluable to the ascendancy of Luynes and the Brûlarts since his liberation in late 1619. Now with Luynes dead, it was widely assumed that his ambition was to fill the void, dominate the council, and continue the anti-Huguenot policies – in short, as head of a war party, that Condé would make himself the power behind a throne which he might one day actually inherit.[54] Clearly, not everyone could be expected to relish this prospect, least of all Louis XIII, but although Louis was determined to assert his independence, Condé's influence waxed during the first half of 1622. The Brûlarts were equally unwilling to accept Condé's domination, but their political style was marked by extreme caution. Whatever policies Louis XIII might pursue – confrontation with the Huguenots or with the Habsburgs – the stage was set for a shift in the

51 Avenel, *Lettres*, VII, p. 517, Richelieu to anon (late 1621); Zeller, *Richelieu et les ministres*, p. 18, Marie de' Medici to Puysieux, 22 Jan. 1622.
52 Richelieu, *Mémoires*, III, pp. 216–19.
53 *Ibid.*, p. 219.
54 A.A.E., Mems. et docs., France 775, fos. 83v-4r, Marillac to Richelieu, 29 Dec. 1621. P.R.O. SP 78/70, fo. 59, Woodforde to Secretary of State, 17 March 1622. See also Zeller, *Richelieu et les ministres de Louis XIII*, p. 61. Condé was second in line in the succession after Gaston d'Orléans.

existing political alignments. In particular, the Brûlarts slowly began to look for allies against the prince, and, for all their previous enmity towards Marie de' Medici, they could not afford to ignore her and her supporters as a potential source of support. The decision to allow the queen mother a voice, ableit a limited one, in council was among the first illustrations of the rivalries and opportunistic shifts which would characterize the post-Luynes régime.

An important consequence of this was that, although the council chamber remained firmly closed to Richelieu, it was gradually becoming more difficult to continue to deny him the satisfaction of his ecclesiastical ambitions. Probably sensing that his political prospects remained negligible, both he and Marie de' Medici decided to revive their earlier pressure for the red hat, concentrating their attention on the Brûlarts, and especially Puysieux, who had been the main stumbling-block all along. But, in the uncertain political atmosphere after Luynes's death, the Brûlarts were in no great hurry to take any initiative, and the letters of recommendation to Rome on Richelieu's behalf remained distinctly formal and unenthusiastic.[55] However, between May and July 1622, a combination of strong pressure from Marie de' Medici, growing difficulties with Condé, and a more friendly attitude to Richelieu on the part of Louis XIII, produced a decisive shift.[56] Marie de' Medici obtained assurances that Richelieu would henceforth be the sole French candidate.[57] Cardinal Sourdis, then resident in Rome, also obtained a cautiously-worded promise from the pope that he would not make any promotion of cardinals which did not include Richelieu.[58] Although this left the pope free to choose his own timetable, a jubilant Bouthillier was convinced that this was a major concession, and that a decision could not be postponed for long; he even felt he could safely leave Rome before his patron's elevation had been publicly announced. By then, Richelieu himself began to believe that circumstances were changing for the better; cautiously discarding the reticence which Sébastien Bouthillier had so often deplored over the previous year or more, he obtained new royal letters to Rome recommending his candidature.[59] The death of Retz in early August further strength-

---

55 Degert, 'Chapeau de Richelieu', pp. 271–7. This at least was the complaint of Sébastien Bouthillier in Rome.

56 Zeller, *Richelieu et les ministres*, pp. 111–15. Zeller prints several extracts from letters of Marie de' Medici, Sillery and Puysieux concerning Richelieu's promotion. Richelieu's letters to Puysieux are in Avenel, *Lettres*, I, pp. 713 (30 June 1622), pp. 718–19 (late July), p. 719, (6 Aug.), pp. 727–8 (n.d.).

57 A.A.E., Mems. et docs., France 775, fo. 142, Marillac to Richelieu, undated, but probably late April 1622.

58 Degert, 'Chapeau de Richelieu', pp. 277–8.

59 Antoine Aubery, *Mémoires pour l'histoire du cardinal-duc de Richelieu*, 2 vols. (Paris 1660), I, pp. 313–14, for the text of royal letter.

ened his hand, and the remaining obstacles to his case quickly evaporated.[60] The change in attitudes was quite dramatic, and Condé,
the Brûlarts and others were all anxious to claim the credit for
ensuring Richelieu's success.[61] When the news of his elevation finally
broke on 5 September 1622, the faithful Bouthillier was still in
Rome, and from there he wrote what amounted to a *nunc dimittis*: 'it
seems to me that I have nothing further to wish for in this world
now that Monsieur de Luçon is a cardinal'.[62] Such relief and elation
was echoed in France by Richelieu's long-serving valet, Desbournais, who rushed about announcing, 'nous sommes cardinal, nous
sommes cardinal'. Richelieu himself heard the news near Roanne,
while on his way to join the court at Lyon. His formal speech of
acceptance of the red hat in December 1622 was strongly reminiscent
of the one he had made to Henri IV in 1607.[63] But, like his father,
Louis XIII was content to regard Richelieu's renewed offers of his
service as just a rhetorical exercise of the kind that was obligatory on
such occasions. By contrast, Richelieu's gesture of laying his red hat
at Marie de' Medici's feet and acknowledging that he owed it to her,
was a recognition that his place was still with her, however much he
might long to cross the threshold of the king's council again.[64]

IV

It would, however, be wrong to imagine that Richelieu had been
reduced to inactivity, or to simply waiting on the changing intentions and goodwill of popes and ministers during the early 1620s. In
view of the continuing dominance of Luynes until his death and,
more generally, the fragility of ministerial careers during these
years, Richelieu had every reason to concentrate upon the more
mundane but highly serious business of his 'establissement'. This
did not constitute an alternative route to ecclesiastical advancement
or political office, nor was Richelieu naïve enough to imagine that it
had the capacity to unlock the door to the royal council. Neverthe-

---

60 It was not until mid-July that Puysieux finally bowed to pressure, which included a few
    anti-Puysieux outbursts from Louis XIII, and ensured that despatches to Rome would be
    far more positive than hitherto: A.A.E., Mems. et docs., France 775, fos. 172–4,
    Marillac to Richelieu, 3 June 1622; fos. 179v–80, same to same, 3 July.
61 The details can be followed in Louis de Marillac's letters to Richelieu, in A.A.E., Mems.
    et docs., France 775, fos. 179v–80r (3 July 1622); fos. 187–8 (2 July); fos. 189–91 (25 July);
    fos. 196–7 (31 Aug.); fos. 198–203 (4 Sept.). For Condé's claim, *ibid.*, fo. 202v.:
    'Monsieur le prince se vante d'avoir esté cause des dernières depesches de Rome en faveur
    de l'evêque de Luçon. Il est vray qu'il y a bien parlé, mais sans luy tout ne laissoit pas
    d'estre fait'. How far Condé's change of attitude towards Richelieu prefigured their
    political reconciliation of 1626 has not been established.
62 Degert, 'Chapeau de Richelieu', p. 285, letter to Claude Bouthillier.
63 Avenel, *Lettres*, I, pp. 745–7, for the text of his speech, 12 Dec. 1622.
64 *Journal d'Arnauld 1622*, p. 84; Degert, 'Chapeau de Richelieu', p. 287.

less, for one who wished to *paraître* to the degree that he did, such an 'establissement' was now indispensable. In the language of the day, it was a question of 'se rendre puissant', which implied the capacity to impress, to inspire loyalty and service, and to bind individuals to him through a variety of ties and obligations – all of which required much more than mere personal charisma.

There were a variety of ways by which Richelieu could work towards this end. It should come as no surprise that he was busy strengthening his position in the French church during the early 1620s. On his departure from office in 1617, he was a somewhat isolated figure who, as we saw, had his critics among the upper clergy. Paradoxically, while the events of 1619–20 brought him into constant contact with some of the most politically active ecclesiastics of his time, he still found himself at a tangent to normal ecclesiastical politics. Thereafter, he was anxious to capitalize on his political prominence in order to enhance his 'reputation' among the French clergy. It is clear from a constant stream of correspondence that, both before and after the Ponts de Cé, his principal confidant and intermediary at court was, in fact, Archbishop du Perron. Until du Perron's death in October 1621, Richelieu depended upon him to defend him and keep him informed of changes there, even on one occasion styling him as his 'confessor'.[65] How far he relied on the offices of the Jesuit confessors of Louis XIII and Marie de' Medici is less apparent, but it is worth remarking that, in his advice of 1621, the strongly gallican Fancan may have been implicitly criticizing Richelieu when he recommended him to frequent the Jesuits less, and the other orders and the Sorbonne more.[66] On the death of Retz in 1622, Richelieu was only too pleased to accept the invitation to succeed him as provisor of the Sorbonne, a post which enabled him to keep an eye on religious controversies and to recruit valuable collaborators in subsequent years.[67] It was as provisor, for example, that he became actively involved in the 1623 disputes concerning Edmond Richer, the combative gallican syndic of the theology faculty, though it was not until 1629 that he finally managed to silence him.[68] Likewise, Richelieu was among the clergy directly involved in the papacy's abortive efforts during 1622 to revive the

---

65 Avenel, *Lettres*, VII, pp. 498–500, letter of 23/24 July 1621: 'Si je vous escris quatre fois contre une, vous ne le trouveres pas estrange . . .'. The reference to du Perron as confessor is at p. 499.
66 *Ibid.*, I, p. 689.
67 See *Correspondance de Rubens*, ed. C. Ruelens and M. Rooses, 5 vols. (Antwerp 1887–1907), III, pp. 31–2, Nicolas Peiresc to Rubens, 8 Sept. 1622. Peiresc claimed that Richelieu had defeated Cardinal La Valette and 'other leading prelates' whom he did not name.
68 Jacques, *Philippe Cospeau*, pp. 155–6.

idea of having the decrees of the Council of Trent accepted by the monarchy as part of French law.[69] Opportunities of this kind increased once he had become a cardinal, as important papal commissions were usually addressed to cardinals in the first instance. Throughout 1623 and early 1624, he was heavily involved in one of the bitterest 'church-state' conflicts of the decade, that between the *dévot* and ultramontane Bishop Miron of Angers and the *parlement* of Paris over episcopal jurisdiction, a dispute in which the papal nuncio, Corsini, found Richelieu a valuable ally.[70] It need hardly be said that these activities, and many others, also enabled him to extend his clientèle among the ranks of the French clergy, which in turn served to reinforce the clerical and *dévot* character of Marie de' Medici's entourage. It is not surprising that, when he returned to office in 1624, several senior clerics such as Miron would choose to work closely with him – and indeed see him as the best hope for church reform and the restoration of ecclesiastical autonomy.[71] More important still, the relations which he cultivated in 1620 and following years with men like Retz, Archbishop du Perron, Bérulle and many others indirectly served another purpose – his political rehabilitation. As *dévots* who were *personae gratae* both to the queen mother and to Louis XIII and his entourage, they helped to soften the king's visceral dislike and distrust of a prelate whose ambition had made him the orchestrator of the largest noble revolt of his reign so far.

There was another, more material but equally indispensable element in Richelieu's quest for ecclesiastical advancement. As one who appeared destined for 'princely' rank within the church, it was only natural for him to pay particular attention to the opportunities provided by the French church's ample network of benefices. His endowment in benefices had not altered, let alone improved, since receiving the abbey of Ile Chauvet around 1609. In this respect at least, he cut a poor figure beside his rival for the red hat, La Valette, who by 1620 was one of the best-beneficed clerics of his generation. In that year, as we saw earlier, Richelieu asked for Luçon to be entrusted to his vicar-general, Flavigny, but with enhanced powers as a suffragan-bishop. Such a move makes it clear that although residence there was no longer practicable, Richelieu felt that it was both too soon and too risky to consider resigning the see outright. Instead, he concentrated his attention on accumulating abbeys *in commendam* – that is to say, on acquiring the title and (often sub-

69 A.S.V., Nunz. Fr. 58, fos. 97–8, Corsini to Ludoviso, 9 Feb. 1622.
70 Nunz. Fr. 60, fo. 15, Corsini to Cardinal Barberini, 7 Jan. 1624; fos. 70–1, to same, 23 Feb.; fo. 214, to same 20 May; IBID., vol. 61, fo. 175, to same 29 April; fo. 214, to same, 20 May.
71 See Blet, *Clergé de France et la monarchie*, II, pp. 414ff.

stantial) revenues of the office of abbot, but without the duties of residence or personal performance of the office's functions. Beginning in 1621, he acquired five substantial abbeys, mostly in western France, which dwarfed his existing endowments, virtually tripled his income from church sources alone, and enhanced his standing among his fellow-churchmen. Some of these abbeys, like St Benoît-sur-Loire, Pontlevoy, and St Pierre de Chalons, were well known and distinguished Benedictine houses. These transactions acquired added significance in May 1623 when he finally divested himself of Luçon: by then his rank of cardinal more than compensated for no longer being an incumbent bishop, and he could at last safely do what had first been reported many years earlier – 'to put awaie his bishopricke and to exchange the same for some abbeys'.[72] Apart from a substantial pension off the see of Luçon, the 1623 exchange made him dean of St Martin of Tours and abbot of Notre Dame du Vast near Le Mans. How much this accumulation of benefices owed to Marie de' Medici's favour or intervention is not wholly clear: only one of the abbeys he received, that of Redon in Brittany, was actually in her gift, but even there the king could have, had he wished, vetoed her wishes. However, it is worth stressing that, on the matter of benefices at least, the king and his ministers seem to have been only too ready to gratify Richelieu and his patron. The papacy, too, even while playing its part in blocking Richelieu's progress towards a red hat, also went out of its way – perhaps in order to dampen his suspicions? – to emphasise how readily his provisions to these abbeys were granted.[73]

However customary and inexpensive Richelieu's accumulation of benefices might be, his 'establissement' was not limited to what the church had to offer. It was during the same years that he laid the foundations of that immense fortune which would continue to grow during his long ministry and make him the richest man in French history to date.[74] It has often been said that Richelieu restored the fortunes of his house. But this is to assert both too much and too little: too little because Richelieu did infinitely more than that – there is simply no comparison between his family's economic and social position in 1642 and in either 1590 or 1619; as we have seen, too much in that the real work of 'restoring' the family's wealth was the work of his tenacious elder brother, Henri. By the time of his death, Henri had managed to recover nearly all of the family's lands and

72 B.L., MS. Stowe 176, fo. 70, Thomas Edmondes to Ralph Winwood, 10 Dec. 1616. One of the abbeys originally promised him in 1616, Moreille, finally became his in 1621: Avenel, *Lettres*, I, p. 677, letter to M. de Sceaux (1621).
73 A.A.E., Rome 23, fo. 38v., Sébastien to Claude Bouthillier, 6 June 1622.
74 The account which follows is drawn from Bergin, *Richelieu*, passim.

properties, and to buy out most of his father's creditors. Admittedly, there was still considerable uncertainty about Henri's personal finances, and in 1619–20 Richelieu's fellow heirs were extremely nervous about having anything to do with the estates of his brother and father. Yet despite the political turmoil of these years, Richelieu applied himself to the complex business of preserving his brother's acquisitions and protecting the family's name and reputation against a combination of former business agents and creditors. The reconciliation of Marie de' Medici and Louis XIII, and Richelieu's growing political stature, undoubtedly weighed in the balance during the ensuing litigation. As a result, a younger son who had hitherto been entirely dependent on the church for his income, now became a *seigneur* and landowner in his own right, albeit a relatively modest one at first. It seems entirely fitting that his first independent land purchase should have been of the *seigneurie* of Richelieu itself, which was finally auctioned off to satisfy the remaining creditors of François de Richelieu in February 1621. His son lost no time in adding to these family lands, whether by purchases or exchanges, but the additions he was able to make in the early 1620s were on a modest scale compared to what he would achieve during his years as a minister. Despite such ancestral attachments, by far the largest of Richelieu's investments during the early 1620s occurred elsewhere, and can be regarded as a fitting symbol of his widening horizons and ambitions. The *comtés* of Limours and Montlhéry, which cost him 270,000 *livres* in early 1623, were essentially prestige purchases situated within easy reach of the royal court at Fontainebleau; their main attraction lay in their capacity to provide him with an imposing estate and residence where he could hold court, but also relax, in the manner of a grand *seigneur*.[75] He would wait until the following year before acquiring his own town house in the fashionable St Honoré district of Paris, which he would subsequently transform beyond recognition in order to build the Palais Cardinal.

If Richelieu resembles his brother rather than his father in his pursuit of landed investments, the influence of his courtier-father is nonetheless visible in his interest in the royal domain. Under Louis XIII, the sale of domain – land, offices, fees and so on – escalated very sharply, and from an early date Richelieu showed a keen appreciation of the value of such investments. It was in 1621 that he made his first modest purchase of domain offices, and not a single year would pass until 1635 during which he would not make further domain investments, all on an increasing scale.

75 Avenel, *Lettres*, VII, p. 527, letter to Claude Bouthillier, 26 April 1623. The residence, he promised, would be 'fort gaye au beau temps'.

By the time he returned to office in 1624, the evidence of Richelieu's 'establissement' was plain to see. Admittedly, he could not yet rival a Guise or a La Valette, but his social 'puissance' was undoubtedly commensurate with his new rank of cardinal and minister. The church was still the prime source of such aggrandizement, a fact which was underscored by the royal pension of 10,000 *livres* given to him shortly after he became a cardinal. By 1624, his conservatively estimated income from known sources was in the region of 85,000 *livres*, over three times the level of only four or five years earlier. On his return to office in 1624, the Venetian ambassador, in listing his principal traits, had no hesitation in describing him as a 'lover of riches'.[76]

Of course, Richelieu's 'establissement' was greatly facilitated by his role as Marie de' Medici's right-hand man. This is true in more than just a general sense. The accepted image of Richelieu *l'homme politique* generally pays little attention to the fact that in the decade after 1619, he was the queen mother's *surintendant des finances*, and thus her principal *homme d'affaires*, as well as her grand almoner (1621) and president of her council (1623). Working through her secretariat and personal council, Richelieu the *surintendant* supervised financial transactions which varied from the routine administration of Marie's scattered, existing interests to the receipt of her pensions and other sums assigned to her by the crown. These sums were especially substantial after the reconciliations of 1619 and 1620, and only a modest proportion of them was payable in cash directly from the treasury. The rest had to be raised from the proceeds of the sale of newly created offices (e.g. those of *commissaire des tailles* or councillors in the *parlement* of Toulouse) or parts of the royal demesne (fees chargeable by notaries or collectors of the salt tax). The sale of the offices of *commissaire des tailles*, for example, involved most of the *generalités* of northern and central France, and was conducted through contracts with financiers; like unpopular fiscal edicts generally, they caused endless business for the queen mother's household officials, all of whom constantly referred the difficulties they encountered to Richelieu for his decision between 1620 and 1622. Although his published correspondence does provide fleeting evidence of his dealings with financiers and leading tax farmers, it is only by looking at the great mass of his unpublished papers that it is possible to see how far they commanded his attention during the early 1620s. By comparison, his political activities generated relatively meagre amounts of paperwork.[77] Under his aegis, there

---

76   See Chevallier, *Louis XIII*, p. 275.
77   Avenel, *Lettres*, I, pp. 674–5, to d'Argouges (mid 1621); p. 695, to comte de St Aignan (?Oct. 1621). Dozens of letters from magistrates, financiers and household officials to

developed a 'shadow' financial administration with valuable agents and 'connections' throughout the realm, many of whom would be associated with him during his subsequent ministry. He even played a part in recovering monies sent abroad to Florence by the queen mother and Léonora Galigaï years earlier.[78] In the final analysis, Richelieu came to know far more about the king's finances than he would ever wish to admit, and most of that knowledge was acquired before 1624; it was knowledge which he would put to good use when he would later invest his own wealth in royal domain and other ventures.

Richelieu's activities in Marie de' Medici's service also constituted his apprenticeship as a builder and patron of the arts. After her return to Paris from exile in 1620, she resumed the building of her great palace, the Luxembourg, buying up properties, commissioning works of art, and hunting for antiques in France and Italy.[79] Richelieu was directly concerned in all these vast and expensive projects: in the summer of 1621, he was entrusted by his absent patron with supervising the completion of the construction work on the Luxembourg.[80] Thereafter, he was in close contact with those overseeing building and decoration, buying antiques or having copies made of major works of art.[81] It was in late 1621 and early 1622 that Rubens was contracted to paint his famous series of paintings on the history of Marie de' Medici, which raised the still sensitive question of how to characterize her regency.[82] It is likely that Richelieu, who was Rubens' paymaster, played a significant part in commissioning pictures which, in symbolic form at least, gave Marie the declaration of satisfaction that Louis XIII and Luynes had always refused her.[83]

An important corollary of all these activities is that Richelieu's princely rank of cardinal was far from dispensing him from his

---

Richelieu, as well as the relevant memoranda, are scattered throughout A.A.E., Mems. et docs., France, vols. 774–8, and are too numerous to cite individually.

78 A.A.E., Mems. et docs., France 775, fos. 99, Marillac to Richelieu, 16 May 1622. Avenel, *Lettres*, I, pp. 760–4, Richelieu to Des Roches St Quentin, 22 May 1623; p. 770, to Puysieux, 1 Aug. 1623; pp. 771ff., to Des Roches, late Aug. 1623.

79 A.A.E., Mems. et docs., France 778, fo. 3v, Des Roches to Richelieu, 27 Sept. 1623.

80 Avenel, *Lettres*, I, p. 673, 675.

81 See A.A.E., Mems. et docs., France 774, fos. 112–13, Claude Maugis, abbot of St Ambroise, to Richelieu, 18 Aug. 1621; vol. 775, fo. 47, Jean de Bérulle to Richelieu, 8 May 1621. See Zeller, *Richelieu et les ministres de Louis XIII*, pp. 328–30, for the Florentine ambassador's letters of late 1624 concerning the queen mother's search for works of art in Florence.

82 See Carmona, *Marie de' Medicis*, pp. 417–21.

83 The most sensitive subjects were the five 'reserved' paintings depicting events from the fall of Concini to the Treaty of Angers, and it was made clear to Rubens that his treatment of them would have to be judged on grounds of 'raggion politica' rather than artistic criteria: *Correspondance de Rubens*, III, pp. 37–40, Peiresc to Rubens, Paris, 15 Sept. 1622.

'domestic' responsibilities. On the contrary, after the events of the summer of 1620, he again needed to demonstrate that his mastery of the queen mother's political and private affairs was intact, and to show that a perfect union of mind and heart obtained between himself and the queen mother. It was for this reason that, as has been noted earlier, he would go out of his way, even in correspondence with friends, to claim that he had no wish or ambition beyond her service.[84] By presenting his own ambitions under such a cover, he hoped to blunt hostility towards him, and to take advantage of Marie's slow political recovery. When he joined the council in 1624, English commentators, admittedly not the best placed of observers, only vaguely recognized him as one of Marie de' Medici's household.[85] If, unlike Luynes, Buckingham, or Olivares, Richelieu did not seek household office in the service of his king after 1624, it was less because of any principled objection on his part, than because his association with Marie de' Medici down to 1630 continued to have just such a 'household' element to it, and any move away from it would have been perceived by his jealous, possessive patron as a form of betrayal.

V

During the two years that he had been made to wait for his red hat, Richelieu had ample time to realize that neither the king's entourage nor the papal curia could be taken by storm. Just as importantly, he also learned to accept that excessive pressure for his political advancement would jeopardize his ecclesiastical prospects, and with them his capacity for political survival in the longer term. The patience and self-discipline that this demanded of a naturally impetuous temperament were considerable, and the strain showed in 1621 and especially 1622 – as it would later in his career – in illness, nervous exhaustion, and severe headaches.[86] All of this was no doubt exacerbated by the need to restrain the queen mother's own frustrations and outbursts, which continued to damage relations with the king's entourage.[87] Although the continuing hostility of Louis XIII and his ministers to Richelieu's *political* ambitions is too well docu-

---

84 See, for example, Avenel, *Lettres*, VII, pp. 520–1, letter to Claude Bouthillier, early Nov. 1622: 'J'ay bien peur d'aller jusques en Avignon . . . ne voulant pas faire un pas qu'elle n'en soit advertie, puisque je depends, comme je dois, de ses volontez et de ses commandemens'.

85 I owe this point to Professor Thomas Cogswell.

86 *Correspondance de Rubens*, II, p. 402, Peiresc to Rubens, 6 May 1622. See also Deloche, *Maison du Cardinal de Richelieu*, p. 198; Marvick, *Young Richelieu*, p. 126.

87 For example, a blistering row erupted in March 1622 when Marie banished Rucellaï from her sight, in a fashion reminiscent of her disgrace of Richelieu during the Day of the

mented to be doubted, it has rarely been noted that by the summer of 1622, some ministers were at least prepared to acknowledge the value of his services in steering Marie away from political adventurism, a change which probably helped to dissipate the remaining resistance to his becoming a cardinal.[88] They were quite prepared to see him continue in that – or some other – role which posed no direct threat to them, and various offers (such as residence in Rome) would be made to him over the next few years. But what all, from Louis XIII downwards, strongly resisted was the ambition of Marie and her favourite to translate his services to her into a place in the king's affairs – an ambition which it was impossible to ignore at a time when changes in the ministry and in policy were again about to multiply.

The first skirmish came in August 1622 with the death of Cardinal de Retz. By then, as he admits in his *Mémoires* for the first time, Richelieu sought to succeed Retz, not just in the college of cardinals, but also in Louis XIII's council. Retz was one of several ministers to die on campaign with Louis XIII but, more importantly, he was also one of the few remaining ministers to have whole-heartedly championed the anti-Huguenot campaigns themselves. Although Retz was an undistinguished figure, circumstances ensured that filling his place in council would be a more than usually contentious matter. It was assumed by now that his seat was virtually an ecclesiastical preserve, and the papal nuncio had obtained a commitment from Louis XIII to replace Retz with another churchman.[89] On learning of his death, Marie de' Medici immediately renewed her pressure for the red hat for Richelieu, and presumably, though direct evidence has not survived, for his ministerial position also. In the king's entourage near Montpellier such a prospect was as unwelcome as ever, but not merely for personal reasons.[90] The account in Richelieu's *Mémoires*, which claims that Condé and Schomberg combined to prevent Retz's place from being given to him, essentially because of Condé's personal aversion to him, is excessively restricted and personalized.[91] It ignores the fact that Retz's death came at a partic-

Dupes in 1630, an incident which subsequently played into the hands of adversaries of the queen mother, like Condé. See *Journal d'Arnauld 1622*, pp. 16–17.

88 A.A.E., Mems. et docs., France 775, fo. 173v, Marillac to Richelieu, 3 June 1622. Ministers feared that Richelieu's illness prevented him from serving Marie properly, and that someone else might tempt her into more dangerous courses of action. The king's contentment with Richelieu at this time was probably similarly inspired: *ibid.*, fo. 185, Marillac to Richelieu, 15 July 1622.

89 Bergin, *La Rochefoucauld*, p. 62.

90 See Hanotaux, *Richelieu*, II, p. 517, n. 2, letter from Marie de' Medici to Puysieux, Aug. 1622.

91 Richelieu, *Mémoires*, III, pp. 248–9.

ularly sensitive moment. With important successes already recorded against Soubise and numerous Huguenot towns, the military effort had reached the point where the decision of whether to besiege the major stronghold of Montpellier could not be postponed much longer. Even some of those who wished to continue the war against the Huguenots were hesitant, mindful of the failure at Montauban the previous year, while others were more concerned about the effect of this war on France's position abroad, and would have welcomed an attempt to intervene in the Valtelline.[92] Condé remained, as ever, the most ardent spokesman for pressing home the anti-Huguenot crusade, but his influence had dwindled in previous months, leaving him quite seriously isolated.[93] It was thus vital for him that Montpellier be blockaded and made to surrender; success would vindicate both his aims and his authority.[94] Crucially, he had the support of Schomberg, who at this juncture was at least as much a minister for war as he was a finance minister.[95] Retz's own anti-Huguenot record meant that failure or unwillingness to pick a like-minded successor would be a further blow to the war party. The Brûlarts, Condé's principal adversaries, might at last be willing to see Richelieu become a cardinal, but they were in no mood to accord him the triumph of a double promotion.[96] The choice as Retz's successor of the elderly Cardinal de La Rochefoucauld, a strongly pro-Jesuit and anti-Huguenot figure but a mediocre politician, also owed something to the efforts of the nuncio and the royal confessor.[97] Thus, however much Richelieu might deplore what he viewed as a narrowly based conspiracy to frustrate him and, especially, Marie de' Medici, there was little objective chance of his securing his political recall in this particular context. Though Louis de Marillac repeatedly regretted that he and the queen mother were not in Languedoc in mid-1622, where he was convinced they could have directly influenced the king's decisions, they were, in fact, too detached from the politics of the war effort to engineer a sudden transformation in their fortunes.[98] In the event, the choice of La Rochefoucauld had little or no

92 Lublinskaya, *French Absolutism*, pp. 205–7.
93 A.A.E., Mems. et docs., France 775, fo. 176, Marillac to Richelieu, 3 July 1622; fos. 189–91, same to same, 25 July. See Zeller, *Richelieu et les ministres*, pp. 72–7, 107–8, 116–26.
94 A.A.E., Mems. et docs., France 775, fo. 195, Marillac to Richelieu, 26 Aug. 1622; Bassompierre, François de, *Journal de ma vie*, ed. A. de Chantérac, 4 vols. (Paris 1870–7) III, pp. 111–16. See Zeller, *Richelieu et les ministres de Louis XIII*, pp. 121ff.
95 Bassompierre, *Journal*, III, p. 164. He was in fact *grand maître de l'artillerie*, a key post during a war consisting largely of sieges.
96 See n. 5, above.
97 Bergin, *La Rochefoucauld*, p. 62.
98 A.A.E., Mems. et docs., France 775, fos. 185–6, to Richelieu, 15 July 1622; fos. 194–5, to same, 20 Aug.; fos. 196–7, to same, 31 Aug.; fos. 204–5, to same, 5 Sept.

direct effect on political developments – he remained in Paris, and the war effort continued – nor, as we shall see, was it an outright disaster even from Richelieu's own point of view.

Over the next few months, attention was focused on the siege of Montpellier, but as the prospects of success evaporated, so did the last vestiges of Condé's and the war party's influence.[99] Both the king and Rohan were increasingly anxious, for very different reasons, to extricate themselves from the stalemate, and Condé decamped to Italy on 'pilgrimage' even before the conclusion of the negotiations leading to the treaty of Montpellier (18 October 1622).[100] By then, Richelieu and Marie de' Medici were at Lyon, ready to rejoin Louis XIII's itinerant court. From Richelieu's point of view, the ceremonies normally associated with the reception of the red hat were doubtless reason enough for the journey, but with Condé gone, he may also have sensed there was a chance of more than just pomp and ceremony.

The court remained in the Rhône valley until New Year 1623, as the king and his advisors tried to take stock of recent events. The military campaign had significantly enhanced royal control of the western and southern provinces; above all, unlike the 1621 campaign, it had produced a general settlement with the Huguenots severely restricting their freedoms and incorporating recent royal gains.[101] Inevitably, foreign policy questions now seemed all the more urgent, and the prospects anything but reassuring. The problems to be faced, particularly in Italy and the empire, were ones which would dominate French politics for many years to come, and shape the course of Richelieu's ministry, with the *bons français* opposed to the *bons catholiques* over the proper aims of foreign policy. The Habsburgs had not only failed to honour their earlier promises to restore the status quo in the Valtelline, but they had taken full advantage of French domestic entanglements in 1621–2, and in a manner which sharply illuminates the different capacities of the two monarchies at that point. While Louis XIII was regularly short of troops during 1622, and was even unable to fully besiege Montpellier, the Spaniards and Austrians mounted an intimidating show of force which enabled them not just to occupy the Valtelline forts, but to overrun the lands of its Protestant overlords, the Grisons, as well.[102] Meanwhile, France had also lost one of its most important

---

99 Bassompierre, *Journal*, III, pp. 148–9.
100 Lublinskaya, *French Absolutism*, pp. 209–10; Zeller, *Richelieu et les ministres*, pp. 132–5.
101 Moote, *Louis XIII*, p. 130.
102 Pithon, 'Les Débuts difficiles du ministère de Richelieu et la crise du Valtelline 1621–1626' *Revue d'Histoire Diplomatique* 74 (1960), p. 307; Geoffrey Parker, *The Thirty Years' War* (London 1984), p. 66. The Grisons were forced to abandon their claims to the Valtelline, and to acknowledge Austrian overlordship of their own lands.

partners in the Empire, the Palatinate, which had been similarly overrun in 1620–1 and its elector driven into exile; its electoral title was about to be transferred to Bavaria (February 1623). But, as the experience of subsequent years – including those of Richelieu's own ministry – would show, resolving the contradictions besetting French foreign policy was far less easy than dealing with the Huguenots. The pro-Catholic foreign policy of 1618–20 and the anti-Huguenot campaigns that followed undoubtedly damaged France's interests and reputation abroad. Nor was it at all obvious how France could effect a change of course and regain the confidence of its allies while at the same time avoiding the Scylla of an open break with Spain and the Charybdis of a predominantly Protestant set of alliances: the first of these prospects would, and with good reason, long remain virtually unthinkable, and the second was anathema to Catholic opinion in general. Meanwhile, traditional allies like Venice and Savoy were powerless to resist Habsburg advances on their own and, in their negotiations at Louis XIII's court in late 1622, they pressed strongly for some positive commitment from him. Both Marie de' Medici and Richelieu were present during these discussions, but it is not clear how far either took part in them.[103] Richelieu was, in any case, as careful as ever to pose merely as Marie's spokesman. Once again, hardly any independent, contemporary clues as to his thinking at this juncture have survived, although his *Mémoires* portray the queen mother as taking a middle-of-the road position on foreign questions. She argued that France should station troops on its Italian and Flanders borders with the intention, not of intervening abroad, let alone of breaking with Spain, but of obliging the Habsburgs to respect their engagements, and of giving encouragement to France's allies; the king should also revive the Dutch alliance, and do everything to undermine negotiations for an Anglo-Spanish marriage.[104] The upshot of these deliberations was a defensive and offensive alliance with Venice and Savoy (Treaty of Paris, 7 February 1623) designed to force the Spaniards to surrender the Valtelline fortresses and liberate the Grisons.[105] But the slowness of the French response gave the régime in Madrid ample time to react, and only a week after the treaty, Olivares formally agreed, with French consent, to hand over the Valtelline forts to papal troops, pending a definitive solution of the religious question.[106] Such unilateral action

103 Chevallier, *Louis XIII*, p. 241. There is no record of Marie's attendance at the meetings of the *conseil élargi* at Avignon or Lyon in Nov.-Dec. 1622.
104 Richelieu, *Mémoires*, III, pp. 264–9.
105 Chevallier, *Louis XIII*, p. 241. A final decision on what to do had been twice postponed.
106 Parker, *Thirty Years' War*, p. 66.

by France dismayed its allies.[107] In the event, the Spaniards retained some of the more strategic forts, and it soon became clear that the pope was anxious to ensure free passage for *all* parties through the Valtelline – the very antithesis of French policy since Henri IV, which had insisted on such a right remaining exclusively French![108] The Brûlarts' handling of the resulting difficulties throughout the rest of 1623 and early 1624 seemed to verge on appeasement of Madrid and Rome, providing their critics with damaging ammunition against them. Foreign problems were set to play an increasingly significant role in domestic politics.

But the post-Montpellier period was not given over purely to questions of high policy. It coincided with a second round of ministerial changes which further altered the political balance. These changes were engineered essentially by the Brûlarts, whose brief political supremacy dates from early 1623. Their opportunity came with the discomfiture of Condé, with whom they had been at loggerheads during most of the previous year. They scored their first success in early September 1622 (even before Condé's departure for Italy), when they prevented his and Schomberg's candidate, Étienne Aligre, from obtaining the keepership of the seals.[109] Thereafter, without the prince to sustain him in office, Schomberg was increasingly vulnerable to attack and, in subsequent months, the Brûlarts gradually undermined his standing as Louis XIII's most trusted minister. Not for the last time, Louis XIII proved only too susceptible to whispering campaigns, and ready to allow individual ministers to become scapegoats for policy failures. Despite strenuous efforts to save him, Schomberg was finally disgraced in late January 1623, and replaced by a Brûlart protegé, La Vieuville: having come to court to air his personal grievance against Schomberg – an unpaid pension – La Vieuville soon found himself leading the attack on Schomberg's financial record, and suggesting remedies which only he himself, as the son-in-law of a leading financier and royal treasurer, seemed capable of implementing! To complete the Brûlarts' triumph and underline their political control, Sillery regained the seals after the sudden death of Schomberg's principal ally in council, Lefebvre de Caumartin, and also assumed the presidency of the council of finance to which La Vieuville was obliged to report.

107   Pithon, 'Débuts de Richelieu', pp. 308.
108   Lublinskaya, *French Absolutism*, p. 255.
109   Bassompierre, *Journal*, III, pp. 131–40; *Journal d'Arnauld 1622*, pp. 70–1; A.S.V., Nunz. Fr. 60, fo. 59, Corsini to Barberini, 10 Feb. 1624. See also Bonney, *The King's Debts*, p. 106.
110   *Journal d'Arnauld 1623*, ed. E. Halphen (Paris 1900), p. 6.

It is not clear how much Richelieu or Marie de' Medici contributed to these political changes. But there are enough signs to suggest that, for the first time since the reconciliation of 1620, their influence and support could no longer be discounted. The fact that both Condé and the Brûlarts had, as we saw, attempted to claim the credit for Richelieu's red hat is one early indication of this. More to the point, some kind of rapprochement occurred between Marie de' Medici and the Brûlarts in the second half of 1622 but, though it was much commented on, its exact scope or purpose is difficult to gauge from surviving allusions to it. By Christmas 1622, the Venetian ambassador was reporting a formal oath of mutual fidelity and service between Puysieux and Marie de' Medici, but one which, at Puysieux's insistence, deliberately excluded Richelieu from its terms. Yet simultaneously, the same ambassador wrote that Louis XIII had made it clear that he was the master, and wished to discourage his mother's ambitions.[113] However opportunistic her alliance with the Brûlarts might be, it almost certainly provided the latter with the insurance they needed in order to evict Schomberg, recover the seals, and install La Vieuville as *surintendant* in late January 1623 – a clean sweep all the more remarkable as Louis XIII's lack of regard for them was no secret.[114] According to one well-placed source, Louis XIII announced his decision to sack Schomberg in Marie's apartments, and then asked for her counsel in choosing a successor.[115] Even if the Schomberg succession was not as open as this account suggests, nor Marie's the decisive voice in the outcome, the king's gesture was itself significant of the changing political equilibrium. That something more than mere stage management was involved is evident from the resolution of a related conflict a few weeks later, also in early 1623. Although Cardinal de La Rochefoucauld had succeeded Retz in council in September 1622, a decision as to what his position there should be was deferred until the king's return to Paris in early January 1623, La Rochefoucauld having himself remained there during the absence of the court. It was the Brûlarts who objected most strongly to the nominal presidency held by

111   Bassompierre, *Journal*, III, pp. 164–80, is the most circumstantial account of this protracted affair. For a broader consideration of the issues, see Bonney, *The King's Debts*, pp. 108–11.

112   *Journal d'Arnauld 1623*, pp. 8, 11.

113   Zeller, *Richelieu et les ministres de Louis XIII*, pp. 164–6, for an analysis of two despatches of 20 Dec. 1622.

114   B.N. MS. Ital. 1779, p. 148, Venetian ambassador to Senate, 21 Jan. 1621, reporting close co-operation between Puysieux and the queen mother, whose power was on the increase.

115   *Journal d'Arnauld 1623*, pp. 8–9. Arnauld was Schomberg's *premier commis* in the finance ministry.

Retz being transferred to a cardinal who owed his position to their enemies, Condé and Schomberg. There was a deadlock during which intermediaries such as Michel de Marillac, the nuncio, and Richelieu's early patron Bertrand d'Eschaux, searched for a solution, but in the end it was Marie de' Medici who was credited with ensuring that La Rochefoucauld would take precedence in council over the constable, the chancellor and the other ministers.[116] The victory was admittedly more symbolic than real, for La Rochefoucauld was not aiming to seize control of council business or policy-making, yet it was a pointed reminder to the Brûlarts of the limits of their hegemony and of the queen mother's ability to restrict their ambitions. Even if there is no reason to believe that La Rochefoucauld's stance over the presidency was in any way 'put up' by Richelieu – his views on ecclesiastical privileges were too well known for that to be necessary – the verdict in La Rochefoucauld's favour must have been some consolation to Richelieu, for all that he remained firmly excluded from preferment. Irrespective of its practical consequences for the business of government, it upheld the 'privileges' of French cardinals at a moment when Richelieu needed every available instrument in his efforts to return to high office;[117] one of his very first moves on entering the council in 1624 would be to secure a similar royal declaration in his favour, for which La Rochefoucauld's success served as a ready-made precedent.[118]

It was one thing to be capable of tipping the scales either way in what were essentially other people's causes, and quite another to exercise significant influence over the conduct of politics. If we can extrapolate from the strong language of Richelieu's *Mémoires*, where the Brûlarts are accused of rank ingratitude towards the queen mother and of remembering her only when they needed her support, it would seem that Marie de' Medici obtained far less than she had expected in return for her services at critical moments in 1623.[119] Yet despite Marie's bitter reproaches, as echoed by Richelieu, it is not sufficiently realized that there was no open break with the Brûlarts, and that their fall, when it came, was only secondarily the consequence of her exertions or those of Richelieu. It seems, for all Richelieu's reluctance to acknowledge it, that Marie de' Medici still needed the Brûlarts' assistance with her own affairs, as for example

116 See Bergin, *La Rochefoucauld*, pp. 62–3. The reference to Eschaux's involvement is in A.S.V., Nunz. Fr. 60, fos. 184–6, Corsini to Barberini, 28 April 1624.
117 B.N. MS. Ital. 1779, p. 188, Venetian ambassador to Senate, 4 Feb. 1623, stating that all of the French cardinals supported La Rochefoucauld's action; *ibid.*, p. 261, letter of 20 Feb.
118 *Les Papiers de Richelieu. Section politique intérieure: correspondance et papiers d'état*, ed. Pierre Grillon (Paris 1975, in progress), I, pp. 85–8. See also Bergin, *La Rochefoucauld*, p. 64.
119 Richelieu, *Mémoires*, III, pp. 275, 277–9.

with the monies she was still trying to recover from her own family in Florence, and that such considerations helped to preserve an admittedly tense peace between the two sides.[120]

But there is a more fundamental reason for this state of affairs, which stems from the queen mother's paradoxical situation after the fall of Schomberg. She had at last returned to court, where the atmosphere was genuinely more receptive than in earlier years, thus enabling her to firmly re-establish her position there during 1623; it is also undeniable that she and her still-expanding entourage were the objects of considerable attention and respect by the court aristocracy, ministers, and foreign ambassadors. To take just one example – Marie felt confident enough to act on her own initiative in late 1623 in exploring the possibilities of an English marriage for her daughter, Henriette-Marie.[121] More importantly, her relations with Louis XIII steadily improved to the point where, it was generally agreed, little trace of past antagonisms seemed visible, in sharp contrast with the alienation of Louis from his queen, Anne of Austria.[122] But, from a political perspective, the new entente had a crucial flaw – it could not be translated into clear political advantage for herself or Richelieu, not because of any lack of effort on their part, nor because of the Brûlarts' alleged ingratitude. This was due essentially to the fact that for most of the Brûlarts' period of supremacy, Louis XIII remained sullenly detached from the business of government. His initial enthusiasm for the duties of kingship after Luynes's death did not of itself suffice to produce a satisfactory definition of his role in government, nor to establish a harmonious division of labour between him and his ministers. His lack of involvement was especially pronounced during 1623, compounding the widely-felt sense of political drift. One of its consequences was to deny the queen mother any effective political leverage against the Brûlarts. Perhaps unwittingly, Richelieu's *Mémoires* illustrate this impotence: her attempts – conceived by himself – to channel advice to Louis XIII on foreign questions at various times during that year were fruitless; the same fate befell her efforts to voice the grievances of the sovereign courts and critics of the Brûlarts. On both counts, Richelieu laid the blame at the door of a ministerial gerontocracy that was averse to exerting itself and preferred the pursuit of its own private interests.[123] Yet this was only a partial explanation. Given Marie's good relations

120 Zeller, *Richelieu et les ministres de Louis XIII*, p. 213.
121 Thomas Cogswell, *The Blessed Revolution. English Politics and the Coming of War 1621–1624* (Cambridge 1989), p. 123.
122 Ruth Kleinman, *Anne of Austria, Queen of France* (Columbus, Ohio 1985), p. 52; Batiffol, *Louis XIII a vingt ans*, pp. 382–3.
123 Richelieu, *Mémoires*, III, pp. 289–90, 298–300.

with the king, it is not altogether surprising that certain foreign ambassadors, such as those of Venice, Tuscany or Savoy, should have continued to frequent her entourage, in the hope that she might be able to counteract the Brûlarts and persuade Louis to give a new impetus to French foreign policy. It was in the course of such encounters that they came to see more and more of Richelieu, to realize the extent of his *governo* of the queen mother and, consequently, to regard him as a political figure with whom they could do business should the ministry change again.[124]

If Richelieu generally emerges as a political sage in most accounts of the Brûlarts' régime, it is due more to the close interest in him taken by foreign ambassadors than it is to the opinions of his fellow countrymen; even Fancan, forever in search of a political figure who would champion royal authority at home and abroad, was extremely slow to regard Richelieu as a potential candidate for such a mission.[125] Were it not for the interest of Florentine, Venetian and other envoys, we should know even less than we do about the Cardinal during the final year or so before his second ministry, a problem which has always made it difficult to provide a satisfactory analysis of the short-term background to his recall. But his low profile throughout 1623 and early 1624, which can be readily sensed from his correspondence, was also a consequence of activities which were no less dangerous for being 'literary' in character. The conflicts of 1619–20 had sharpened the pens of the political pamphleteers, but Richelieu's own uncertain political position at the time had obliged him, as we have seen, to steer a cautious, not to say highly ambiguous, course when it came to exploiting their skills. Pamphlet attacks on Luynes continued unabated, though by no means all of them were written by supporters of Marie de' Medici.[126] Perhaps the most incisive as well as the most damaging were those which appeared after Luynes's death, such as the corrosive *Chronique des favoris* of early 1622. Its author, Fancan, was the most fiercely independent of the government's critics; he had slowly gravitated towards the queen mother's milieu, not in search of service like so many others, but because of his desire to see the political maxims of Henri IV revived, especially in foreign matters.[127] His truculence and his frankly anti-clerical, pro-Protestant sentiments made him very different both from Marie and Richelieu, but this did not prevent each man from seeing advan-

124 Zeller, *Richelieu et les ministres de Louis XIII*, p. 267, quoting the Venetian ambassador, 28 Nov. 1623.
125 Deloche, *Autour de la plume de Richelieu*, pp. 224–5.
126 *Ibid.*, pp. 214ff.
127 Gustave Fagniez, 'L'Opinion publique et la presse politique sous Louis XIII, 1624–1626', *Revue d'Histoire Diplomatique* 14 (1900), pp. 366–7.

tages in the other's talents.[128] Richelieu was prepared to give free rein to Fancan's vitriolic pen against the Brûlarts: his savage diatribes would serve to inflict damage on the record, past and present, of the ministry, but could not be readily traced back to Richelieu. During 1623, one of Fancan's best-known pamphlets, *La France mourante*, mercilessly pilloried the Brûlarts, their policies and their private interests at a time when Richelieu and the queen mother were not ready to break with them.[129] The following year, it would be the turn of their successor, La Vieuville, to feel the full force of the pamphleteer's venom. As a minister, Richelieu would be acutely aware of the need to strengthen royal policy through the intensive use of propaganda; in 1623 and early 1624, well-directed propaganda must have seemed especially valuable to a man who as yet had few other political instruments at his disposal.

VI

Yet it was not the invective of pamphleteers nor even Richelieu's own manoeuvres which triggered the changes which would bring him back into office. The political stalemate of 1623 was finally broken, not from outside, but from inside the ministry. If we draw a veil over subsequent events, it is possible to regard Richelieu's entry into the council in late April 1624 as one of several changes that occurred during a brief period of rapid ministerial turnover, the immediate effects of which were to weaken confidence in the government's competence and to sow confusion over conciliar and ministerial responsibilities. Initially the changes had relatively little to do with the ambitions or discontents of Richelieu and his royal patron. However, there was one crucial development, from their vantage point at least: the changes served to bring Louis XIII firmly back into the centre of the political arena, with consequences that neither he nor anyone else could have predicted.

Throughout 1623, as we have just seen, the Brûlarts had become the targets of increasingly stinging criticism, and they could point to no policy successes that might limit the damage to their reputation. Meanwhile, their protegé, La Vieuville, had been consolidating his position through effective management of the royal finances. The policy which he had proposed to Louis XIII in January 1623 was one of financial retrenchment, and in his attempts to honour his contract he was particularly favoured by circumstances. The military establishment was cut back in the months following the treaty of Mont-

128   Deloche, *Autour de la plume de Richelieu*, p. 218.
129   Geley, *Fancan*, pp. 137ff.

pellier; enjoying the crucial advantage of peacetime conditions, La Vieuville never had to peer into the bottomless pit of war finance. But it was his plans to cut back on court pensions which, as his predecessors Jeannin and Schomberg had discovered before him, were potentially the most troublesome in political terms. At a *conseil élargi* in March 1623 held in the presence of the great nobility, he obtained the king's approval of his plans to restore financial rigour.[130] This gathering, at which La Vieuville complained about the importunity of the aristocracy, revealed clearly where he expected resistance to come from, and the outcome justified his tactic in summoning it. If royal approval was not more spontaneously given, it was probably because of the king's limited affection for La Vieuville as a Brûlart minister, and not because of his opposition to cutting pensions. The parsimonious Louis XIII was a lifelong enemy of profligacy, and he continued to support La Vieuville until mid-1624 because his financial policy was essentially the one he himself wanted. As a result, La Vieuville's ministerial position gradually strengthened, and with it his ambition to supplant his erstwhile patrons.[131] Indeed, almost as soon as he was appointed, he had unsuccessfully tried to prevent Sillery from recovering the seals, wanting, as had Schomberg before him, a personal ally as keeper.[132] The Brûlarts initially excluded him from the king's inner council, but he subsequently secured a place there.[133] By late 1623, he was convinced that Louis XIII could be persuaded to discard the Brûlarts, and he proceeded, as they themselves had done the previous year in the case of Schomberg, to marshal evidence of embezzlement, the alteration of royal decisions and so on, for use against them.[134] But, because his personal power base was so limited, he had first to take steps to ensure that his coup would have wider support; quite how widely he cast his net is unclear, but he seems to have had little difficulty by that point in persuading Marie de' Medici and Richelieu that it was in their interests to see the Brûlarts go.[135] To what extent the queen mother used the opportunity to obtain even informal promises from him regarding Richelieu's future has never been established, and no doubt La Vieuville was as reluctant as other

130 *Journal d'Arnauld 1623*, pp. 18–19. According to Arnauld, Louis XIII would only give La Vieuville six months in which to achieve his objectives.
131 Fontenay-Mareuil, *Mémoires*, p. 558, '. . . il ne songea plus qu'à se défaire de Monsieur le chancelier et Monsieur de Puysieux . . . qui servoient de barrière à son ambition'.
132 Richelieu, *Mémoires*, III, pp. 274–5. Marie de' Medici, according to Richelieu, supported the Brûlarts at this juncture against La Vieuville, and later complained her support had not been rewarded.
133 Bassompierre, *Journal*, III, p. 180; Richelieu, *Mémoires*, III, p. 275.
134 *Journal d'Arnauld 1624*, ed. E. and J. Halpen (Paris 1902), p. 5.
135 Bassompierre, *Journal*, III, p. 183; Fontenay-Mareuil, *Mémoires*, p. 560.

ministers had been in the past to commit himself to the Cardinal's advancement. But if we are to believe the account that the decision to disgrace Sillery was taken in the presence of Marie and Richelieu, then it is reasonable to suppose that these efforts to at least associate them with – and thus implicitly gain their approval of – ministerial changes gave them serious grounds for expecting some kind of satisfaction.[136]

But if La Vieuville intended to make a clean sweep and establish personal control of the administration, he was unsuccessful. A brief account of what happened should make it clear why, from the out-set, the results spelt trouble for the victor as well as for the van-quished. Initially, Louis XIII agreed only to demand that Sillery, whom he despised, return the seals to him. Sillery protested, but his son Puysieux, believing that prompt compliance would keep him in his post and perhaps even save his father's reputation as well, secured the chancellor's grudging compliance. The king then waited several days before announcing his choice of a keeper of the seals. The delay was intended to make it clear that the decision was his alone, and when he finally presented the seals to Étienne Aligre on 6 January, he stressed the personal nature of the choice.[137] To that extent, La Vieuville was not being allowed to dictate ministerial changes in his own interest, all the more so as he had insisted that a keeper 'à sa dévotion' was essential in council, in view of the financial measures he had to take as *surintendant*.[138] Indeed, before the king's delayed announcement of Aligre's appointment, the different factions had suggested several candidates for the seals; even Sillery himself did so, proposing the name of Michel de Marillac, perhaps as a way of retaining Marie de' Medici's goodwill, and staving off further dis-grace.[139] Puysieux, for his part, was determined to hold on as the principal secretary of state, and hoped that the transfer of the seals from his father would satisfy royal vengeance against them.[140] It was only five weeks later, after foreign ambassadors had been ordered not to deal with Puysieux without first discussing their business with the council, that both Brûlarts were actually disgraced and exiled to their estates.[141]

136 This was reported by the Venetian ambassador: see Zeller, *Richelieu et les ministres de Louis XIII*, p. 241.
137 *Journal d'Arnauld 1624*, pp. 5–6. See David Sturdy *The D'Aligres de la Rivière. Servants of the Bourbon State in the Seventeenth Century* (Woodbridge, Suffolk 1986), pp. 32–3.
138 *Journal d'Arnauld 1624*, p. 6.
139 A.S.V., Nunz. Fr. 60, fos. 11v-13, Nuncio Corsini to Cardinal Borghese, 5 Jan. 1624; *ibid.*, fos. 16v-17r, to same, 8 Jan.
140 P.R.O., SP 78/72, fo. 6, Herbert to Naunton, 29 Jan. 1624: 'They [the Brûlarts] keep their places and consequently will render themselves necessary, unlesse some further arguments of disfavor do appeare.'
141 Zeller, *Richelieu et les ministres de Louis XIII*, pp. 236–41.

This was hardly a ruthless, let alone an efficient piece of political surgery. But the ensuing changes in ministerial divisions of labour were no less indecisive. Puysieux's replacement in the secretaryship, Beauclerc, was not given foreign affairs at all, but was confined to the embryonic war department and the *taillon* tax, which had been one of Richelieu's responsibilities in 1616–17.[142] Instead, the foreign affairs portfolio was now split up along purely geographical lines and shared out between the three other secretaries, only one of whom, La Ville-aux-clercs, had been in post for any length of time; none of the three had any formal experience of foreign questions. The resulting complications were not eased by the decision to recall all of the ambassadors appointed during the Brûlarts' period of dominance.[143] The consequences of such changes at a time when the challenges facing France abroad were again becoming urgent, need hardly be underlined; fragmentation was occurring precisely when a unified approach to problems in several parts of Europe – the Valtelline, the Palatinate, and the English match – was vital.

This unexpected division of responsibilities was probably the work of La Vieuville, who was anxious to extend his personal control to foreign questions.[144] In this respect, at least, his example was followed by Richelieu, who would keep the foreign affairs portfolio vacant for a number of years. But, as we shall see, La Vieuville's ambition was also founded on a determination to prosecute a much more vigorous foreign policy than had the Brûlarts. At the same time, he was convinced that his financial policies, especially of retrenchment, themselves required such control, and that these could be undermined if foreign policy could not be subordinated to domestic financial exigencies.[145] Yet, however coherent this approach might appear, it was also potentially dangerous: apart from the question of his own competence beyond the financial sphere, La Vieuville risked assuming in effect the powers and responsibilities of a chief minister, but without the administrative arrangements needed to manage them effectively. In broader political terms, there were risks, too. The removal of the Brûlarts had arguably weakened rather than strengthened the king's council by denuding it further of men of political experience; elderly figures like Constable Lesdi-

---

142 Michaud, 'Aux origines du secrétariat à la guerre', p. 412.
143 A.S.V., Nunz. Fr. 60, fo. 58, Corsini to Barberini, 10 Feb. 1624. Corsini thought that foreign ambassadors in Paris were taking advantage of the secretaries' lack of knowledge to feed them information favourable to their own interests. See Zeller, *Richelieu et les ministres de Louis XIII*, pp. 242–3.
144 Louis XIII claimed that the division was necessary 'per haver maggior sicurità nella fede' in handling foreign affairs, with the three secretaries keeping a check on each other: B.N. MS. Ital. 1781, p. 295, Venetian ambassadors to Senate, 11 Feb. 1624.
145 Lublinskaya, *French Absolutism*, pp. 253–4.

guières or Cardinal de La Rochefoucauld were not men of energy or resolution. La Vieuville might not lack either of these virtues, but his relatively narrow political base meant he could do little enough to enhance the authority of the council. It is, therefore, not surprising that, even before the Brûlarts' disgrace was complete, there should have been widespread talk of enlarging the council or, alternatively, of creating a special *conseil des dépêches* which would co-ordinate the entire range of foreign affairs.[146] The Venetian ambassadors reported in mid-February a flutter of activity by those, of whom Richelieu was one, seeking places in council, while a month later the new papal nuncio, Spada, learned of similar suggestions as far away as Lyon.[147] In fact, it was the presidency of a planned *conseil des dépêches* that La Vieuville was prepared to offer Richelieu in February 1624, when he was still unwilling to see him take a full seat in council. Richelieu's response was firmly negative, and his arguments were irrefutable – the seriousness of foreign policy questions made it impossible for such a subordinate body to take major decisions when none of its members had access to the council of state which, in turn, might be making and implementing foreign policy decisions of its own.[148] But however unsatisfactory, from Richelieu's point of view, the actual form which La Vieuville's offer took, it was an implicit admission of the need for wider participation in government business; once made, its effect was to strengthen Richelieu's resolve to keep up the pressure on La Vieuville and to hold out for the altogether more attractive alternative of a full place in an enlarged council of state.

As foreign issues loomed ever larger, Richelieu's strategy seemed vindicated. In mid-April, the final instalment of the Brûlarts' handling of the Valtelline conflict – an agreement with Urban VIII negotiated by ambassador Sillery in Rome to allow Spanish troops the right of passage through the valley – caused a furore when its terms were brought to France for ratification. Louis XIII again felt the need to hold his council in the presence of the leading nobles in order to demonstrate widespread support for rejecting the terms out of hand.[149] A few days later, he received a Dutch embassy, and talks began which would lead to the Treaty of Compiègne of June

---

146 P.R.O., SP 78/72, fo. 16, Herbert to Calvert, 5 Feb. 1624. This letter was written before Herbert learned of the Brûlarts' disgrace; A.S.V., Nunz. Fr. 60, fo. 57v, Corsini to Barberini, 10 Feb.

147 B.N. MS. Ital. 1781, pp. 308–10, letter to Senate, 16 Feb.; A.S.V., Nunz. Fr. 401, fo. 24, Spada to Barberini, 18 March.

148 Avenel, *Lettres*, I, pp. 783–6, letter to La Vieuville (Feb. 1624).

149 A.S.V., Nunz. Fr. 60, fos. 166–72, Corsini to Barberini, 18 April 1624. See Pithon, 'Débuts de Richelieu', p. 309.

1624.[150] Since February, there had also been an English envoy, Viscount Kensington, in Paris, whose mission was to sound out French interest in an English match and, more importantly, a treaty of alliance, but the initial French response was to reveal as little as possible of their intentions.[151] Thus, quite apart from the political factions angling for power, the coincidence of major questions like these, all of which required sustained attention, seemed to support the case for strengthening the authority of the royal council.

The principal difficulty lay in persuading Louis XIII to accept the force of that case. Before August 1624, he showed few signs of dissatisfaction with La Vieuville, especially in financial matters, and while his well-known capacity for dissimulation makes confident judgement hazardous, he was not one to dissimulate for months on end. The king's role and predicament was best captured by the English ambassador, Herbert, who remarked in early March 1624 and without any obvious paradoxical intent, that although Louis had matured and was giving more direction to his council than previously, there was apprehension as to what results his return to active kingship would produce. Sensing that this could lead to further changes in council, Herbert put his finger on the real problem when he observed that the king 'is betwixt being able to give good counsel himself and being able to receave it from others'.[152] Among those who had been offering him counsel, particularly on foreign policy, was Richelieu, but as it still had to be channelled through Marie de' Medici, Louis was entirely free to feign ignorance of its true source. The surviving evidence does not suggest that the counsel so given softened royal dislike of the Cardinal, any more than it enables us to know how far the king was influenced by widespread speculation about further ministerial changes.[153] Although it may be an illusion induced by hindsight, it seems that it was only when the queen mother and Richelieu rejoined the court gathered at Compiègne in mid-April 1624, that pressure to give them satisfaction intensified. But as so often throughout his reign, Louis XIII remained impassive until he actually announced his decision – at Marie de' Medici's *lever* on 29 April – to admit Richelieu to the council. As a result, most historians have ascribed the final impetus for Richelieu's return to the council to La Vieuville. Needing, for

150 *Journal d'Arnauld 1624*, p. 18. The first audience took place on 17 April.
151 Fontenay-Mareuil, *Mémoires*, pp. 560–1. See Thomas Cogswell, 'Crown, Parliament and War 1623–1625' (Ph.D. dissertation, Washington University, St Louis, 1983) pp. 372–3. I am grateful to the author for permission to consult and cite his thesis.
152 P.R.O., SP 78/72, fos. 37–8, Herbert to James I, 5 March 1624.
153 On the other hand, anecdotes abound concerning Louis XIII's fear of Richelieu's 'esprit altier et dominateur'. See Chevallier, *Louis XIII*, p. 273.

reasons we shall see presently, to strengthen his ties with the queen mother, the *surintendant* agreed to present Richelieu's promotion as a consequence of the need to relieve Richelieu's fellow cardinal, La Rochefoucauld, then seriously ill and unable to travel to Compiègne.[154] As for the king's own motives – apart from a widely reported desire to satisfy his mother – they may be deduced from the instructions given to his secretary the day after Richelieu's appointment, for communication to the prince of Condé, which referred almost exclusively to the major foreign questions that needed to be dealt with in council.[155] Nor were these two sets of motives unconnected. Marie de' Medici's eagerness to propel Richelieu into government again was itself part of her determination to have a significant role in any negotiations for her daughter's marriage to the Prince of Wales, which both she and her *dévot* supporters hoped would bring advantages to English Catholics. Likewise, the rejection of papal mediation in the Valtelline and the restoration of France's position in the valleys, was fraught with difficulties which required sensitive handling. Richelieu's *Mémoires* are also of disconcertingly little value in providing an explanation of such a key moment in his career: having recounted some of La Vieuville's manoeuvres after the fall of the Brûlarts, they simply state that 'La Vieuville persuaded the king to appoint the Cardinal to his councils'.[156] Indeed, to the extent that the *Mémoires* offer any kind of extended commentary, it is on Richelieu's quite elaborate attempts to refuse the honour being offered to him, largely on the grounds of poor health![157] If such a *mise en scène* did occur, its real purpose was very different from its ostensible one – namely, to elicit from a rather frosty monarch some declaration which would make it plain that he personally desired to promote Richelieu, who could then point to it as evidence of Louis's goodwill and protection. In the absence of any such royal gesture, it is not surprising that the *Mémoires* make no mention at all of the most important but least flattering aspect of Richelieu's appointment – the fact that he was empowered merely to give his views (*opiner*) in council, and was specifically debarred from handling the king's business outside the council chamber. Given the king's instinctive reluctance to admit him to his council, La Vieuville probably did not need to press him particularly hard to circumscribe Richelieu's

154 Grillon, *Papiers de Richelieu*, I, p. 65; A.S.V., Nunz. Fr. 61, fo. 182, Spada to Barberini, 2 May. Like other commentators, Spada initially tnought La Rochefoucauld had been disgraced in order to make way for Richelieu, and was only disabused later: *ibid.*, fo. 71, to same 3 May; P.R.O., SP 78/72, fos. 163–4, Herbert to Calvert, 4 May 1624.

155 Grillon, *Papiers de Richelieu*, I, pp. 65–6. See also Zeller, *Richelieu et les ministres de Louis XIII*, Appendices nos. 9–10, pp. 316–19, letters of Florentine ambassador, 10 May 1624.

156 Richelieu, *Mémoires*, IV, p. 23.

157 *Ibid.*, pp. 24–36.

activities in this way. Such a step was by no means unheard of, and had been taken in several instances during the Luynes years.[158] La Vieuville's tactic, designed to safeguard his own predominance in council, probably enjoyed the tacit approval of the other ministers, who could not have been expected to welcome the addition of a new member to their ranks.

VII

Richelieu's second ministerial career thus began on a low key; when the king formally introduced him in council, he did so briefly and entirely without ceremony. Since no one had had to be disgraced to make room for him, there was no question of his presenting a political programme, which would have been both unwelcome and damaging to himself.[159] Where La Vieuville had begun his ministerial career by eliminating Schomberg and proposing his own financial policies, Richelieu began his more prosaically by joining his main rival in council, and only later did he engineer his fall. Within a week or so, Richelieu was joined in council by La Rochefoucauld, who continued to serve as its nominal president; just as promptly, Richelieu himself obtained royal confirmation of the precedence rights of cardinals over the constable and other members of the council.[160] In his ambition to supplant La Vieuville, which all observers took for granted, his best bet lay, not in attempting to besiege Louis XIII, but in biding his time and allowing La Vieuville to commit the kind of errors which the political challenges of mid-1624 made it very difficult to avoid in all cases. Although the Florentine ambassador detected considerable bitterness in Richelieu over the conditions of his appointment, they proved to be a useful shield against what he viewed as La Vieuville's attempts to discredit him.[161] Richelieu proved patient enough and La Vieuville sufficiently fallible for the widely-anticipated outcome to materialize.

In one sense, the ministry of La Vieuville represents the *reductio ad absurdum* of French politics following the death of Luynes, when a

158 Louis Batiffol, 'Louis XIII et le duc de Luynes', *Revue Historique* 102 (1909), pp. 258–60.
159 Louis Batiffol, *Richelieu et le roi Louis XIII. Les véritables rapports du souverain et de son ministre* (Paris 1934), pp. 1–2.
160 B.N. MS. Ital. 1782, p. 196, Venetian ambassadors to Senate, 9 May 1624. Avenel, *Lettres*, II, pp. 6–10, for memorandum on the 'préséance des cardinaux'. There is a copy of the royal *brevet* in Richelieu's favour in P.R.O., SP 78/72, fo. 176. See also Richelieu, *Mémoires*, IV, pp. 36–7.
161 Zeller, *Richelieu et les ministres de Louis XIII*, Appendix no. 9, pp. 316–18, letter to Grand Duke, 10 May 1624.

succession of political figures suffering from varying combinations of a lack of support, respect, and ability, exercised increasingly transitory dominance while never appearing, even at the time, as if they could last the course. La Vieuville's own attempts to bolster his political position were blessed with less success than those of Schomberg or the Brûlarts. On the contrary, his efforts seem fated to backfire, constantly leading observers to wonder how long he could survive.[162] From the outset, he possessed a slender power base within the government; his original alliance with the Brûlarts was purely tactical, and his efforts to capitalize on their decline and removal yielded meagre results, at least in the form of a personal clientèle. He failed, as we have seen, to obtain the seals for his wife's relative, *président* Le Jay, or to find a political role thereafter for either Le Jay or the duc d'Angoulême, another ally.[163] Attempts to secure additional influence over the king also came to nothing, as is evident from his lack of success in replacing Séguiran as royal confessor by Arnoux or some other figure; he only seems to have attracted the enmity of the Jesuits for his pains.[164] Several other manoeuvres by La Vieuville only provoked bitter hostility. Placating the queen mother by bringing Richelieu into the council was thus an attempt to redress the balance; the result, however, was neither gratitude nor support, but a sense of grievance, owing to the restrictions placed on Richelieu's role in council. Nor did La Vieuville's political skills improve much thereafter. He created a quite unnecessary row in May–June 1624 when he insisted on sacking and exiling Gaston d'Orléans's governor and confidant, Ornano, an episode which poisoned his relations not only with leading members of the court nobility, but also with Gaston and Marie de' Medici.[165] At the same time, and no less damagingly, he also contrived to alienate close favourites of Louis XIII, such as Bassompierre.[166]

These straightforward political blunders were compounded by the fact that La Vieuville's financial reforms, which cut expenditure substantially and did enjoy royal support, nevertheless exposed him

---

162 A.S.V., Nunz. Fr. 60, fo. 18v, Corsini to Barberini, 8 Jan. 1624. See also Zeller, *Richelieu et les ministres de Louis XIII*, pp. 243–4.

163 *Journal d'Arnauld 1624*, pp. 6, 12.

164 *Ibid.*, p. 12; B.N. MS. Ital. 1781, p. 295, Venetian ambassadors to Senate, 11 Feb.; MS. Ital. 1782, pp. 31–2, same to same, 15 March. P.R.O., 30/53/6, fo. 38, Daniel Mercier to Calvert, 11 March. One of the candidates mentioned was Philippe Cospeau, Richelieu's old mentor, and the Venetians believed he and the queen mother supported his candidature.

165 *Journal d'Arnauld 1624*, pp. 19–50. See Zeller, *Richelieu et les ministres de Louis XIII*, p. 320, letter of Venetian ambassadors, 2 Aug. 1624. After La Vieuville's fall, Richelieu would quickly take steps to end this dispute, and to recall Ornano.

166 Zeller, *Richelieu et les ministres de Louis XIII*, p. 319, letter of Venetian ambassador, 2 Aug. 1624.

to the ire of the *grands* and other courtiers, leaving him with few natural supporters when he found his position challenged and the king turning against him. His handling of major foreign issues, which saw him pursuing *bon français* policies without securing adequate support, and taking independent personal initiatives, also left him vulnerable to denunciation. The reinforcement of the Dutch alliance in June 1624, and the resurrection of the alliance with Savoy and Venice, the massing of troops near Lyon, and the despatch of the marquis de Coeuvres to the Valtelline in order to engineer an anti-Habsburg insurrection there, made the *bons catholiques* at Louis XIII's court distinctly uneasy.[167] But it was La Vieuville's conduct of the negotiations for the English match which provided his opponents with the opportunity to sink him. The talks, which formally began in late May 1624, quickly reached deadlock because the French were proving as intransigent as the Spaniards by making the match conditional on James I's publicly guaranteeing religious toleration for English Catholics. La Vieuville, fearful that a breakdown would both damage his credibility and undermine his foreign policy by driving England back into the arms of Spain, took it upon himself to give an undertaking, for which he thought he had the support of Louis XIII, that a private promise of toleration by James I would be acceptable, and that few questions would be asked subsequently about its implementation.[168] This concession had the desired effect in London, but by the time the English were ready to resume negotiations in Paris, La Vieuville was on the brink of disgrace, and Louis XIII was denying all knowledge of the offer![169] The more La Vieuville appeared to be moving France closer to Protestant powers and into a break with the papacy and Spain – which both the English and the Dutch were really after – the more susceptible he became to a backlash from the *dévots* around the queen mother, who were busily involved in the affair of the English match.

Richelieu was perfectly placed to exploit this turn of events. The restrictions placed on his role in council meant that he could not be blamed for La Vieuville's mistakes, and he was shrewd enough to behave accordingly. But, despite La Vieuville's precautions, he did manage to make some useful gains. The declaration of 9 May concerning his rank in council was a demonstration that, as a cardinal, he could defend his own interests there without La Vieuville's patronage. It was also logical, given the religious issues at stake, for him to become a member of the commission appointed in May 1624

167 Moote, *Louis XIII*, p. 135.
168 Cogswell, 'Crown, Parliament and War', pp. 392–3; Cogswell, *Blessed Revolution*, pp. 279–80; Roger Lockyer, *Buckingham* (London 1981), pp. 199–200.
169 Cogswell, 'Crown, Parliament and War', pp. 402–11.

to handle negotiations over the English match. His role in the exchanges was, it appears, one of extreme caution and his views were indistinguishable from those of the *dévots*.[170] But it is not sufficiently appreciated that, at this juncture, he had a direct interest in English affairs, and that, as a consequence of it, he was probably better briefed on them than anyone at the French court. From April 1624 onwards, he was personally pressing to have his long-standing client, Richard Smith, made bishop of the English church, and he finally succeeded in obtaining papal approval in October of that year. This appointment was intimately connected with the question of the English marriage and toleration for English Catholics.[171] Moreover, Smith himself, who was in London in April–May 1624, hurried back to Compiègne ahead of the returning English ambassadors, and immediately rejoined Richelieu at court in order to inform him of conditions in England, and to press him to demand significant religious concessions from James I.[172] This, as well as his membership of the commission to negotiate the marriage, provided Richelieu with an unrivalled vantage point from which to shadow La Vieuville; and not surprisingly, it was to him that La Vieuville's *dévot* enemies passed on the highly compromising information about the *surintendant*'s independent diplomacy concerning the question of toleration for English Catholics.[173]

With several possibilities open to him, Richelieu galvanized Fancan into renewed action; his pamphlets, *Le Mot à l'oreille* and *La Voix publique au roi*, published in May and early August respectively, delivered a devastating and widely remarked attack on La Vieuville's ineptitude, while pointing quite clearly at the same time to the obvious candidate as his successor; the stir produced by the second pamphlet was such that Louis XIII himself had publicly to deny that the campaign presaged La Vieuville's imminent disgrace.[174] But Fancan's rhetoric did not limit Richelieu's options, nor prevent him from playing the *dévot* card to full effect. The attack on La Vieuville which followed was two-pronged, and proved all the more suc-

170 Richelieu, *Mémoires*, IV, p. 63.

171 A.F. Allison, 'Richard Smith, Richelieu and the French Marriage', *Recusant History* 7 (1964), pp. 148–211, for a well-documented study of this issue.

172 *Ibid.*, pp. 170–1. He quotes Smith's letter of 2 June 1624 to Rome: 'I am comen to my Cardinal Richelieu for to request him for to help us to get an other Bishop . . . and to obtaine as good conditions for Catholiks in case our Prince marie here in France as the Spaniards had obtained.'

173 Zeller, *Richelieu et les ministres de Louis XIII*, pp. 320–1, letter of Venetian ambassadors, 6 Aug. 1624; Cogswell, *Blessed Revolution*, pp. 279–80. At one point, La Vieuville is reported as saying: 'ces clercs me gastent tout'.

174 The English envoy, Carlisle, directly linked the publication of the *Voix publique* to the rumours of La Vieuville's disgrace: P.R.O., SP 78/72, fos. 388–91, letter to Secretary Conway, 8 Aug. 1624. See also Geley, *Fancan*, pp. 176ff; Lublinskaya, *French Absolutism*, pp. 265–6.

cessful because it reached two different, but complementary, targets. With the assistance of La Ville-aux-clercs, the secretary of state who handled English affairs, Richelieu proceded to hit the rawest royal nerve of all by persuading Louis XIII that his leading minister was operating behind his back and, in watering down the terms under which Henriette-Marie could be married to the future Charles I, effectively conducting a foreign policy of his own invention.[175] This highly-dangerous accusation was accompanied by a more general attack, directed towards public opinion, on La Vieuville's financial record. Fancan had already shown the value of such attacks in his pamphlets, alleging that La Vieuville's family connections and personal behaviour had sacrificed France and the king's finances to a race of bloodsuckers.[176] Both Fancan and the political attack on La Vieuville which followed, conveniently ignored the fact that his unpopularity was due essentially to his tightfistedness, not to his corruption or profligacy.[177] But, as on other occasions of a similar kind, finance ministers found such accusations extremely difficult to counter, and a well-orchestrated campaign, especially where it gave rise to a special *chambre de justice*, could both mobilize opinion and inflict serious damage on political opponents at relatively little risk to its beneficiaries.[178]

La Vieuville lost out to Richelieu, not just because he was dealing with a more accomplished political operator, experienced at surviving in unfavourable conditions, but because he overreached himself, being effectively chief minister, foreign minister, and finance minister all in one until August 1624. Signs of his discomfiture became increasingly visible in July and early August, and included altercations between himself and Richelieu, no doubt because of La Vieuville's suspicions of the Cardinal's involvement in the propaganda campaign against him.[179] His arrest and imprisonment on 13 August followed a familiar pattern of speculation, rumour and royal dissimulation until the last moment.[180] Richelieu, who as a

175 Zeller, *Richelieu et les ministres de Louis XIII*, pp. 293–5.
176 Geley, *Fancan*, pp. 196–200.
177 Fagniez, 'L'Opinion publique et la presse politique sous Louis XIII', p. 368; Lublinskaya, *French Absolutism*, pp. 269; Bonney, *The King's Debts*, pp. 111–12.
178 ·J.F. Bosher 'Chambres de justice in the French monarchy', in *French Government and Society 1500–1850*, ed. Bosher (London 1973), pp. 19–40; Françoise Bayard, 'Les Chambres de justice dans la première moitié du xviiᵉ siècle' *Cahiers d'Histoire* 19 (1974), pp. 121–40; D. Dessert, *Argent, pouvoir et société au grand siècle*, ch. 11.
179 Zeller, *Richelieu et les ministres de Louis XIII*, pp. 319–21, Venetian ambassadors to Senate, 2 and 6 Aug. 1624.
180 *Journal d'Arnauld 1624*, pp. 51–2; A.A.E., Mems. et docs., France 778, fos. 195–6, for a contemporary account of his arrest. The official version is contained in royal circular letters to provincial governors, the sovereign courts and foreign envoys: Grillon, *Papiers de Richelieu*, I, pp. 101–2, letter to governors 13 Aug. 1624. See also Zeller, *Richelieu et les ministres de Louis XIII*, pp. 326–7, letter from Venetian ambassador, 22 Aug.

minister would acquire a great deal of experience in identifying, and coping with, the susceptibilities of Louis XIII, passed the first of many tests and achieved an essentially 'political' victory over La Vieuville: neither principles – with the possible exception of that of 'conciliar' government in which ministers were not free to act on their own initiative – nor policies were really at stake. One consequence was that Richelieu decided it was necessary to proceed more, not less, cautiously in foreign matters than had La Vieuville, although the policy itself remained remarkably similar. The English marriage would go through under conditions not so very different from those La Vieuville had offered and, ironically in view of the charges against the latter, Richelieu, too, would have to resort to separate, secret talks with the English envoys in order to make sure of the outcome.[181] The Dutch alliance of June 1624 would also be maintained, while military intervention in the Valtelline later in 1624 would provide the spectacle of French troops actually firing on those of the pope.[182]

Richelieu was effectively installed as *principal ministre* from mid-August 1624, but few contemporaries could yet fasten a distinctive political style or set of priorities to him. It was not until La Vieuville had fallen, and a full-scale attack on him and a purge of his administration had been launched, that ideas and proposals for change began to circulate, and Richelieu himself began to respond to the need for reform and reorganization in the government of the realm.[183] Meanwhile, in sharp contrast to what we have seen in the case of Schomberg, the Brûlarts and La Vieuville, there was surprisingly little speculation about how long, or indeed whether, Richelieu could survive in his new position; in fact, there was a widespread belief that he would succeed where others had failed, and would establish himself firmly in power.[184] This belief was based on more than respect for his intelligence and political skills. Given the uncertainty about Louis XIII's own leanings, Richelieu understood the need to avoid the political isolation that had befallen the likes of Schomberg and La Vieuville, and realized that the most obvious way to achieve this was to strengthen his own position in the council. He seems to have experienced little difficulty in his dealings with Aligre, the keeper of the seals, who was happy enough to see the end of La

---

181 Cogswell, 'Crown, Parliament and War', pp. 412–20. He shows how far Richelieu systematically backed away from clarity in the terms of the marriage treaty, and indeed that his preference for vague, ambiguous articles would bedevil Anglo-French relations in the coming years.

182 Pithon, 'Débuts de Richelieu', p. 312.

183 See the memoranda in Grillon, *Papiers de Richelieu*, I, docs. nos. 62–3, 88–9 for the year 1624, in addition to the extensive plans for reform in 1625.

184 P.R.O., SP 78/73, fo. 5, Kensington and Carlisle to Conway, 17 Aug. 1624.

Vieuville; only two months later, in October 1624, Aligre became chancellor on the death of Sillery. Schomberg was recalled from disgrace amidst considerable publicity, and regained his place in council, where Richelieu could expect the support of a man who still enjoyed royal approval. But Schomberg was not restored to the post of *surintendant*, which Richelieu was anxious to see reduced in status and power. Whatever the financial reasons for this design, recent history had probably convinced him that a unified *surintendance* could serve as a launching pad for potential political challengers; the result was a collegial system of financial administration, with Michel de Marillac and Bochart de Champigny as joint *surintendants*, and Richelieu himself assuming overall responsibility.[185] As we have seen, he assumed a similar role in foreign affairs.

Important as these moves were, the confidence that the Cardinal would survive longer than his recent predecessors rested above all on the knowledge that, unlike them, he could count on an extensive and increasingly influential power base. Previous ministries had been so effectively destroyed by the queen mother's rising influence, that there seemed, to one observer at least, no competition left capable of denying her and her circle the power to which they had aspired for so long.[186] Whatever conflicts the more distant future might bring, Richelieu's skill in rebuilding and managing the queen mother's power now seemed to guarantee the kind of political stability and protection from those anxious to take his place which would permit him to devote his energies to the business of government.

185 Bonney, *The King's Debts*, pp. 115–17.
186 Zeller, *Richelieu et les ministres de Louis XIII*, p. 324, letter of Florentine ambassador, 15 Aug. 1624.

Conclusion

'Guardate, se potete, più alle mani degli homini che alla bocca'
(Take care to observe men's hands more closely than their mouths)[1]

RICHELIEU's second experience of ministerial office was to be as unforeseeably long as his first was dramatically short. His eighteen years as Louis XIII's leading minister obviously possess a unity of their own, and as such they have consistently both challenged and attracted historians. Yet despite the attention lavished on his ministry, a considerable amount of work still needs to be done if we are to understand fully his career, his policies and his achievements. Amid often sharp disagreement over the nature of those policies and achievements, one undisputed success has perhaps not always received the attention that it deserves – the simple fact that he kept his grip on power for an unprecedented period of years, and that he did so in an age which detested ministers of the kind he represented. It may be that historians and biographers have taken this obvious fact too much for granted, and hastened to turn their attention instead to more 'elevated' issues. There can be no question of attempting here even a cursory explanation of how Richelieu managed such a feat, which by any criterion must be as remarkable as even his most undisputed successes, but any satisfactory account would need to acknowledge some of the lessons of the odyssey outlined in the preceding pages.

Neither the focus nor the time-scale of the present study should be taken as suggesting that Richelieu's ministerial career after 1624 ought to be regarded as no more than an epilogue to his ascent to high office. Yet it will be no less obvious that the political skills which enabled him to survive disgrace and make a political comeback between 1617 and 1624 were indispensable to him in later years. As we have seen, all he had managed to achieve in April 1624 was a place in the king's council, a position which several others had obtained in previous years, but which they had been unable to consolidate for any length of time after their initial success. Richelieu would have ample opportunity to realize, especially in the early

---

1 Cardinal Cervini, later Pope Marcellus II, writing in 1545, quoted in Barbara McClung Hallman, *Italian Cardinals, Reform and the Church as Property 1492–1563* (Los Angeles, Calif. 1985), p. 3.

years of his ministry, how fragile such a position could be. From this vantage point, he differs from his rivals essentially by the manner in which he succeeded in gradually transforming his initial toehold through the successive, piecemeal conquests of power which eventually made him such a dominant figure in government during the last decade of his career. Although the context and circumstances would be very different, this stage-by-stage advance mirrors the pattern of his political apprenticeship which we have attempted to trace in this book.

Of course, if Richelieu the political operator has not received sufficient attention from historians, this is partly because the waters have long been muddied by arguments about the nature of the political objectives of Richelieu the minister. These arguments began, as is well known, with his own *Testament Politique*, in which he claimed that he had from the outset of his second ministry proposed a clear set of goals for Louis XIII to follow. Such an assertion can no more be taken on trust than the idea that his *Mémoires* represent an objective account of the reign of Louis XIII as a whole. The question of Richelieu's objectives in or after 1624 is also one which cannot be answered from the evidence of the foregoing pages, but they do constitute a warning against accepting traditional accounts on trust. As we saw in the final chapter, Richelieu remained extremely reticent, and with good reason, about divulging his ideas prematurely; the political circumstances in which he came to office in 1624 obliged him to behave with the utmost circumspection, especially on foreign issues. Moroever, it seems extremely unlikely that he would have risked committing himself to a set of specific, but very ambitious goals in the way which had proved highly damaging to some of his predecessors.

This does not mean that Richelieu had no idea of what to do with power apart from enjoying the exercise of it, but rather that he would wait until he had obtained office and begun to experience the realities of government again before formulating objectives. On a more general level, even when, in subsequent years, he drafted memoranda, submitted *avis*, and conceived projects, we should be extremely wary of taking them as evidence of a complete unity of thought and action in Richelieu. Whatever his perceptions of the problems he faced, and whatever the remedies he prescribed for them, it is increasingly obvious that he always allowed himself as much freedom as possible when it came to deciding what to do and when to do it.[2] If such caution owed much to the need to retain the favour of a wilful and exacting Louis XIII, it also reflected his own

---

2 This is especially clear from the successsive discussions in Moote, *Louis XIII*.

highly pragmatic outlook and sense of political reality. It was those among his contemporaries – and perhaps among historians, too – who took his words too literally who were to be most disappointed by him.

Interesting and instructive as it might be to pursue such questions further, they could only be adequately treated in the context of Richelieu's exercise of ministerial power. What the present study has attempted to show is that the Richelieu who returned to ministerial office in 1624 was neither a saviour-figure and statesman who was the exception to every rule, nor a genius who could blithely defy the ordinary laws of political gravity. His route to power was infinitely less dramatic and more conventional than such venerable *images d'Épinal* imply. In his methodological study of the élites of early seventeenth-century Rome, Wolfgang Reinhard saw kinship, friendship, common geographical origins and patronage as the main contributory factors admitting individuals to the different networks which made up these élites. While he did accept that individual talent – the 'via della virtù' in contemporary language – could operate as a supplementary factor, which might even make up for the absence of the others, Reinhard insisted, crucially, that, in the long term, talent could not free able or outstanding individuals from the constraints governing membership of the élites in question; on the contrary, talent and ability would lead the individuals in question into, rather than away from, networks of patrons and clients.[3] Even allowing for the differences between Rome and France in the seventeenth century, it can be suggested that the career of Richelieu fits comfortably into such a pattern.

The early history of the Richelieu family shows the presence of a range of traditions of activity and service – arms, the court, the law, and the church. The main threads of that history were service to the Montpensier family and, to a lesser degree, at the court of the kings of France. It was really only when François de Richelieu opened a new chapter by becoming *grand prévôt de France* that the direct service of the king beckoned, but it did not do so to the exclusion of everything else. As we saw, it was at just that juncture that wider connections and opportunities also opened up to him; and he proved as quick as any nobleman to seize the openings provided by royal service to enrich himself and promote his family. Unfortunately, his early death curtailed most of these developments before they could be exploited to the full, and specifically before he had had the opportunity to shape the careers of his own children. His final bank-

3 Wolfgang Reinhard, *Freunde und Kreaturen. 'Verflechtung' als Konzept zur Erforschung historischer Führungsgruppen. Römische Oligarchie um 1600* (Munich 1979), esp. p. 72.

ruptcy and the absence of a strong extended family left the younger generation in a very uncertain and difficult position. It should also be remembered that inherited patterns of service and patronage were themselves disrupted by the effects of the religious wars. By the time the young Richelieu became bishop of Luçon, the house of Montpensier was reduced to a single heiress, and that of Joyeuse to a celibate cardinal who spent most of his time in Rome or Toulouse. Nor was there much prospect, after the events of the Catholic League, of the rising generation of the Richelieu family attempting to emulate their La Porte grandfather by seeking to revive the patronage of the Guises which had, apparently, lapsed with La Porte's death in 1572. It was thus crucial to the family's survival that the Cardinal's elder brother, Henri, established himself at court and patiently rebuilt its shattered fortunes. Royal goodwill apart, we know all too little about the patronage networks to which he belonged, and which enabled him to pursue his objectives so effectively.

One of his principal objectives was to preserve the see of Luçon for a younger brother, whether it be Alphonse or Armand. Of the available family traditions, the ecclesiastical – and especially the episcopal – was the most recent and least developed, which left a young bishop like Richelieu an appreciable measure of liberty to make his own way in his chosen profession. His undoubted intelligence, solid academic record, and personal appeal enabled him in his early days to compensate for the scarcity of obvious, inherited protectors, and gradually to build up a circle of personal servants, friends and associates. But it would be fatal to conclude from this that Richelieu was able, or even sought, to remain sovereignly free of the normal ties and constraints of patronage; the isolated loner was just as likely to remain rooted to the spot in the upper reaches of the French church as elsewhere in French society. Luçon may have deserved Richelieu's disparaging description of it, but as a bishop, he was a member of perhaps the best organized corporate group in France; it had considerable experience of united action, enjoyed enviable status and privileges, and was criss-crossed with powerful networks of patronage, friendship, and protection. Thus, although our information is extremely scanty, it was quite realistic for Richelieu the young bishop, given his academic background and aspirations, to begin by seeking out the patronage of a scholar-cardinal who also enjoyed visible royal favour, du Perron. During his years in Luçon, he continued and broadened that quest, as he patiently built up his circle of protectors, friends, disciples, and clients, essentially among the first- and second-order clergy. But even here, we should not prejudge the results, which took a considerable time to materialize; many of those most closely associated with him during these years were in no sense his dependents or 'créatures'. As we saw, Richelieu failed in his early attempts to change diocese, attract new benefices, or secure an ecclesiastical post at court; and to the leaders of the clergy at the Estates General of 1614, he was a valuable, but not especially powerful or influential, middle-ranking bishop. Thereafter, he continued to use his ecclesiastical support to make his way at court and into the council chamber. Although he would gradually extend that support to include more and more laymen, it is no exaggeration to say that during the ensuing decade, when he emerged into the limelight, Richelieu was at his most vulnerable when isolated from his ecclesiastical milieu, and at his most effective when firmly anchored in it. The extent to which he could mobilize it and make it serve his purposes was convincingly demonstrated during the events of 1619; in the isolation which followed his dismissal from office in April 1617 or which preceded the revolt of 1620, he relied heavily on his ecclesiastical support to sustain him and deflect criticism. His subsequent quest for cardinal's status was a natural culmination of his efforts: success would guarantee greater insurance in the event of future difficulties or setbacks, but at the same time open the door to a wider world of power and patronage.

This *modus operandi* was not merely a product of unusual circumstances, nor was it confined to the ecclesiastical sphere: it was one which Richelieu would continue to practice even more effectively throughout his second ministry. He did not surround himself with clients and supporters out of mere vanity or an elemental *libido dominandi*. Here, too, myth and reality seem to diverge sharply, leading to a one-sided perception of him. The Richelieu so powerfully portrayed in the iconography is withdrawn and aloof, a superior being; the Richelieu who emerges from the archives is one who needed, and constantly surrounded himself with, an entourage – whether it be secretarial, domestic, intellectual, or even ministerial – which he constantly prompted to work for him, generating ideas and projects from which he could then make his own selection. The foundations of this pattern of behaviour, which is abundantly documented in his published papers, were clearly laid, as we saw, during his years at Luçon, and they may ultimately go back to his years at university.

Other features of Richelieu's political style owe a great deal to his ecclesiastical background. However superfluous it may seem to do so, it is worth noting that he relished both the responsibilities and the challenges of power, whether ecclesiastical or political. He expressed himself relatively little on the responsibilities of being a bishop, and he did so mostly in a matter-of-fact way in letters to friends. But his later writings as a minister would strongly stress the vocational, and even sacrificial, character of the exercise of power in a monarchy such as France. It is not hard to see the religious origins of such thinking. On a less elevated, but perhaps more decisive, plane, such high seriousness also enabled him to become, despite Louis XIII's continuing ambivalence towards him, virtually confessor to the king, whose conscience he directed far more effectively than the nominal royal confessors who came and went during his ministry. Certainly, it is difficult to imagine a king as conscious of his royal dignity as Louis XIII allowing anyone else – and in particular a layman – to lecture him on personal and political issues to the extent that Richelieu was to do; such patronizing behaviour was acceptable only in a respected churchman. In the struggle to gain and keep power, Richelieu the priest, bishop, and cardinal, possessed some formidable advantages over his lay rivals, and he learned how to use them to the full.

If the ecclesiastical dimension is more important than has usually been assumed, because it provided the essential framework for so much of Richelieu's career, it cannot of itself explain everthing. It has been a central thesis of this book that Richelieu was profoundly and enduringly marked by the specific experiences of his political apprenticeship in the 1610s and early 1620s. When he returned to office in 1624, he was anything but an inexperienced tyro; he was nearly forty and, therefore, unlikely to drastically change his political style or values. His previous experiences had ranged all the way from high favour, as represented by ministerial office, to sudden disgrace, suspicion, and defeat; the cumulative effect of all this was to make him a master of the arts of political survival. His later career would show again and again that his greatest skill was undoubtedly the capacity to survive in a hostile political climate. This was far more crucial to his record as a minister than any political philosophy which he had allegedly developed during the decade or so before 1624. His first brief experience of ministerial office was, in any case, dominated by the need to deal with a serious internal revolt, and his own position as a second-rank figure precluded any attempt at a wider vision of government and its needs. It was only when he returned to office in 1624 that he had to face the challenges of government again, and it was only then that he was gradually led to enunciate both the policies and the principles with which his ministry is associated. On the basis of the surviving evidence, it is fair to say that he was not given to weaving elaborate theories or projects when there was no point in doing so. Appropriately enough for a man who carried relatively little ideological baggage, the goals which he would set himself as Louis XIII's minister were primarily responses to the challenges of government, not the consequences of a highly-defined political philosophy.

It is no secret that Richelieu would scathingly criticize and deplore the political excesses, mistakes, and weaknesses of France after the death of Henri IV, particularly in his *Mémoires*. But it is essential to grasp in what sense he did so, for it never amounted to a fundamental rejection of the political practices and values of the day. His understanding of politics and power remained rooted in the history of that period. His early experiences of political institutions and practices reinforced his pragmatic realism. Later, as he strove to establish himself as chief minister to Louis XIII, he would outdo both his predecessors and his rivals in his efforts to accumulate as many sources of power as possible. He was not a new political broom determined to rewrite the rules governing the distribution and exercise of power; where ministers, nobles, and courtiers lost favour and office on his account, it was due almost entirely to short-term political considerations or conflicts, and not to any blueprint for a transformation of government. The bitter struggles over provincial governorships, *places fortes*, royal domain, pensions, and other perquisites which he witnessed under Marie de' Medici, Concini and Luynes profoundly shaped his own perceptions of the location and hierarchy of power. By comparison, the theories of royal power and reason of state so long associated with him, seem less crucial to our understanding of his ministerial style. Moreover, as he demonstrated in his service of Marie de' Medici before 1624 and then during his years as minister, both his understanding and his accumulation of power extended in practice far beyond the sphere of the political. The search for appropriate historical comparisons is thus far more likely to point backwards towards the Renaissance past rather than forward to the *grands commis* and *hommes d'état* of future generations.

In this as in so many other respects, 'le grand cardinal' was far more a man of his own time than a man for all political seasons.

Genealogy of La Porte Family

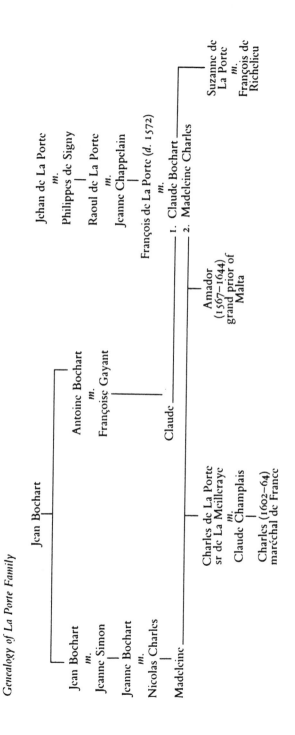

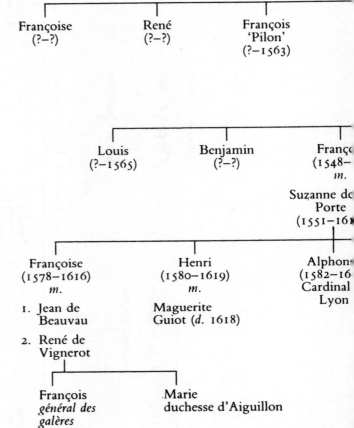

Françoise
(?–?)

René
(?–?)

François
'Pilon'
(?–1563)

Louis
(?–1565)

Benjamin
(?–?)

Franç(
(1548–
m.

Suzanne de
Porte
(1551–161

Françoise
(1578–1616)
m.

1. Jean de
Beauvau

2. René de
Vignerot

Henri
(1580–1619)
m.

Maguerite
Guiot (*d.* 1618)

Alphons
(1582–16
Cardinal
Lyon

François
*général des
galères*

Marie
duchesse d'Aiguillon

*Having previously accepted the evidence for the e
sceptical as to its value, and prefer to leave the question

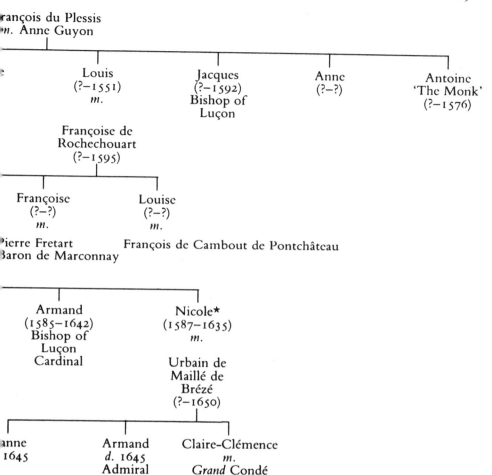

François du Plessis
m. Anne Guyon

Louis
(?–1551)
m.

Jacques
(?–1592)
Bishop of
Luçon

Anne
(?–?)

Antoine
'The Monk'
(?–1576)

Françoise de
Rochechouart
(?–1595)

Françoise
(?–?)
m.

Louise
(?–?)
m.

Pierre Fretart
Baron de Marconnay

François de Cambout de Pontchâteau

Armand
(1585–1642)
Bishop of
Luçon
Cardinal

Nicole*
(1587–1635)
m.

Urbain de
Maillé de
Brézé
(?–1650)

anne
1645

Armand
d. 1645
Admiral

Claire-Clémence
m.
Grand Condé

a third daughter of François de Richelieu and his wife, I am now more

Bibliography

MANUSCRIPT SOURCES

Paris

Archives des Affaires Étrangères (A.A.E.)
Correspondance politique, Rome, vols. 23, 28.
Mémoires et documents, France 767–79, 841.

Archives Nationales (A.N.)
G 8* 632b; O1 1907b, P 5651, S 4073, TT 262, V⁵ 1225, 1227, 12294 (ii), Y 137,
    A.P. 120, vol. 11.
Minutier central (M.C.), Étude III, 488; VIII, 102–3; XIX, 173; XXIII, 244;
    LXXIII, 277, 321; LXXVIII, 118; XC, 131–48; XCIX, 56; CVII, 109, 113.

Bibliothèque Nationale (B.N.)
Manuscrits français, (MS. Fr.) 3722, 4328, 6379, 15699, 18002, 18012, 18155, 26169,
    31808.
MSS. Nouvelles acquisitions françaises, 3538, 3644.
Pièces originales, vol. 2302, dossier 52053, Richelieu family.
MSS. Latin (MS. Lat.) 9957, 17389, 18384, 18389
MS. Fichier Charavay, s.v. La Rocheposay.
Cabinet d'Hozier 271, dossier 7332.
MS. 500 Colbert 91.
MSS. Clairambault 365–77
MSS. Italiens (MS. Ital.) 1779, 1781–2.

Sorbonne, Bibliothèque Victor Cousin (B.V.C.)
Fonds Richelieu, vol. 14; box 22.

London

Archives of the Archdiocese of Westminster (A.A.W.)
Series A, vols. 11–16; Series B, vol. 26.

British Library (B.L.)
Additional MS. 22052; Sloane MSS. 2059, 2089; Stowe MS. 175–76.

Public Record Office (P.R.O.)
State Papers, series 78 (=France), vols. 65–73; series 30/53, vol. 6.

Rome

Archivio Segreto Vaticano (A.S.V.)
Acta Miscellanea 97.
Fondo Borghese III, 127e.
Fondo Consistoriale, Acta Miscellanea 53.
Miscellanea Armarium XII, 145; XLV, Epistolae ad Principes 2.
Nunziatura di Francia 60, 61, 401.
Processus consistoriales 34.

Malta

Archives of the Order of Malta, vol. 3180, *preuves de noblesse* for Amador de La Porte.

PRINTED SOURCES

Arnauld d'Andilly, Robert, *Journal inédit 1614–20*, ed. Achille Halphen. Paris 1857.
Arnauld d'Andilly, Robert, *Journal inédit 1620–1624*, ed. E. and J. Halphen, 5 vols. Paris 1888–1902.
Aubery, Antoine *Mémoires pour l'histoire du cardinal-duc de Richelieu*, 2 vols. Paris 1660.
Bassompierre, François de, *Journal de ma vie. Mémoires du maréchal de Bassompierre*, ed. A. de Chanterac, 4 vols. Paris 1870–7.
Birch, Thomas, *An Historical View of the Negotiations between the Courts of England, France and Brussels from the Year 1592 until 1617*. London 1749.
Brantôme, André de Bourdeille, sieur de, *Discours sur les colonels de l'infanterie de France*, ed. Etienne Vacheret. Paris/Montreal, 1973.
Calendar of State Papers Foreign, ed. W.B. Turnbull et al., 23 vols. London 1861–1950.
Camus, Jean-Pierre, *Homélies des États Généraux (1614–1615)*, ed. Jean Descrains. Geneva 1970.
La Chambre des Comptes de Paris. Pièces justificatives pour servir à l'histoire de ses premiers présidents (1506–1791), ed. A.M. de Boislisle. Nogent-le-Rotrou 1873.
Correspondance de Pierre de Bérulle, ed. Jean Dagens, 3 vols. Louvain 1937–9.
Correspondance de Rubens, ed. C. Ruelens and M. Rooses (*Codex Diplomaticus Rubenianus*), 5 vols. Antwerp 1887–1907.
Correspondance du nonce en France Innocenzo del Buffalo, évêque de Camerino (1601–1604), ed. Bernard Barbiche. Rome-Paris 1964.
Correspondance du nonce Girolamo Ragazzoni 1583–86, ed. Pierre Blet. Rome-Paris 1962.
Déageant, Guichard, *Mémoires envoyés à Monsieur le Cardinal de Richelieu contenant plusieurs choses particulières et remarquables arrivées depuis les dernières années du roi Henri IV jusqu'au commencement du ministère du cardinal de Richelieu*. Paris 1756.
Extrait des raisons et plainctes de la Reyne mère du Roy. n.p., n.d.
Flavigny, Jacques de, *Briefve et facile instruction pour les confesseurs*. Fontenay 1613.
Fontenay-Mareuil, François Duval, marquis de, *Mémoires*. ed. C.B. Petitot. Paris 1826.
Gallia Christiana in provincias ecclesiasticas distributa, 16 vols. Paris 1715–1865.
Hierarchia Catholica medii et recentioris aevi, 5 vols., ed. Eubel, C. et al., Munich 1898–1958.
Histoire du syndicat d'Edmond Richer, par Edmond Richer lui-même. Avignon 1753.
Histoire ecclésiastique des églises réformées, ed. G. Baum and E. Cunitz, 3 vols. Paris 1883.
La Nunziatura di Francia di Guido di Bentivoglio, ed. Luigi Steffani, 4 vols. Florence 1863–70.
La Rochefoucauld, François de, *Maximes*, ed. Jacques Truchet. Paris 1967.
Le Bret, Cardin, *Decisions de plusieurs questions notables traitées en l'audience du parlement de Paris*. Paris 1630.
Ledain, Bélisaire, ed., 'Lettres adressées à Jean et Guy de Daillon comtes du Lude gouverneurs de Poitou de 1543 à 1574 et de 1575 à 1585', *Archives Historiques du Poitou* 12 (1882), pp. 1–396.
L'Estoile, Pierre de, *Journal pour le règne de Henri IV et le début du règne de Louis XIII*,

ed. L.R. Lefèvre and A. Martin, 3 vols. Paris 1948–60.

——— *Journal pour le règne de Henri III 1574–1589*, ed. L.-R. Lefèvre. Paris 1943.

Lettres de Catherine de Médicis, ed. H. de La Ferrière and G. Baguenault de la Puchesse, 10 vols. Paris 1880–1905.

Lettres de Henri III, ed. Michel François, 4 vols. to date. Paris 1959–84.

Lettres missives de Henri IV, ed. J. Berger de Xivrey and J. Guadet, 9 vols. Paris 1843–76.

Lists and Analysis of State Papers, ed. R.B. Wernham, vol. i. (Aug. 1589-June 1590). London 1964.

Lucinge, René de, *Lettres sur la cour d'Henri III en 1586*, ed. A. Dufour. Geneva, 1966.

Malherbe, François de, *Oeuvres*, ed. A. Regnier, 5 vols. Paris 1862–9.

Mémoire d'Armand du Plessis de Richelieu(sic), évêque de Luçon écrit de sa main, l'année 1607 ou 1610, alors qu'il méditait de paraitre à la cour, ed. A. Baschet. Paris 1880.

Miraumont, Pierre de, *Le Prévost de l'hostel et grand prévost de France avec les édits, arrests, règlements et ordonnances concernans son iurisdiction*. Paris 1615.

Molé, Mathieu, *Mémoires*, ed. A. Champollion-Figeac, 4 vols. Paris 1855–7.

Monluc, Blaise de, *Commentaires 1521–1576*, ed. Paul Courteault. Paris 1964.

Morgues, Mathieu de, *Très-humble, très véritable et très importante remonstrance au roy*. n.p., (c. 1631).

Murdin, William, ed. *A Collection of State Papers relating to Affairs in the Reign of Queen Elizabeth from the year 1571 to 1596*. London, 1759.

Négociation commencée au mois de mars de l'année 1619 avec la reine mère Marie de Medicis par M le comte de Béthune et continuée conjointement avec M le cardinal de La Roche-foucauld. Paris 1673.

Négociations, lettres et pièces relatives à la conférence de Loudun, ed. L. Bouchitté, Paris 1862.

Oeuvres de Saint François de Sales (Annecy edition), 26 vols. Lyon-Annecy 1892–1932.

Pontchartrain, Paul Phélypeaux, sieur de, *Mémoires*, ed. C.B. Petitot. Paris 1822.

Rapports et notices sur l'édition des Mémoires du cardinal de Richelieu, 3 vols. Paris 1907–14.

Registres des délibérations du bureau de l'hôtel de ville de Paris, ed. F. Bonnardot et al., 23 vols. Paris 1883–1984.

Répertoire des visites pastorales de la France. Anciens diocèses jusqu'en 1790, 4 vols. Paris 1977–86.

Richelieu, Armand-Jean du Plessis, Cardinal de, *Instruction du chrestien par Révérend Père en Dieu Messire Armand Jean du Plessis Cardinal Duc de Richelieu*. Paris, 1636.

——— *Lettres, instructions diplomatiques et papiers d'état du cardinal de Richelieu*, ed. Denis-Louis-Martial Avenel *(Collection de documents inédits sur l'histoire de France)*, 8 vols. Paris 1853–76.

——— *Mémoires*, 10 vols. (ed. Société de l'Histoire de France). Paris 1907–31.

——— *Ordonnances synodales*, in Flavigny, Jaccques de, *Briefve et facile instruction* (s.v. Flavigny)

——— *Les Papiers de Richelieu. Empire allemand*, ed. Adolf Wild, vol. i. Paris 1982.

——— *Les Papiers de Richelieu. Section politique intérieure: correspondance et papiers d'état*, ed. Pierre Grillon, 6 vols. to date. Paris 1975–85.

——— *Principaux points de la foy de l'église catholique défendus contre l'escrit addressé au Roy par les quatre Ministres de Charenton*. Paris 1617.

——— *Testament politique*, ed. Louis André. Paris 1947.

Sully, Maximilien de Béthune, duc de, *Oeconomies Royales* (ed. Michaud and Poujoulat), 2 vols. Paris 1837.

Teulet, A., ed., *Relations politiques de la France et de l'Espagne avec l'Ecosse au xvi*ᵉ *siècle*, 5 vols. Paris 1862.

Vérités chrestiennes au roy très-chrestien. Paris 1620.

SECONDARY WORKS

Allier, Raoul, *La Cabale des dévots*. Paris 1903.

Allison, A. F. 'Richard Smith, Richelieu and the French Marriage', *Recusant History* 7 (1963–4), pp. 147–211.

—— 'Richard Smith's Gallican Backers and Jesuit Opponents. Part II: Smith at Paris as Protegé of Richelieu, 1631–*c.*1642', *Recusant History* 19 (1989), pp. 234–85.

Aubery, Antoine, *Histoire du cardinal-duc de Richelieu*. Paris 1660.

Aumale, Henri d'Orléans, duc d', *Histoire des princes de Condé*, 8 vols. Paris 1863–96.

Avenel, Denis-Louis-Martial, 'La Jeunesse de Richelieu' *Revue des Questions Historiques* 6 (1869), pp. 146–224.

—— 'L'Evêque de Luçon et le connétable de Luynes', *Revue des Questions Historiques* 9 (1870), pp. 77–113.

Barnavi, É., *Le Parti de Dieu: Étude politique et sociale des chefs de la ligue parisienne*. Louvain-Paris 1980.

—— and Descimon, Robert, *La Sainte ligue, le juge et la potence. L'Assassinat du président Brisson*. Paris 1985.

Batiffol, Louis, 'Le Coup d'état du 24 avril 1617', *Revue Historique* 95 (1907), pp. 292–308; 97 (1908), pp. 27–77, 264–86.

—— 'Louis XIII et le duc de Luynes', *Revue Historique* 102 (1909), pp. 241–64; 103 (1910), pp. 32–62, 248–77.

—— *La Vie intime d'une reine de France au xviie siècle*, 2 vols. Paris 1931.

—— *Louis XIII a vingt ans*. Paris 1910.

—— *Richelieu et le roi Louis XIII. Les véritables rapports du souverain et de son ministre*. Paris 1934.

—— *Richelieu et les femmes*. Paris 1931.

Baumgartner, Frederic J., *Change and Continuity in the French Episcopate*. Durham, N.C., 1986.

Bayard, Françoise, 'Les Chambres de justice dans la première moitié du xviie siècle' *Cahiers d'Histoire* 19 (1974), pp. 121–40.

—— *Le Monde des financiers au xviie siècle*. Paris 1988.

Bergin, Joseph, *Cardinal de La Rochefoucauld. Leadership and Reform in the French Church*. New Haven and London, 1987.

—— *Cardinal Richelieu. Power and the Pursuit of Wealth*. New Haven and London, 1985.

Blet, Pierre, *Le Clergé de France et la monarchie*, 2 vols. Rome 1959.

Bonney, R.J. , 'Cardinal Mazarin and the Great Nobility during the Fronde', *English Historical Review* 96 (1981), pp. 818–33.

—— *The King's Debts. Finance and Politics in France 1589–1661*. Oxford 1981.

Bosher J.F., '*Chambres de justice* in the French monarchy', in *French Government and Society 1500–1850*, ed. Bosher (London 1973), pp. 19–40.

Boucher, Jacqueline, *La Cour de Henri III*. Rennes 1986.

Bourgeon, Jean-Louis, *Les Colbert avant Colbert. Destin d'une famille marchande*. Paris 1973.

Boutier, Jean, Dewerpe Alain, Nordman Daniel, *Un Tour de France royal. Le voyage de Charles IX (1564–1566)*. Paris 1984.

Bouwsma, William J., *Venice and the Defense of Republican Liberty*. Berkeley, Calif. 1968.

Brockliss, L.W.B., *French Higher Education in the Seventeenth and Eighteenth Centuries. A Cultural History*. Oxford 1987.

Burckhardt, Carl J., *Richelieu and his Age*, 3 vols. English translation. London 1967–70.

Carmona, Michel, *Marie de Medicis*. Paris 1981.

———— *Richelieu: le pouvoir et l'ambition*. Paris 1983.

———— *Une affaire d'inceste: Julien et Marguerite Ravalet*. Paris 1987.

Champion, Pierre, *Henri III roi de Pologne*, 2 vols. Paris 1943–51.

———— *Jeunesse de Henri III*, 2 vols. Paris 1941–2.

Châtellier, Louis, *The Europe of the Devout. The Catholic Reformation and the Formation of a New Society*. Cambridge 1989.

Chevallier, Pierre, *Henri III*. Paris 1985.

———— *Louis XIII*. Paris 1979.

Church, William F., *Richelieu and Reason of State*. Princeton 1972.

Clarke, J.A., *Huguenot Warrior: The Life and Times of Henri de Rohan 1579–1638*. Hague, 1966.

Cogswell, Thomas, *The Blessed Revolution. English Politics and the Coming of War 1621–1624*. Cambridge 1989.

———— 'Crown, Parliament and War 1623–1625'. Ph.D dissertation, University of Washington, St Louis 1983.

Cornette, Joel, 'Fiction et réalité de l'état baroque', in *L'État baroque*, ed. Henri Méchoulan (Paris 1985), pp. 7–87.

Crouzet, Denis, 'Recherches sur la crise de l'aristocratie au xviᶜ siècle: les dettes de la maison de Nevers', *Histoire, Économie, Société* 1 (1982), pp. 7–50.

Dagens, Jean, *Bérulle et les origines de la restauration catholique (1575–1611)*. Paris 1952.

Davis, Natalie Zemon, *Fiction in the Archives*. Oxford 1988.

De Pure, Michel, *Vita Eminentissimi Cardinalis Arm. Joan. Plessei Richelii*. Paris 1656.

Degert, Antoine, 'Le Chapeau de cardinal de Richelieu', *Revue Historique* 118 (1915), pp. 225–88.

Delhommeau, Louis, *Documents pour l'histoire de l'évêché de Luçon*. Luçon 1971.

Deloche, Maximin, *Autour de la plume de Richelieu*. Paris 1920.

———— *La Maison du Cardinal de Richelieu*. Paris 1912.

———— *Les Richelieu. Le Père du Cardinal*. Paris 1923.

———— *Un Frère de Richelieu inconnu*. Paris 1935.

Dessert, Daniel, *Argent, pouvoir et société au grand siècle*. Paris 1984.

———— *Fouquet*. Paris 1987.

———— *Louis XIV prend le pouvoir: naissance d'un mythe?* Brussels 1989.

Dez, Pierre, *Histoire des protestants et des églises réformées du Poitou*, vol. 1 (new ed.). La Rochelle 1936.

Duchesne, André, *Histoire de la maison royale de Dreux et de quelques autres familles*. Paris 1631.

Dumolin, Maurice, 'Les Académies parisiennes d'équitation', *Bulletin de la Société Archéologique Historique et Artistique, Le Vieux Papier*, 16 (1925).

Elliott, J.H., 'Richelieu, l'homme' in *Richelieu et la culture*, ed. R. Mousnier (Paris 1987), pp. 187–98.

———— *The Count-Duke of Olivares*. New Haven and London, 1986.

———— *Richelieu and Olivares*. Cambridge 1984.

Estrées, François-Annibal, duc d', *Mémoires*, ed. Paul Bonnefon. Paris 1910.

Evans, R.J.W., *The Making of the Habsburg Monarchy*. Oxford 1979.

Fagniez, Gustave, 'Fancan et Richelieu', *Revue Historique* 107 (1911), pp. 59–78, 310–22; 108 (1911), pp. 75–87.

———— *Le Père Joseph et Richelieu (1577–1638)* 2 vols. Paris 1894.

———— 'L'Opinion publique et la presse politique sous Louis XIII, 1624–1626', *Revue d'Histoire Diplomatique* 14 (1900), pp. 352–401.

Fontenelle de Vaudoré, A.D. de la, *Histoire du monastère et des évêques de Luçon*, 2 vols. Fontenay-le-Comte 1847.

Geley, Léon, *Fancan et la politique de Richelieu de 1617 à 1627*. Paris 1884.

Girard, Guillaume, *Histoire de la vie du duc d'Épernon*. Paris 1655.

Greengrass, Mark, 'Mary, Dowager Queen of France', *Innes Review* 38 (1987), pp. 171–94.

———— *France in the Age of Henry IV*. London 1984.

Griselle E., 'Louis XIII et sa mère', *Revue Historique* 105 (1910), pp. 302–31; 106 (1911), 82–100, 295–308.

———— 'Un cardinalat différé', *Documents d'Histoire* 2 (1911), pp. 527–43.

———— *Profils de jésuites au xviie siècle*. Paris 1911.

———— *Etat de la maison de Louis XIII*. Paris 1912.

———— *Louis XIII et Richelieu*. Paris 1911.

Hanotaux, Gabriel, and La Force, duc de, *Histoire du cardinal de Richelieu*, 6 vols. Paris 1893–1947.

Harding, Robert, *Anatomy of a Power Elite. The Provincial Governors of Early Modern France*. New Haven and London, 1978.

Hayden, *France and the Estates General of 1614*. Cambridge 1974.

———— 'The Uses of Political Pamphlets: The Example of 1614–15 in France', *Canadian Journal of History* 21 (1986), pp. 143–65.

Hayem, Fernand, *Le Maréchal d'Ancre et Léonora Galigaï*. Paris 1910.

Hickey, Daniel, *The Coming of French Absolutism*. Toronto 1986.

Hildesheimer, Françoise, *Richelieu, une certaine idée de l'état*. Paris 1985.

Holt, Mack P., *The Duke of Anjou and the Wars of Religion*. Cambridge 1986.

Houssaye, Michel, *Le Père de Bérulle et l'Oratoire de Jésus 1611–1625*. Paris 1874.

Ingold, A.M.P., *Un Sermon inédit de Richelieu (Noël 1608)*. Luçon 1889.

———— *L'Oratoire à Luçon*. n.p., n.d.

Jacques, Émile, *Philippe Cospeau. Un ami-ennemi de Richelieu 1571–1646*. Paris 1989.

Jourdain, Charles, *Histoire de l'université de Paris au xvie et au xviie siècle*. Paris 1867.

Kleinman, Ruth, *Anne of Austria, Queen of France*. Columbus, Ohio 1985.

Lacroix, Lucien, *Richelieu à Luçon, sa jeunesse, son épiscopat*. Paris 1890.

Lockyer, Roger, *Buckingham*. London 1981.

Lublinskaya, A.D., *La France au temps de Richelieu. L'Absolutisme français*. Moscow 1982.

Lutz, Georg, *Kardinal Giovanni Francesco Guidi di Bagno. Politik und Religion im Zeitalter Richelieus und Urbans VIII*. Tübingen 1971.

Major, J. Russell, 'The Revolt of 1620. A Study of the Ties of Fidelity', *French Historical Studies* 14 (1986), pp. 391–408.

———— *Representative Government in Early Modern France*. New Haven and London, 1980.

Martineau, Aimé, *Le Cardinal de Richelieu*, vol. 1 (only vol. published). Poitiers 1866.

Marvick, Elizabeth Wirth, *Louis XIII: The Making of a King*. New Haven and London, 1986.

———— *The Young Richelieu. A Psychoanalytical Study in Leadership*. Chicago 1983.

Meurisse, Martin, *Histoire des Evêques de Metz*. Metz, 1633.

Michaud, Hélène, 'Aux origines de sécrétariat d'état à la guerre: les règlements de 1617–1619', *Revue d'Histoire Moderne et Contemporaine* 19 (1972), pp. 389–413.

———— 'L'Ordonnancement des dépenses et le budget de la monarchie 1587–1589', *Annuaire-Bulletin de la Société de l'Histoire de France* (1970–1), pp. 87–150.

Mousnier, Roland, *La Vénalité des offices sous Henri IV et Louis XIII*. 2 ed., Paris 1971.

Muchembled, Robert, *L'Invention de l'homme moderne*. Paris 1988.

Orcibal, Jean, *Jean Duvergier de Hauranne, abbé de St Cyran, et son temps*. Louvain-Paris 1948.

Parker, Geoffrey, *The Thirty Years' War*. London 1984.

Parrott, David, 'The Administration of the French Army during the Ministry of Cardinal Richelieu'. Oxford D.Phil thesis, 1985.

Pavie, Eusèbe, La Guerre entre Louis XIII et Marie de Médicis. Angers 1899.

Pérouas, Louis, Le Diocèse de La Rochelle. Sociologie et pastorale 1648–1724. Paris 1964.

Perroy, E., 'Social Mobility among the French Noblesse during the Later Middle Ages', Past and Present 21 (1962), pp. 25–38.

Pillorget, René, Paris sous les premiers Bourbons (Nouvelle Histoire de Paris). Paris 1988.

Pithon, Rémy, 'Les Débuts difficiles du ministère de Richelieu et la crise du Valtelline, 1621–1626', Revue d'Histoire Diplomatique 74 (1960), pp. 298–322.

Potter David and Roberts, P.R., 'An Englishman's View of the Court of Henri III, 1584–1585: Richard Cooke's "Description of the Court of France"', French History 2 (1988), pp. 312–44.

Pozzo di Borgo, Cécile, 'Denis Simon de Marquemont, archévêque de Lyon et cardinal (1572–1626). La carrière d'un prélat diplomate au début du xviiᶜ siècle, Archivum Historiae Pontificiae 15 (1977), pp. 265–94.

Ranum, Orest, Artisans of Glory. Writers and Historical Thought in Seventeenth-Century France. Chapel Hill, N.C., 1980.

———— Richelieu and the Councillors of Louis XIII. Oxford 1963.

Rebelliau, Alfred, 'Un Épisode de l'histoire religieuse du xviiᶜ siècle. La Compagnie du Saint Sacrement' Revue des Deux Mondes, 5 ser., 16 (1903), pp. 49–82, 540–63; 17 (1903), pp. 103–35.

Reinhard, Wolfgang, Freunde und Kreaturen. "Verflechtung" als Konzept zur Erforschung historischer Führungsgruppen. Römische Oligarchie um 1600. Munich 1979.

Richet, Denis, 'La Polémique politique en France de 1612 à 1615', in Roger Chartier and Denis Richet, Représentation et vouloir politiques. Autour des états-généraux de 1614 (Paris 1982), pp. 151–94.

Sauzet, Robert, Les Visites pastorales dans le diocèse de Chartres pendant la première moitié du xviiᶜ siècle. Rome 1975.

Solé, Jacques, Le Débat entre protestants et catholiques français de 1598 à 1685, 4 vols. Paris 1985.

Sturdy, David, The D'Aligres de la Rivière. Servants of the Bourbon State in the Seventeenth Century. Woodbridge, Suffolk. 1986.

Tallon, Alain, La Compagnie du Saint-Sacrement (1629–1667). Spiritualité et société. Paris 1990.

Tapié, Victor-Lucien, La Politique étrangère de la France et le début de la guerre de trente ans (1616–1621). Paris 1934.

Thuillier, Jacques, Nicolas Poussin. Paris 1988.

Trevor-Roper, Hugh, Renaissance Essays. London 1985.

Venard, Marc, 'The Influence of Carlo Borromeo on the French church', in John M. Headley and John B. Tomaro, eds., San Carlo Borromeo. Catholic Reform and Ecclesiastical Politics in the Second Half of the Sixteenth Century. Washington 1988.

Wood, James B., The Nobility of the élection of Bayeux. Princeton, N.J., 1980.

Wootton, David, Paolo Sarpi. Between Renaissance and Enlightenment. Cambridge, 1983.

Zeller, Berthold, Louis XIII, Marie de Medicis chef du conseil 1614–1616. Paris 1898.

———— Richelieu et les ministres de Louis XIII, de 1621 à 1624. Paris 1880.

Index